INFAMOUS
MURDERERS

INFAMOUS
MURDERERS

by
RODNEY CASTLEDEN

timewarner paperbacks

A Time Warner Book

This first edition published in 2005

ISBN 0-7515-3648-2

Produced by Omnipress, Eastbourne

Printed in the EU

Time Warner Books
Brettenham House
Lancaster Place
London WC2E 7EN

Photo credits: Corbis
Front cover images: *Richard III, Ruth Ellis,*
and *Lee Harvey Oswald*

For John and Trudi Urmson

CONTENTS

Introduction 7

PART FIVE: POLITICAL ASSASSINATIONS

PART SIX: CHILD VICTIMS

PART SEVEN: THE LADY-KILLERS

PART EIGHT: BODIES IN BOXES

PART NINE: MURDER FOR PROFIT

Introduction

Murder!

Infamous murder!

It is the stuff of high drama and melodrama, the epicentre of most crime thrillers and detective stories and many other novels besides – but it is and always has been part of the fabric of every-day life in most societies. Luckily murder does not happen frequently and does not involve very many people but it will, however infrequently, always go on happening and when it happens it causes terrible psychological and emotional pain to every-one it touches. In any society, murder is the one ultimate taboo, the one universally forbidden act.

Everyone knows what murder is: the unlawful killing of one person by another. Under British law, murder is only committed when the killer acts 'with malice aforethought', either intending to kill or cause serious injury, or realising that this will be the likely result. Manslaughter is a lesser crime; the killer may be mentally ill and therefore have diminished responsibility for his or her actions, or may have killed by accident in the course of committing another crime or behaving recklessly. In the USA there is a third type of crime, which is halfway between murder (in the British sense of the word) and manslaughter: that is called second-degree murder.

It is not quite so easy to define what an 'infamous murder' is. I suppose it is a murder that inspires horror, a murder that revolts everyone, as in Shakespeare's phrase 'murder most foul'. An infamous murder is one that makes you shudder when you hear about it. Infamous murderers are not just the people who commit infamous murders; they are horrible, repulsive figures, with something of the demonic about them. We normal people find it impossible to understand how they could do such terrible things – though we have to try to understand.

Infamous murderers have always held a strange fascination, probably because they seem to be people who dare to do that most outrageous thing of all, wantonly kill a fellow human being. That puts them apart, because most of us could not and cannot do it; our better judgement prevails, or the calculating judgement that we would not get away with it. For hundreds of years infamous murderers were publicly executed, and the huge crowds who turned out to watch them hanged or beheaded are an indication of the degree of fascination they have always inspired. Many of them became by-words for evil, almost figures of folklore.

Another source of interest is that the circumstances have often been recorded in the sharpest detail, showing snippets of history and sociology, and glimpses of contemporary or historic values. The dark deeds of infamous murderers are sharply focused film clips of very specific events happening in very specific places; reading about them transports us back to those times and places as if we ourselves were witnesses. They are mini-melodramas acted out by players functioning at the highest pitch of emotion; many of them are real-life melodramas, and a surprisingly large number of them have been turned into plays, films and even operas.

The deeds of infamous murderers have been a constant source of inspiration for fiction. The great crime writers P. D. James and Dorothy L. Sayers were (and are) both fascinated by real-life crimes. Films too have often drawn on the stories of real-life murderers. *Another Life* (2001) portrayed the life of Edith Thompson. *All This and Heaven Too* portrayed the circumstances surrounding the murder of the Duchesse de Praslin in Paris in the 1840s.

Many infamous murders have gone unsolved. The murderer of May Daniels near Boulogne in 1926 has never ben identified. The May Daniels murder was investigated by Dorothy Sayers and her husband Mac Fleming, the crime correspondent of the *News of the World*. Dorothy representing crime fiction and Mac representing crime fact went to Boulogne to investigate. The facts of the case were simple to the point of starkness. May Daniels was a London nurse who went on a day trip to France with a friend, Staff Nurse McCarthy, on 6 October, 1926. Towards the end of the day, May went into a cloakroom while her friend waited for her outside. She waited and waited, and May never came out. May was never seen alive again. She had vanished. The French and

British police were called in and a search was mounted.

May's badly decomposed body was found in open country outside Boulogne on 26 February, 1927, four months after she had gone missing. A hypodermic syringe and an empty morphine box were found nearby. Journalists reporting this bizarre case speculated that May Daniels had died of a morphine overdose during an illegal abortion, but the post mortem showed that she had died of strangulation or suffocation. The syringe and the morphine became even more puzzling. Who murdered May Daniels has remained a total mystery down to the present day. There are all kinds of questions arising from this case. Did Staff Nurse McCarthy know more than she admitted to the police? What happened to May in the cloakroom? Was she abducted by someone waiting for her – or any victim – inside? How was she removed without McCarthy knowing? Why was May killed?

There are hundreds of such real-life murder mysteries – murders without murderers. Because they are incomplete stories, they have a magnetic appeal to crime writers, who love devising scenarios to explain all the known facts. Dorothy Sayers' solution to the May Daniels' puzzle is hinted at in an incident in *Unnatural Death*, where a woman disappears from a cloakroom. In the novel, the woman reappears in disguise, fooling the man waiting for her outside.

Dorothy Sayers was equally interested in cases where the murderer was known to all, such as the 1930 novel, *The Documents in the Case*, which was based heavily on the scandalous Thompson-Bywaters case of 1922. Sayers based her 1939 short story *In the Teeth of the Evidence* on another notorious real-life murder, the Blazing Car Murder at Hardingstone near Northampton.

The murders in this book were nearly all committed by known murderers. Sometimes there is doubt, though, especially in the older ones, and sometimes we can tell that the infamous deed has been done by someone else entirely. The awful murder of Edward II was committed by two or three men whose names can be discovered but very few people have ever heard of them.

The documents about infamous murders and their perpetrators are infamously unreliable, and that sometimes creates problems for us. Some people, inevitably, have not told the truth. The case of Edith Thompson could be presented from transcripts of her trial, but we now know that the evidence was partial, in both senses, and that the judge was biased. But we have other evidence; the letters Edith wrote to her lover, sympathetic accounts of Edith written by her friends, a hostile account written by her brother-in-law, the victim's brother, and even a piece written by her hangman. The murder happened in 1922, and eighty years on from there the case as a whole looks very different. Both murder and murderer look different depending on your vantage point. With the older murders, it becomes harder to work out what happened, but we should always be ready for surprises; the standard versions of events are not always the only way of looking at them.

Authorities have often been in difficulties when hunting for murderers – the recent case of Caroline Dickinson, the British schoolgirl murdered in a French youth hostel, is typical – and there is always public pressure to produce a result. Often a scapegoat is put on trial. Most murders are not witnessed, except by the victim, who in the nature of things cannot give evidence. So there have been many cases of the wrong people being arrested, tried, condemned, vilified and even executed. Some of the most infamous murderers were innocent. Rather too frequently, the police have doctored evidence to make the case against a particular suspect more convincing in order to get a conviction. In cases like these, it is the nameless, faceless officers of the law who are the infamous murderers. I have become painfully aware while researching this book that the police have been far more prolific as murderers than any of the well-known figures that have made their alarming waxen way through the Chamber of Horrors in Baker Street.

In a sense William Calcraft, the principal British hangman for several decades in the nineteenth century, was a prolific murderer. In his black suit, dark hair and bushy white beard, he cut a terrifying figure. The photograph on his visiting card – as if anyone would want a visiting card from an executioner! – shows him posing with his right hand resting on a waist-high cenotaph decorated with a wreath on the front. It is distinctly sinister. Calcraft executed his prisoners using the short drop, so that they died slowly of strangulation.

His successor, William Marwood, invented the long drop method of hanging, in which the weight of the falling body broke the prisoner's neck and caused instant death. Marwood's long drop was calculated by dividing the required energy level, 1,260 foot–pounds, by the prisoner's weight in pounds. A man weighing 112 pounds required a drop of eleven and a quarter feet to kill him instantly. There were some early mistakes with the long drop method, which resulted in unintended decapitation, but Marwood's approach was far more humane. Some hangmen hated their work and some enjoyed it. The last surviving British hangman, Syd Dernley, who died in 1994, loved it; he kept a model guillotine and three working models of gallows in his bedroom. He positively enjoyed hanging people.

But, whatever we think of executioners, they are technically not murderers, simply because they are instruments of the law and they therefore kill their victims lawfully. Inevitably, the executioner is hovering in the shadows throughout most of this book, simply because few people get away with murder. People have never been happy about leaving murders unsolved, so they are always thoroughly investigated, though not always competently.

As Shakespeare said, 'murder cannot be hid long'.

PART ONE

ANCIENT
MURDER
MYSTERIES

King John and the death of Prince Arthur

KING JOHN HAS become a byword for wickedness. He is England's infamous 'bad king', yet most of us would be hard pressed to point to any particular act of great wickedness. In folkloric history, John was the bad brother of good King Richard the Lionheart; he was the cowardly stay-at-home brother who was supposed to look after England while the brave Lion-hearted brother went off on the crusade; he was the deceitful brother who plotted to take Richard's throne while he was away. He was in dispute with his barons, and he lost the crown jewels in the Wash. The folkloric version of John's reign looks pathetic and ineffectual rather than positively evil. Other medieval kings did far worse things without getting such bad press.

John was born at Beaumont Palace in Oxford on Christmas Eve 1167. He was the youngest son of Henry II. The eldest son, Prince Henry, was appointed titular king during Henry II's lifetime, but this great and unprecedented honour went to his head. He led a rebellion against their father in which he was killed. Richard, the second son, succeeded and he too died early after being shot by a French archer during a siege at Chalus. In this way, John, the third son who should never have reached the throne, became king of England. He did indeed try unsuccessfully to seize the throne during Richard's absence. This may have been dishonourable, but was also less costly to England than the alternative, which was paying the extortionate ransom demanded by Richard's captors. England's interests might have been better served by leaving Richard (who was in reality a useless absentee head of state, however glamorous) in captivity and letting John take the throne early. When Richard returned, John was banished for a time, but the brothers were soon reconciled.

Like all rulers, John made some bad decisions. For instance, he rejected the Pope's candidate for the Archbishopric of Canterbury, Stephen Langton. The Pope's response was spectacular; England's churches were closed and King John was excommunicated, and this forced him to give in.

John antagonized his barons and caused a civil war. This led directly on to the signing of Magna Carta, which limited royal power and outlined the rights of barons and freedmen; it could be argued that this was an achievement of his reign, however inadvertent. But he did lose the crown jewels and the rest of his baggage train when he was taking a short cut across the Nene estuary at Sutton; a fast incoming tide overwhelmed the baggage train and John and his retinue had to scramble to safety without their possessions.

Overall, the story of King John's reign does not

look any more disastrous than that of any other monarch. While he was evidently fairly unscrupulous and unpleasant, on this evidence he does not appear to have been any worse than the others.

Shakespeare, in his play *King John*, has John instructing Hubert to murder the boy-prince Arthur. Hubert is unable to bring himself to kill the boy, but Arthur later leaps to his death from the castle walls in a vain attempt to escape. Shakespeare's John is far from blameless, but he does not actually kill Arthur; Arthur kills himself. Part of this was drawn from genuine medieval traditions.

Arthur I, Duke of Brittany, was born in 1187, the posthumous son of Geoffrey Plantagenet and Constance, Duchess of Brittany. In the reign of Richard, he was designated heir to the English throne, in direct line of succession after Richard, who had no children of his own. Just as Prince John took some liberties in England while Richard was away on crusade, Constance took the opportunity to seize a greater measure of independence for Brittany. In 1194, Constance had her young son Arthur, then aged seven, proclaimed Duke of Brittany.

When Richard died in 1199, his brother John immediately usurped the English throne, but there was a problem in the French possessions. Many of the French noblemen refused to recognize the new King John of England as their king also. They preferred to recognize Duke Arthur, who declared himself vassal of Philip Augustus. This was sufficient provocation for John to invade France in 1202.

Philip Augustus recognized Arthur's right to rule Brittany, Anjou, Maine and Poitou, so Arthur set about asserting his right in fact. He was doing so in Poitou when he was surprised at Mirabeau, where he was holding as a hostage King John's mother, Eleanor of Aquitaine.

Arthur was captured by King John's army and imprisoned at Corte. Early in the following year, 1203, he was transferred to Rouen under the charge of William de Braose. He vanished mysteriously in Rouen in April 1203.

The mystery of Arthur's disappearance gave rise to many stories. According to one contemporary account, the gaolers were ordered to murder him, but they could not bring themselves to harm him (this was the story Shakespeare used). When it was clear that the gaolers would not do the deed, King John himself murdered Arthur and had his body dumped in the River Seine. This outrageously melodramatic scenario might sound too bad to be true, but there are reasons for believing that it is what happened.

When Arthur disappeared in Rouen he was formally in the charge of William de Braose. William de Braose therefore in effect hosted the murder and must have known about it either before or after the event. William de Braose was evidently greatly in favour with King John following Arthur's disappearance; in fact he rose so high that many contemporaries drew the conclusion that he must have been involved in a conspiracy to do away with the Duke of Brittany.

Many years later, back in England, William de

Braose's wife Maud directly accused King John of murdering Arthur. It is difficult to imagine why she did this; it was an incredibly foolhardy thing to do. Given that she was de Braose's wife, and he knew what had happened in Rouen, she was almost certainly speaking from inside knowledge. It was nevertheless an extraordinarily rash accusation to make, and John lost no time in silencing her. He had her and her eldest son, who John presumably suspected knew too much as well, both locked up in prison and starved to death. The incredible force and cruelty of John's response strongly suggests that Maud's accusation was true.

William de Braose, so recently in high favour, knew that his life would not be spared, and he fled to France. Once he had reached a place of safety, he wrote a statement, describing what had happened to Arthur. Unfortunately, no copy of this document has yet been found. It may have been a confirmation of his dead wife's accusation; it may have been an attempt at damage limitation, explaining how he himself was innocent, and knew nothing about the murder until it was all over.

The balance of the evidence points to King John as a usurper, since Arthur was next in line to the English throne, and it also points to King John as the murderer of Arthur, the rightful King of England, in Rouen in April 1203. Shortly after the Wash fiasco, John himself died.

According to one account he too was murdered, under peculiar circumstances. He was staying overnight at Swinestead Abbey in Lincolnshire when he was presented with a cup of spiced ale. The King took the ale and was about to drink it when he noticed the precious stones he had about him changing colour – taken at the time as a sure sign that there was poison about. The monk who had brought the ale took a hearty drink of it himself, which reassured the King that all was well. King John soon began to feel seriously unwell – he was in fact dying – and his lords went to search for the traitor who had given the King the poisoned drink. They found him lying in a corner, already stone dead. The monk had committed suicide in his zeal to kill King John.

John de Nottingham
killing by magic

THE PLOT OF this strange story begins on a snowy winter's night, way back in 1324. It was a Wednesday night, as it happens, just before the Feast of St Nicholas – and what we would now more mundanely call 6 December. On this night twenty-seven men, or more specifically 'gentlemen' as the documents carefully record, converged on the house of John de Nottingham. His house was at Shortly, which is now part of the Charterhouse area of Coventry.

The mysterious twenty-seven visitors gathered at John de Nottingham's house for a specific purpose, so serious a purpose that they had to swear both John de Nottingham and his assistant Robert Mareschal to secrecy before they would state their business. The number twenty-seven has an occult significance. Three is a pre-Christian (Celtic) magic number, and it is also a Christian sacred number, the number of the Trinity. Twenty-seven is three, three times over: 3 x 3 x 3 = 27. Perhaps the choice of twenty-seven gentlemen was a deliberately significant choice.

It was strange business, because John de Nottingham was a magician, a necromancer, and to dabble in necromancy was to risk terrible punishment at the hands of the authorities. Given the nature of the business, the punishment might come from church or state; either way, all of those present were risking their lives by being there and implicating themselves in acts of witchcraft. The penalties for witchcraft were extreme.

The twenty-seven gentlemen were all wealthy merchants, tradesmen and landowners, and they were all smarting from the crippling taxes they had to pay to the King, Edward II, the Prior of Coventry, Hugh le Despenser and his son (who were both favourites of Edward II), and the Earl of Winchester. Their spokesman was Robert Latoner and he asked John de Nottingham if, for a sum of £20 and maintenance in any religious house in England, together with £15 for his assistant, he would do as he asked.

When the matter later came to court, in a trial held at Coventry Priory, Robert Mareschal gave evidence that Latoner had then asked his master to take on the work of killing the King, the Earl of Winchester, Hugh le Despenser, the Prior of Coventry and others he would name. His master was to do these deeds by witchcraft. John de Nottingham agreed and was once again sworn to secrecy. Seven days after the Feast of Saint Nicholas the two men were given part payment for their work, together with the materials they had requested in order to create images of the victims: four pounds of wax and two rolls of canvas.

Robert and John then set about making seven images out of the materials provided, one of King

Edward wearing a crown, one of the Earl of Winchester, one of the Prior of Coventry, one each of his cellarer and seneschal, one of Hugh le Despenser and finally one of Robert de Sowe. Robert de Sowe was a minor favourite of the King, and as such well hated by a great many people who saw such creatures as parasites.

At midnight on the Feast of the Holy Cross, John de Nottingham began to demonstrate his very considerable skills as a black magician. First he took the doll of Robert de Sowe and cast a spell over it. He ordered Robert Mareschal to push a lead nail through the image's head. The first bewitching was accomplished. Then they went to bed.

The next morning, Mareschal went round to Sowe's house to see whether the spell had worked or not. Robert de Sowe, he found, had gone mad in the night, shouting and screaming, unable to recognize any of his servants or members of his family. Sowe stayed in that state until the Sunday before the Feast of the Ascension. Then, with the agreement of the twenty-seven gentlemen, Mareschal withdrew the lead nail from the head of the image and drove it into the heart. A few days later, Robert de Sowe dropped dead.

By this stage Robert Mareschal, who was proving to be a diffident sorcerer's apprentice, was becoming uneasy about the whole business. Not only had he been involved in murdering a man by black magic, the plans were in place to go on and murder the King himself. Evidently it could be done quite easily, with just a spell and a pin. He knew that this would almost certainly lead him to an unspeakably horrible execution. Mareschal decided to do what many others had done before and many others would do later, and that is to sneak off to the authorities and tell all in the hope of saving his own neck. He went to Simon Croyce, who was coroner of the King's household, and told him of the whole affair.

By the King's command, John de Nottingham was arrested and the gentlemen concerned in the case were informed of developments. All of them surrendered themselves to the Sheriff of Coventry. Robert Mareschal was then asked to repeat his earlier accusation in front of them, which he did.

All denied the charges and were then committed to the care of Robert Dumbleton, the Marshal. Within a few days, nineteen more gentlemen from the Midlands and London went to Dumbleton and offered him bail to allow the prisoners out, on condition that they returned the fifteenth day after Easter. All except Nottingham and Mareschal were released on bail. So far, Mareschal's decision had not worked in his favour. Turning King's Evidence had been a bad idea. Twenty-four knights were appointed to act as a jury at the trial.

The trial started on 15 March, 1325. John de Nottingham was summoned to appear. He was to be the star witness. The Marshal, Robert Dumbleton, had to inform the court that Nottingham had died suddenly and unexpectedly in prison. Given the revelations he might have made, it seems likely that he was murdered, and that his murder was a contract killing commissioned by one of the twenty-seven gentlemen. The trial was postponed and reconvened two weeks later. Mareschal gave his evidence. Numerous gentlemen swore that the accused gentlemen were not guilty of anything at all. Not surprisingly, no-one would speak on behalf of Mareschal, and he was handed back to Dumbleton. Mareschal was never heard of again, and it must be assumed that he too was murdered in prison. The twenty-seven gentlemen were acquitted.

The outcome was extraordinary, given that treason, murder, magic and the destruction of the monarch were all part of the plan. But they walked out of the courtroom free men. The ultimate aim of the conspiracy was undoubtedly the assassination of Edward II. He had become an extremely unpopular king, partly because of his homosexuality, partly because of the power he handed over to his favourites, partly because of the poor way he treated Queen Isabella, who had a great deal of influence in Coventry. The fact that the twenty-seven gentlemen were let off suggests that there were plenty of people in positions of great authority who were ready to turn a blind eye to any attempt to assassinate Edward II.

The John de Nottingham plot to kill Edward II failed, but the king had so many enemies that there was bound to be another way, another opportunity. Eventually he was indeed despatched – though not with a lead pin.

Who killed Edward II?

EDWARD II MET an appalling end in Berkeley
Castle on 21 September, 1327. He was 43,
constitutionally strong, and his murderers – there
must have been more than one of them – tried
several different ways of killing him before he
eventually died. The road to this terrible death
was a long and complicated one, involving power
struggles among nobles, personal rivalries,
personality clashes, heterosexual and homosexual
love affairs, and an adulterous Queen who was
ready to depose her own husband out of revenge.

Edward II was born in Wales. He was the baby
born in Carnarvon Castle to Eleanor of Castile in
1284, and presented by Edward I to the Welsh as
their Prince of Wales; he was the first 'English'
Prince of Wales. He was regarded as a weak king
because he preferred rustic pursuits to soldiery.
He enjoyed gardening, basket-making and ditch-
digging to the noble arts of government, warfare
and jousting; his chosen hobbies were of course
of the wrong class, which made him an object of
sheer contempt among his courtiers. When he
chose a lover, it was not just the fact that it was a
gay lover that drew contempt, but a low-born gay
lover. Piers Gaveston was just too low-born to be
countenanced at the royal court. That Gaveston

could beat any and all of them at jousting only made it worse. He was also arrogant and sarcastic.

So it was that Edward II antagonized his barons very early in his reign. A group of them, headed by Thomas Earl of Lancaster, seized Gaveston and executed him in June 1312. Edward adopted two new favourites, Hugh Le Despenser, father and son. These were very different men from Gaveston; they were able administrators, but Edward allowed them far too much power, so they too became objects of hatred among the barons. In 1322, Edward led an army against Roger Mortimer, and succeeded in capturing him and imprisoning him in the Tower of London. Then Edward marched on Thomas of Lancaster, defeating, capturing and summarily beheading him.

Meanwhile, the queen began to cultivate a relationship with Roger Mortimer, the prisoner in the Tower. It was probably with Queen Isabella's help that Roger Mortimer escaped from the Tower to create new problems for the King.

In the end, Edward's most dangerous enemy turned out to be his queen, whom he had married when she was twelve. Even then, French observers at the wedding said that Edward loved Gaveston more than Isabella. She had put up with his slights and infidelity for many years. The last straw was when the Despensers tried to persuade Edward that Isabella was a bad influence. In 1325 Isabella offered to undertake a diplomatic mission to her brother the King of France. It was really a ruse to escape from the English court. She arranged a treaty between the two kings, but indicated that Edward would have to come to France to sign it. He was persuaded not to go by the Despensers, who feared that he might be turned against them if he spent a significant amount of time talking to other people; they also feared what might happen to them, the Despensers, without the protection of the King. So a compromise was to send the young Prince Edward, which was exactly what Isabella wanted. She then had her son safely with her and could mount a small invasion without fear of her son being taken as a hostage. In September 1326, with a company of only 700 men, Isabella landed at Harwich and succeeded in pulling off a coup d'etat. Edward fled to Wales rather than fight her. The Despensers were hunted down and killed. Then the King himself was captured and imprisoned in Kenilworth Castle.

The usurpers, Isabella and her lover Roger Mortimer, needed to get rid of Edward II so that her son Prince Edward could become king. She approached Parliament with a request to depose her husband. They refused, but indicated that she could persuade him to abdicate in favour of his son. This she succeeded in doing; he abdicated five days later, on 25 January, 1327. Ex-King Edward II was then taken to Berkeley Castle.

In 1327, Lord Berkeley, the owner of Berkeley Castle, was commissioned jointly with Sir John Maltravers to guard the royal prisoner. Lord Berkeley was not residing at his castle at the time of the king's murder, but was ill elsewhere. He made much of this later, when he was on trial. It is not clear whether Isabella or Mortimer or the two of them together had decided to kill Edward from the start. Certainly at least one of them came to this decision after there was an attempt to rescue Edward. Obviously all the while he lived, he might be reinstated. It was too risky to let him live. Initially the orders, probably directly from Mortimer, were to keep Edward in such poor living conditions that he would just die of neglect. But Edward had a strong constitution, and the living conditions were made even worse. Still he would not die. In the end he was held down and a red-hot poker inserted into his bowels – a slow and agonizing death that would leave no outward mark on his body.

On the night of 21 September, 1327, the inmates of the castle were terrified by shrieks coming from the king's apartment. The next day the king was found dead. His body was put on display in Gloucester and people were encouraged to go and see the body. Mortimer wanted everyone to believe that the deposed King was dead and could never regain the throne. The citizens of Gloucester were rounded up to look at this odd lying-in-state, but they were kept a good distance back from the corpse. Was this because there were, after all, some tell-tale marks on the body after all? Or was it because the body smelt so awful?

Some people have suggested that Edward II was not really killed at Berkeley Castle at all, but was rescued and lived out the rest of his life abroad. The body briefly displayed and then buried in a royal tomb at Gloucester might have been a substitute: a body, yes, but someone else's. That might be the reason why the crowd was kept at a distance. There was a significant delay before Edward's funeral took place, on 20 December 1327, but that could be explained by the military expedition in Scotland. One reason for believing that Edward lived on is that some of his contemporaries believed it. Edmund, Earl of Kent, said that Edward still lived and was imprisoned at Corfe Castle. There was even a plot to free him, which led in turn to arrests, treason trials and executions. The Earl of Kent himself was executed in 1330. Another piece of evidence that Edward survived is a letter dating from 1337, written by the papal notary Fieschi; Fieschi claimed in this letter that he actually met Edward II in Italy, describing his life on the run until he ended up at a monastery near Milan. The document could be a forgery, but there is no reason to think so; Fieschi may even have been exaggerating when he said he met the ex-King, but the possibility remains that the story about Edward's death was a sensational cover-up, designed by Roger Mortimer and Isabella to bring Edward's supporters to heel. If Edward was dead, he was literally a lost cause.

On balance it is more likely that Edward II died at Berkeley Castle, not least because the story of the manner of his death was extremely destructive to the Mortimer cause. It inspired pity for the dead king and sympathy for his cause, anger and disgust at the Queen and her paramour. If Mortimer and Isabella had wanted to invent a story, then a 'natural causes' death would have been far better. The story about the red-hot poker is too awful to have been made up. Thomas Deloney's *Strange Histories* (modernized spellings) give us the fully developed late medieval horror of Edward's sufferings, beginning with the failed attempt to poison him, then going on to the foul-smelling pit before the final horror of the red-hot poker:

Loathing his life at last his keepers came,
into his chamber in the dead of night:
And without noise they entered soon the same,
with weapons drawn and torches burning bright,
Where the poor prisoner fast asleep in bed
lay on his belly, nothing under his head.

The which advantage when the murderers saw,
a heavy table on him did they throw:
Wherewith awaked, his breath he scant could draw,
with weight thereof they kept him under so,
Then turning up his clothes above his hips,
to hold his legs, a couple quickly skips.

Then came the murderers, one a horn had got,
which far into his fundament down he thrust.
Another with a spit all burning hot,
the same quite through the horn he strongly pushed,
Among his entrails in most cruel wise,
forcing hereby most lamentable cries.

And while within his body they did keep
the burning spit still rolling up and down,

Most mournfully the murdered man did weep,
whose wailing noise waked many in the town,
who guessing by his cries his death drew near,
took great compassion on that noble peer.

And at each bitter shriek which he did make,
they prayed to God for to receive his soul:
His ghastly groans enforced their hearts to ache,
yet none durst go to cause the bell to toll:
Ah me, poor man, alack, he cried,
and long it was before he died.

Strong was his heart and long it was God knows
ere it would stop unto the stroke of death.
First was it wounded with a thousand woes,
before he did resign his vital breath.

Once the slow murder was completed, Lord Maltravers was the one who rode to court to bring the Queen the news that her husband was dead. He expected to be welcomed and well rewarded, but Isabella wept and wrung her hands, calling him a traitor for killing her noble wedded lord. Maltravers was thoroughly shaken when he was turned away from court in this way, and returned to tell Sir Thomas Gourney and the other murderers that the Queen had outlawed them all. Suddenly their lives were in peril, and they had to leave England as quickly as possible.

Then farewell England, where we were born,
our friends and kindred which hold us in scorn.

At Lord Berkeley's trial, Sir Thomas Gourney and William Ogle were specifically named as the King's murderers, but they had fled the country. There is no record of Ogle ever being found. Perhaps he successfully changed his identity and vanished. Sir Thomas was detained in Spain and brought back to England, but there is no record of his having been punished. According to one version of the story, Gourney was taken ill after his arrest and died under guard, in France, on his way back to England. According to another version, picked up by Thomas Deloney, he was returning to England voluntarily because he missed his wife and children, was recognized on the boat and beheaded before landing.

Commandment was sent by one called Lea,
he should be beheaded forthwith on the sea:
Alack and alack and alas did he cry,
that ever we forced King Edward to die.
Thus was Sir Thomas despatched of life,
in coming to visit his sorrowful wife.

Maltravers was accused of murdering Edward, acquitted, but later executed for committing a similar crime elsewhere. On balance it looks as if Berkeley knew what was going to happen, had qualms about regicide, and made himself scarce so that he could not be accused of murdering the King. All those concerned except Gourney were eventually given formal pardons, which tells us nothing about their guilt. Gourney, Ogle and Maltravers were most likely the regicides, the men who carried out the murder that must rank among the cruellest in history.

These regicides could not conceivably have acted on their own initiative, though. They must have been instructed to do away with Edward, and that instruction can only have come from Roger Mortimer or Queen Isabella. Ultimately the responsibility for Edward's death must be theirs.

Richard III and the Princes in the Tower

RICHARD III (1452--1485) is one of the most infamous murderers of all time, but most of what we think we know about him comes to us via Shakespeare's play. But playwrights often bend history to make a better play, and Shakespeare certainly 'improved' the case against Richard.

Richard III, King of England, was born on 2 October, 1452 at Fotheringhay Castle near Peterborough. As far as the outside world was concerned, he was the fourth son of Richard Duke of York (who himself had a strong claim to the throne of Henry VI) and his wife, Cecily Neville. Within the family it was an open but unspoken secret that his older brother Edward was illegitimate; his very low-key christening was an admission that his birth was not altogether welcomed. Once that older brother became king, as Edward IV, it became a very dangerous secret.

Richard spent much of his childhood at Middleham Castle, which when he married he later made his home.

During the turbulence of the Wars of the Roses, the Yorkists were sometimes in great danger and in February 1461, his mother sent Richard and his brother George overseas, to Utrecht, for safety. They returned in April and at the coronation of Edward IV Richard was created Duke of Gloucester.

Richard's father was killed when Richard was still a boy, and after that he was taken into the care of Richard Neville, Earl of Warwick, 'Warwick the Kingmaker'. Warwick was strongly implicated in turning Henry VI off the throne and replacing him with Richard's oldest brother, Edward, as Edward IV, and therefore indirectly responsible for making Richard king too.

As a boy, Richard was of no consequence until 1469, when he supported his brother against Warwick, shared his exile and took part in his triumphant return. He fought loyally and effectively on his family's behalf, the Yorkist cause, in several battles in the Wars of the Roses.

During his brother's reign, Richard worked with steadfast loyalty, using his great skills as a military commander to support the king, and was rewarded with huge estates in the north of England and the title of Duke of Gloucester. He thus became the richest and most powerful nobleman in England. The other surviving brother, George Duke of Clarence, was by contrast disloyal to Edward IV, who had him executed for treason. It is possible that George tried to use his knowledge of Edward's illegitimacy as a justification for leading a full-scale revolt in an attempt to supplant him. Edward saw him as too dangerous and had him removed. Richard played a more intelligent game, showing his older half-brother nothing but loyalty.

After the Battle of Tewkesbury, which the Yorkists won, Richard married Prince Edward's widow, Anne Neville. It was Richard and his brother George who in cold blood stabbed Prince Edward to death after the battle. Richard was also present in the Tower of London shortly afterwards, on the night of 21 May 1471, when Henry VI was murdered, and may have been responsible for that assassination too.

Edward IV died, completely unexpectedly, in April 1483. The king's sons (Richard's nephews), the 12-year-old Prince Edward and the 9-year-old Prince Richard, were apparently next in the order of succession. In view of Richard's conscientious loyalty to his brother's cause, it seems remarkable that he moved to claim the throne for himself. Richard arranged for the young king, Edward V, to be escorted to Stony Stratford, where he took personal charge of the two boys. He accompanied them to London and lodged them in the Tower, then more a royal residence than a prison.

Richard declared himself Lord Protector and Chief Councillor. Something even more extraordinary followed. At a meeting of the Royal Council in the Tower on 13 June, 1483, Lord Hastings was arrested for treason. He was a known anti-Ricardian. A few minutes later, he was executed by beheading outside. Three other alleged conspirators, Lord Rivers, Richard Grey and Sir Thomas Vaughan, were executed elsewhere.

After ruthlessly removing all possible opposition at court, Richard had a statement read out, declaring that he was the rightful king, that his brother Edward IV had been illegitimate and that therefore the two princes were excluded from the line of succession. The declaration was startling for many reasons – not least that Richard was not just denouncing the boy-king as illegitimate but his elder brother as well, the brother he had served with unswerving loyalty.

A few days later, some evidence was produced, probably by the Bishop of Bath and Wells, to show that Edward IV's marriage to Elizabeth Woodville had been bigamous, and therefore all their children were bastards anyway. If Edward's two sons were illegitimate they could have no right to the throne. The children of George Duke of Clarence had lost their right on account of their father's treason. That left Richard. He was crowned King Richard III at Westminster Abbey on 6 July, 1483.

The two princes were seen a few more times in the Tower shortly after that, then never again. According to the Great Chronicle of London, the boys were seen several times in the summer of 1483, shooting and playing in the Tower garden. According to another account, by the French spy Dominic Mancini, they were seen less and less frequently that summer, at windows and behind bars 'till at length they ceased to appear altogether'. The two accounts contradict one another and it is not possible to be sure what happened. It is usually assumed that the boys were murdered that autumn, in the Tower, in secret, much as Shakespeare portrays it, but they may simply have moved elsewhere, to a place of safety where they would be less visible.

Richard's reign was a very short one, and when Henry Tudor usurped the throne in 1485 at Bosworth he had even less title to the throne than Richard III. He therefore had a very strong motive for removing the two princes if they were then still alive. Henry's mother, Lady Margaret Beaufort, was a latter-day Livia, scheming on her son's behalf. When she heard of the reported death of the two princes, she was pleased because she supposed 'that that deed would without doubt prove for the profit of the commonwealth'. If it was known that the princes were alive during the regime-change, they would have been a focus for rebellion. The Crowland Chroicle says that it suited the Tudors to spread the rumour 'that King Edward's sons, by some unknown manner of violent destruction, had met their fate.'

It is not known what the princes' mother, the ex-Queen Elizabeth Woodville, was told about her sons' fate, but she evidently was, and because of this she agreed that her eldest daughter Elizabeth of York could marry Henry Tudor.

Eventually, some skeletons assumed to belong to the two murdered princes were discovered, hidden under a stone staircase in the Tower. The forensic examination of the skeletons in 1933 was inconclusive. The skeletons seemed to be closer together in age than the two princes were, and there was a strong chance that the bones belonged to two girls instead. Nor was there any possibility, then, of dating the bones. Now, radiocarbon dating could resolve the question fairly conclusively. The remains were found in a complex of buildings running along the southern side of the White Tower, and now demolished.

Sir Thomas More gives the most detailed account of the alleged murder, and he says that the bodies were removed from the place where they were initially buried 'at the stair foot' to a better (more dignified) site by a priest of Sir Robert Brackenbury, who then died taking the knowledge with him. But the position of the skeletons found in 1674 was 'at the stair foot', where they should no longer have been, casting doubt on the rest of More's account. The problem becomes even more complicated by the earlier discovery, in 1603, of another pair of skeletons; these too were assumed to be the remains of Edward V and his brother. The 1603 bones were found in the substantial fore-building that stood in front of the south-west corner of the White Tower, not far from the two skeletons found in 1674. Obviously all four skeletons could not be authentic. Maybe none of them were.

It is at least equally likely that Richard III did not kill his nephews, but sent them abroad. He had himself needed to flee to Flanders, and he may well have sent the boys to the care of his sister, the Dowager Duchess of Burgundy, who held her own court at Malines. For a time, it is likely the boys lived quietly with their mother at Gipping Hall near Stowmarket, the home of the Tyrell family. Tyrell is named by Shakespeare as one of the princes' murderers, but he was Richard's 'knight of the body', his secret agent. He might well have been entrusted with looking after the princes for a time, while arrangements for spiriting them across to the Continent were made. That is the tradition within Sir James Tyrell's family. The princes lived at Gipping Hall 'by permission of their uncle', Richard III. There were widespread rumours circulating in 1486 that the princes had not been murdered, but were yet living. There are even documents dated 1484 in the Harleian Manuscripts which may tell us some of the arrangements for the secret transfer of the boys overseas. There is a tantalizing entry late in 1484 referring to a journey made by Sir James Tyrell 'over the Sea into Flanders for divers matters greatly concerning our well-being.'

Although it is generally assumed that Perkin Warbeck was an impostor, it is just possible that he really was Richard Duke of York. He may have been lodged with the Werbecque family of Tournai. What happened to the elder brother is less clear, and although chroniclers are able to say where Richard/ Perkin went they seem unable to follow Edward. One actually says, 'I find no mention of the elder brother being in Flanders, but very frequent mention of his younger brother's being there.'

There was a great deal of confusion over the identity of Lambert Simnel, the pretender who appeared in 1486. Four early chroniclers gave conflicting accounts of his claim. One said that he was the genuine Edward Earl of Warwick, son of George Duke of Clarence; another said he claimed to be Edward V but was an impostor; another said he was an impostor claiming to be the Earl of

Warwick; another said he first claimed to be York, then changed his claim to Warwick. It has even been suggested that the original claimant (whoever he was and whatever he claimed to be) was actually killed in the Battle of Stoke in June 1487 when his army of supporters was annihilated, and that the 'Lambert Simnel' who was afterwards treated as the claimant was a substitute.

The identity of Perkin Warbeck is a shade clearer, though still not certain. He looked strikingly similar to Edward IV, spoke flawless English, wrote English well, bore himself in a princely manner; it was – and still is – hard to believe that he was merely the son of a Tournai boatman. After close questioning, he was acknowledged by Margaret of Burgundy as her nephew and was acknowledged as the Duke of York by many others too. It was only after he fell into the hands of Henry VII that his fate was sealed.

But if the two pretenders were not Edward V and his brother, it is difficult to see what else might have happened to them other than an untimely death. If they were murdered, they might have been murdered at Richard III's orders, or Henry VII's. As we have seen there is some indirect evidence that that the two princes did survive Richard III's reign. When they were murdered, by whom and at whose orders is still not known, though it has usually been assumed that Richard III was responsible for ordering their murder. Richard was only in power for two years, and Henry VII, who would equally have wanted rival claimants out of the way, was around for much longer.

Because of the way he had removed potential opposition, Richard was left with too few friends to govern safely. His was a very short and troubled reign. His own loyal supporter, Buckingham, turned against him and was promptly executed. Richard's enemies finally united against him on the battlefield at Bosworth on 22 August, 1485. He was killed fighting bravely in the battle, and his body was carted naked through the streets of Leicester before being buried at Greyfriars Church.

Richard III is still one of the most controversial English kings. Shakespeare was a mouthpiece for Tudor propaganda, and his play *Richard III* is in effect a justification for Henry VII's usurpation of the throne; but Henry VII's right to the throne was not as strong as Richard's. Shakespeare blames Richard for the murder of his brother, the innocent George Duke of Clarence, but history records a very different story – that Clarence did indeed plot against Edward IV and it was Edward IV himself who had him executed.

Some have excused the (alleged) murder of the two princes on the grounds that England needed to be governed by a man. As for the accusation that Prince Edward (the boy-king) had no right to the throne, that turns out to have been doubly true. Edward IV was a bigamist, so his son Edward V was illegitimate. Edward IV was himself illegitimate. His mother was Cecily, but she conceived Edward while her husband was away and she had an affair with an archer called Blaybourne. It was a matter of general comment that Richard and George were slightly built like the Duke of York, but Edward IV was huge. He was 6 foot 4 inches tall. Richard would certainly have known this, but kept quiet for safety's sake, during Edward IV's lifetime. Once Edward IV was dead, it was not only safe for Richard to expose the illegitimacy of Edward IV's sons, he may have seen it as his family duty to the purity of the bloodline and his patriotic duty to the integrity of the Crown. We can see here a very different Richard III from the crook-backed villain of Shakespeare's play – not quite as infamous as we thought.

Who killed Mary Queen of Scots?

ON 7 FEBRUARY, 1587, the Earls of Shrewsbury and Kent arrived at Fotheringhay Castle and demanded to see Mary Queen of Scots, who had been Elizabeth I's prisoner for eighteen years. Mary was ill in bed but they sternly told her that she must die the following morning. She calmly asked if she could see her chaplain and if she could have a few more hours to prepare herself. Shrewsbury and Kent refused; she now had a reputation as devious and conspiratorial and it might be that even at this late stage she hoped to be rescued. She took supper, made her will and wrote letters far into the night, not going to bed until 2 a.m. She was unable to sleep because of the noise of hammering from the Great Hall below, where her scaffold was being built through the night. Mary rose at 6 a.m. to wash, dress and pray. At 8 a.m. she was summoned to execution. She said goodbye to her old friend Andrew Melville, who was deeply upset, and tried to comfort him before going down the stairs into the Great Hall. She looked tremendous in her State Robe of black satin heavy with gold embroidery and a massive gold crucifix hanging from her neck. The dark hall was lit only by the leaping flames of a huge log fire. At the far end stood the scaffold, the wooden platform of standard design with wooden rails and a block, the whole structure draped in black cloth. The axe was leaning against the rail, while the black-clad executioner and his assistant waited menacingly in their black masks and white aprons.

Mary stepped up onto the scaffold and sat on a chair, half-smiling as she listened to the executioner reading her aloud the warrant for her execution. The Earls of Shrewsbury and Kent, the Dean of Peterborough and the local Sheriff joined Mary on the scaffold. Mary knelt to pray. When she got up the executioners knelt to ask her forgiveness. Mary's ladies in waiting helped her to disrobe, until she stood in a petticoat and bodice of crimson velvet; she quickly added a pair of sleeves in the same material. Spectacularly dressed in blood red from head to foot, she lay blindfolded on the black-draped cushions and put her head on the block. The executioner's assistant gently drew her hands away from her chin and held her still while the executioner struck. Unnerved by the gravity of the situation – he was after all killing a queen – the executioner aimed badly and hit the blindfold knot by mistake. Mary was only slightly cut, still alive, still conscious. She did not move or make a sound, but waited for the next blow, which cut her head clean off. As the executioner held up her head, Mary's chestnut-coloured wig fell off. The onlookers were horrified. All the glamour and majesty had gone;

they saw the head of a grey, wrinkled old woman. She was forty-five but looked thirty years older.

The story of the execution of Mary Queen of Scots for plotting against Elizabeth I is one of the great costume-dramas of history. And the conventional verdict of history is that Mary was foolish, vain and ambitious, and brought her own death upon herself by ungratefully conspiring to have her hostess assassinated. She deserved to die.

But the truth may turn out to be very different. Mary was rightful Queen of Scots, but as many Scots saw it she had connived at the murder of her husband, Lord Darnley, and she had eloped with her lover, Lord Bothwell; for this unacceptably unroyal behaviour she was in effect outlawed. Mary had to leave Scotland in fear of her life and sought refuge in England.

Elizabeth I's attitude to this unwelcome refugee was very ambivalent. She did not want Mary in her kingdom, but if she was going to be there she needed to supervise what she was doing. There were English Catholics who were plotting to overthrow Elizabeth, and no doubt many of them would have been glad to see the Protestant Elizabeth removed by any means available and Mary installed as a Catholic queen in her place. She was in any case next in line to the English throne, which her son James was eventually to inherit. Mary was thus a focus for English Catholic rebels and conspiracies. For her own safety, Queen Elizabeth I could not afford to allow Mary complete freedom of action within her kingdom. Elizabeth's ministers were Protestants like Elizabeth, and they too were against the idea of a Catholic queen and the prospect of a Catholic dynasty.

Elizabeth's ministers were often heard trying to persuade Elizabeth to have Mary killed, but she was reluctant to do this, remembering her own rather similar plight as a threatened Heir Apparent during the reign of Queen Mary of England. She was also reluctant to kill the rightful monarch of a neighbouring kingdom. She was nevertheless tempted several times after 1572 to return Mary to Scotland, where the Scots would almost certainly have done away with her. If she had done that, she would have been just as guilty of Mary's death as having her judicially murdered, or secretly assassinated, in some English castle.

In 1584, the members of Elizabeth's Privy Council signed a Bond of Association, an extraordinary document which was designed to destroy Mary Queen of Scots. This was a bomb with a very short fuse. What it said was that any claimant to the throne on whose behalf anyone plotted against Elizabeth should be excluded from the line of succession and put to death – even if the claimant was entirely unaware of the plot. In this way any Catholic plot set up in Mary's favour was bound to result in her death – and that is what the Bond was intended to achieve. Hundreds of Englishmen signed the Bond. In 1585 the terms of the Bond were made law by an Act of Parliament, the Act of Association; the one change was that the claimant had to know about the plot in order to qualify for the death penalty. From that point on, Mary was doomed. Elizabeth's ministers had only to uncover a plot on Mary's behalf and they could politically disable her by excluding her from the succession, and possibly kill her as well. They knew that they would need to implicate Mary in the plot to a significant extent, as Elizabeth would be called to account for a judicial murder by Catholic monarchs elsewhere in Europe. The King of Spain in fact did use the execution of Mary as a pretext for sending the Armada.

Poor Mary had arrived in England as a royal refugee. Her cousin responded by locking her up, admittedly in some comfort, for eighteen years. All that time, she was seen by the Protestant courtiers surrounding Elizabeth as a threat to the English queen's safety.

There had to be a plot, and it had to implicate Mary herself. Sir Francis Walsingham was Elizabeth's Secretary of State and spy-master, and he set himself the task of destroying Mary – for Elizabeth – with incredible subtlety and cruelty. Born in 1530, Walsingham was a zealous Protestant, and, like many other zealous Protestants, he had had to take refuge abroad to save his skin during the reign of Bloody Mary and he had no wish to see England return to a regime like that.

Walsingham used two agents provocateurs, Gilbert Gifford and Bernard Maude, and their task was to manipulate two other men, John Savage and John Ballard, who believed that the assassination of a tyrant was a lawful act. It may be that Gifford first approached Savage to incite him to kill Elizabeth on his own initiative, and that

Walsingham's spies caught Gifford and black-mailed him under threat of torture and death into becoming a double agent. Walsingham learned through his agents that Sir Anthony Babington was plotting to rescue Mary, and this seemed an ideal platform for his entrapment of Mary. Babington was a young English Catholic gentleman who, because of his Catholic faith, had been in contact with Mary and smuggled letters from others to her. Walsingham worked cunningly and methodically towards combining the two plots: the Babington plot to rescue Queen Mary from Chartley Hall and the Gifford plot to kill Queen Elizabeth.

Babington was accordingly approached by Ballard with the additional, and crucial, extra proposal that Elizabeth should be assassinated. Walsingham almost misjudged the situation. Babington was greatly troubled by the idea of killing Elizabeth. The murder of tyrants might be morally justifiable, but was Elizabeth really a tyrant? Babington was not convinced and he wrestled with his conscience. He was probably encouraged by Ballard to write to Mary herself to resolve this, and in July 1586 he wrote a letter asking her to authorize the assassination. The letter caused her downfall. Babington described her planned rescue from imprisonment by 'ten gentlemen and a hundred followers' and wrote of 'six gentlemen' who, with Mary's authorization, would assassinate Elizabeth.

Babington's ciphered letter was smuggled into Chartley Hall, though not before Gifford had intercepted it and shown it to another Walsingham agent, Thomas Phelippes, who deciphered it. Mary got the letter on 14 July. On 17 July she replied to Babington. It was a long letter, explaining that the rescue attempt would only work if it had foreign aid; she clearly doubted the workability of Babington's plan. More significantly she did not give her authorization for the murder of Elizabeth. Instead she left it to Babington to decide what to do. Mary's letter was intercepted by Gifford and once again decoded by Phelippes. The story now becomes more complicated, as Phelippes was a good forger. He sent a copy of the letter with a forged postcript and possibly additions or alterations to the main text as well. In the forged postscript, Mary offered to take an active part in the assassination.

Babington and the other conspirators were arrested, tried and executed, even though most of them had wanted only to free Mary and were opposed to the assassination. Mary herself was put on trial at Fotheringhay Castle on 14 and 15 October, 1586.

The trial of Mary Queen of Scots was illegal and unprecedented. No court had ever put the crowned head of another kingdom on trial. Mary understandably at first refused to attend the trial on the grounds that an English court had no jurisdiction over her. She was assured she would be allowed to record that protest, so she agreed to attend and demonstrate her innocence. This suggests that she was innocent as she must have guessed that her letter to Babington had been intercepted. She was not expecting to be confronted in court with anything incriminating in her letter – simply because she had not written anything incriminating in it. She had no suspicion that Walsingham would stoop so low as forgery and perjury.

Mary admitted plotting to escape, but repeatedly denied consenting to the plan to assassinate Elizabeth. She demanded to see the evidence of her complicity – her notes for the letter to Babington. But no firsthand evidence was produced. The verdict of the trial was a foregone conclusion. When the commissioners reconvened nine days later at the Star Chamber in Westminster they gave their guilty verdict. Only Lord Zouche declined to go along with the verdict, declaring himself dissatisfied with the evidence. He was right to be dissatisfied. Maybe other lords were also dissatisfied, but knew what the queen – and Walsingham – required of them.

Mary was allowed no defending counsel at her trial. She was not allowed to see any of those who bore witness against her. Her secretaries were not produced at the trial. Babington, a potential key witness, was dead and in several pieces. Most important of all, Mary was not confronted with the original letter that she had written. A copy was read out, but almost certainly a version edited in such a way as to incriminate her. The original intention had certainly been to read out Phelippes' forged postscript, but by the time the trial came round, Walsingham thought better of it. Perhaps he thought it was just too incredible to be taken seriously and would actually weaken the force of the evidence against Mary. Phelippes kept the original letter, which he evidently showed to Curle, Mary's secretary, so that Curle could be pressed to identify his own handwriting. Since then, no-one has ever seen the original letter, and it is likely that Phelippes – or Walsingham himself, if Phelippes felt the responsibility was too great – destroyed it immediately afterwards. None of those involved could afford to allow the genuine and probably innocent letter Mary Queen of Scots wrote to Babington to see the light of day. Almost certainly it would have been kept from Elizabeth herself, who had had doubts about executing her cousin, and Walsingham needed the English queen to believe that the Queen of Scots really had been plotting against her. The very fact that the original letter was never produced as a vindication of the verdict and execution is suspicious. Similarly, Mary's drafts for the letter, in French, vanished during the trial.

Scholars who have analyzed the text of the doctored letter believe that the two references 'Mary' made to the assassination were added by Walsingham. Stylistically, these two references sit awkwardly in the text. The first is 'By what means do the six gentlemen proceed?' and it stands out by being a direct question in a list of indirect questions. A second reference says that the assassination should take place before the attempt to rescue Mary, but it is followed a little later by Mary's speculation about what Elizabeth would do to her if the rescue failed, a comment implying that Elizabeth would still be alive to exact revenge. The inconsistency suggests that the assassination sentences were insertions by Walsingham. Mary was careful elsewhere in her letter not to answer Babington's questions about the assassination. Babington for instance asked for Mary's undertaking to 'reward' the six assassins. In her reply, Mary emphatically referred 'to yourself in particular' and made it clear that she would be grateful for her freedom. Nothing about rewarding assassins.

Even if the jolting question 'By what means do the six gentlemen proceed?' is the genuine and authentic voice of Mary, she may have been asking a rhetorical question and trying to warn Babington that, to her, assassinating Elizabeth did not sound practicable. Even if all of the main text is the authentic work of Mary, evidently Sir Francis Walsingham did not think it was incriminating enough on its own, or he would not have had the incriminating postscript added. It may be that Walsingham decided in the end make only small changes to the original text, so that Curle and Nau (Mary's two secretaries) would not notice when they attested that the copy was a 'true' copy. Changing the odd 'ten gentlemen' (rescuers) to 'six gentlemen' (assassins) would almost certainly have gone unnoticed by the secretaries, who might not have understood the dire significance of the changes. The copy was shown to and attested by Babington; after torture, it is unlikely that he would have noticed these apparently minor changes either. He wrote on it,

'This is the verie trewe coppie of the Queenes letter laste sente unto me. Anthony Babington.'

A copy of the forged postscript, the one Walsingham decided should after all not be read out at the trial, has survived. It is written on a stray sheet of paper endorsed by Phelippes and is stored in the Record Office.

Where Mary was foolish was in leaving Babington to decide whether to assassinate Elizabeth. That was a kind of complicity. She should have flatly refused to countenance that action. She wrote in a letter to the Spanish ambassador in France that she had not wanted to get involved in the assassination but left that part of the plot to providence. Knowing of the plot to kill the Queen of England and failing to report it to the English authorities was a serious moral offence; she was in effect an accessory before the fact. To put herself in the clear she should have forbidden Babington to proceed with the assassination; she should, ethically, have notified Elizabeth of the danger to her life, though because she was the queen of a neighbouring state and not an English subject she had no legal duty to do so. Mary was in a very cleverly set trap, and whichever way she stepped it would have been sprung. It was a trap with both freedom after eighteen years in prison and the Crown of England as the bait. Even if she had not replied to Babington, even if she had remained absolutely silent, by the Act of Association Walsingham could still have blocked her succession to the English throne. Once she had received Babington's letter, she was in effect condemned to death, and it could be argued that acquiescing in the destruction of Elizabeth was nothing more than an act of self-defence. Once she had Babington's letter, it was her life or Elizabeth's.

Who was Mary's murderer? Technically, Bulle, the headsman who wielded the axe, was her killer, but he was only the instrument carrying out the illegal sentence passed by the court. Ultimately, the whole chain of events was instigated and orchestrated by Sir Francis Walsingham, who took the view that Elizabeth was not safe on her throne while Mary lived. So Mary had to die. He, not so simply, arranged it. Walsingham was the murderer.

Walsingham's stratagem to bring about the destruction of Mary Queen of Scots had worked. Elizabeth showed him no gratitude whatever for removing the danger, and he died in poverty only three years after his most famous victim.

But there is another man who must take his share of the blame for Mary's execution – her own son and heir, James – James I of England and VI of Scotland. After the commissioners gave their guilty verdict, there was a three week delay before this awesome news was given to Mary. Even at this late stage, Elizabeth was uneasy about ordering Mary's execution. The repercussions for England might be terrible. What retaliation might there be from the Catholic kings and princes of Europe? In particular, Elizabeth was afraid of Prince James's reaction. Would the execution of his mother precipitate a Scottish invasion of England with a furious new young King of Scots in the lead, thirsting for revenge? Elizabeth sounded James out. She was surprised to find that he was not nearly as concerned about his mother as he was about his inheritance. Once Elizabeth reassured him that he would be the Heir Apparent to the English throne after the execution, he 'digested' his resentment at the way his mother was about to be treated. It was an extraordinary situation. If James had reacted as Elizabeth anticipated, Mary's life just might have been spared. James's unconcern about his mother's death meant that the last barrier was removed; Elizabeth signed the death warrant on 1 February 1587 knowing that she had James in her pocket, and his mother's head was cut off a week later.

PART TWO

POISONOUS WOMEN

Frances Howard

'that filthy, base woman'

FRANCES HOWARD WAS the daughter of Lord Thomas Howard, who was created Earl of Suffolk when James I succeeded Elizabeth I in 1603. The normal route to preferment of this kind was unscrupulous double-dealing and the judicious betrayal of friends at court. Suffolk was no exception. In common with many others in high office at that time, he fell prey to the many temptations to dishonesty. People in high positions were approached with massive bribes on a daily basis; there were many opportunities for corrupt money-making. Suffolk's career ended in disgrace when he was accused of embezzling public funds. Frances Howard's mother was also greedy.

Frances was brought up at the family home of Audley End, not far from Saffron Walden. She was charming and beautiful and for a long time people were completely unaware of her true character, which was evil, cunning and ruthless. It was Lord Northampton, her great-uncle, who first noticed that there was a devilish, destructive side to Frances.

At the age of fifteen she was married to Robert Devereux, the glamorous Earl of Essex, but she was separated from him almost straight away;

King James had taken the good-looking boy under his wing as one of his favourites. He insisted that Robert should complete his degree course at Oxford and then serve in the army – abroad. This had the effect of releasing the Countess of Essex for her own wicked pastimes at court. She was free to take any lovers she liked and where possible she used these affairs to her own political advantage.

The first affair she had was with the young Prince of Wales, Prince Henry. She soon lost interest in him when she met Robert Carr, who had come south with the King on his accession to the throne of England. Robert Carr was the King's favourite, and he had been made Viscount Rochester. Frances' great-uncle, Lord Northampton, was aware that Frances was attracted to Carr and arranged for them to meet. Carr was wary at first, not unnaturally because he knew of the King's affection for Devereux, and did not want to antagonize the King. Favourites could very quickly become ex-favourites. Even so, it was not long before he gave in to the charms of the Countess of Essex, insisting only that they should meet well away from court.

There was one problem. Though spectacularly handsome and now ennobled, Robert Carr was not an educated man. He lacked the literary skill of a Walter Ralegh. He could not write a love letter at all. He needed a go-between, someone who would write the letters for him. He chose Thomas Overbury, whom he had first met in Edinburgh when he, Carr, was page to the Earl of Dunbar.

They became the closest of friends and travelled south together to King James's court in London.

The letter-writing arrangement with Overbury worked well for a time, as did the secret liaison with the Countess away from court gossip. But then Devereux returned from abroad and was keen to bed the beautiful eighteen year old wife from whom he had been forcibly separated. She was not at all keen. At first she made out that she was shy, then she made out that she was frigid. She was obliged to sleep in the same room and the same bed with Devereux, but she would not have sex with him. She now felt that Rochester was her husband and the idea of having sex with Devereux was repulsive to her.

Devereux took the drastic step of speaking to her father, asking him 'to remind his daughter of her obedience as a wife'. The father could do little. Frances must have been grateful for a reprieve when Devereux caught smallpox, and was too ill for a while to worry about his conjugal rights. It gave her some time to work out a solution. There were two things she wanted; one was to damp down Devereux's desire for her, the other to raise Carr's to still greater heights. She decided the most effective way to achieve her ends was through witchcraft.

Frances was given the address of a Mrs Ann Turner, who was the widow of a London doctor and who worked closely with the notorious magician Dr Simon Forman. Under cover of darkness, the Countess visited the den of Ann Turner and Simon Forman, and took away some powders and potions that were supposed to do what she wanted.

When Robert Devereux recovered from his bout of smallpox, Frances started giving him the poison Forman had prescribed. She expected him to become debilitated by the poison, but it had no effect whatever. She increased the dosage, but still he remained healthy, lively and over-interested in her. She sent a note to Mrs Turner, asking her to burn it after she had read it, begging her to send a more effective remedy. She foolishly added the words, 'I cannot be happy as long as this man liveth'.

The Countess of Essex was desperate to be rid of this pestering husband, and she consulted another witch, this time in Norfolk, a witch called Mary Woods. Mary Woods was given a diamond ring and a promise of a thousand pounds if she could supply a poison that would rid the Countess of her Earl within four days.

Rochester was a powerful figure at court because of the King's favour, and Frances could see that he could have any woman he chose. She felt she was in danger of losing him. She was also irritated by Rochester's determination not to be found out by associating openly with her; in fact it was better for both their sakes that he insisted on discretion. She fell back increasingly on spells and potions. Dr Forman even made wax figures of Frances and Robert making love. It seemed to Frances that the magic was working, because Rochester was more strongly drawn to her than ever. They met at Ann Turner's lodgings in

Hammersmith or at a house in Hounslow which Frances had bought specially.

Only one other person knew of their affair, and that was Thomas Overbury. Rochester spoke favourably to the King about Overbury's staunch friendship – in general terms only – and the King knighted Overbury. The problem was that Overbury, now Sir Thomas Overbury, did not like what he was involved in at all. He positively hated Frances, seeing her as a wicked and dangerous woman who would bring his friend down. When he discovered that Frances was planning to divorce her husband in order to marry his friend Carr, he finally blurted out all his misgivings to Carr, calling Frances 'that filthy, base woman'. This naturally put a distance between the two men and also put Overbury himself in considerable danger.

Frances heard what Overbury had said and decided to destroy him. At that moment, the King had some sympathy for her request for a divorce, but if he heard a different version of events from Overbury he might decide differently. Sir Thomas Overbury must die. The Countess turned to her great-uncle Lord Northampton for help. Together they managed to turn Rochester against his former friend. They persuaded Rochester that Overbury was now very much in the King's favour and might supplant him.

The King offered to send Overbury as Ambassador to the Low Countries, and in the circumstances it would have been far safer for him to accept this posting than to refuse it, but he did not want it. He turned it down. The King regarded this as a high-handed snub and wondered what ulterior motive he had. He sent Overbury to the Tower for 'contempt'.

The Countess of Essex now worked to ensure that Overbury never came out of the Tower alive. She hired an agent called Weston and succeeded in getting him a posting at the Tower. She even arranged for him to become Overbury's servant in the Tower. Then it became Weston's job to poison Overbury's food. The first attempt at poisoning was a disaster. Weston was caught in the act by the Lieutenant of the Tower, Sir Gervase Elwes. Elwes was unsure what to do. Evidently there was a plot afoot to kill Sir Thomas Overbury, but he could not tell where the plot originated; for all he knew the King himself might be behind it. He decided it was safer, for himself, if he did not expose the attempt to kill Overbury. At the same time, the poisoning offended Elwes' sense of what was right and just, and he was determined to prevent Overbury's assasination if he could.

The Countess sent in all kinds of food for Overbury, all laced with poison, and Elwes managed to intercept it before it reached his prisoner. The Countess was working very hard on this project, and she was sending in seven different poisons in huge quantities. She could not understand why Overbury was still alive. She had sent in enough poisoned food to kill twenty men. Indeed there was even talk of his being released. She decided that Weston was useless and replaced him with a young man called William

Reeve. Reeve was the assistant to the physician attending the prisoners in the Tower. Frances offered Reeve £20 to steal a solution of mercury sublimate and give it to Sir Thomas Overbury as a medicine.

Unsuspecting, Overbury swallowed the poison and died in agony shortly afterwards.

By this stage, Frances Countess of Essex had formally petitioned for divorce. On 16 May, 1613 a commission was appointed to investigate her claim that her marriage to the Earl of Essex was void because he was impotent. Essex naturally denied this emphatically, and there was general support for his version of events. The King found the whole business distasteful and wanted it over with, and intervened to have the marriage nullified. Essex's pride had been badly bruised and he felt he had been ill-treated, but he had, in reality, had a lucky escape. Frances had really wanted him dead.

Rochester was now created Earl of Somerset, and he was able to marry Frances Essex later in 1613. She wore white, with her long fair hair flowing freely down her back – the picture of innocence. It was a great occasion, attended by both the King and his Queen. Rochester himself was blissfully ignorant. He still did not know that his new wife was a murderess.

There was not to be a happy ending. She had worked with too many accomplices to feel safe. There were Turner and Forman, the Norfolk witch, and Weston and Reeve at the Tower – too many people who knew her secret. They were small people who knew how rich she was. It was inevitable that that they would blackmail her. She became tense and nervous. Rochester, now Somerset, was also in difficulties of a different sort. The King thought he had become too grand and over-bearing, and was showing more interest in a new favourite, George Villiers.

It was in the autumn of 1615, two years into her marriage to Somerset, that Frances' secret came out. William Reeve, the man who had fatally dosed Sir Thomas Overbury with poison for twenty pounds, fell seriously ill. He thought he was going to die and decided he had to confess. He told his secret – and then recovered. News of what had happened to Sir Thomas Overbury filtered back to the King, who wanted justice done. Somerset and his wife were put under house arrest while the stories were investigated. Then they were formally arrested on a charge of murder.

Somerset insisted throughout that he had known nothing about the murder of his friend. He was found guilty and sentenced to death, but there was a general feeling that he was not guilty; at the last moment before his execution he was granted a pardon. A pardon seemed less likely for the Countess, yet James I did grant her one, on the extraordinary grounds that her family had done the country great service and that she was truly penitent.

The people of England did not believe that she was penitent and saw her as thoroughly guilty. She was mobbed in the streets. On one occasion, a mob attacked a coach in which the Queen was travelling with a young friend. They had believed it to be 'that vile woman' and her mother.

Both Somerset and his Countess were lodged in the Tower. She pleaded with the Lieutenant not to put her in the chamber where Sir Thomas Overbury had died. They were kept there until 1621, after which the King allowed them to go and live at Grey's Court in Oxfordshire, where Frances' brother-in-law offered them accommodation. But they were to stay there, under house arrest, for the rest of their lives.

It was a terrible punishment for Somerset, who had by this time come to hate the scheming murderess he had married, the woman who had poisoned his mind against his best friend and then arranged, elaborately and in cold blood, to have his best friend killed. Somerset barely spoke to Frances again. She contracted a wasting disease which slowly killed her. She eventually died in August 1632, while he watched her, unmoved.

Eliza Fenning

'the cruellest thing in the world'

ELIZABETH FENNING, WHO was always known as Eliza, was an attractive young woman of twenty-one employed as a domestic servant by Robert and Charlotte Turner. The Turners lived in Chancery Lane in London and were well off enough to employ several servants, including Eliza as their cook.

It was on 21 March, 1815 that Eliza prepared the fateful meal. It was steak and dumpling casserole. Robert Turner's father came to dinner that day. They all ate the casserole and all were soon suffering from severe stomach pains and vomiting. Roger Gadsden, one of the apprentices, and Eliza herself suffered the same symptoms. The doctor was called, and everyone made a full recovery.

Old Mr Turner had a suspicion that they had been deliberately poisoned. A packet of arsenic he kept in his desk drawer had gone missing, he said. Arsenic was easily available at this time, and commonly used as a rat poison. Mr Turner asked the doctor to examine the contents of the pan Eliza had used to cook the dumplings. As he thought, it was found to contain arsenic. Eliza was arrested and charged with attempted murder.

Eliza was made to appear before a magistrate, who committed her for trial at the Old Bailey. She was remanded in custody in Newgate Prison. There was only circumstantial evidence against her, yet the result of her trial was a foregone conclusion. An accusation had been brought, the judge was against her and there was the hostile testimony of Mrs Turner. Eliza did not stand a chance. Mrs Turner told the court that Eliza had been seeking revenge on the family ever since she, the mistress of the househould, had discovered her partially dressed in one of the apprentice's rooms one night. She had threatened to dismiss Eliza and the girl wanted revenge on them.

Eliza had no defence lawyer. No-one represented her. While she was awaiting sentence in Newgate, she wrote to the man she had hoped to marry, 'They have, which is the cruellest thing in the world, brought me in guilty. I may be confined six months at least.' She was horrified when the following day she was sentenced to death. Reporters described an appalling scene. 'She was carried from the dock convulsed with agony and uttering frightful screams.'

In 1815, it was not just murder that carried the death penalty but a ranger of other offences as well, including attempted murder. Attempted murder remained a capital offence in England until as late as 1861.

Even so, there was considerable public feeling that this was not a fair verdict. Appeals arrived from various quarters, aimed at the Prince Regent, the Home Secretary and the Lord Chancellor. All appeals were rejected. The date of poor Eliza's execution was set: Wednesday 26 July, 1815.

Early that morning, the large portable gallows was taken out and assembled outside the Debtor's Door of Newgate Prison, in readiness for the triple hanging. It was quite normal for prisoners to be hanged in lots of three, even for entirely unconnected crimes, or as in this case for no crime at all. This one was to be the only triple hanging of 1815; in fact only twelve people were hanged there altogether that year.

Denied any hope of a reprieve, Eliza was taken out into the prison yard, where her hands were tied. She was dressed in a white muslin gown with a high waist tied with a ribbon, a white muslin cap, and high-laced lilac boots. This pretty outfit, to add further poignancy to the occasion, was for her wedding. This, the day of her execution, was to have been her wedding day.

Probably still not quite believing what was happening to her, Eliza Fenning was led to the steps of the scaffold. The prison chaplain, the Revd Horace Cotton, accompanied her and asked her if there was anything she had to tell him. She said, 'Before the just and Almighty God, and by the faith of the Holy Sacrament I have taken, I am innocent of the offence with which I am charged.' She mounted the steps and the crowd fell silent. John Langley, the hangman, tried to pull the white hood over her head, but her large muslin cap got in the way. He tried instead to tie a muslin handkerchief over her face but it was too small. Then he pulled out his own large, but filthy, pocket handkerchief and tied that over her face. Eliza was disgusted by this final humiliation. 'Pray do not let him put it on, Mr Cotton! Pray make him take it off. Pray do, Mr Cotton!' Cotton told her that he must put it on.

She now had two others beside her, a forger called Abraham Adams and a rapist called William Oldfield; the rapist had apparently asked to be hanged beside Eliza Fenning.

At about 8.30 a.m., Langley pulled the bolt, which gave the three prisoners a short drop of about twelve inches. Eliza died fairly quickly. Her father had to pay fourteen shillings to the executioner to get his daughter's body back for burial. Eliza Fenning's funeral took place on 31 July, 1815 at St George the Martyr in London. Several thousand people attended, which is an indication of the amount of feeling there was for Eliza Fenning's cause. There was a general feeling that justice had not been done. The conduct of the trial was loaded against her and an entirely innocent young woman had been hanged. In this case it was not so much the murderer who was infamous as the trial judge and the 'justice' system he represented.

What had happened at the Turners' house? Given that Eliza was so close to marrying, it is very unlikely that she was having an affair with one of the apprentices as Mrs Turner alleged. Mrs Turner was almost certainly not telling the truth, so what motive could she have had for lying? It might have been jealousy. Eliza was a very good-looking young woman. Perhaps Mrs Turner was aware that her husband was on the point of infidelity; perhaps she had noticed his roving eye. She may have thought for some time that it would be better if Eliza Fenning was out of the way. The poisoning incident may just have been a heaven-sent opportunity. Some have suggested that the younger Mr Turner had become mentally ill and decided to kill the whole family, but there is no evidence of this.

One thing is certain and that is that Eliza is very unlikely to have deliberately poisoned the food; she was eating it herself and, with her forthcoming marriage, she evidently had every-thing to live for. It cannot even be known for certain whether the Turners' doctor was telling the truth about finding arsenic in the dumpling pan. As just another of the Turners' employees, he was evidently under pressure from Mr Turner to find arsenic, and may simply have given in and said what was required of him.

There may have been no poison as such at all in the dumplings. Refrigeration was not invented until later in the nineteenth century and was not in general domestic use in England until well into the twentieth century. It was quite common for people to eat food that was 'off'. In the summer months especially food poisoning leading to gastro-enteritis was a very common ailment, and it seems odd that the Turners' doctor did not make that diagnosis. It seems likely that a stronger minded doctor would have made that diagnosis – in spite of what the Turner family clearly wanted – a scapegoat.

Madeleine Smith

POISON HAS ALWAYS been the preferred weapon of the murderess; poison has been the death of choice. This may be because it does not require physical strength, but perhaps for a purely psychological reason, that it does not involve contact or physical confrontation. Poison is indirect. Poison was also a more intelligent way of killing people; in the days before forensic science, poison was often difficult to detect. Murder by poison was therefore also difficult to detect.

The two greatest Victorian poison cases are those of Madeleine Smith and Florence Maybrick. Both cases are complex, both, in spite of a hundred years of scrutiny, remain unsolved. What may look like a straightforward murder on closer inspection turns out to be an accident or a suicide. At the time of their trials, Madeleine Smith and Florence Maybrick were both branded murderesses, and they were both demonized, but did they commit murder?

Madeleine Smith was tried in Glasgow in July 1857. Her trial failed to establish whether she had committed murder or had been framed by her insane and suicidal lover. She was on trial for the murder of her ex-lover Emile L'Angelier, who died as a result of arsenic poisoning.

Madeleine was the elder daughter of one James Smith, a successful Glaswegian architect. He was able to afford to maintain a comfortable household with six servants, but like the head of many a Victorian paterfamilias he ruled it with a rod of iron. For much of the time there was nothing for Madeleine to do. Along with many other Victorian girls she was expected to occupy herself with lady-like pursuits such as painting and piano-playing.

Madeleine was bored stiff and ready for a romantic adventure.

The adventure came in the unlikely shape of a packing clerk called Emile L'Angelier. She first saw Emile in the street, when their eyes met by chance. He later found an opportunity to send her a flowery message of love. She rather foolishly replied that she had worn it next to her heart. It would have been better if she hadn't.

A correspondence started that would prove very damaging to her at her trial. Conversations written down can be read out in court, as she was to discover to her great embarrassment. After the initial flush of novelty, she knew it was silly and she tried to break off the relationship, but Emile was by then obsessed. In July 1855 he wrote in threatening tone: 'Think what your father would say if I sent him your letters for perusal.' Given the stern character of Mr Smith, this must have frightened Madeleine. She was already virtually imprisoned in the family home, and her father would certainly be shocked if he was given her letters to read. They were full of barely suppressed sexuality, and this at a time when women in her class were supposed to put up with sex, not enjoy it. When L'Angelier lay dead and his lodgings were searched, more than five hundred steamy letters from Madeleine were found.

It was obvious from the letters that they had had sex. 'If we did wrong last night, it must have been in the excitement of our love. I suppose we should have waited until we were married.'

When they moved out to their country house at Row in the summer of 1856, Madeleine asked for a ground floor room. Then she could just step out of the window to meet Emile. They met again and again at night without Madeleine's parents knowing. But then a middle class suitor appeared on the scene, William Minnoch. He was a businessman in his thirties, and began 'calling on' Madeleine. She received these calls without finding Minnoch attractive, she told Emile.

At the end of that summer the Smiths returned to India Street in Glasgow. Secret meetings were more difficult there because Madeleine's bedroom was in the basement, with the window at pavement level covered by bars. There was no longer any possibility of slipping out to have sex with Emile. He came each night for a whispered conversation through the barred window, but it was scarcely enough. Emile went into a depression. Worse still, Madeleine's letters began to talk of their love as if it was over. She was seen in public with Minnoch and her letters to Emile were getting shorter. On 28 January she seems to have decided to marry Minnoch. This was a decisive moment. She had to end the affair with Emile. She wrote him a letter that was cold in tone. 'We had better for the future consider ourselves as strangers. I trust to your honour as a gentleman that you will not reveal anything that has passed between us.' And she asked him to return the deadly letters.

Emile became hysterical. He would not give her up. He would show her father the letters. If he couldn't have her, no other man would either. Madeleine in her turn became frantic when she realised that Emile was not going to return the letters. 'Hate me, despise me – but do not expose me.' She asked him to come to the house so that she could talk to him through the window. He kept that appointment, on 11 February, 1857. Madeleine was playing a game with L'Angelier, playing for time, keeping his hopes alive so that he would not show her father the letters. She seems to have agreed to marry him in the autumn, which she cannot have intended to do.

Mrs Jenkins, Emile's landlady, went to his room on 20 February to call him for breakfast and found that he was unwell. During the night he had been very sick after feeling violent stomach pains on the way home. Four days later Mrs Jenkins was awakened by Emile's groans. He had the same symptoms as before. The symptoms were those of arsenic poisoning. It emerged at her trial that Madeleine had been shopping for arsenic at exactly this time. The chemist gave it to her mixed with soot according to the law, and he was surprised that Madeleine was concerned about the colour of it; why would it matter if she was giving it to rats, as she said?

Emile said to the trusted go-between, Miss Perry, that he couldn't understand why he was so ill after taking coffee and chocolate from Madeleine. He even speculated that the drinks might have been poisoned. On 22 March he arrived at his lodgings very late, presumably after seeing Madeleine again. This time he was doubled up with pain. A doctor was fetched, but Emile died the next morning.

Emile had enough arsenic in his stomach to kill forty men, and the presence of arsenic throughout his body showed that he had taken several doses.

At her trial, Madeleine pleaded not guilty and changed her explanation about the arsenic; she had bought it for cosmetic reasons. The prosecution explored the idea that she had used the sooty arsenic to lace the coffee and chocolate and fed them to Emile L'Angelier through the bars. She had got herself into such a difficult position that murder seemed the only way out. But the defending advocate argued that Emile was vain, unable to accept rejection. He had also boasted of being an arsenic eater. It is possible that in his depressed and desperate state Emile took the arsenic hoping to incriminate Madeleine. If he couldn't have Madeleine, no other man would have her either, as he had threatened. If he could commit suicide in a way that reflected badly on Madeleine, so much the better. If he could make it look as if she had murdered him, best of all.

But the coldness of Madeleine Smith at her trial

was incriminating in itself. She showed no feeling when the sufferings of Emile L'Angelier were described. She showed the same indifference to William Minnoch's sufferings. The whole affair had made Minnoch ill. Yet when asked about the welfare of the man she had said she would marry, she said, 'My friend I know nothing of. I hear he has been ill, which I don't much care.' The jury in Glasgow in 1857 could not decide – they gave a verdict of 'Not Proven' – and it is no easier for us to decide now. Could she possibly have committed that cold-blooded murder? If she did, she was indeed evil. It was noted at the trial that her defending advocate, normally a courteous man, pointedly left the courtroom after the verdict without so much as a glance at his client, implying that he thought her guilty.

Guilty or not, Madeleine Smith was a free woman. She moved to London, married an artist and led an interesting and fulfilled life. She spent her later years in America, where she died, of natural causes, at the age of ninety-one. There is a photograph of Madeleine Smith, taken when she was an old lady in America. She is fastidiously and beautifully dressed, giving the camera a sunny, direct and guilelessly innocent smile. She looks happy, untroubled, innocent. But appearances often deceive.

Florence Maybrick

FLORENCE MAYBRICK STARTED life as Florence Chandler. She was a Southern belle, a headstrong eighteen year old travelling across the Atlantic with her mother, Baroness Caroline von Roques, when she met James Maybrick, a wealthy cotton broker. The two women had travelled from their home at Mobile, Alabama to board the Baltic on 12 March, 1880 and the ship was to take them to Liverpool, but their eventual destination was Paris. During this fateful voyage, Florence fell in love with the 42-year-old Englishman and decided to marry him. It was a decision she no doubt came to regret over and over again in later life. It was a decision that led her to the condemned cell.

The next year, 1881, Florence and James Maybrick were married at St James's, Piccadilly. The newly wed couple settled down at Battlecrease House, a mansion in Aigburth, a wealthy Liverpool suburb, where they produced two children, a boy called James Chandler (or 'Bobo') and a girl named Gladys Evelyn. They were born in 1882 and 1885. To begin with, all was well, but in 1887 things began to go sour.

Behind the gentlemanly facade of James Maybrick's outward life there was another, darker life. He spent much of each year in Norfolk,

Virginia. This meant that he was often away from home, so to begin with Florence had no suspicions when he went off on secret visits to Whitechapel, where the mistress lived. But eventually Florence discovered that her husband had a mistress, and not only that but he had had a mistress all along. He had five children by the mistress, and two of them had been born during the time he had been married to Florence. He was supporting the mistress with payments of £100 a year.

Florence was furious. She stopped sleeping with Maybrick and their relationship froze, although they kept up the outward appearance of their marriage, probably for the sake of their children.

Florence was still young and not unnaturally began to take an interest in other men. In particular she enjoyed the company of one of her husband's friends, Alfred Brierley, a handsome young man nearer her own age. James went on visiting his mistress. He also went on eating arsenic and strychnine, which had become an addiction with him. On one of his visits to Virginia, James had contracted malaria, which had spread widely during the Civil War. He had made a recovery from the malaria – but not from the treatment. He became addicted to the ingredients of Fowler's Medicine for the rest of his life. One of the chemists Maybrick used as a supplier, and who gave evidence at Florence's trial, said Maybrick had visited his shop as many as five times a day to get his pick-me-up. By 1887, the arsenic and strychnine pick-me-ups were having a disastrous effect on Maybrick's personality.

Arsenic was a common ingredient in a range of medicines and potions in the nineteenth century. Many women used it as a base for cosmetics (Elizabeth I had famously used it in the preparation that made her face white and corpse-like). Victorian chemists used it to make flypaper. It was only when Florence found caches of white powder hidden in various places round the house that she realised her husband was a drug addict. But, as with the mistress, it took her several years of marriage to find out. James Maybrick, a man with a double life, was not the man she thought she had married.

That Florence had taken a lover, Alfred Brierley, came as no surprise to anyone who knew the Maybricks. But when Maybrick himself discovered what was going on he was furious. It was a classic case of the Victorian double-standard. It was fine for him to deceive his wife and take a mistress; it was outrageously immoral for Florence to deceive him by taking a lover. He was also mortified that everyone who mattered knew that Florence had a lover. He beat her for it.

James Maybrick often went to London to visit his brother Michael, better known as the popular composer Stephen Adams. Michael might be able to write best-selling songs like *The Holy City*, but he could not soothe his brother's savage breast. By June 1888, James Maybrick started to experience health problems. He had always been a hypochondriac, so his doctor thought nothing was wrong. He saw his doctor twenty times that summer. If modern testing techniques had been available, Dr Hopper would probably have diagnosed the drug-taking as the cause of the problem. Maybrick was suffering from years of serious drug abuse. As it was he got no diagnosis and prescribed himself ever-larger doses of arsenic and strychnine. These had the effect of producing increased physical strength and stamina, but his personality disintegrated and there were ever -greater emotional problems.

James Maybrick was a fully-fledged 'arsenic-eater'. He told a friend about his arsenic addiction. 'It is meat and drink to me. I don't tell everybody. I take it when I can get it, but my doctors won't put any in my medicines except now and then. That only tantalizes me.' This remark could explain his apparent hypochondria; he was going back to his doctors as frequently as possible in the hope that they would prescribe something with arsenic in it. 'You would be horrified, I dare say, if you knew what this is – it is arsenic. We all take some poison, more or less. For instance I am now taking arsenic enough to kill you.'

It was in March 1889 that Florence spent her first illicit weekend with Alfred Brierley in London. Maybrick was suspicious. On 29 March, the couple were seen quarrelling openly at the Grand National. The row continued and intensified when they got home. Maybrick beat his wife and dragged her round the bedroom that night. The following day the doctor came to treat Florence's black eye and she told him she was going to seek a separation from Maybrick. The row simmered on into April. Just before Maybrick became seriously ill, Florence made her biggest mistake. When she lost her arsenic-based cosmetic prescription, she made up the preparation herself by soaking a dozen flypapers to dissolve out the arsenic. It was quite a common stunt at the time, and she made no attempt to hide what she was doing. All the servants saw what she was up to – which should have proved to them that she had no evil intent. At the trial, Florence's defence counsel, Sir Charles Russell, made this very point, emphasizing that Florence had bought the flypapers openly at shops where she was well known. Nevertheless, the nurse, the aptly named Alice Yapp, started to gossip about her, putting the rumour about that Mrs Maybrick was trying to poison Mr Maybrick. The servants had never liked Mrs Maybrick.

On 28 April, Maybrick was violently sick after eating a lunch his wife had prepared. He was dazed, numb in the legs. He recovered the next day but had repeated relapses the following week. Florence visited another chemist and bought another two dozen flypapers. On 7 May, Maybrick collapsed, vomiting so badly that he could keep no food down. He experienced a horrible and persistent sensation that he had a hair in his throat.

James Maybrick's condition deteriorated so sharply that Nurse Yapp's suspicions seemed to be confirmed. The flypaper poisonings of Mrs Flanagan and Mrs Higgins were still fresh in the minds of Liverpudlians, and it was obvious to the servants that Mrs Maybrick was another Mrs

Flanagan. She had a word with a family friend; 'Thank God, Mrs Briggs, you have come, for the mistress is poisoning the master.' Mrs Briggs sent a telegram to Maybrick's brother: 'COME AT ONCE. STRANGE THINGS GOING ON HERE.'

Michael came up from London and took charge. He assumed that Florence was indeed poisoning his brother, and he saw to it that James changed his Will. Michael was also given Power of Attorney, so that he had the authority to handle Maybrick's estate. The new Will greatly reduced Florence's inheritance, which was a simple expedient measure to remove Florence's incentive to kill Maybrick.

Maybrick was closely supervised so that he could not be given any more poison, and Florence was virtually banned from entering his room. One evening, the servants saw Florence furtively removing a bottle of meat juice from Maybrick's bedside table. She put it back, equally furtively, a few minutes later. What had she put in it? The bottle was handed to a doctor for analysis. But the actions that were seen as 'furtive' may just have been the quiet solicitude people often show towards a sick person who is trying to sleep. All through this, Florence went on seeing Alfred Brierley. Then she made another terrible mistake. She wrote Brierley a letter, which she – equally rashly – gave to Nurse Yapp to post. Alice Yapp walked to the post office with little Gladys holding the fateful letter. Gladys dropped the letter in a muddy puddle – at least that was Alice Yapp's story. On the pretext that the letter would need to be put into a new envelope, Alice Yapp opened it – and read it. The letter included some incriminating sentences.

Dearest,

I cannot answer your letter fully today, my darling, but relieve your mind of all . . . fear of discovery now and in the future. M. has been delirious since Sunday, and I know now that he is perfectly ignorant of everything . . . Excuse this scrawl, my own darling, but I dare not leave the room for a moment, and I do not know when I shall be able to write to you again.

In haste, yours ever,
Florie.

The letter was never sent. Alice Yapp kept it and within hours everyone at Battlecrease House knew what she had written to her lover. Why should Alfred Brierley relieve his mind of all? Was the obstacle to their marriage about to be removed? What was it that Maybrick was perfectly ignorant of? Not their relationship, as he knew all about that. The letter also included the remark that Maybrick was 'sick unto death'. How did she know he was going to die, unless she was the one who was going to make sure that he did? Much was made of the phrase at her trial. But the English lawyers and jurors were making no allowance for the fact that Florence Maybrick was an American. In her 'Southern' usage, the deadly phrase was a common exaggeration and meant no more than 'very ill'. It should not have been taken literally.

Maybrick's condition got worse. His doctor prescribed meat juice, specifically with nothing added. But Maybrick was desperate to have something added. He wanted the arsenic poisoning. Servants overheard wisps of conversation between the Maybricks. Maybrick: 'Don't give me the wrong medicine again.' Florence: 'What are you talking about? You never had the wrong medicine.' This was interpreted as meaning that Maybrick knew he was being poisoned and was telling Florence to stop adding poison. But now that we know he was an arsenic-eater, he may have been accusing her of not giving him arsenic. This is exactly what Florence said at her trial; that her husband had nagged her to give him one of the powders, that she had at first refused but he had begged her so piteously that she in the end agreed.

On the evening of May 9, Maybrick asked Florence to add some of his powder to the juice. It is not clear how much she added, and with what intention. Maybrick's food and urine were tested earlier in the day and they contained no arsenic.

On 11 May, 1889 James Maybrick died. His brother Michael took charge immediately, in effect putting Florence under house arrest. Two days later, the coroner found that Maybrick had died of 'inflammation of the stomach and bowels set up by some irritant poison'. At the trial, the distinguished forensic expert Dr Tidy said that Maybrick had died of gastro-enteritis caused by an irritant. There was no mention of arsenic poisoning. The next day, inevitably, Florence Maybrick was arrested for the murder of her husband.

Baroness von Roques hired Sir Charles Russell, a lawyer who had been a great barrister in his day but was now past his prime. He had had a string of losses and was less than fresh when he came to Florence's case; he had just finished fighting another long gruelling trial. Florence was also unlucky in her trial judge. Mr Justice James Stephen was only two years away from being committed to a lunatic asylum in Ipswich. During the Maybrick trial, he did and said a number of inappropriate things, including denouncing Florence Maybrick's statement as a lie. He was at least half-mad. The trial is viewed by many as a model of legal impropriety.

The Maybrick trial began on 31 July, 1889 in a flurry of public interest; it was a major event. Florence Maybrick played up to this magnificently and melodramatically by wearing black crepe in the dock. She was a widow, after all: some would say determinedly so. The public had decided that, like Mrs Flanagan, she was guilty, and they booed and jeered the black van that took her to the Liverpool courthouse. The trial, which lasted seven days, at first seemed to go well for Florence. Right up until the last couple of days it looked to most observers as if there would be a 'not guilty' verdict. Then it suddenly switched to 'guilty'. It seems almost incredible that at no point during the trial were the jury told about Maybrick's serious addiction to arsenic and strychnine. Florence's lawyer made the mistake of calling her as a witness at the end of the proceedings and allowing her to make a statement, in which she attempted haltingly and tearfully to explain that she had only tried to use the flypaper to make a cosmetic preparation. It sounded lame, like a feeble and inadequate excuse. She also unwisely said that she had confessed her adultery to her husband the day before he died, and 'received his entire forgiveness for the wrong I had done him'. That underlined her role as a betrayer, which was unhelpful. The effect was made even more devastating to Florence's chance of acquittal by Mr Justice Stephen's comment that she was lying. He was profoundly prejudiced against Florence because of her affair with Brierley; it was really the adultery he was denouncing. She was a wicked women – and therefore killed her husband.

The trial verdict was a bombshell. The jurors had in effect been directed to find against Florence Maybrick and after only 35 minutes of deliberation they decided she was guilty. Mr Justice Stephen put on his black cap and passed the sentence of death on Florence Maybrick. She was doomed. In 1889, Britain had no Court of Criminal Appeals. Defendants who lost their cases, like this one, had no recourse whatever, even if the verdict had been arrived at through the blunders of an incompetent barrister or an insane judge. There was always Queen Victoria, but she did not have a reputation for pardoning criminals. Following the verdict, there was a huge public demonstration of public support for Mrs Maybrick, with several petitions for clemency.

The speech Florence had made before collapsing in a faint in the dock had been badly judged in terms of a verdict, but it won her enormous popular support. She received several proposals of marriage while she waited in the condemned cell. Just four days before she was due to be hanged, the Home Secretary issued a reprieve; the death sentence was commuted to life imprisonment.

Florence went to prison, where she was never visited by her children. Michael Maybrick was in complete control of the family now, and he evidently still believed that Florence had killed his brother. When the children were old enough to make up their own minds, they still did not visit her, presumably by then conditioned to regard her as a treacherous murderess, their father's killer. She never saw them again.

The major miscarriage of justice led directly to some significant reforms in the British legal system. In 1907 a Court of Criminal Appeals was set up. When Florence was finally freed, in 1904, she spent six months at a convent in Truro before returning with her mother to America. She wrote the dramatic story of her life, *My Lost Fifteen Years,* and made a living by giving lectures, until she tired of going over and over her sad story. She reverted to her maiden name, Florence Chandler, and got a job as a housekeeper in Connecticut. As an old lady, she was taken up as a cause by the boys at a nearby school in South Kent, which is where she died on 23 October, 1941 at the age of 79. She had lived in Connecticut in complete anonymity, thanks to one great act of kindness. Twenty years before her death, she had given a black lace dress to a friend, Genevieve Austin. Genevieve noticed the old name-tag, which Florence had somehow over-looked. It read 'Florence Maybrick'. Genevieve was a real friend, and she kept the secret for twenty years, only revealing to the press after Florie's death exactly who the old 'cat lady' of South Kent had been. They buried her in the South Kent School cemetery.

That might be the end of the story, but there is a tailpiece to it. In 1993 a diary was discovered, purporting to be James Maybrick's diary, and revealing that he was Jack the Ripper. A second piece of evidence has also emerged: a man in Liverpool bought a pocket watch as a present for his granddaughter. There was tiny writing scratched on the inside cover which could only be deciphered with a microscope. It consisted of the signature '*J. Maybrick*', '*I am Jack*', and the initials of the Ripper's victims. There is also a police drawing based on eye witness reports that looks remarkably like Maybrick.

The circumstantial evidence that Maybrick had a mistress living in Whitechapel and that he was therefore in Whitechapel, on and off, during the period when the Ripper murders took place cannot seriously be used as evidence against Maybrick. Even so, a hypothesis that Maybrick was the Ripper has been floated. Could Maybrick have been the Ripper? We know from the events that led up to his death that he was leading at least a double life, and possibly a more complicated life than that. He covered up a mistress and five children, and in effect a second home in White-chapel. He also covered up a serious addiction to strychnine and arsenic. What else was he covering up? There was a dark side to Maybrick, we know. Was it even darker than we thought? The first entry in the diary is undated. It includes the sentence, 'I long for peace of mind but I sincerely believe that that will not come until I have sought my revenge on the whore and the whore master.' The whore is presumably Florence and the whore master Brierley.

Maybrick's alleged diary gives us a first Ripper murder in Manchester, which is a trial run for the Whitechapel murders. 'The whore is now with her maker and he is welcome to her.' Then came the most infamous murders in English criminal history, the Whitechapel murders that took place in the autumn of 1888. According to the 'Ripper diary' the Ripper was interrupted during the murder of Elizabeth Stride, 'Long Liz', early in the morning of 30 September. A passer-by saw what he was doing and ran off. 'I find it impossible to believe he did not see me. In my estimation I was less than a few feet from him. The fool panicked, it is what saved me.'

October was a quiet month in Whitechapel, and in the 'Ripper diary' too. In the diary, Maybrick records taking very large doses of drugs. 'The more I take the stronger I become.' Then came the final and most savage of the Ripper murders, the killing of Mary Kelly. This caused a great uproar of disgust and anger in

Whitechapel. The Ripper diary says that London was no longer a safe place for Jack the Ripper to operate in. Maybrick decided to return to Manchester, where he killed another victim in late December 1888. This killing 'did not amuse me. There was no thrill.'

It was in March 1889 that Florence Maybrick became concerned about her husband's health, telling Dr Humphreys, the family doctor, that Maybrick was taking a white powder which she thought was strychnine. Humphreys told her that if Maybrick should die he would tell the authorities about their conversation. He was clearly aware that suspicion could otherwise fall on Mrs Maybrick – as indeed it did with a vengeance. When it came to court, Humphreys failed to give Florence the support he had promised.

The last entry in the 'Ripper diary' is dated 3 May, 1889 and it anticipates death.

Some think Florence Maybrick was guilty, though the balance of evidence is (just) in favour of her innocence. Some, including Maybrick's relatives, believe that James Maybrick was Jack the Ripper, but most think the diary is a fake. If it was genuine, and Maybrick was the Ripper, and if Florence too was guilty, then Florence Maybrick turns out to have done the world a massive favour – by murdering Jack the Ripper!

It is an attractively sensational theory. Regrettably, there is an important inconsistency and that is the idea that Maybrick wanted to exact revenge on Florence and Alfred. Surely, the obvious thing to do was to kill the pair of them at once – not to go off and kill a random selection of strangers hundreds of miles away. This aspect of the 'Ripper diary' does not ring true. Another flaw in the hypothesis is that it has not been possible to identify a Ripper murder, or Ripper-like murder, in Manchester.

Was Florence Maybrick guilty? The truth is that we still can't be sure. Many studying the case have felt that if she did kill her husband, she was very nearly justified in doing so – and he was certainly begging to be fed arsenic. The thriller writer Raymond Chandler looked closely at all the evidence and his verdict was: 'I am pretty well convinced the dame was guilty.' I am not so sure. What I am sure of is that on the evidence presented she should have been acquitted.

PART THREE
MADMEN

Major John Oneby

'the quarrelsome gambler'

JOHN ONEBY WAS the son of a successful lawyer at Burnwell in Leicestershire. His father intended John to follow him into his own profession, and arranged an advantageous marriage with the niece of Sir Nathan Wright, Lord Keeper of the Great Seal of England. Sir Nathan appointed the young John Oneby as his train-bearer, which was intended as an honour but was actually well below what John aspired to or expected. John kept this position for some time, waiting for preferment, but no preferment came.

Tired of waiting for promotion, John bought a commission in the army, serving under the Duke of Marlborough in Flanders. He did well as a soldier, and was promoted. While in winter quarters at Bruges he quarrelled with another officer and they fought a duel in which the other officer was killed. Oneby was tried before a court-martial and acquitted.

The regiment was posted to Jamaica, and John Oneby naturally went with it. While at Port Royal, he got involved in another duel with another officer. This time he fatally wounded the other officer, who died several months later. Because the death did not immediately follow the duel, no action was taken against Oneby, who in effect had got away with a second murder.

By now John Oneby was Major John Oneby, but the Peace of Utrecht meant that the military campaigning was over. He was returned to England and reduced to half-pay. He found himself at a loose end in London and started drifting round the gaming-houses. He lived the life of a professional gambler, carrying dice and packs of cards in his pockets everywhere he went.

He met some men at a Covent Garden coffee-house and they adjourned to the Castle Tavern in Drury Lane, where they started a card-playing session. One of the group, Mr Hawkins, declined to play cards. Another, Mr Rich, asked who would accept a bet of three half-crowns. Mr Gower accepted, but as a joke laid down only three halfpence. Oneby was angry at this facetiousness and threw a bottle at Gower. In retaliation, Gower threw a glass back. Both men drew their swords, but Mr Rich intervened to restore peace. They sat down again to playing cards. Gower destabilized the truce by saying he accepted it, but irritated Oneby by adding that Oneby had been the aggressor. Predictably, Oneby rose to this, saying he would have his blood.

Mr Hawkins left the card party at three o'clock in the morning. After that, Oneby said to Gower that he wanted a word with him. They went into another room and shut and locked the door. The sound of clashing swords was heard. The waiter broke the door open and within they saw Oneby holding Gower with his left hand and his sword in his right hand; Gower's sword was lying on the floor. A doctor was called and he found that Oneby's sword had passed through Gower's intestines. Gower died the next day and Oneby was arrested immediately.

The trial was inconclusive. The jurors were in doubt, so they brought in a special verdict, which was to defer to the opinion of twelve judges. Oneby was detained in Newgate Prison while this could be arranged. He remained there for two years, and naturally became impatient. On a writ of habeas corpus, which declares that prisoners have a right to have their case tried, Oneby had a new trial before the Court of King's Bench. Lord Chief Justice Raymond and three other judges presided. They heard his case and told Oneby they would let him know their verdict.

Oneby was taken back to Newgate, where he gave 'a handsome dinner' to his custodians. He was evidently confident that he would be acquitted. The judges met again, this time without Oneby, to discuss the case for a further day. Throughout this day, the mad Major caroused with his warders, still confident of his imminent release. The judges broke their hearing up at ten in the evening, still without having come to a decision.

Shortly after this, the warder arrived in Oneby's cell to tell him he must be double-ironed to prevent him from escaping and that he would have to be moved to a more secure room unless he could pay for a full-time attendant. Oneby was shaken by this news, because it implied that he was not after all going to be released, but agreed to pay for an attendant. The man appointed was John Hooper. Hooper was an extraordinary man with a strong and entertaining sense of humour, but also terrifying in appearance. He would soon become an executioner, and already looked like one. When Oneby first set eyes on Hooper, he was terrified. 'Whenever I look at him I shall think of being hanged!' Hooper turned out to be a sympathetic character with a fund of funny stories, and Oneby found him a very good companion.

At last the judges came to a decision. Major Oneby was indeed guilty of murder. Proof of this was embedded in his declaration earlier in the evening that he would 'have the blood' of Gower. That proved an intention to kill. A few days after this sentence of death was passed and Oneby was ordered to be executed.

A couple of days before the appointed date of his execution, Major Oneby received a letter:

HONOURED SIR, This is to inform you that I follow the business of an undertaker in Drury Lane, where I have lived many years and am well known to several of your friends. As you are to die on Monday, and have not, as I suppose, spoken to anyone else about your funeral, if your honour shall think fit to give me orders, I will perform it as cheap, and in as decent a manner, as any man alive. Your honour's unknown humble servant, G. H.

The Major went into a spasm of fury. When the undertaker heard about the mad Major's anger and his notorious reputation as an impulsive killer, he decided to leave town for a few days and come back after the hanging. When John Hooper arrived in the evening to attend Oneby, he heard about the undertaker's letter, and agreed with Oneby (or pretended to agree with Oneby) that it was an insult.

All that was left to the Major now was to find a way of evading the humiliation of the gallows. He woke up at four in the morning on the Sunday and asked Hooper for a glass of brandy-and-water. Sitting up in bed he wrote a note:

> COUSIN TURVILL, Give Mr Akerman, the turnkey below stairs, half-a-guinea, and Jack, who waits in my room, five shillings. The poor devils have had a great deal of trouble with me since I have been here.

He gave the note to John Hooper and asked to be left alone to sleep. At about seven he had a visitor, accompanied by Oneby's footman. Oneby called out, 'Who is that, Philip?' As the visitors approached the Major's bed they could see that he had slashed his wrist; he was drenched in blood. They sent for a doctor, but he died before the doctor arrived.

The mad Major had committed three murders and was not hanged for any of them.

Matthew Henderson

'the servant who trod on a Lady's toe'

MATTHEW HENDERSON WAS born at North Berwick in Scotland, where he received a liberal education. When he was fourteen he went into service in the household of Sir Hugh Dalrymple, MP, who took Henderson with him to London. When he was only eighteen, Matthew married one of his master's maids, very much against Sir Hugh's wishes, although Sir Hugh did not dismiss him for his action. This shows Sir Hugh as an enlightened master because, in those days, masters expected to control their servants' private lives and regarded unilateral action of this sort as a gross impertinence.

Matthew liked his master and mistress. He thought Sir Hugh a very worthy gentleman. Lady Dalrymple, he said, was lady of great humanity and kindness, and she was greatly liked by all the other servants too.

A few days before the murder took place, Sir Hugh was due to leave town for a month and summoned Matthew Henderson to help him dress. While he was performing this customary task, Lady Dalrymple came into the room. Matthew was no doubt preoccupied with what he was doing and accidentally trod on her toe. He apologized profusely, and explained that it was entirely unintentional. Lady Dalrymple nevertheless boxed his ear and said he would be dismissed from their household. Matthew said it was unnecessary to dismiss him, as he was ready to go without compulsion.

Matthew Henderson thought it likely that Lady Dalrymple would recover from her anger and that his position would in the long term be safe. He sat it out and continued working as Sir Hugh's servant as before, just as if the toe-treading incident had never happened.

But Matthew still felt insulted and aggrieved. His much-loved mother had died several years earlier and he reflected that if she had known of the incident it would have broken her heart; he thanked Providence that she was dead and had seen none of this awful business. Although Lady Dalrymple had let the incident go, Matthew had not. He brooded on the insult and it grew and grew in his imagination, like the destructive grudge in William Blake's *Poison Tree*. As he fumed inwardly, he considered ways of exacting revenge on Lady Dalrymple for her insult. He came to the insane conclusion that she must die.

Left alone one night after the other servants had gone to bed, he stayed in the kitchen to clean some plate. Then he went into the back-parlour, which doubled as his bedroom, and let down his folding bed. He prepared for sleep by taking off his shoes and tying up his hair with his garter. The thought suddenly came to him that this was the right moment to go and kill Lady Dalrymple. He would do it now. He went into the kitchen to get a small iron cleaver and then went upstairs to the first landing. After a few moments he came down again, shocked at the idea of what he had proposed to do. Then he went up again, this time entering his lady's bedroom. He pulled back the curtain round her bed and saw that she was fast asleep.

Still, he was unable to carry out the dreadful deed. Twice he went back to the bedroom door in a turmoil of indecision. Then he stood over her and silently mimed the murder, bringing the cleaver down twelve or fourteen times, but stopping short of hitting her. She was still asleep. Then he repeated the cleaver action, but this time hitting Lady Dalrymple. She woke up at once and instinctively started struggling, falling out of the bed onto the floor. Then, as the poor woman lay helpless on the floor, Matthew Henderson delivered the blow that killed her.

Henderson went back to his own bed and sat on it for ten minutes. Then it came to him to rob the house. Presumably, in his disturbed mental state, he thought he might as well be hanged for a sheep as for a lamb. He went back up to Lady Dalrymple's room and took a gold watch, two diamond rings and some other things.

Matthew Henderson was hanged at Tyburn on 25 February, 1746. There was no question of Matthew Henderson's guilt, and in those days no question of diminished responsibility. He was clearly mentally ill. The many changes of mind during the half hour running up to the murder show that Henderson's mind was profoundly disturbed, that he did not know what he was doing, that he was not really responsible for his actions.

Laurence, Earl Ferrers

'and his unfortunate steward'

QUEEN ANNE CREATED Robert, Lord Ferrers, Viscount Tamworth and Earl Ferrers in 1711. This lord had huge estates, but he also had a huge family – fifteen sons and twelve daughters, the children of two wives – and he reduced his estates considerably by making dutiful provision for all these offspring. At the death of the first Earl, his title descended to his second son, who died childless, and then to the tenth son, who was the father of Laurence, Earl Ferrers.

Laurence, Earl Ferrers was married in 1752 to a daughter of Sir William Meredith. He was an unremarkable man when sober, and it would indeed have been better if he had remained sober. When he was drunk he behaved with the brutal and wild abandon of a madman. When he was first married, all seemed well, and his wife saw nothing wrong with him. But as time passed, he behaved more and more cruelly towards her, so that in the end she was forced to leave him and return to her parents; she also applied to Parliament for redress.

An Act was passed which allowed her a separate income to be generated out of her husband's estate. Trustees were appointed to supervise this arrangement, and Mr Johnson, who lived and worked within the Earl's household as his trusted steward, was proposed as the receiver of rents for the Countess's use. He was at first reluctant to do this, but the Earl himself urged him to take on this extra role.

The Earl ran a rather unusual household at Stanton, his seat just outside Ashby-de-la-Zouch in Leicestershire. He lived with a Mrs Clifford and her four illegitimate daughters. He had three maidservants and five menservants. Mr Johnson lived at the Lount, the Ferrers 'home farm' about half a mile from his lordship's house. In the course of his work he visited his lordship from time to time to settle the accounts. After a while the Earl came to dislike Johnson, associating him with the unpalatable notion of having to hand over part of his estate to his estranged wife. He accused Johnson of conspiring to stop him getting a coal contract and called him a villain, telling him to get out of the farm.

Johnson was unwilling to leave the farm, and the Earl found that he was unable to get him out; the trustees had already granted him a lease on the house in fulfilment of a promise by the Earl himself. So the Earl now had a steward he hated and distrusted, living in what he regarded as his farm, and he was unable to get rid of him. It was probably at this time that the Earl decided to get rid of Johnson in some other way.

On 13 January, 1760 Earl Ferrers went to the Lount. After some conversation with Johnson, the

Earl told him to come to him at Stanton the following Friday, 18 January at three in the afternoon. On the day when Johnson was expected, Ferrers had his lunch and then went to the still-house to tell Mrs Clifford to take the children off for a walk. She prepared herself and the girls for a walk, and set off to her father's house, not far away; she was told to return at half past five. The menservants were then sent off on various errands. Ferrers was then left in his house with only the three maids.

Then Mr Johnson arrived and was admitted by one of the maids, Elizabeth Burgeland. The Earl asked him to wait in the still-room. After about ten minutes the Earl called him into his room and locked the door. Then he started accusing him of various offences and ordered him to kneel down. Johnson went down on one knee. Then the Earl shouted, loud enough for the maidservants outside to hear, 'Down on the other knee! Declare that you have acted against Lord Ferrers! Your time is come – you must die!'

Then Earl Ferrers suddenly drew a pistol from his pocket and fired it at Johnson. The ball hit Johnson, but he got up, begged the Earl to do him no more violence. Hearing the shot, the maids came to the door in alarm, and Ferrers left the room. A messenger was sent to fetch Mr Kirkland the surgeon from Ashby-de-la-Zouch.

Johnson was put to bed. Ferrers went to his bedside and asked him how he felt. Johnson told him he was dying and asked Ferrers to send for his family. Johnson's daughter arrived soon afterwards. While she was there, Ferrers pulled down the bed clothes and bathed Johnson's wound with a pledget or compress.

After that, the Earl went off to do some hard drinking. It appears that when he shot the fatal bullet he was perfectly sober, but he became fighting drunk shortly afterwards. When Mr Kirkland arrived, Ferrers told the surgeon he had shot Johnson but believed Johnson was frightened rather than hurt. He also said he had intended to shoot him dead because he was a villain and deserved to die. But since Johnson's life had been spared, he now wanted Kirkland to save him. He warned Kirkland that if anyone tried to take him into custody he would shoot him. Kirkland saw how things stood and promised him he would not be seized; then he went to attend to the wounded man.

Kirkland found the ball lodged in Johnson's body. Ferrers was surprised at this, saying that he had tried the pistol a few days before and fired a ball right through a deal board an inch and a half thick. The evidence for premeditation was mounting. The drinking continued and the Earl went through a range of different passions. The fleeting bout of compassion gave way to rage, fear and malice. At one point he attacked the wounded Johnson in his bed, trying to pull the bedclothes off so that he could hit him; he had to be restrained.

Mrs Clifford sensibly suggested that Mr Johnson should be taken home, but Ferrers wanted to keep him at Stanton, 'to plague the villain'. He spoke to Miss Johnson, telling her that if her father died, he would take care of her and her family – so long as they did not prosecute. Eventually, towards midnight, Earl Ferrers went to bed. In spite of the Earl's orders, Kirkland was keen to get Johnson home. He went to the Lount, fitted up an armchair with poles to make an improvised sedan chair, and returned to Stanton at about 2 o'clock in the morning to collect Mr Johnson.

Mr Johnson died seven hours later. His neighbours set about arming themselves, and then went to Stanton to take the murderer. As they entered the yard, they met Earl Ferrers, partly dressed, going towards the stable as if he was going to take out a horse. One of the men, Springthorpe, approached the Earl with a pistol, telling him to surrender. Because the Earl put his hand in his pocket, Springthorpe thought he might be going for his own pistol and stepped back. The Earl escaped into the house.

By now a great crowd had gathered at Stanton, shouting at Earl Ferrers to come out. Two hours later, Ferrers appeared at the attic window and called, 'How is Johnson?'

'Dead!' they shouted, but Ferrers refused to believe them. He told them to disperse. He would let them in and give them food and drink. Then he said no-one would take him and disappeared from the window. Another two hours passed before the Earl was spotted, outside once more, on the bowling-green, armed to the teeth with a blunderbuss, a dagger and a brace of pistols. One of the men, Curtis, walked boldly up to him – so boldly that the Earl calmly surrendered to him.

Earl Ferrers was immediately taken into custody by the crowd, who took him to the public house at Ashby, where a coroner's inquest was held. The jury brought in a verdict of wilful murder against him and he was committed to Leicester Gaol.

But Ferrers was an Earl and therefore entitled to be tried in the House of Lords. Two weeks later, he was taken in his own landau, drawn by six horses, to the Lords. Black Rod ordered him to go the Tower, where he was admitted at six o'clock on 14 February. Earl Ferrers was now behaving very calmly and properly. He was imprisoned in the Round Tower. Two warders were with him all the time, one at the door; two guards were posted at the foot of the stairs and another on the drawbridge – with fixed bayonets.

His behaviour in the Tower showed that he was mentally ill. He was calm a lot of the time, but he would also suddenly start and tear his clothing. Mrs Clifford and her daughters followed him from Leicestershire, taking lodgings in Tower Street. Mrs Clifford went to the Tower, but she was not allowed to see Ferrers.

On 16 April, after waiting in the Tower about two months, Earl Ferrers was put on trial before his peers. There was no dispute about the murder having been committed. What was at issue was the Earl's state of mind. The Earl himself called witnesses whose testimony was to show that he was not of sound mind. But none of them could prove a level of insanity that relieved him of responsibility for his conduct. He defended himself with remarkable sensitivity and persuasiveness, even mentioning the curious situation he was in – of being reduced to the need to prove himself a lunatic.

It did not work, and then he admitted that he had done this only to gratify his friends. The peers gave their guilty verdict. He was to be hanged on 21 April and then his body dissected. He was given a short stay of execution in view of his rank. Earl Ferrers used this time to make a will, distributing his wealth among Mrs Clifford and her children, but also leaving £1,300 to Mrs Johnson's children. Because of his conviction, the will was not legally valid, but in fact provision was made as he asked.

A scaffold was erected under the gallows at Tyburn. A part of the platform, about a yard square, was raised eighteen inches above the rest of the floor, with a contrivance that would cause it to sink on a given signal. The whole was covered in black baize. The Earl was conveyed to Tyburn in his own landau. When at the outer gate of the Tower the Earl was formally put in the charge of the Sheriffs of London and Middlesex, Mr Sheriff Vaillant expressed concern at having such a sad duty to perform. But Ferrers said he was much obliged to him and took it kindly that he would accompany him.

Earl Ferrers was dressed in a spectacular white suit, richly embroidered in silver. It was the suit in which he had been married. The landau moved off with a guard of grenadiers. There were so many people out in the streets to see the spectacle of an Earl being taken to the gallows that the landau could scarcely move. In fact it took nEarly three hours to cross the City of London from the Tower to Tyburn. Ferrers remained calm, but said he wanted to have the whole affair over with; passing through such crowds was worse than death itself. He told the Sheriff sitting with him in the carriage that he had written to the king asking that he should be executed where his ancestor, the Earl of Essex, had been executed. He specifically mentioned to his majesty that he and the king shared part of the same arms, which was by no means a happy or a tactful thought. The king in any case turned down Ferrers' request. Ferrers thought it was hard that he had to die at the place set aside for common felons. But that was probably exactly the point his majesty was trying to make. Ferrers had behaved like a common felon; he therefore was a common felon.

At Tyburn, Earl Ferrers remained calm and dignified as he walked up onto the scaffold. Mr Humphries invited him to say the Lord's Prayer with him, so they knelt on two baize-covered cushions. Then Ferrers shouted, 'Oh God, forgive me all my errors! Pardon all my sins!' The executioner took his neckcloth off, put a white cap on his head, tied his arms with a black sash and put the noose over his head. Lord Ferrers walked three steps to the raised part of the scaffold and stood under the cross-beam. He asked the executioner, 'Am I right?' The white cap was pulled down over his face. The sheriff gave the signal (Ferrers' having declined to give one) and the raised section of the platform sank, leaving the bad Earl swinging in space.

He left a short piece of verse behind in his apartment, which included the line, 'In doubt I lived, in doubt I die.' There is no doubt that Earl Ferrers was a profoundly unstable man, certainly not mentally normal. If his case had come up two hundred years later, he might well have been diagnosed as a paranoid schizophrenic, and the charge would have been reduced to manslaughter.

George Allen

'a family massacre'

THE ALLENS WERE a poor family in Uttoxeter at the beginning of the nineteenth century. George Allen, the father of the household, was a troubled man given to epileptic fits and not altogether responsible for his actions. He had a wife and four children: a boy of ten, a girl of six, a boy of three and a babe in arms.

At eight o'clock in the evening on 12 January, 1807, George Allen went to bed for a rest. When his wife went up about an hour later, she found him sitting up in bed smoking his pipe. This was their usual ritual.

In another bed in the same room the three eldest children lay fast asleep. When his wife got into bed with the baby at her breast, he asked her what other man she had in the house. It was an irrational question. The house was very small and no other man could have been there without his knowing about his presence. She answered simply that no man had been in the house except him. He would not believe her, insisting that someone else was there. She insisted that there was no-one.

George Allen jumped out of bed and went

downstairs. Mrs Allen followed him, fearing what he would do, and asked where he was going in such a hurry. He ordered her to go upstairs. He went into their bedroom, and turned down the bedclothes of the bed where the three children were sleeping. She sensed that he was going to harm them and tried to hold him. He told her to leave him alone or he would 'serve her with the same sauce'. He straight away tried to cut her throat, but her neckerchief gave her a certain amount of protection and the wound was not fatal. He also wounded her in the chest.

Still clutching her baby, Mrs Allen managed to free herself from his grip, and escaped from him by half-running, half-tumbling downstairs. Before she had managed to recover herself and get to her feet again, the little girl fell at her feet with her head almost cut off. Allen had murdered her and thrown her body after his wife down the stairs. Mrs Allen got the house door open and screamed for help, shouting that her husband was cutting off their children's heads.

A neighbour quickly came to help her. When he went in with a light, he could see George Allen standing in the middle of the living room, holding a razor. The neighbour asked what he was doing. Allen said coolly, 'Nothing yet. I have only killed three of them'. When they all went upstairs they saw a truly dreadful sight in the bedroom. The two boys' heads were very nEarly severed, their bellies were cut open and their intestines pulled out and thrown on the floor.

George Allen made no attempt to escape, and

was taken into custody without giving any trouble. He said it had been his intention to kill his wife and all the children – and then kill himself.

An inquest was held on the children's bodies by Mr Hand, the coroner of Uttoxeter. Allen admitted he had killed the children, but expressed no regret. When he was questioned, he promised to confess something that preoccupied him. The coroner assumed this might refer to some earlier crime he wanted to own up to, and arranged for him to be examined by a group of men. But instead of confessing to other murders, he told a mad tale about a ghost in the shape of a horse. This horse had enticed him into a stable, where it injured him, drawing blood, and then flew up into the sky. 'With respect to the murder of my children', he observed to the coroner with apparent unconcern and detachment, 'I suppose it is as bad a case as ever I've heard of'.

There was no doubt that George Allen had committed the murders. He was found guilty and sentenced to death. He was hanged at Stafford on 30 March, 1807. It was known that Allen had epileptic fits, but no allowance was made for these. The preoccupation was with the horror of the killings and Allen's apparent detachment from them; but the detachment may itself well have been a symptom of the epilepsy. A modern court would not have found Allen guilty. In fact it would probably have found him unfit to plead. Certainly there was diminished responsibility on the grounds of insanity.

PART FOUR

A FAMILY
AFFAIR

KILLING HUSBANDS, WIVES,
PARTNERS AND PARENTS

Alice Arden of Faversham

'tell-tale footprints in the snow'

THOMAS ARDEN LIVED at Faversham in Kent, in the sixteenth century. He was a tall, good-looking man, married to a good-looking young woman, and seemed on the face of things destined for an ordinary and unremarkable happy marriage. But his wife began an affair with a servant of Lord North's called Mosbie. This affair was a turbulent one. At one stage they fell out and they had nothing to do with one another for a time. It would have been better for all concerned if it had stayed that way, but she wanted a reconciliation and sent him a present of some silver dice.

It was not long before Mosbie, who was described as a 'black swarthy fellow', was a constant guest at the Ardens' house. The affair between Mosbie and Mrs Arden became more and more open. Thomas Arden must have been as aware of it as the rest of Faversham, but he seems to have turned a blind eye, apparently in the hope of gaining some advantage from his wife's family. Alice Arden was having sex with Mosbie all the time now, and began to take a violent dislike to her husband. She wanted him out of the way and looked around for ways of getting rid of him.

She heard of a painter in Faversham who was a poisoner. He was ready to help and gave her a dose of poison with instructions to put it in the bottom of a porringer and pour milk on it. Alice forgot the instructions and poured the milk out first with the poison on top. That morning, Thomas was due to ride to Canterbury and before setting off he took a spoonful or two of milk. He didn't like the colour or the taste of it. He said, 'Mrs Alice, what sort of milk is it you gave me?'

She threw the dish down and said, 'I find nothing can please you.' Thomas set off for Canterbury, but along the way he stopped to vomit. In this way he escaped being fatally poisoned.

Then Alice got to know a servant of Sir Anthony Agers. His name was Green, and Green had a grudge against Thomas Arden because of a dispute over land. Arden had got hold of a piece of land that he himself wanted behind Faversham Abbey. Alice exploited Green's hatred of Thomas to get him to agree to find someone to murder him; Alice would pay him ten pounds. Green was sent on an errand to London and because he had to carry some money with him he got his neighbour to ride with him, Bradshaw, a Faversham goldsmith. After a while, he and Bradshaw saw a terrifying-looking man coming up the hill from Rochester towards them. Green saw him as a potential hired killer. Bradshaw recognized him as Black Will, whom he had known at Boulogne where he was a soldier and Bradshaw had been in the service of Sir Richard Cavendish. Bradshaw knew him as a robber and murderer, and was unwise enough to pass this crucial information to Green. He would later come to regret it. Soon they all met, Black Will accenting almost every word with an oath. They asked him where he was going. 'By my blood, I neither know nor care. I'll set up my stick and go as it falls.'

Bradshaw invited him to accompany them to Gravesend, where they would give him supper. Black Will remembered Bradshaw from Boulogne, but Bradshaw for some reason pretended not to remember him. Green invited Black Will to join him at his lodgings for a drink after he had supped. And so it went. Green took Black Will apart from Bradshaw and offered him ten pounds to kill Thomas Arden. Black Will was very eager to murder for money and asked only to have Arden pointed out to him. Sending word to Alice Arden that, 'thanks to Bradshaw', they had found their assassin, Green took Black Will to St Paul's the next day and pointed out Thomas Arden. Will wanted to know who it was that followed Arden. When Green told him it was one of Arden's servants, Will was all for killing him too. Green told him in no uncertain terms that he was not to kill anyone except Arden.

Green then told Arden's servant, a man called Michael, about the plot and about the conversation with Black Will. Michael realised that he too was in considerable danger as, in spite of Green's prohibition, Black Will might in the heat of the moment decide to kill him as well. Black Will was obviously ready to kill anyone at all, and extremely dangerous. Michael was considered a safe man to tell, because he was in love with a kinswoman of Mosbie's.

Thomas Arden was lodging at a parsonage in London, and Michael and Green agreed that Black Will should go there at night, find the doors open and go in and kill Arden. Michael helped Thomas Arden to bed, left the doors open as arranged, went to bed, and then was overwhelmed by the fear that Black Will would come in and kill both of them. He went straight downstairs again and bolted the doors. When Black Will arrived, he was unable to gain entry and went away in a fury. The next day, in a frenzy of swearing, Black Will confronted Green and threatened to kill Michael for locking him out. Green told him to let him find out from Michael what had gone wrong. Michael ingeniously explained the situation; his master had, unusually, got up to check the doors, found that Michael had left them open, locked them himself and reprimanded Michael for his slackness.

The next plan was to kill Thomas Arden on Rainham Down. Michael deliberately lamed his horse so that he could lag behind his master; he was still afraid that Black Will would kill him if he saw him with his master. As Michael hoped, Thomas urged him to stop off at a blacksmith's to have the horse's shoe attended to. Thomas rode on ahead to the place where Black Will was waiting to ambush him. Just as he got there, he was overtaken by several men that he knew, so Black

Will was unable to attack; he was thwarted again.

Another ambush was planned, between Faversham and the ferry. Black Will unfortunately waited for Arden in the wrong place and missed him altogether.

The scheme to murder Thomas Arden was turning into a farce. A new plan was thought up. At about six o'clock one evening, Black Will was hidden in a cupboard in the parlour of Arden's house, all the servants were sent away on a pretext, and Mosbie went and stood by the door in a silk night-gown. Thomas Arden had been visiting a neighbour called Dumpking, to do some business with him. When he got home and encountered Mosbie he asked him if it was supper time. Mosbie said he thought supper was not yet ready. Arden suggested that they play a game before supper, and took Mosbie through to the parlour. Alice was there but said nothing to her husband. Thomas Arden and Green sat down to play at the table; Michael stood behind his master holding a candle in such a way that Arden would not see Black Will, come out of the cupboard.

As they played, Mosbie said, 'Now, sir, I can take you if I please!' That was the signal for Black Will to jump out of the cupboard. He threw a towel round Arden's neck. Mosbie had a fourteen-pound pressing iron by him and hit Arden over the head with it. Arden gave a loud groan and fell down. Mosbie and Black Will carried him from the parlour into the counting-house and laid him down, still groaning. Black Will used a knife to gash his face and killed him.

He took the money from his pocket and the rings from his fingers. He emerged from the counting-house, immediately asking for his money. Alice Arden gave him the agreed sum of ten pounds, then he went to Green's to borrow a horse, and rode away.

After Black Will had gone, Alice went into the counting-house, took a knife and stabbed her husband in the chest seven or eight times, just to make sure he was dead. Then she and Mosbie cleaned the parlour, wiping up blood with a cloth. The bloody cloth and the bloodstained knife were thrown into a tub beside the well. After this, Alice coolly sent for two people from London who were staying in Faversham to come to supper; they had been invited some time earlier. Their names were Cole and Prune and they were grocers. She pretended to be expecting her husband at any moment, and suggested that they should start without him. Mosbie's sister was sent for to join the party.

After supper, Alice asked her daughter to play the virginals for them, frequently asking, 'I wonder Mr Arden stays so long.' Eventually the guests went back to their lodgings and Alice and Mosbie, together with Michael, a maid and Mosbie's sister, set about disposing of her husband's body. It was snowing that night, but they took the corpse out into the field next to the churchyard and left it about ten paces in. The dead body of Mr Arden was dressed in his night-gown and slippers and left lying on its back. Tucked into his slippers were a couple of tell-tale rushes.

Mosbie and Alice thought they were safe now. When the servants who were not in on the plot returned, she sent them out to look for Mr Arden. Neighbours were roused, as Mrs Arden was now pretending to be distraught at the non-appearance of her husband.

Thomas Arden was not a popular man in Faversham. He had managed to keep the fair wholly inside the abbey ground, which he himself owned, and this brought him the greatest benefit. As a result of this commercial opportunism, Faversham hated him bitterly. Faversham would not be distraught to find Thomas Arden lying dead in the snow, as was shortly to be the case, but it would avenge his death just the same.

It was Prune the grocer who spotted Arden's body first and called the rest of the searchers over. They found the rushes sticking out of his slipper and also the footprints in the snow of several people round the corpse and a trail of footprints leading to the garden door. The mayor told everyone to stand still, and then asked one person to go round to the other side of the house to pick up the trail of incriminating footprints. The mayor knew all about Alice Arden's irregular relationship with Mosbie and could see at once the motive. He suspected her and questioned her closely about her husband's murder. She denied it at first, but when the bloody cloth and the knife were found and shown to her she confessed. She cried out, 'Oh, the blood of God help me, for this blood I have shed!' She also confessed on behalf of all her co-conspirators.

Mrs Arden, Michael, the maid, Mrs Arden's daughter – all were taken off to prison. The mayor then went to the Flower-de-Luce (Fleur-de-Lys) and found Mosbie in bed there. It was not long before the mayor discovered smears of the murdered man's blood on his clothes. Mosbie wanted to know why they were in his room. The mayor said, 'You may easily see the reason. This is our evidence.' Mosbie confessed and was taken to prison. Green and Black Will remained at liberty, as did the poisoning painter, who was never heard of again.

At the assizes at Faversham, the prisoners were tried and condemned. The conspirators were all brought to justice. There was just one man who suffered who ought not to have suffered – and that was Bradshaw. The letter Green sent to Alice Arden implicated Bradshaw, as having introduced him to the assassin, but what had actually happened was that Black Will approached them on the road, and Bradshaw was simply able to tell Green who – and what – he was. Bradshaw was represented in court as the procurer of Black Will. Bradshaw tried as hard as he could to protest his innocence. He asked to see all the condemned people. He asked each of them if they had ever had any conversation with him and they all said no. Even so, poor Bradshaw was condemned and hanged on the strength of Green's letter.

The murderers were, unusually, executed in several different places. Michael was hanged at Faversham. One of the maids was burnt there, bitterly denouncing Mrs Arden, who had brought her to this terrible end. Mosbie and his sister were hanged at Smithfield. Alice Arden was burnt at Canterbury. Green returned to the area some years later, perhaps thinking it was safe to do so, and was taken up and hanged on the highway south of Faversham; but at least before his death he proclaimed that Bradshaw had been innocent. Black Will was burnt on a scaffold at Flushing in the Low Countries.

Abbé Guerra and the Cenci family

'the nail killers'

FRANCESCO CENCI WAS one of the most vicious criminals in Italian history. He was the son of Pope Pius V, in the days when popes had only a slight pretence at celibacy, and he had inherited a huge fortune when his father died. Cenci discovered that the money bought him not only whatever pleasures he fancied but immunity from legal action as well. He saw a beautiful young woman, and did not have to go through the laborious business of a seduction; he simply had her kidnapped so that he could rape her. He did this repeatedly. When arrested, as he was more than once, he simply bought himself out and re-offended.

Cenci had twelve legitimate children by his first wife. He disliked them all and when two of his sons died he said he would not be satisfied until the others were dead too. But he made an exception for his daughter Beatrice. With his penchant for girls, he began to notice the pale skin, the auburn hair, the budding beauty. He became sexually infatuated with her and at the same time frightened that some other man might come and take her from him, so her sent her off to La Petrella, an isolated castle near Naples. There he was able to visit his beautiful daughter without fear of competition.

Or so he thought. A rich young aristocrat called Guerra, an abbé, proposed marriage several times. Cenci refused, and eventually gave him the reason; he told Guerra baldly that he wanted his daughter for himself. 'She is my mistress.' Guerra could not believe it. He assumed Cenci was just trying to put him off, and went on pressing to gain access to Beatrice. Eventually he met her and she told him that what her father had said was true. Guerra was appalled and disgusted, as well as thwarted, and declared that Cenci must die.

Beatrice agreed with Guerra. She had been ill-used by her father in more ways than one. Her two brothers Giacomo and Bernardo also wanted to see their father dead. They were all thoroughly disgusted by their father's behaviour, and they were also alarmed at the rate of his spending. Before long there would be nothing left for them to inherit.

Giacomo Cenci hired two soldiers called Marzio and Olimpio to do the deed. Marzio was infatuated with Beatrice. Olimpio had already had sex with Beatrice while he was the castellan of La Petrella – until, that is, Francesco Cenci had understandably dismissed him. Both men had strong motives for hating Cenci. Both were ready to kill him.

On the evening of 9 September, 1598, Beatrice and her stepmother, who was living at La Petrella with her, mixed opium with Francesco's wine. Old Cenci drank a lot and without suspecting anything at all he passed out. He was carried to his bedroom. Marzio and Olimpio entered and drove two large nails into Cenci, one through an eye and into his brain, the other into his throat. It is not clear why they did this, as they then threw the still-living Cenci out of the window to try to make his death look like an accident. Francesco Cenci landed in a tree and he was found there, dead, the next day. In spite of the fact that this was very obviously a murder, everyone seemed happy to pass the incident off as an accident. The old man had perhaps leant out of his window while drunk, they said, and fallen from his balcony.

All seemed to have gone smoothly, but there were rumours spreading during the weeks that followed. The siblings had had much to gain from their father's death. The court in Naples sent a commissioner to investigate Francesco Cenci's death. But the only evidence he was able to get was the statement of a washerwoman who had washed a bloodstained sheet for Beatrice, but that had been explained to her as a menstrual accident. There was no evidence to go on. Everyone at La Petrella was content to connive at the murder because old Cenci was such a horrible man. Even the Neapolitan authorities would have gone along with it but for one thing – the taboo against parricide. Killing was one thing, but killing your father was quite another. The fabric of Italian society was threatened by such a crime.

The court of Naples decided to move the

enquiry on a step, by resorting to the favoured sixteenth century police enquiry method – torture. Guerra heard of the plan and decided that Marzio and Olimpio were now the weak links. They had to be removed. He hired two more soldiers to murder them. They successfully killed Olimpio at Terni, but Marzio was arrested before they could reach him. Marzio was tortured and confessed the details of the plot to kill Cenci.

Beatrice, Giacomo and Bernardo were arrested and they too were subjected to torture. Beatrice was subjected to a form of torture called the strappado. She was stripped, her wrists were tied behind her and a rope attached to them. Then she was hoisted up into the air on a pulley. Her arms were pulled up behind her and her shoulders were dislocated. In spite of the intensity of the pain, Beatrice denied murdering her father. She fainted, was lowered to the ground, revived, then hoisted up again for another bout of questioning. Bernardo was tortured, and he confessed. Giacomo was tortured too, and he too confessed. Giacomo's flesh had been ripped from his body with red-hot pincers.

The Cencis appealed to the Pope, Clement VIII. He was inclined to show leniency and was ready to grant the three siblings a reprieve. Unfortunately another case of parricide came up at the same time: the Marquis of Santa Croce was stabbed to death by his son. It looked as if parent-slaying was turning into a fashion. The Pope decided he had to allow the death sentences to be carried out.

On 11 September, 1599, nearly a year after the murder, the Cencis were executed. Beatrice was beheaded on a scaffold; the executioner held up her head to show it to the crowd. Next came Lucrezia, Cenci's second wife. Next came Giacomo, who for some reason was killed in a different way. His head was smashed with a mace. Bernardo was given a last-minute reprieve by the Pope, who changed his sentence to life imprisonment. For some reason he was freed after only a year in prison. Marzio was already dead, having died in the torture chamber. Guerra, the instigator of the plot, was ironically the only one to escape. He managed to get out of Italy, changed his identity and was never heard of again.

It is an extraordinarily grim and brutal story, the sort of thing we expect to find in the plot of a Jacobean tragedy, but it shows that playwrights were simply reflecting the gruesome events of their time. The story was taken up by Shelley as the subject of his tragic verse-drama, *The Cenci*. Those who died on the scaffold were the real victims. There is no doubt that old Francesco Cenci was an irredeemably evil criminal and that the rest of the family were driven to take an extreme measure to get rid of him. He is perhaps the only one in the story to have received true justice.

Alexander Balfour

'escaping the maiden'

ALEXANDER BALFOUR WAS born near Kinross in 1687, at the house of his father, Lord Burleigh. He was educated at a village school in Orwell, close to Burleigh's house, and then at the University of St Andrew's. Alexander Balfour was a good, conscientious student and pursued his studies with great success.

Alexander's father planned to put him into the army. In Flanders he would serve under the command of the great Duke of Marlborough. Lord Balfour reasonably expected that his son would have an assured career in the army. In those days, preferment and promotion depended heavily on family connections, and Alexander Balfour had blood connections with the Earl of Stair and the Duke of Argyll, who were themselves both high-ranking army officers.

Lord Burleigh's scheme did not come to fruition. During the university vacation, Alexander returned to his father's house and fell in love with the governess appointed to teach his two sisters. The governess was called Anne Robertson. She was a talented, refined and well-educated young lady, but when Lord Burleigh heard about the liaison developing between his son and Miss Roberston he did everything in his power to end it. He dismissed her at once and sent his son off on the Grand Tour.

Before Alexander Balfour left for France and Italy, he wrote a letter to Anne telling her to wait for him and warning her that if he returned to find her married he would kill her husband.

In due course, Miss Robertson met and married a schoolmaster from Inverkeithing in Fifeshire, not thinking that Balfour meant so literally what he had written in his letter. But when Balfour did return, the first thing he did was to ask after Miss Robertson. When he was told that she had married, he went straight to Inverkeithing. He saw Anne, now Anne Syme, sitting at her window, nursing her child. As soon as she saw Balfour, she remembered the awful threat he had made and screamed in terror, realising what was about to happen.

She shouted to her husband to protect himself, but Mr Syme had done nothing wrong and could not conceive why anyone should be about to do him harm. In any case, within moments, Balfour was in the schoolroom, confronting Syme. As soon as he found him he shot him through the heart. Syme fell dead.

There was a scene of great confusion in which Alexander Balfour escaped from Inverkeithing. But it was not to be long before he was apprehended. In a few days he was arrested at an inn four miles outside Edinburgh.

Balfour was tried, found guilty, sentenced to death. Because he came from an aristocratic family, Balfour was not sentenced to die by hanging but by the maiden. This was a beheading machine very similar to the French guillotine, and in fact the forerunner of the guillotine; the main difference was that the guillotine had a diagonally sloping blade edge – a refinement designed by Louis XVI – whereas the maiden had a horizontal blade edge.

The scaffold was built in Edinburgh for Alexander Balfour's execution and it seemed certain that he would lose his head. But on the day before the execution his sister visited him in prison. His sister looked very much like him in height and their faces were alike too. They changed clothes, and so Alexander Balfour was able to walk free from prison, disguised as his own sister. His friends provided a horse for him and a servant at the west gate of the city, so that they could ride away to a distant village. There Balfour changed clothes again and left Scotland.

Lord Burleigh, Balfour's father, died during the reign of Queen Anne, but not before working to obtain a pardon for his son. In this way, Alexander Balfour was able to succeed to the family title, honours and property. Balfour expressed repentance for the murder of Mr Syme, and lived on until 1752, a full fifty years after he should have been beheaded by the maiden.

Catherine Hayes
'the unwanted husband'

CATHERINE HAYES LIVED in Birmingham with her parents, a poor couple called Hall, until she was fifteen. She quarrelled with her parents and set off from Birmingham with the idea of making her way to London. On her way she met some officers who told her they liked the look of her and flattered her into going with them to their quarters at Great Ombersley in Worcestershire. Catherine stayed with them for some time before wandering off into Warwickshire, where she became a servant in the house of a Mr Hayes, a respectable farmer.

It was not long before she started an affair with Mr Hayes's son, and they were married in secret in Worcester. The officers attempted to trap young Hayes into enlisting, and he found he had no choice but to tell his father the whole story. Mr Hayes did not approve of the marriage, but saw there was no point in opposing his son and tried to set him up in business as a carpenter. But Catherine wanted him to enlist, so he did. The regiment was posted to the Isle of Wight, and she followed him there. Then old Mr Hayes bought his son out of the army, which cost him sixty pounds.

Six years later, Catherine pressed her husband

to move to London, where he bought a house. Part of it was let as lodgings. He also opened a shop in the chandlery and coal trade, which was profitable enough. He also earned quite a lot by lending small sums of money on pledges. At this time anyone could set up as a pawnbroker; there was no regulation at all.

Mr Hayes had by now realised that his wife was a restless woman who would never be contented. Her main pleasure now seemed to be in instigating quarrels with the neighbours. She also seemed inconsistent in her attitude towards her husband. Sometimes she spoke of him with affection to her friends, sometimes with contempt. She said on one occasion that to kill him would be no more of a sin than to kill a dog. Mr Hayes became uneasy about her and decided to move away. He moved his business to the Tottenham Court Road, then again to Tyburn Road (which is now called Oxford Street).

Hayes was a good businessman and he soon had enough money to retire from business. He took lodgings near Oxford Street. A man who was presented to Hayes as a son of Catherine's by her former lover, a man called Billings, lived in the same house. Both Billings and his 'mother' got into the habit of eating well at Hayes's expense. On one occasion when Hayes was out of town, Mrs Hayes and her son were so extravagant that the neighbours thought they should tell Hayes. He rebuked her. This led to a quarrel breaking out, and this in turn developed into a fight. She then decided she would kill him, and enlist the help of her son.

A man named Thomas Wood, who was up in town from Worcestershire, sought out Hayes to see if Hayes would give him accommodation, as he was afraid of being 'impressed', or compulsorily enlisted by the press gangs. Wood had only been in London a few days when she told him of her plan to kill Hayes. Wood was shocked at the idea initially, and had no wish to join in a scheme to murder his friend and benefactor. Catherine Hayes was taking an enormous risk but eventually persuaded Thomas Wood that her husband was an atheist who had murdered two of his children, one of whom was buried under an apple tree, the other under a pear tree. She added that fifteen hundred pounds would come to her when her husband died, and that this would be divided among her accomplices. Wood caved in and agreed to the murder.

Thomas Wood left London for a time, then returned to find Mr and Mrs Hayes and Billings drinking together convivially and apparently getting on well. Hayes asked Wood to join them and the three conspirators went off to buy more alcohol. When they were out in the street they agreed that this was a good time to kill Hayes. Mrs Hayes bought half a guinea's worth of wine for Hayes, which he drank while the others sipped beer. After a while Hayes started dancing drunkenly round the room, but he was not completely stupefied. Mrs Hayes sent out for another bottle. After Hayes had drunk that too he fell down senseless on the floor for some time before dragging himself into another room and falling onto a bed.

While he slept, Catherine Hayes told her associates that this was the time to kill him. Billings went into the room with a hatchet and hit Hayes hard over the head with it, fracturing his skull. Hayes' feet were hanging off the edge of the bed onto the floor, and the pain of the blow made him stamp repeatedly on the floor. Thomas Wood heard the stamping, went in, took the hatchet off Billings and gave Hayes two more blows, which killed him.

In the room above the one where the murder was committed, there was a lodger named Mrs Springate. She heard the noise of the stamping and assumed it was more of the drunken quarrelling, went downstairs and told Mrs Hayes that the noise had woken her up, as well as her husband and child. Mrs Hayes said that some visitors had had too much to drink but were on the point of leaving, and Mrs Springate went back to her room satisfied.

The three murderers then had to discuss how to dispose of the body and escape detection. Mrs Hayes proposed that they should cut off the head, so that if the body was found it would not be possible to identify it. The others agreed, so she fetched a bucket and a candle. The men pulled the body partly off the bed, Billings held the head while Wood used his pocket-knife to cut it off, and Catherine Hayes held the bucket to catch the blood. Then she emptied the bucket of blood into a sink by the window and several buckets of water after it.

Catherine Hayes then suggested they should

boil the head in order to lose the flesh and make it unidentifiable, but the others thought this would take too long and thought throwing it into the River Thames to be carried away by the tide would be better. The head was put in the bucket and hidden under Billings' greatcoat. Billings and Wood went out together, disturbing Mrs Springate once more. Mrs Hayes called out that it was only her husband going on a journey; she then put on a playlet for Mrs Springate's benefit, enacting a leave-taking scene with her husband.

Wood and Billings went first to Whitehall, but they found the gates shut. Instead they went to a wharf near Horse Ferry at Westminster. Wood threw the head into the river and they both returned home. Mrs Hayes decided that the body should be packed in a box and buried. A box was purchased, but they found it was too small, so they had to dismember the body to make it fit. Then they found it was quite difficult to carry the box, so they abandoned the box and carried the mangled body wrapped in a blanket to a field in Marylebone and threw it into a pond.

By this time, the head had been picked up by a waterman, and it was seen as the clearest evidence that a murder had been committed. The magistrates wanted to find out whose head it was, so they had it washed clean and the hair combed. After that it was mounted on a pole in the churchyard of St Margaret's, Westminster, so that the general public could have a good look at it. Several people in the crowd recognized it as Mr Hayes's head. Some of them mentioned it to

Billings, but he ridiculed the idea, saying that Hayes was alive and well and gone out of town for a few days. After the head had been on show for four days, it became necessary to take steps to preserve it. A chemist called Westbrook was directed to put it in a jar of spirits.

Mrs Hayes soon afterwards changed her lodging, taking Mrs Springate with her. Wood and Billings went too. Now she devoted her energy to collecting the debts due to her husband, using the proceeds to supply her associates with money and clothes.

Among the many who saw the head was a poor woman from Kingsland. Her husband had gone missing at about the time the murder had been committed. After looking very closely at the severed head she became convinced that it was her husband's. A search was made for his body, in the belief that she would be able to identify the clothes if not the body.

Mr Hayes had been missing for a time now and his friends began to make inquiries. There was a Mr Ashby in particular, who had been a close friend, and he called on Catherine Hayes to demand what had had happened to him. She rashly accounted for his absence by telling Ashby that Hayes had murdered somebody, that the dead man's wife had agreed to say nothing so long as Hayes paid her an agreed annual allowance. He had not been able to make this promise good, so she had threatened to expose him, so he had decided to disappear. Mr Ashby did not accept this explanation. He asked Mrs

Hayes if the head on the pole in the churchyard was the head of the man Hayes had killed. No, she said, because the murdered man had been buried intact. Ashby then asked her whereabouts, roughly, Mr Hayes had gone. She said he had gone to Portugal with some other man, though she had as yet not received a letter from him.

Mr Ashby thought the whole story was highly improbable, and he went to see a Mr Longmore, who was a relative of Mr Hayes. It was agreed that Longmore should call on Catherine Hayes and ask her the same questions and see whether the answers were the same. Longmore duly knocked on her door and was told a story that was different in detail from the tale told to Ashby. Mr Eaton, another friend of Hayes, was consulted, and they agreed that they should all examine the head on the pole. After they had closely examined the head they came to the conclusion that it must belong to their friend Hayes, and went to a magistrate, Mr Lambert. Lambert immediately issues warrants for the arrest of Catherine Hayes, Mrs Springate, Wood and Billings.

The magistrate went himself to the house where they all lived, and told the landlord what their business was. Lambert was shown to Catherine Hayes's room. He knocked on the door. She did not open up at first, saying that she was undressed, but soon opened the door. Billings was sitting on the side of the bed, with bare legs, the implication that Catherine Hayes had been in bed with Billings. Some people stayed with Mrs Hayes and Billings, while Longmore and Lambert went upstairs to take Mrs Springate into custody. All were taken to Mr Lambert's house.

The magistrate interviewed them all for some time, but they all persisted with the story that they knew nothing about the murder of Hayes. They were committed to prison before being re-examined. Catherine Hayes said she wanted to see the head, so she was taken to Westbrook's house where the head was now kept and shown it. She cried out, 'Oh, it is my dear husband's head!' She took the jar in her arms and wept as she embraced it. It was suggested that they could take the head out of its jar so that she could have a better look at it. She readily agreed to this. She pretended to be deeply moved, kisisng it several times and asking for a lock of its hair. Westbrook, incensed by her hypocrisy, expressed the view that she had had too much of his blood already, and she became hysterical.

By chance it was on this very day that the rest of the body was discovered. A gentleman and his servant were crossing the fields at Marylebone when they saw something lying in a ditch. When they went nearer they saw that it was parts of a human body. Help was summoned, and it was quickly found that all the parts of a human body were there except the head. The magistrate was informed. This was obviously the rest of the unfortunate Mr Hayes.

Mrs Hayes was committed to Newgate for trial. The committal of Mrs Springate and Billings was put off until Thomas Wood had been caught. Wood soon returned to Mrs Hayes's lodgings, where he was re-directed to the house of Mr Longmore. Longmore's brother seized him immediately and had him taken before Mr Lambert, but he admitted to nothing. Once he knew that the body had been found he changed his position. He told everything. He said that from the moment the crime had been committed he had not had a moment's peace. He had been terrified at the sight of everyone he met and that he was in terrible inner turmoil. He too was committed to Newgate for trial. The guilt of Mrs Hayes, Billings and Wood was now emerging clearly, as was the innocence of Mrs Springate, and she was released at this point.

At the trial, Wood and Billings pleaded guilty. Catherine Hayes faniced she had a chance of being acquitted if she made no plea, but she was found guilty anyway by the jury. Wood seemed to be genuinely remorseful and said he was ready to suffer any punishment to atone for the terrible crime he had committed. He became feverish and died in prison before he could be executed. Billings too admitted his guilt and accepted his fate. He was executed and hung in chains close to the pond where Mr Hayes's body had been found.

Mrs Hayes managed to get hold of a bottle of poison, but a woman who was imprisoned with her casually tasted it, presumably hoping it was alcohol, and realised what was going on.

On the day of her execution, 9 May, 1726, Catherine Hayes was dragged to the appointed place on a sledge. An iron chain was hung round her body. Usually, when women were burned for treason, it was the merciful custom to strangle them before they were burned. A rope was looped round the neck and pulled from behind by the executioner before the flames reached them. But on this occasion, by mistake, the prisoner was burned alive. The flames leapt high too quickly and the executioner had to let go of the rope for fear of burning his own hands. The fire burned fiercely round her. She desperately tried to push the faggots away from her, to no avail, and she screamed as she burned.

John Vicars

'a strange final request'

JOHN VICARS' FATHER and grandfather were both born in Oxford, and the family had a good name there. The father seems to have got into debt and the family was obliged to move to Dodington on the Isle of Ely in the Fens. John's father died when John was still a boy. His mother remarried and he was consequently given very little education. At the age of thirteen he was apprenticed to a gardener, Mr Aaron, who was himself gardener to the famous 'improver' Thomas Coke, later Earl of Leicester, at Holkham. The young John Vicars served his apprenticeship conscientiously and was employed as a gardener until he began a liaison with a married woman and was obliged to leave.

He was given a good reference and was then taken on by Mr Bridgeman, a gardener at Kensington, where he worked for a time. Then he went to sea, engaged by Captain Duroy of the man-o'-war Exeter, where he served for nine months. After that he went into crime.

He joined a band of smugglers and worked with them for a year until he was taken prisoner by a custom-house smack in the English Channel near the Sussex port of Rye. John Vicars was committed to the New Gaol in Southwark and tried and acquitted.

Vicars now had a second chance to go straight. He was very lucky. He was taken on by Mr Miller, gardener to the Earl of Oxford at Chelsea, where he worked for a year.

He fell in love with a woman named Anne Easom and married her. They lived happily together in Whittlesea for seven years, though without producing any children. At about that time, Anne became ill, and her illness altered her temperament. She became harder to live with and there was increasing tension between them. He decided to enlist for a year with the Duke of Bedford's regiment, mainly to get away from his difficult wife. Then he returned to her and lived with her until she died, which was about a year after that.

John Vicars lived as a widower for a while. He noticed a woman called Mary Hainsworth leading a busy social life, chatting merrily and flirting with lots of men. He asked her teasingly one evening if they were all sweethearts, She said they were not, so he offered to be one himself. She was very taken with him and their relationship quickly developed, she 'refusing him nothing'. He never offered to marry her and never had any intention of marrying her. They had sex frequently for a while, and she pressed him to marry her. He said there was no hurry to marry, but she said she was pregnant and if he refused she would bring in the law and force him to marry her.

Vicars must have been very angry at being entrapped in this way. He had known the woman only a short time, and he had been having sex with her for a fortnight. Now it turned out she was pregnant, obviously by someone else, and was looking to him to support her. He kept out of her way for a couple of days. Then a coachman came to town, and she seemed so friendly with him that a woman who worked in his garden told him that he had lost his sweetheart. Vicars was very relieved to think that she was latching onto someone else instead. He had had a narrow escape.

But he was not so lucky. Three days later the coachman left and she accosted him. Vicars was foolish enough to begin the relationship all over again, though, as he thought, making it clear that it was not to lead to marriage. Once again, after they had had sex a few times, she threatened him with the law if he would not marry her. She assured him she would be a careful and hard-working wife and he foolishly agreed to marry her so long as he was convinced that she was not secretly harbouring a love for someone else.

They lived quite happily together as man and wife for two months, but after that there were frequent quarrels, often arising from Mary following some very bad advice from her mother and others. She even admitted to him that some of her friends had advised her to poison him. It was a short step from fighting each other with words to fighting with blows. Eventually she left him and went to live with her mother. He pleaded with her to return, but she refused, which was ironic, given that the marriage had been all her idea.

One day Vicars was passing Mary's mother's house, saw her inside and went in to her. He offered her some fruit, kissed her and asked for a reconciliation. Mary's mother came in and gave Vicars a piece of her mind, beating him and swearing she would kill him. She screamed at her daughter to stab him with the knife she had in her hand. Mary did as she was told by her mother and tried to stab him. He felt something push against his stomach, ran to the door, tripped and fell on the threshold. The old woman was quickly on him, but he managed to push her off. He got up, found that his thumb was cut, that his shirt had a hole in it, and ran back home.

Mary and her mother accused him of a breach of the peace and took action to get him arrested. On 24 April, to avoid being taken into custody, Vicars left Whittlesea and sought the advice of a man who lived about three miles away; the advice he got was to sell up and move away, which was good advice. Vicars decided to act on this and went back to Whittlesea that evening. On the way home, he saw his wife in the new shop her mother had provided for her, and he decided once again to try to reason with her. As he moved towards the shop, his emotion shifted from affection to resentment and anger. He went into the shop, where Mary was sitting working – she was a glover – and put his left hand under her chin. She seemed to smile in anticipation of the kiss she thought he was about to give her. He pulled his knife from his pocket with his right hand and tried to cut her throat. When she felt the knife she realised what was happening, put her hands up and stopped him, but he still managed to stab her deeply under the left ear.

Mary shouted, 'Murder!' Vicars told her, 'Molly, it is now too late. You should have been ruled in time.' He ran out into the street, calling hysterically for someone to take him prisoner. At first they were afraid to do so, but he begged them to arrest him before he did any more mischief. Then at last Thomas Boone took hold of him and he was taken into custody. Vicars raved until the next day, when he became very calm.

He was then naturally regarded in Whittlesea as a dangerous criminal and rumours quickly spread that he had committed more murders in the past. There was a grain of truth in this. He had had a career in crime, though not as a murderer, and he had been instrumental in the killing of another man. Vicars made a statement to try to clarify and explain what had happened. While he was gardener to Mr Man, the garden was often robbed, so his master set him to watch one night, armed with a gun and a sword, and fixed a trap at the place where they supposed the thief was entering the garden. The thief duly appeared, saw Vicars and tried to run off, but Vicars managed to cut him in the leg with his sword. The thief was also unfortunate enough to run onto the man-trap. The teeth of the man-trap caught him savagely in the midriff. The thief had been taken before magistrates, and committed to Maidstone Gaol, but died shortly afterwards of his wounds. 'But', as Vicars himself argued, 'this cannot be deemed a murder'.

While he languished in prison, Vicars said how much he loved his wife, but that she had greatly provoked him. He could not live with her, but he also could not live without her – a common enough complaint. He also said that he would do the same again under similar provocation.

At his execution, John Vicars was very steady and penitent, praying with the minister and singing Psalm 6. Then something peculiar happened. A woman called Amy Hutchinson had been convicted for the murder of her husband. She was there too at the gallows, sentenced to be strangled and burnt for her crime. Vicars wanted to see her die first. It was a very peculiar request. The crowd was there to watch a public execution, enjoying the spectacle from their assumed position of physical and moral safety; but here was one of the victims also wanting to savour the spectacle – or at least half of it.

Remarkably, John Vicars got his request. Amy Hutchinson's face and hands were smeared with tar; she was already wearing a garment daubed with pitch. The executioner strangled her, left her for twenty minutes, and then kindled the fire, which burned for half an hour. Then the executioner went to Vicars, who helped him fix the knot and then obligingly threw himself off the ladder. Why on earth had he wanted to watch Amy Hutchinson die first? Was it for the simple sadistic pleasure of watching a woman suffer? Or was it just that he saw it as a way of staying alive – for one more precious hour?

Lydia Adler

'one of four wives'

LYDIA ADLER WAS tried at the Old Bailey in London in June 1744, for the wilful murder of John Adler, her husband. It was alleged that she had thrown him down on the ground, kicked him in the groin and stamped on him, and in this way bruised and injured him mortally. John Adler languished in St Bartholomew's Hospital from 11 May until 23 May, 1744 , when he died.

Lydia Adler was charged with manslaughter. Her own daughter gave evidence that John Adler had told her himself that it was Lydia who had injured him.

Another witness was Benjamin Barton. He said that John Adler had come to his house on 11 June, 1744 with a bloodstained handkerchief tied round his head. John had asked him for a spare bed, and said, 'This infernal fiend will be the death of me'. The infernal fiend was his wife. But Barton was afraid to take John Adler in; he knew all too well that his wife was a fiendishly violent woman, and for his own safety refused to give him a bed. After this, he had visited John in hospital every day. John had said to him, 'I wish, Mr Barton, you would be so good as to get a warrant to secure this woman, for she will be the death of me'. Just two hours before he died he asked if the warrant had been obtained, and pressed Barton to bring her to justice. Barton promised to do it if it lay within his power.

The Adlers' daughter Hannah said her father had said about two hours before he had died, 'I am a dead man, and this lady has killed me'. After that he repeatedly stated that his wife was his murderer, and begged that she should be brought to justice. He went on saying this until about ten minutes before he died.

Lydia said in her defence that her husband had two wives besides herself, She said that there had been a quarrel between her and one of the other wives and that John had tried to separate them. In doing this he fell down, and then the other woman had fallen on top of him. She herself had never laid hand or foot on him. In the circumstances it was a pathetically poor defence.

Another witness said that John Adler had had four wives and that he was kind to them all at first, but afterwards he began to beat them. The witness had seen John and Lydia fighting frequently.

The jury found Lydia Adler guilty of manslaughter. Her punishment was to be branded on the hand.

Mary Blandy

'and the dishonourable William Cranstoun'

THE CASE OF Mary Blandy, who was executed in 1752, is perhaps the classic English parricide. Her father – her victim – was Francis Blandy, a lawyer in Henley-on-Thames. He was a proud and conscientious father and he was keen to make a good marriage for his daughter. He allowed it to be known around Henley that he was putting up a dowry of £10,000, which was a huge sum of money at that time. Unfortunately, he was over-egging his daughter's marriage prospects, as he had less than half that sum, and it is not clear how he hoped to get away with this scam.

In the short-term, the deception was predictably effective, at least in terms of pulling in large numbers of interested men. The suitors queued up for Mary Blandy's dowry, though each in turn was rejected by Mr Blandy as unsuitable. Time passed, and Mary Blandy's birthdays came and went. She was approaching thirty, which in the eighteenth century was a very late age to be getting married, at least for the first time. Then she met Captain William Cranstoun.

The Hon. William Cranstoun looked to be no

great catch. He was short and he had bandy legs, but he was pleasant and well-mannered, and altogether appealed to Mary, who seems to have been an amiable and placid woman. It was not long before Cranstoun told Mary he loved her, but added that he had a problem: he had a mistress who claimed to be his wife. Mary told him she would marry him as long as he sorted this problem out.

This time, Francis Blandy agreed that Mary could marry. Although Cranstoun was not marvellous to behold, and although he was poor, he was well-connected. Cranstoun was the son of a Scottish earl, and that suited Francis Blandy's aspirations well enough. He would have his daughter married into the aristocracy. Cranstoun was allowed to move into the Blandy household as a guest and his relationship with Mary was allowed to develop.

Then there was a setback. A relative of Cranstoun's wrote to Francis Blandy to tell him that the mistress Cranstoun claimed to be keeping was in fact his wife, not pretending to be his wife but actually his wife. It looked to Blandy as if Cranstoun was a lying opportunist who simply hoped to get his hands on a large dowry, and he was right. Francis Blandy confronted Cranstoun, who eventually managed somehow to convince him that he really was unmarried. He continued to live with the Blandys for six months, and during that time, almost inevitably, Mary Blandy became his mistress.

The abandoned mistress or wife, 'Mrs Cranstoun', took legal action against William Cranstoun. A

Scottish court found in her favour; she was declared to be indeed the legal wife of William Cranstoun. Francis Blandy now turned Cranstoun out of his house in Henley and told his daughter to forget all about him.

Mary Blandy had always been a dutiful and obedient daughter and she wanted to do what her father asked, but she was in love with William Cranstoun and could not forget him to order, even if he was an adulterer and a proven liar. Mary and William Cranstoun exchanged letters. Cranstoun had an idea. The obstacle in the way of their living together was Mary's father. With Francis Blandy removed from the picture, all would be well. It was a peculiar and peculiarly mischievous suggestion, as it must have been obvious to all parties involved that the obstacle was actually Mrs Cranstoun. Cranstoun should, if anything, have worked towards ridding himself of her. But no, it was Mr Blandy who must go.

Cranstoun gave Mary a powder which he said would make her father more amiable. She put the powder into her father's tea and it really seemed to have the effect that William Cranstoun predicted. For some days afterwards, her father was in a better temper. Cranstoun sent her some more powder, and because of the earlier success Mary did not hesitate to put this in his tea as well.

Poor Mary Blandy. She was trying to overlook the lies William Cranstoun had told her about the mistress or wife he had left behind in Scotland, when now it emerged that he had another mistress in London. Even at this point she did not relinquish him. She forgave him. She does seem to have been a very simple and gullible person. When one of the servants drank some of her father's 'powdered' tea and became ill immediately afterwards, she still did not realise what Cranstoun was trying to do. She added Cranstoun's powder to her father's soup. He became ill straight away. The maid, Susan, had a taste of the soup and she was sick for two days as a result. The maid realised what was happening and took the soup to a chemist. The chemist analyzed it and as a result the maid warned Mr Blandy that he was being poisoned.

Francis Blandy loved his daughter and just wanted her to stop poisoning him. He hinted heavily to Mary that he knew what was going on. She was frightened by this into throwing the rest of the powder onto the fire. But as Mary left the kitchen, the maid pulled out what was left of the powder and took that off to the chemist. The chemist confirmed that the powder was arsenic.

Mary then wrote a fateful letter to her lover, telling him to be careful. The letter turned out to be deeply incriminating at her trial. She gave the letter to a clerk to post, but the clerk opened it and gave it to the chemist for safe-keeping.

On 14 August 1751 Francis Blandy finally died. Before he died he told Mary that he believed she had poisoned him and he forgave her for it. When William Cranstoun heard Mr Blandy was dead, instead of rushing to her side he fled to France, leaving Mary to face trial alone.

The trial was an interesting one for its time,

because it leant heavily on forensic evidence. Mary depended for her defence on her belief that that the powder was a love potion that would sweeten her father's disposition and make him change his mind about William Cranstoun. From today's vantage point, this would seem to be true. Mary made no attempt to get rid of the remains of the incriminating poisoned soup and tea. If she had known they contained arsenic she would surely have seen to it that no trace remained. But the jury did not believe her and she was found guilty of murder.

Mary asked the hangman not to hang her too high, 'for the sake of decency'. She did not want the crowd looking up her skirt. William Cranstoun died in poverty only half a year later.

While Mary was in prison she heard about another woman in the same plight, Elizabeth Jefferies. Elizabeth had plotted with her lover to murder her uncle. The motive behind the murder was that the uncle had had sex with the niece. Mary opened a sympathetic correspondence with Elizabeth. Just before her execution, Elizabeth confessed to her part in the murder. Mary was evidently shocked and sent her a letter reproaching her. This suggests very strongly that she had assumed until that point that what they had in common was their innocence. It is fairly clear now that Mary Blandy was rather simple-minded, trusting, obedient to her menfolk, and probably innocent of any intent to murder. It was the untried and unpunished Captain William Cranstoun who was the real murderer.

John Williamson

'and the tortured wife'

JOHN WILLIAMSON WAS a child of a poor family in mid-eighteenth century London. When he was old enough, he was apprentice to a shoemaker. He completed his apprenticeship and pursued his trade earnestly and conscientiously. He married a sensible and sober young woman, by whom he had three children.

Then things started to go wrong. Mrs Williamson died. For a time Williamson kept his family going on his own, but must have realised that his children needed a mother. He then met a simple-minded young woman. It was said that she 'bordered on idiocy', but she did have an income. She had had sufficient money left to her to maintain her without any need for her to work. It was the money alone that made Williamson propose marriage. She accepted the proposals, but when the banns were read in church her guardian blocked the marriage; his reason is not known.

Williamson managed to get a licence to marry the young woman in spite of the guardian's opposition. As a result he was able to get hold of the income due to his new wife.

Only three weeks into the marriage, Williamson

began to abuse his wife. He beat her. He threw water over her. Then he pulled her hands behind her back, secured them with handcuffs, passed a roped through a staple and pulled her hands up so high that only the tips of her toes were touching the ground – a medieval form of torture. She was confined in a closet and fed on small amounts of bread and butter; she was allowed a small amount of water each day. She was subjected to this appalling treatment repeatedly and was once kept like this for a whole month.

Luckily there were other people in the house, and she occasionally got help from a woman lodger and a little girl, Williamson's daughter by his first wife, who felt sorry for her. The little girl once released her stepmother, and Williamson gave her a beating for it. While the father was out, the little girl frequently gave her stepmother a stool to stand on to relieve her suffering. Again, when Williamson found out he beat the child without mercy.

Williamson released his wife a few days before she died. At dinner he gave her some meat, though she was only able to eat a small amount because of her very low state. Williamson expected that by showing his wife this consideration he would be treated more kindly when she died. He clearly intended her to die. Her hands were now very swollen, partly because of the cold, mainly because of the handcuffs, and she asked to be allowed to sit near the fire. The little girl asked Williamson on her behalf as well. Williamson agreed. After a few minutes, he noticed that she was picking off the vermin that swarmed on her clothes and throwing them into the fire. In disgust, he ordered her to go back to her kennel.

The poor woman went back into her closet, where she was locked in until the next day. She was then found to be delirious, and she remained so for about twenty-four hours until she died.

At the coroner's inquest, evidence emerged that incriminated Williamson, and he was committed to Newgate Prison. He was brought to trial before Lord Chief Justice Parker and sentenced to death. From this point on, Williamson reverted to behaving like a normal, decent human being, showing regret for what he had done. He was hanged in Moorfields on 19 January, 1767. Just before he was executed, he sang a psalm and said some prayers, showing every sign of being a law-abiding and God-fearing citizen. There was no explanation for his systematic cruelty to a wife who had done nothing whatever to provoke this maltreatment.

Even Williamson's children suffered. They were placed in the Cripplegate Workhouse.

Revd James Hackman

'and his dangerous obsession'

JAMES HACKMAN WAS born in Gosport in Hampshire and his early intentions were to go into trade, but his temperament was against this line of work. He was too impatient and too volatile to put up with the routine work of a shop or counting-house. His parents were sufficiently well off to buy an ensign's commission in the army, in the 68th Regiment of Foot.

He had not been in the army very long when he was put in charge of a recruiting party at the town of Huntingdon. While there, he was often invited to dine with Lord Sandwich, who had a house nearby. It was at Lord Sandwich's house that the volatile James Hackman first set eyes on Miss Reay.

Miss Reay was the attractive daughter of a humble stay-maker in Covent Garden and was serving an apprenticeship in George's Court, St John's Lane, Clerkenwell, when she was noticed by Lord Sandwich, who took a fancy to her. He took her under his protection, giving her a place in his household at Huntingdon.

When Hackman saw her, he fell in love with her. By this time, Miss Reay had lived for nineteen years with Lord Sandwich. Hackman meanwhile had lost patience with the army career his parents had bought him; he was not getting promoted. He then thought of entering the church. He took holy orders and obtained the living of Wiverton in Norfolk, but he was not to enjoy this living for very long – he would soon be dead.

Miss Reay loved music. Her protector, Lord Sandwich, indulged her with concerts at his country seat, and she also attended concerts in London. Hackman was still in attendance in the country, and he contrived to be not too far away in London either. Miss Reay, in short, had a stalker. Hackman had lodgings in Duke's Court in St Martin's Lane, which he used as his London pied-à-terre.

On 7 April, 1779, James Hackman spent the morning in his London lodgings reading Dr Blair's *Sermons*. He had lunch with his sister and then, in the afternoon, he wrote a letter to his sister's husband, Mr Booth, who was a barrister, to tell him that he intended to commit suicide. Why he did this is not clear. What did Hackman expect Booth to do with this information? Hackman was by now in a very disturbed state indeed. The infatuation with the unattainable Miss Reay had taken him over completely. In the evening he walked to the Admiralty, where he spotted Miss Reay entering a coach with Signora Galli. The coach took her to Covent Garden Theatre, where she watched a performance of *Love in a Village*. Hackman went into the theatre too, but was unable to contain his violent emotions. He returned to his lodgings. There he loaded two pistols, which shows a good deal of premeditation, and went back to the theatre. He waited on the pavement outside until the play was finished.

When the play was over, the audience drifted out of the theatre onto the street. Miss Reay appeared and was about to step up into her coach when Hackman stepped forward and fired one of his pistols at her, killing her instantly. The other pistol he turned on himself, but for some reason it would not fire. He then tried to beat himself to death with the butt-end of the pistol, which must rank among one the most futile attempts at suicide of all time.

There was a brief struggle while Hackman was restrained, and he was taken away to have his injuries attended to. He was then taken before Sir John Fielding, who committed him to Bridewell Prison. Hackman was then transferred to Newgate Prison.

The outcome of his trial was a foregone conclusion. The jury found him guilty of wilful murder, and Hackman listened to the judge passing sentence on him with calm resignation.

During the procession to the gallows at Tyburn on 19 April, 1779, James Hackman appeared to be in the grip of strong emotions, but he said very little. He climbed onto the cart, took his leave of the officials who had accompanied him, and spent a little time in prayer. After his body had hung on Tyburn tree for the customary hour, it was taken down and handed over to the surgeons for dissection.

Bartholomew Quailn
'the wife-beater'

BARTHOLOMEW QUAILN WAS a poor labourer who lived in the Fens. He and his wife visited a pub in Hadgrane in Cambridgeshire. He was seen carrying his infant child under one arm and a bag under the other, following his wife out of the pub. Not long after this, the two of them were seen quarrelling in the road. She was lying in the road, complaining bitterly because he would not give her the bag he was holding. They shouted abuse at each other for a time until Quailn was so incensed by her abuse that he kicked her very hard as she lay on the ground.

Mrs Quailn got up and tried to run away, but Quailn ran after her, caught up with her and she again fell to the ground. He again kicked her violently. She managed to get to her feet and run a short distance, but Quailn followed her and kicked her yet again. An onlooker rebuked Quailn; how could he treat his wife so barbarously? Quailn replied that he would do it again – and he did. Once more Mrs Quailn managed to struggle to her feet and get away, but Quailn followed her and kicked her several times more.

This time he did her some serious damage. Mrs

Quailn clutched her side with her hand and cried, 'Oh, Bat, now you have done for me!' Shortly after that the poor woman died. Her spleen had been ruptured.

When Bartholomew Quailn's case came to court, as it did in March 1791 at Ely Assizes, there was no doubt whatever as to who had caused the poor woman's death. She had been killed by her husband in the road in full view of several shocked onlookers. Counsel for the Crown (prosecution) discussed definitions of murder, and argued that Quailn had shown 'his heart to be regardless of social duty, and his mind deliberately bent on mischief'. If he had killed his wife as a result of genuine provocation, that might be a mitigating circumstance, but there was no evidence of any provocation by Mrs Quailn that was sufficient to justify his kicking her to death. She had moreover made no resistance whatever to her husband; on the contrary, she had made several attempts to get away from him. He was evidently deliberately bent on mischief.

It would be interesting to know what was in the bag, and also exactly what the quarrel was about, but all the surviving records tell us is that there were 'high words' exchanged.

The trial developed into an argument between the lawyers about these technicalities. The lawyers – this was the eighteenth century – happily accepted that there was such a thing as 'reasonable chastisement'; it was acceptable, given the social mores of the time, for husbands to go in for a certain amount of physical correction when their wives were disobedient. Men expected to be allowed to hit their wives. The point at issue was whether the level of chastisement was *reasonable*, and in this case it evidently was not.

It was argued that this case was like another contemporary case where a park-keeper tied a boy to a horse's tail, then hit the boy, which caused the horse to bolt, dragging the boy to his death. The boy's death may not have been intended, but the method of punishment was too violent and it was also a deliberate act; what the park-keeper did could have been predicted to end in the boy being killed. The park-keeper was found guilty of murder, and so it should be, the argument ran, in this case of Bartholomew Quailn. Other parallel cases were quoted as well, supporting the idea that Quailn was guilty.

The argument continued as to whether Quailn had committed murder or manslaughter. The jury arrived at a special verdict; they found that they were unable to choose between the two crimes of manslaughter and murder in this case. The judge stated that this amounted to finding the accused guilty of wilful murder.

The Clerk of the Crown called upon the prisoner and, after reading the proceedings to him, he asked him what he had to say why the Court should not pass judgement on him to die according to the law. There was nothing he could say. Mr Justice Ashurst solemnly pronounced the sentence of death. Bartholomew Quailn was hanged at Ely on 7 March, 1791.

Elizabeth Marsh

'who killed her grandfather'

Not much is known about Elizabeth Marsh, beyond the one appalling fact that she killed her grandfather, John Nevil, for no apparent reason.

She was a Dorset village girl, only fifteen years old, living with her grandfather. While he was asleep, she gave him two savage blows on the head, killing him outright.

When Elizabeth Marsh was questioned about the killing, it emerged that she had no knowledge whatever of the difference between good and evil. This was, at the time, put down to 'extreme ignorance', but in more recent times Elizabeth Marsh might well have been declared insane under the McNaghten Rule. As it was, she was condemned as not only ignorant but malicious, and found guilty of wilful murder.

At Dorchester Assizes in March 1794, Elizabeth Marsh was sentenced to death and ordered to be executed forty-eight hours later.

The Duc de Praslin
'wife-murder in Paris'

CHARLES-LOUIS THÉOBALD de Choiseul, the Duc
de Praslin, was at the centre of one of the greatest
sex and murder scandals in nineteenth century
France. The story has an enduring fascination and
was the basis of a powerful Anatole Litvak film,
All This and Heaven Too, starring Charles Boyer
as the duke and Bette Davis as Henriette.

The duke was born in Paris in June 1805. When
he was nineteen, he made his first and perhaps
biggest mistake in marrying Fanny, Françoise
Sebastiani-Porta, who was sixteen and had been
born in Constantinople in 1807. Fanny, the new
duchess, was a choice Théo must soon have come
to regret. She was a woman of fiery temperament,
lesbian inclinations and fanatical obsessions; she
was neurotically possessive and overbearing.

By the time she had reached the age of thirty-
four, and had given birth to nine children, she
had lost her youthful charm. She had become fat
and wrinkled. The duke was a self-contained,
withdrawn, introverted man, and he increasingly
found his wife's charmless, domineering ways
insufferable. He no longer sought out her bed. At
the same time there is no doubt that the duchess

continued to love him in her neurotic, over-possessive way. The marriage was strained almost to breaking-point.

Then Henriette Deluzy arrived. She was engaged as the children's governess. It was soon very obvious that the duke was strongly attracted to her. The duchess assumed the worst – that the governess had become her husband's mistress. She told her husband to dismiss the young woman. He replied that if Henriette went he would go too. He had enough of being told what to do by the duchess.

Normal communication between husband and wife seems to have come to a halt, as the duchess was reduced to writing him letters. They were pathetic in tone, and made it clear that this was not the first time Thæo had shown an interest in other women. In spite of all the problems she still loved him.

In the end the duchess got her way and the governess was dismissed, and without a reference. The duke had not abandoned her, though. He went on calling on her. His affair with Henriette became a great Paris scandal. In 1847, the duchess announced that she was going to seek a divorce. Théo's adultery with Henriette was common knowledge in Parisian high society and she could take the humiliation no longer. The duke was not relieved at the prospect of being rid of his wife at last, as might have been expected; instead he was absolutely furious. Divorced by his wife, he would lose his social status – and his children too.

On the evening of 17 August, Théo went to see

Henriette Deluzy, and did not return home, to his house in the Rue Faubourg St Honoré, until the small hours of the next morning. At dawn on 18 August, the servants were alarmed to hear a piercing scream. The bell connected to the Duchess's room began to ring. Evidently she needed help. There was another piercing scream. The duke's manservant and the duchess's maid crept discreetly to the duchess's door and heard the noise of furniture falling over. It sounded as if there were burglars in the duchess's bedroom. They knocked and called. There was no answer. They tried another door, but that seemed to have been wedged shut.

Several servants went out into the garden to see what they could see from there. They looked up at the bedroom window and several of them saw a man they recognized as the duke, opening the shutters. They assumed that he too had heard the noise of the burglars and rushed into his wife's bedroom to deal with them. The servants went back inside to go to the duke's aid. To their surprise, the bedroom door was now open. The duchess's room was in a state of chaos; furniture had been overturned and there were splashes of blood on the walls. They saw the duchess herself sitting on the floor, propped against her bed, evidently dead. Her face was battered and bruised. Her throat had been cut.

While the stunned servants were examining and taking in this appalling sight, the duke walked in and cried out as he saw his dead wife. 'Some monster has murdered my beloved Fanny!

Fetch a doctor.' He said he had only just been woken up by the noise. The servants knew better; they had seen him at the window a few minutes before.

Two policemen passing in the street noticed that the front door was open, which was unusual, and decided to come in to investigate. Before long the house in the Rue Faubourg St Honoré was overflowing with policemen. Among them was Monsieur Allard, head of the Sureté. He rejected the burglar theory almost at once. If the place had been burgled, why did the burglars leave the duchess's jewels? He also found a Corsican pistol underneath the sofa; it was covered in blood. Allard asked the obvious question; 'Does anyone know who this pistol belongs to?' He was very surprised by the answer. The duke said, 'Yes, to me'.

Allard asked the duke how the pistol had got there. The duke said he had heard cries for help and rushed to his wife's bedroom waving his pistol. Seeing that she had been attacked and was covered in blood, he had dropped his pistol to raise her up. In consequence, he too had become covered in blood. Then he realised his wife was dead, so he went back to his own bedroom to wash off the blood. It was just about possible, but he had already told the servants that he had only that moment woken up, and he had also cried out in pretended surprise when he had come into the room after the servants arrived.

Allard went next to the duke's bedroom and pointed out that the trail of blood splashes and stains led to his door. The duke explained that he had been dripping with his wife's blood as he had returned to wash. But then there was further evidence in the duke's bedroom. There was a bloodstained handkerchief, the bloodstained hilt of a dagger, and a piece of bloodstained cord. Then Allard found the severed end of the bell-cord from the duchess's bedroom hidden inside the duke's shirt. At this point, Monsieur Allard arrested the duke for his wife's murder.

There was the strong possibility that the duke would persist with his version of events. It would be very difficult to prove that what he was saying was untrue – even though Allard and the duke's own servants all knew the duke was lying. It might well be that the case could not be made to stand up in court. He could claim that the servants in their confused and emotional state had misunderstood what he had said about when he was awakened. Even the severed bell-pull could be explained as an irrational, deranged response to the trauma of finding his wife savagely murdered. No-one in court might believe his fabrication, and yet it might still be impossible to get a conviction.

Then another key figure came into the story – a brilliant pioneering forensic scientist. Ambroise Tardieu had written the first scientific treatise on hanging. He had also discovered the 'Tardieu spots', the spots of blood that form under the hearts of people who have been suffocated. What M. Allard wanted to find out was whether the pistol had been dropped in the duchess's blood, as the duke claimed, or actually been used as a murder weapon. Tardieu approached the problem with characteristic thoroughness. He studied the pistol with a magnifying glass, then under a microscope. He found a chestnut coloured hair near the butt. Near the trigger guard he found skin tissue. Then he found a human hair root and more pieces of human flesh. Tardieu also found that some of the contusions on the duchess's head had been made by beating with a blunt instrument – like a pistol stock. Tardieu had no doubt; the duchess had been severely battered with the duke's pistol. He could prove scientifically that the duke had lied.

Tardieu's painstaking work on the duchess's bedroom as a whole enabled him and Allard to piece together the horrific story of Fanny's murder. He produced a detailed plan of the room, noting and labelling every sign of disorder and violence, every trace of blood. The plan gives an horrific picture of the way Fanny was chased round and round the room, suffering more and more injuries, her blood was everywhere.

The Duc de Praslin had quietly entered his wife's bedroom through the bathroom, probably intending to kill her instantly with a single slash across the throat. He took the precaution of cutting off the lower part of the bell-pull, just in case Fanny tried to summon help. Perhaps his nerve failed him. Perhaps, even more poignantly, Fanny woke up as he stood over her bed and she hoped for just a moment that this was the start of a reconciliation. Perhaps he unintentionally made a sound while he was cutting the bell-pull and that woke Fanny up. He made an attempt to cut her throat and managed to cut deep, but it was not a fatal cut; he missed the artery. He also missed the windpipe, and that was when she screamed and started to fight him off. She knew then that she was fighting for her life. The duke had locked the doors, so that wherever she ran she could not escape her fate.

The duke stabbed the duchess again and again with his dagger, still without inflicting a mortal wound. Then he began beating her with the butt of his pistol. He had her down on the floor at this stage, but still the fiery Fanny fought back. She bit Théo in the leg. There was so much noise by this time, with the screams and the knocking over of furniture, that the servants were roused.

Originally, the duke had planned to kill the duchess and open the front door and try to make it look like a burglary. But now the servants were outside the room, directly on the escape route. He had to create another way out of the house for his imaginary burglars. That was when he opened the window and shutters; that was why the servants in the garden saw him briefly at the window. The duke in his turn saw the servants in the garden and realised he had to return to his own bedroom.

This was when he made another mistake. He rushed into his wife's bedroom pretending for the servants' benefit that the noise had just woken him, when they knew that he been at the window of the duchess's bedroom several minutes earlier. It was the inconsistencies between what he said and what had been seen that undid him. That – and Tardieu's analysis of the pistol stock.

Now the Duc de Praslin was finished. He was arrested and preparations were made to take him to the Luxembourg Prison. He was watched by the police, but not closely enough. He surreptitiously managed to swallow a dose of arsenic. He died three days later, without admitting to the murder, but everyone knew he had done it.

Poor Henriette Deluzy was suspected of complicity in the murder, but she clearly knew nothing about it and was acquitted. She left France for America, where she married Henry Field. A letter dated 1864 tells how an American went to a soirée and 'made a most interesting acquaintance'. The American met a Mrs Henry Field, and was bowled over to discover that this was none other than the 'much-talked-about' femme fatale in the Duc de Praslin case. She had been the cause of the duchess's death, because the duchess had refused to give her a reference and it was this that enraged the duke to the point of murdering his wife. The American letter ends with two possible cautions: 'Warning to young women: Don't love your husbands too much, or don't engage too attractive a governess.'

Elizabeth Martha Brown

'the original Tess'

ELIZABETH MARTHA BROWN was a woman of humble birth who worked as a servant. It is not known where she was born, or when. Her two claims on our attention are that she was the last woman to be publicly hanged in Dorset, in 1856, and that she became the model for the tragic heroine of Thomas Hardy's *Tess of the D'Urbervilles*. It is for these things, and these only, that this unfortunate woman is remembered.

Elizabeth was about eighteen years older than her husband, John Brown. The two met when they were both in service. It was said by gossips at the time that John married Elizabeth for her money. They set up home at Birdsmoorgate near Beaminster in Dorset. Their marriage was a turbulent one. John was not faithful and Elizabeth caught him in bed with another woman. Not surprisingly, an outspoken quarrel broke out, the older Elizabeth probably feeling seriously threatened by her younger husband with his more than roving eye. Later the same day, words gave way to physical violence.

Elizabeth struck out at John with her fists. He responded by lashing her with his whip. Elizabeth was not accepting that. She grabbed the axe they used for chopping firewood, and hit him hard over the head with it. The blow smashed his skull and killed him outright.

Elizabeth Brown was arrested for killing her husband, but she claimed he had been kicked in the head by a horse. The police did not believe her and she was charge with murder. Whether the outcome would have been any different if she had come clean at the beginning is doubtful, but the deception certainly did not help her to win the sympathy of the jury.

She went to trial at the Dorchester Assizes. The jury did not believe Elizabeth's yarn about the horse any more than the police did and returned a verdict of guilty. She was automatically sentenced to death, the sentence to be carried out three weeks later. There were obviously mitigating circumstances, including the provocation of her husband's infidelity and the further provocation of his whipping her. The killing was also unpremeditated. There was agitation for a reprieve. Reprieves for murder were rare in the middle of the nineteenth century, but not completely unknown. She had a good deal of public sympathy because of the way her husband had behaved. Unfortunately the plea of diminished responsibility was not available to her; it would be a hundred years before she could make that plea in an English court.

The Home Secretary refused a reprieve,

perhaps because Elizabeth had not owned up. She had gone on claiming it was the horse and that lie undid her. The case is similar to the case of Tracy Andrews, who in 1997 claimed that her boyfriend had been stabbed in a road rage attack by an unknown stranger, whereas she had stabbed him herself. Tracy Andrews later retracted her lie, which must have been very difficult for her to do. Once a lie, a big lie, is told as part of a defence it is psychologically very difficult to get out of. Elizabeth Brown unfortunately became locked into her lie and was unable to retract it.

Eventually, in the condemned cell, she did confess that she had killed her husband with the axe. She knew she was responsible for his death and went to her death with great courage.

The sheriff of Dorset prepared for her execution, appointing the notorious William Calcraft as her hangman. Calcraft was Britain's principal hangman from 1829 until 1874, the longest serving hangman known in history. He was even so not a very good hangman, using the 'short drop' that caused his victims to die unnecessarily slow and agonizing deaths. He was an infamous killer; because he had the licence of the law behind him he was, technically, not a murderer. Tell that to his victims.

Elizabeth Brown's execution was due to happen at 9 o'clock on 9 August, 1856. Calcraft came to Dorchester from London by train the day before, as required by the Home Office, to make the necessary preparations. Elizabeth meanwhile was well looked after in her cell by two matrons.

The gallows was built outside the gates of Dorchester Prison, on what is now the prison car park in North Square, and it was very impressive structure.

Elizabeth was an attractive woman, who looked younger than her years. She had lovely hair. She chose a long, tight-fitting black silk dress for her hanging. People often wore their Sunday-best for what was a major public event. A crowd of up to four thousand gathered to see her hang. At the prison gates she shook hands with the prison officials. She was offered a ride to the place of execution in the prison van, but she preferred to walk to the gallows even though it was raining.

She climbed the eleven steps to where Calcraft was waiting for her. He pinioned her hands in front of her, then led her up the next nineteen steps, across a platform and then on up a final flight of steps onto the trap. Calcraft put the white hood over her head and the noose round her neck. He then set off to go below the trap to pull back the bolts, when it was pointed out to him that he had forgotten to pinion Elizabeth's legs. He went back and put a strap round her legs. This was done for modesty, to stop women's dresses flying up when the trap doors opened and showing their legs.

Elizabeth Brown waited quietly and patiently waiting for the drop. The rain continued falling, and made the white hood translucent, and it stuck to her face. She looked like an alabaster statue. Calcraft went below again and pulled the bolts, releasing the trap doors. Elizabeth fell about a foot. She struggled for a few moments and body wheeled half round and back. Her body was left hanging the regulation hour before it was taken down.

And the connection with Tess? Thomas Hardy was sixteen years old at the time of the execution – and he was there. He and a friend had been able to get a good view perched in a tree very close to the gallows. He remembered all his life 'what a fine figure she showed against the sky as she hung in the misty rain, and how the black silk gown set off her shape as she wheeled half round and back'. Hardy was an impressionable young man at the time of the hanging, and one cannot help sensing a sexual element in his appreciation of the unfortunate woman's death throes. Charles Dickens noticed the unhealthy appeal of the public hanging, 'the fascination of the repulsive, something most of us have experienced'. Hardy managed to turn the macabre sensuality of the memory to some account, at least. His memory of the beauty, the pathos and the anguish of Elizabeth Brown's execution was to cast a long shadow across the most haunting of his novels, *Tess of the D'Urbervilles*. As Sir Michael Tippett once said to me of *Tess*, one of his favourite books, 'Tears to my eyes. . .'

Mary Wheeler

'murder in the family'

THE WHEELER FAMILY is thought to be unique in criminal history, in seeing a father and his daughter hanged for completely separate and unconnected murders.

Thomas Wheeler was hanged at St Albans in Hertfordshire by William Marwood in November 1880 for murdering a local farmer called Edward Anstee. While waiting in the condemned cell, Thomas Wheeler wrote to his victim's widow, asking her to forgive him and praying that his sins should not be visited on his wife and fourteen year old daughter.

Mary Eleanor Wheeler was born in 1866 and very little else is known about her early life. It is not even known what effect her father's trial and execution had on her, though she was certainly to suffer from depression, which may have been related to the early trauma of her father's hanging. When she too was arrested for murder, she was described as being five foot six inches tall with 'lovely russet hair and fine blue eyes'. She was of average build and had shapely hands. She was not a beautiful woman, but she had plenty of male admirers – enough for her never to need to work. She launched herself on a short career as a 'kept woman'.

She had a relationship with a carpenter called John Pearcey. They did not marry, but Mary even so adopted his surname, perhaps to escape from the inevitable stigma attaching to her father's name. She kept Pearcey's name even after their relationship ended, and it ended so that Mary could go off with richer men. It must be significant that Pearcey was ready to give evidence against Mary at her trial: evidence that would help to hang her. One of these better off men, Charles Creighton, rented rooms for her at 2 Priory Street, Kentish Town in North London.

Mary suffered from depression and took to drinking heavily. Mr Creighton visited her once a week, but she also became involved with Frank Hogg; although Hogg was a furniture remover, he had printed business cards and this impressed the class-conscious Mary Wheeler. She needed to make sure Creighton did not catch her while she was entertaining Hogg, so she had a simple arrangement with Hogg; she put a light in the window to show when she was available. He had his own key and could let himself in. Mary seems to have fallen for Frank Hogg and she increasingly saw his family – he had a wife and a daughter, both called Phoebe – as obstacles to her own happiness.

Mary Wheeler had learnt nothing from her father's trial and execution for murder. Just ten years after his execution, she committed her own murder. She murdered Phoebe Hogg, Frank's wife. Phoebe Hogg was thirty-two and had been ill. She had married Frank Hogg only two years before, when she was three months pregnant by him. But Frank had been having an affair with Mary all the time, not only since their marriage but beforehand.

On 24 October, 1890, Mary asked a boy called Willie Holmes to run an errand. That morning she gave him a penny to take a note to Phoebe Hogg inviting her to tea in the afternoon. At 4 p.m., tea-time, a neighbour heard the sound of breaking glass coming from Mary's house and called over the garden fence to see if everything was all right. There was no answer.

Three hours later a woman's body was found lying on a pavement in Crossfield Road by a man walking home from work. He reported it to a policeman. The woman's head was wrapped in a cardigan. When the policeman unwrapped it he found Phoebe's face covered in blood and a deep gash across her throat. At the mortuary it was found that Phoebe had a fractured skull and that the throat had been cut so violently that the head was nearly severed. She also had bruises on her arms where she had tried to defend herself. There was no blood on the pavement where the body was found, so Phoebe had evidently been murdered elsewhere.

The next day, the body of a little girl was found. She had been suffocated. Possibly she had been suffocated deliberately after the murder of her mother. Possibly she had been suffocated inadvertently when the mother's body was dumped into the pram on top of her to wheel it away to dump it somewhere.

Frank and his sister Clara reported Phoebe missing after they read about the finding of a woman's body in the evening paper. Frank sent Clara round to Mary's house to ask if she had seen Phoebe. Naturally she said she hadn't. She then started behaving very oddly. She agreed to go to the mortuary with Clara to identify the body, but when she was there she tried to prevent Clara from identifying Phoebe. She became hysterical when the extent of Phoebe's injuries was shown to them. The pram too had to be identified. One of Mary's neighbours had seen Mary wheeling the pram with a large object in it on the evening when the murder took place.

Frank Hogg was visited by the police, who had to tell him that his wife was dead. He was also inevitably a suspect, so he was searched. The police found the key to Mary Wheeler's house, and he confessed to having an affair with Mary.

Next the police went to interview Mary. They had been suspicious of her behaviour at the mortuary. They searched the house in Priory Street. They found many blood stains and spatters in the kitchen, and a bloodstained carving knife and poker. There was also evidence of a violent struggle in the kitchen. Two of the window panes were broken. During the search Mary Wheeler's behaviour was very peculiar. She sat at the piano singing and whistling loudly. She explained the bloodstains away by saying that she had been killing mice, which obviously was not the true explanation. When Mary herself was examined, her clothes were found to be bloodstained and she had scratches on her hands. She was also wearing two wedding rings, one of which was Phoebe Hogg's.

Detective Inspector Banister arrested Mary Wheeler, and charged her with the murder of the two Phoebe Hoggs, mother and child. While in the police court awaiting her committal hearing, Mary Wheeler made a partial confession to Sarah Sawhill, the woman who was looking after her. She said that Mrs Hogg had indeed gone to her house for tea that afternoon, that Mrs Hogg had made an offensive remark and that a quarrel had developed. At that point, she seems to have realised she was incriminating herself and decided not to say any more.

Mary Wheeler's trial at the Old Bailey under Mr Justice Denman opened on 1 December 1890. Mary entered a plea of not guilty through her defence counsel, Mr Arthur Hulton. Then the prosecution, conducted by Mr Forrest Fulton, outlined its case. Letters were read out to show her passion for Frank Hogg. The suggested motive was jealousy, that Mary wanted to supplant Phoebe and be Frank's wife. The counsel for the prosecution was also mischievously turning the jury against the accused by emphasizing her immorality. Evidence was produced that linked Mary closely to the killing. John Pearcey was able to identify the cardigan wrapped round Phoebe's head as one that he himself had given to Mary. Evidence was also given that the blinds in Mary's house were drawn on the afternoon of the murder, which implied premeditation.

Arthur Hulton was hard pressed to present any kind of case for the defence. He tried to argue that the evidence against Mary was circumstantial and that a woman of Mary's moderate build would be able to inflict the dreadful injuries suffered by Phoebe Hogg, who was similar in size and build to Mary Wheeler.

Mary remained completely impassive throughout her trial and gave no evidence at all. Presumably Arthur Hulton did not feel able to trust her to give a sensible or consistent account of herself; he had perhaps had the experience of hearing Mary singing or whistling when confronted by her crime, and did not want her doing that in court. Just halfway through the third day of the trial, the jury found Mary Wheeler guilty, though it did take them 52 minutes to agree on it. When asked if she had anything to say, Mary said, 'I say I am innocent of this charge'. Denman sentenced her to death.

There was still no Court of Criminal Appeal in England in 1890, so Mary Wheeler's fate was sealed. Her solicitor even so made valiant efforts to save her, alleging that she was not in full control of herself, having had epileptic fits since birth. The Home Office was not minded to change the sentence.

Mary asked if Frank Hogg could visit her the day before her execution in Newgate Prison. Permission was granted, but Hogg did not turn up; it is not known why. Mary was distraught. She wept inconsolably. Apart from this, though, she remained very calm.

On her final evening, she was visited by her solicitor, Mr Freke Palmer. She asked him to deal with her bequests and also to place a personal ad in the Madrid neswpapers, to read, 'MECP Last wish of MEW. Have not betrayed, MEW'. 'MEW' stood for Mary Eleanor Wheeler, but nobody knows what the rest of the message means. It certainly implies that someone else, 'MECP', was being protected. Mr Palmer assumed this was the case, and he pressed Mary very hard to tell him what it was about, telling her that he could still get the Home Secretary to intervene. But she would not say. Nor would she confess to the murders.

The execution, the customary three clear Sundays after the sentence, was to take place on 23 December, 1890. On arrival at Newgate she was, like all other prisoners, made to take a bath, and dressed in prison uniform, a grey shift. She was guarded round the clock by three wardresses. The hangman arrived at the prison on the Saturday before the execution to take a discreet look at the prisoner through the peephole in the door and assess her weight and height for the hanging. Mary noticed this, commenting to the wardresses, 'Oh, was that the executioner? He's in good time, isn't he? Is it usual for him to arrive on the Saturday for the Monday?'

Mary was very calm and composed at her execution – unusually so. Berry entered her cell just before 8 a.m., shaking hands with her and saying, 'Good morning, madam. If you're ready madam I will get these straps round you.' Berry put the leather body belt round her and tied her wrists to it in front. Mary then said, 'My sentence is a just one but a good deal of the evidence against me is false.' She kissed her wardresses and was then escorted by two of them out of the cell, along the corridor, across the yard to the execution shed. The gallows was a big structure capable of taking four victims at once. This time there was a single noose hanging from six links of iron chain. Mary weighed nine stone, and Berry had set a drop of nine feet for her. Her legs were pinioned and a white cotton hood put over her head. The noose was tightened round her neck. Berry pulled the lever as soon as the scaffold was clear. The trap doors crashed down and Mary Wheeler dropped out of sight into the brick-lined pit, dying instantly.

The execution of Mary Wheeler provoked little public sympathy, partly because of the gratuitous murder of the child. Madame Tussaud's made a waxwork model of her to put on display in the Chamber of Horrors, and bought the pram from Frank Hogg to make a gruesome tableau.

If Mary Wheeler had been put on trial a hundred years later, the medical evidence of her lifelong epilepsy would almost certainly have been brought out at her trial. She had also made two attempts at suicide in the ten years between her father's hanging and her own. There was no definite evidence that she had had an epileptic fit that fateful afternoon, but one neighbour said in evidence that she appeared 'boozed' immediately after the murder, and that could easily have been the effect of a fit. There was even so not enough evidence to justify a plea of insanity, which in England was governed by the McNaghten Rule. This rule regarding an insanity plea had been set up as a result of a high-profile case in the 1840s.

In 1843, Daniel McNaghten had tried to kill the Prime Minister, Sir Robert Peel, accidentally shooting his secretary Mr Drummond instead. McNaghten had an imaginary grudge against Peel. The court found him not guilty by reason of insanity; he either did not know what he was doing, or if he did he did not know it was wrong.

Mr Palmer tried hard to persuade the Home Secretary, saying it seemed as if the whole world was against Mary Wheeler. But given the murder of the child and Mary Wheeler's 'immoral' lifestyle, Victorian society was indeed against her. There was no public support for a reprieve. Many saw her death sentence as come-uppance, no less than she deserved.

But several questions remain. Mary was completely resigned to her fate, and even seemed to resent her solicitor's efforts to gain her a reprieve. It is also not absolutely certain that what the hangman reported her as saying is exactly what she said. It was common for people to confess at the last moment, and he may have expected a confession and mis-heard her on that account. Berry thought she said, 'My sentence is a just one but much of the evidence against me is false'. But what if she actually said, 'My sentence is an unjust one and much of the evidence against me is false'? If so, it could be that she knew that someone else had committed the murders, but she was taking the blame. Who was this person in Madrid that she wanted to reassure? Was MECP the real murderer? Or was he just another lover who was anxious not to have his name dragged through the courts?

Another reason for her resignation may have been that Mary was unable to deal with her solicitor's persistent questions about the crime; perhaps she simply had no recollection of it. If she really had had an epileptic fit, she would remember none of the events of those critical hours, and be unable to answer any questions.

On balance, it looks as if Mary Wheeler killed Phoebe Hogg, and with malice aforethought. Mary had a strong motive. She was in love with Frank Hogg and evidently wanted Phoebe Hogg out of the way. It was not a chance meeting; Mary had invited Phoebe round for tea. The house seems to have been set up for the murder by having the blinds pulled down. It is nevertheless very peculiar that Mary seems to have done nothing to escape punishment afterwards. Wheeling the bodies through the streets in a pram in the early evening and dumping them on the pavement was inviting discovery. By wrapping the victim's head in one of her own garments, she was almost deliberately implicating herself. She could also have cleaned up the kitchen and the murder weapons, instead of which she left everything just as it was for the police to find. Maybe that was it. Maybe it was an elaborate way of committing suicide – suicide by proxy. Instead of killing herself, which she had tried to do twice and failed, she would get the public hangman to do it for her.

Lizzie Borden

'who gave her mother forty whacks'

IN JULY 1860 Lizzie Borden was born in Massachusetts. The family, who lived at Fall River, was
at odds with itself from the start. Lizzie's mother
died, leaving Andrew, Lizzie's father, to care for
the two-year-old and her elder sister Emma. Three
years later Andrew Borden remarried. The new
wife, Abby Durfee, was a short, heavy and rather
withdrawn woman. The small town gossip was
that this was a marriage of convenience, and that
all Andrew wanted from Abby was the services of
a maid and child-minder, but the truth is that
Andrew Borden seems to have cared for his new
wife, one of life's non-starters, and wanted to make
proper provision for her. That was at the heart of
the problem.

From the beginning the two girls resented their
new stepmother. The 32-year-old Emma despised
Abby, and for the very specific reason that Abby
was likely to rob her of her inheritance. Andrew
Borden, now seventy, had become wealthy as a
result of his investments but, in spite of being one
of the richest men in town, he and his family lived
frugally in a small house in an unfashionable
district of Fall River. As events developed, she

turned out to be right. First one of Andrew Borden's properties was made over to Abby, then, just at the time of her death, there were plans to make over another. Lizzie and Emma were fully justified in their fears that they were going to be disinherited. As the two girls grew older, things got steadily worse and they refused to eat meals with Abby, pointedly calling her 'Mrs Borden'. Lizzie decapitated Abby's cat after it annoyed her.

Another problem was the narrow focus of Lizzie's life. She was over thirty now and still had no job, no husband, no love life, nothing to distract her from the long-simmering grievance against her father and his second wife. She did some voluntary work and taught at a Sunday school, but those were not enough to distract her from the frustrations that were intensifying in her mind. Then, in 1891, her feud with her parents erupted into physical action. On one occasion when Andrew returned from an outing, Lizzie reported that Abby's bedroom had been broken into and ransacked by a thief who had stolen a watch and jewellery. Mr Borden called the police, then dismissed them halfway through their investigation, once it was obvious that Lizzie herself was the culprit. Again, later in the same year, the Borden's barn was twice broken into. Andrew Borden again assumed that Lizzie was behind the petty crime. He retaliated by cutting the heads off Lizzie's pigeons, probably as a reminder of what Lizzie had done to Abby's cat. It is not known what Lizzie's reaction was to this act. Probably she sat around, as the Bordens tended to, and fumed silently for days afterwards.

Probably Andrew Borden's fate was already sealed, but the double murder of Lizzie's parents did not come until the following summer, the summer of 1892.

Lizzie Borden was known to have 'funny spells' when she behaved totally unpredictably, and those spells became more frequent during the unusually hot year of 1892, when all New England steamed and suffocated. The local drugstore noticed that Lizzie was regularly buying small doses of prussic acid, well known as a lethal poison. By the end of July the entire Borden household was afflicted with stomach upsets. These were probably nothing to do with the prussic acid, but more likely to do with the fact that meat was going off faster than normal in the high temperatures – a common problem in the days before refrigerators.

Abby Borden was nevertheless convinced that she had been poisoned after she had suffered a long bout of vomiting. She made one of her rare trips out, to see the doctor who lived over the road. When she returned she was told off by her husband for her nonsensical behaviour. The doctor pointed out that the whole family was retching, including the maid. Lizzie's hate grew, Abby's apprehension grew, Andrew's irritation grew.

The day of 4 August, 1892 began like any other, only hotter. It was the hottest day of the summer. By mid-morning Andrew and Abby Borden were dead. Exactly what happened in between is still not known. It is not known for certain whether

Lizzie committed the murders – and some investigators have suggested other culprits, such as a discontented employee, or the maid, Bridget – but such evidence as there is points directly to Lizzie.

Luckily for her, Lizzie's sister Emma was out of town. Uncle John Morse, who had been invited to stay for a few days, was up early. The maid, Bridget Sullivan, followed him down to start her chores, but she had to stop to be sick. By 7.30 a.m. Abby and Andrew were dressed and sitting at breakfast with Uncle John. Just over an hour later, Uncle John went into town. Lizzie came down for a light breakfast, Bridget went outside to clean the windows, Abby got on with some dusting. At about 9 a.m. Andrew Borden went into town. He waited outside the bank and then decided to return home, where he arrived at about 10.30.

While Andrew Borden was out, a young man arrived and hung about outside the Borden house. He was noticed by the neighbours. He seemed agitated, then he disappeared. He was never identified.

Inside No 92 Second Street nasty things had started to happen. Someone had crept up behind Abby Borden while she was dusting the guest room and brought a hatchet crashing down on her head. She was killed instantly, but the attacker, whoever he or she was, carried on raining blows on her. There was no noise, at least not enough to alert anyone else in the house that anything untoward was happening up in the guest room. It was then, at 10.30, that Andrew Borden turned the key in the lock on the front door, hot and tired after his walk back from town. Lizzie helped her father settle himself for a rest on the sofa in the sitting room, then went to the outbuilding. She was, according to her own testimony, away for 20 minutes before returning.

It was at 11.10 a.m. that Lizzie officially 'found' the body of her father sprawled on the sofa in the sitting room. Half of his head was shorn away by blows from an axe, and blood was still trickling from his wounds. Lizzie's composure during the next few hours was a matter of comment. Lizzie summoned the maid, Bridget Sullivan, and went to a neighbour to tell her what had happened. 'Oh, Mrs Churchill, do come. Someone has killed Father!' is what the neighbour remembered her saying. She also called the family doctor and the police. Lizzie said her mother had had a note asking her to go and visit a sick person, so she did not know where Mrs Borden was. That was odd, because Abby virtually never went out – and if this was true where was the note?

Even when the police and the doctor arrived, the body of Abby Borden still lay undetected upstairs. Then Lizzie 'remembered that she thought she had heard Abby coming back from town' and a curious neighbour went upstairs to look. It was only then that the body of Abby Borden was found on the floor beside the bed in the guest room. Dr Bowen found that Andrew Borden had been killed, probably with a hatchet, where he lay on the sofa; he had suffered eleven axe-blows to the head, delivered from above and behind. The weather had been oppressively hot for days, so it was understandable that Mr Borden should have reclined on the sofa in the middle of the day. Abby had been attacked from behind while she was cleaning the bedroom. The much-hated Abby received eighteen blows to the head. She had probably died at about 9.30 a.m., Andrew at 11 a.m.

In spite of the heat, a crowd began to gather in the street outside the Borden house. Then a man came walking up the street. It was Uncle John. It was his behaviour that now seemed remarkable. Instead of seeing the crowd and hurrying to see what was wrong at the Borden house, which would have been most people's response, he slowed right down. When he at last reached the house, he went round to the back garden, picked some fruit from a tree and ate it. Even with the evidence of disaster round him, Uncle John was in no hurry to find out what it was. Did he perhaps already know?

Once he was inside the house, Uncle John was a changed man. His story of the morning's events cascaded out of him. His alibi was so watertight that he became the principal suspect. When he emerged, the crowd had already decided he was their man, and they chased him back inside.

Emma was out of town, visiting friends, and Lizzie and Bridget were the only people left alive in the house. Bridget told the police she had been washing windows most of the morning, and then gone up to her room to lie down. Her story never changed, but Lizzie kept on contradicting herself and giving versions of events that could not have been true. She said she had been in the barn loft before returning to the house to discover her father's body, but when the investigators went up to the loft they saw that the floor was covered with an undisturbed layer of dust: nobody had been up there at all recently. In the cellar they found four hatchets. One of them had no handle and was covered in ash; this was the supposed murder weapon that would be presented as an exhibit at Lizzie's trial.

The next day, Emma hired a lawyer. The District Attorney Hosea Knowlton, resisted the pressure from the police to arrest Lizzie but, as he said, 'You don't have any evidence against her'. Five days later, after an inquest had been held, Lizzie Borden was arrested, charged and taken to Taunton Jail. If it had been someone outside the family circle, an intruder, that intruder would have been incredibly lucky to hit a moment when Bridget was outside cleaning windows, and Emma and Uncle John just happened to be out.

The Grand Jury trial, a preliminary hearing, opened on 7 November. One of the Bordens' friends, Alice Russell, gave evidence; she had seen Lizzie burning a dress she said was stained with paint three days after the murders. On 2 December, Lizzie was formally charged on three counts of murder, one for the murder of Andrew, one for the murder of Abby, one for the murder of them both.

Lizzie Borden's trial opened on 5 June, 1893 and lasted fourteen days. Witnesses testified that

Andrew Borden was drawing up a new will, and intended to leave half his estate to Abby, the rest to be divided between his daughters. Another witness testified that Lizzie had tried to buy prussic acid from a drug store, which she could have used to poison her parents. The defence took only two days to present its case, calling witnesses who said that they had seen a mysterious man near the Borden house. Emma Borden – not the most impartial of witnesses, since she had hated Abby as much as Lizzie – confirmed that Lizzie had no motive for killing their parents. Was Emma protecting not only Lizzie but herself? Did she perhaps know that Lizzie was planning the murders?

A leading question related to Lizzie's visit to the outbuilding during the twenty minutes when her father was being murdered. What was she doing in the outhouse? 'To look for a piece of metal with which to mend a window screen, also to get some lead suitable for fishing weights. Detectives searching the house found no broken screens and no lead that could be used for fishing weights. She also claimed that she had eaten three pears while she was in the outbuilding, even though it had been stifling and she had a queasy stomach. None of this sounded true.

In her favour was the lack of bloodstained clothing. If she had done the killings, she would have been soaked in blood, twice in the space of ninety minutes, yet when the house was searched all of Lizzie's clothes were found to be spotless. Alice Russell told a slightly different story. Before the second police search was carried out, Lizzie tore up an old dress and burnt it in the kitchen stove. Alice asked Lizzie why she was doing it. Lizzie said, 'Because it was all faded and paint-stained'. Alice said, 'I wouldn't let anybody see me do that, Lizzie, if I were you.' Alice couldn't see any paint on the dress and obviously suspected that the dress was stained in some other, more incriminating, way.

The court gave two rulings on points of order, which proved decisive as far as the jury was concerned. This is unusual, in that the points of order were technical rather than substantive. Lizzie's inquest testimony was disallowed as trial evidence on the grounds that when she made the statement she had not at that stage been formally charged. The evidence of the drug store assistant was also disallowed because the matter of the poison was irrelevant to the case. This was because no poison had been involved in the murders. These rulings evidently impressed the jury, who were no doubt left feeling that the case for the prosecution had been heavy-handed, illegal and unfair. It took only half an hour for the jury's sense of fair play to prevail. They found Lizzie Borden not guilty on all three counts of murder. The courtrooom reverberated with applause. That night she was guest of honour at a celebration party. She laughed over the collection of newspaper cuttings of the trial that her supporters had kept for her.

If Lizzie was innocent, then who had committed the murders? Was it the agitated young man seen by the neighbour outside the house? And who was he? If it was the agitated young man, how would he have got into the house? The front door was locked.

Lizzie Borden was released, but suspicion still hung in the air at Fall River. In spite of her acquittal, many people believed that she had killed her parents. Lizzie and Emma had to leave the neighbourhood, though surprisingly they did not leave Fall River altogether. Five weeks after the trial, the sisters moved to a house in a more fashionable neighbourhood, and called the house Maplecroft. Lizzie took to calling herself Lizbeth which, in a similar way, was a sort of break with the past but not enough to make any difference. Murders apart, she was evidently a very peculiar person.

Lizzie's underlying criminality, which seems to have been there all along, emerged in a small way again in 1897, when she was accused of shoplifting. The matter of a hundred dollars was settled out of court. Or if we do not want to go as far as calling it criminality, perhaps, as one writer has proposed, Lizzie suffered from temporal epilepsy, which could account for what the family called her 'peculiar turns'.

Lizzie's lifestyle underwent a transformation when she met a young actress called Nance O'Neill. Nance moved into Maplecroft and Lizzie started throwing parties for Nance and her new-found theatrical friends. Emma did not like any of these new developments and moved out; she never spoke to her sister again. Lizzie Borden died at the age of sixty-six on 1 June, 1927, after gall bladder surgery. Just a week later, her sister Emma died after a fall down stairs.

The Borden murders remain officially unsolved. The maid, the doctor, and an illegitimate brother demanding money have all been blamed by various authors, but Lizzie still looks like the obvious culprit. The Borden family was a profoundly dysfunctional family, and it is clear that both the daughters had a strong financial motive for resenting Abby's intrusion and their father's intention to draw up a new will in her favour. Abby could have been killed out of hatred; Andrew because he would have avenged Abby's murder; Andrew had to die before he could sign the new will. There is no need to look outside the immediate family for suspects or motives. We also know enough about Lizzie's criminal tendencies (the faked burglaries and the shoplifting) and her violence (the beheading of Abby's cat) to sense that she was capable of both criminal deception and murder. It is also possible that someone else, a nameless stranger, or a disaffected neighbour, was guilty of the break-ins, and that Lizzie was incensed that her father should blame her for them. Anger at her father's unjust accusations could easily have fuelled her frenzied attack on him.

But there was something else happening that fateful morning. Uncle John was there for a particular purpose. Andrew Borden had already transferred a piece of property to Abby's name and it had led to a massive row, with Lizzie protesting that she was being disinherited. Uncle

John was there to assist in the transfer of another property to Abby Borden. A young man called at about 9 a.m. with a note. He may have left the note just before or just after Andrew Borden left for the bank. Neither Andrew nor Uncle John would have wanted to upset things by telling Lizzie, but let us suppose that the note arrived at 9 a.m. just after Andrew left and Lizzie read it and realised its significance. She could easily have flown into a rage and gone upstairs and killed Abby within the half-hour. That makes more sense than the temporal epilepsy. If it had been temporal epilepsy, Lizzie would have been quite certain she hadn't committed the murders and would probably have gone on living in Second Street.

Lizzie Borden was guilty, beyond all reasonable doubt. This was the general perception in America at the time, and America delivered its own sentence on Lizzie Borden by turning her into folklore. She became, like the Big Bad Wolf, a nursery rhyme hate figure, this girl who 'gave her mother forty whacks. When she saw what she had done, She gave her father forty-one.' She became a jolly cautionary tale. Lizzie Borden quickly turned into a kind of joke-evil which still persists and is in a strange way far worse than the guilty verdict that comes from a court of law.

Dr Crippen

'a runaway caught by wireless'

FOR AN INFAMOUS murderer, Hawley Harvey Crippen was a remarkably quiet and inoffensive man. He was an American by birth, born in Michigan in 1862, though his spectacularly newsworthy murder was carried out in London. He gained his medical qualifications at Cleveland, London and New York. It was after that, while he was working as a doctor's assistant in New York, that he met Cora Turner. She was seventeen, lively and attractive, but also pregnant and the mistress of a stove manufacturer. She had a miscarriage. In spite of the very obvious disadvantages of the liaison, Crippen, who was by now a 31-year-old widower, fell in love and courted her. Love is blind, and Hawley Harvey Crippen was blind to the flaws in Cora's personality, blind to her total unsuitability as a partner. He found that she was not really Cora Turner but Kunigunde Mackamotzki, of Russian-Polish and German parentage, and hoped to be an opera singer. Crippen indulged this pipe-dream, paying for her singing lessons. Cora and Hawley were married in 1893. It was a big mistake for both of them.

In 1900, Crippen was transferred to London to

be the manager of the head office of Munyon's, a mail-order medicine company. Cora followed him across the Atlantic later that year. In London, she decided to lower her sights a little; here she would be a music-hall star. She changed her name, a second time, to Belle Elmore. For reasons unknown, Crippen too changed his name, from Hawley Harvey to Peter. Their new life consisted of a riot of Bohemian parties with the gay, extravert Belle at their centre and the insignificant and slightly lugubrious Peter, with his big sandy moustache and small spectacles, looking dolefully on. Occasionally he treated her to a lavish present – a fur or some jewellery – but life behind the scenes was far from glamorous. Neither of them wanted to do any housework, and they lived in a squalid back kitchen in a tangle of unwashed clothes and heaps of unwashed crockery.

Then things started to go badly wrong. Crippen had to return to America on business and while he was away Cora had an affair with an American music hall entertainer called Bruce Miller. In 1905, the Crippens moved up-market to 39 Hilldrop Crescent in Camden Town, but the move did nothing to heal the damaged relationship. Crippen said, 'There were very frequent occasions when she got into the most violent tempers . . . She went in and out just as she liked . . . I was a rather lonely man and rather miserable.'

Cora worked for the Music Hall Ladies Guild, where she was able to pretend to be a great star helping out less fortunate members of the profession. Cora lived in a world of illusion; one of her fantasies was that her father was titled. Crippen even used his father-in-law's imaginary title in one of his firm's quack remedies: Baron Mackamotzki's Cure for Deafness. She was bored and frustrated with Crippen. She also spent time with a string of lovers. Then Crippen formed a new relationship of his own, with one of the secretaries at Munyon's offices in New Oxford Street. She was much more like Crippen than Cora had ever been, and a much better match; she was quiet, demure, lady-like, respectable. She was just the sort of woman Crippen should have married. But for Ethel Le Neve, getting entangled with Crippen was to become the defining tragedy of her life. At Hilldrop Crescent the situation got progressively worse. Cora started taking in paying guests, for whom Peter was expected to fetch coal, polish boots and do general cleaning. He was close to breaking point by now.

Then Crippen lost his job as manager at Munyon's and was paid only on commission. Cora chose this moment to give the bank notice that she was withdrawing £600 from their joint account. It was a punishment for Peter's philandering, and a kind of threat. Cora's fate was sealed.

On 17 January, 1910, Crippen went to a chemist near his office and ordered hyoscine, a strong depressant. The chemist had none in stock and delivered it two days later. On 31 January, Cora and Peter Crippen were 'at home' to two retired music hall friends, Clara and Paul Martinetti. Paul was a reitired mime artist. There was dinner followed by whist, then death, for Cora. Clara

Martinetti recalled that it was 'quite a nice evening and Belle was very jolly'. They left for home at 1.30 in the morning. Clara's last words to Cora were, 'Don't come down, Belle. You'll catch your death.' After the Martinellis had gone Cora picked a fight with Peter. Within hours she was dead. Crippen never owned up to killing her, and it is by no means clear how Cora Crippen died. The neighbours later claimed that they heard a woman screaming, pleas for mercy and a pistol shot, or perhaps a door being slammed. It must be assumed that he somehow administered a huge dose of hyoscine, waited for her to die, and then set about dismembering her body.

Two days later, Crippen pawned some of his wife's jewellery for £80. He also sent a letter to the Music Hall Ladies Guild to explain that Cora would be missing the next few of their meetings. She had gone to America to attend to a sick relative. A week later, Crippen pawned another £115 worth of Cora's jewels. That was understandable, in that he needed the money, but it was very rash of him to give some of the jewellery to Ethel to wear. Meanwhile, Crippen released increasingly alarming bulletins about Cora. She was out of reach in the mountains of California. She was ill with pneumonia. She was dead. Her body, Crippen put it about, had been cremated in America.

Then Crippen had a piece of really bad luck. A couple of Cora's friends, Lil and John Edward Nash, returned from an American theatre tour and told Crippen they had heard nothing of

Cora's death in California. They asked him some leading questions. Where had Cora died? 'Some little town near San Francisco, with a Spanish name I think,' was all he seemed to be able to come up with, then 'Los Angeles'. They were suspicious of the answers Crippen gave them and decided to go to the police; by chance they had a friend who was a senior officer at Scotland Yard. On 30 June they took the decisive step, and visited the CID at New Scotland Yard.

Chief Inspector Walter Dew wrote a report on the situation as reported to him by the Nashes. 'It will be gathered from the foregoing that there are the most extraordinary contradictions in the story told by Crippen, who is an American citizen, as is Mrs Crippen, otherwise known as Belle Elmore. . . without adopting the suggestion made by her friends as to foul play, I do think that the time has now arrived when "Doctor" Crippen should be seen by us and asked to give an explanation as to when and how Mrs Crippen left this country, and the circumstances under which she died.'

On 8 July, Chief Inspector Walter Dew called at Crippen's office with Sergeant Mitchell to ask him some questions about Cora. Crippen admitted straight away that he had told a lot of lies about Cora's disappearance. 'I suppose I had better tell the truth. All my stories about her illness and death are untrue. So far as I know she is not dead at all.' She had not died. She had left him, run off to America with another man. He made the mistake of mentioning Bruce Miller, but Miller had by this time married and wanted to present a respectable image of himself to his wife. Crippen had lied to everybody in order to protect her reputation and because he felt too ashamed to own up to what had happened. The interview was amicable and the three men went off to have lunch together before Dew asked Crippen if it would be all right for him and his sergeant to have a look at the house. Crippen agreed to this and went with them to Hilldrop Crescent. Dew was bothered by the fact that Cora had left all her finest clothes behind, but on the whole he was satisfied with Peter Crippen's version of what had happened.

It was then that Crippen made his biggest mistake, after killing Cora, that is. After Dew had gone, he panicked, and persuaded Ethel that they should emigrate at once; they must leave the next day for America. He asked his assistant to go out and buy a suit of clothes for a boy and that afternoon the couple left, initially for Europe. As bad luck would have it, Dew decided to go back and ask one or two more questions. He found the house empty. He immediately ordered a much more thorough search of the house and the garden, rightly suspecting that Crippen had murdered his wife and that her body was probably buried somewhere in or near the house. It was at the end of the second day that Dew himself found a loose stone in the coal-cellar floor. Underneath, he found an appalling mess of rotting human flesh, but no bones. Crippen had filleted Cora, disposed of the bones in some other way, probably on the kitchen stove, then dumped all her flesh in this pit.

The pathologists, led by Sir Bernard Spilsbury, who had the horrible task of picking through these remains, found that they were those of a fat woman who bleached her hair. There was also skin from the lower abdomen which included (Spilsbury said, though others disagree) an old scar in a position where Cora was known to have one. Most significantly of all, the flesh contained large quantities of hyoscine. On 16 July, there were arrest warrants out for Crippen and Le Neve. Wanted for murder and mutilation.

In disposing of the body, Crippen had made several mistakes. He treated the flesh with wet quicklime, whereas quicklime only works as a corrosive when dry. If he had used dry quicklime, the flesh might well have disappeared in the intervening five months. Worse still, he in effect gave the police pathologists a date for the remains by wrapping them in a labelled pyjama jacket, which the manufacturers, Jones Brothers, Holloway, were able to confirm was not made until 1909. There was no possibility that these remains could be older than that.

Peter and Ethel, meanwhile, were in Antwerp, boarding the SS *Montrose* for Quebec, blissfully unaware that they were so soon to be run to earth. They noticed the British policemen watching the gangway as they boarded the ship, but thought they had got away with it once the ship set sail. Crippen had shaved off his moustache, removed his glasses and become Mr John Robinson. Ethel was rather unconvincingly wearing the boy's suit, posing as Crippen's 16-

year-old son. The captain of the *Montrose*, Captain Kendall, was suspicious of them. He had read about the gruesome murder at Hilldrop Crescent in the papers, and watched the odd couple carefully. Kendall slipped into their cabin on the first day and saw a piece of flannel torn from a woman's bodice; something was not right about this pair. He noticed that there was more hand-touching between the two than would normally be the case between father and son. The boy ate in a rather too refined and dainty way. Kendall cleverly called to 'Mr Robinson', Crippen's newly adopted pseudonym, and timed the rate of reaction: a little too slow to be the real name. He amiably invited the pair to dine at his table. He cracked lots of jokes to make Crippen bare his teeth. He was described by the police as having false teeth. It turned out that this was wrong information, but it serves to show how thorough Kendall was in chasing his hunch about the Robinsons. Kendall's last doubts were literally blown away when a gust of wind moved the flap on Ethel's jacket, revealing a safety pin inserted to let out the trousers to accommodate her hips.

After a couple of days at sea, Kendall was sure. He used the new wireless telegraph to send a message to the ship's owners, telling them of his conclusions. 'Have strong suspicions that Crippen London cellar murderer and accomplice are among Saloon passengers. Moustache taken off growing beard. Accomplice dressed as boy. Voice manner and build undoubtedly a girl.' On 23 July, Chief Inspector Drew and his sergeant sailed from

Liverpool on the *Laurentic*. This was a faster ship than the *Montrose*, and it was following a more northerly Great Circle (shortest distance) route. Dew hoped that by taking the faster ship by the shorter route he might overtake the *Montrose* before she reached Quebec. The last thing he wanted was to have to chase Crippen and Ethel Le Neve all over North America.

For eight extraordinary days, Crippen lounged in a deckchair on the deck of the *Montrose*, voicing admiration for the wonderful new invention, little suspecting that the wireless telegraph was preparing the trap that would send him to the gallows and break Ethel's tender and innocent heart. 'What a wonderful invention wireless is!' he said to Kendall. Captain Kendall had carefully collected up all the English newspapers he had found at the start of the voyage, so no-one on the ship except Crippen and himself knew what had happened. The outside world, on the other hand, was being told, almost hour by hour, of the net closing on Dr Crippen. There was great excitement about the case, not just because of the grisly murder and the way Crippen had disposed of his wife's body, but because this was turning out to be the very first manhunt triggered and fuelled by wireless. Policing had entered a new era. After 25 July, Kendall's ship was out of receiving range from land, but he was able to listen to reports via other ships fitted with wireless and use them to bounce messages back across the ocean to Scotland Yard. Even the *Laurentic* was out of direct range when it passed the *Montrose* on 27 July.

The newspapers were full of the chase across the Atlantic, full of Crippen and his accomplice, full of the wireless. The sensational success of the radio-assisted chase was a heaven-sent advertisement for wireless. Marconi could not have wished for more. Within a year, the number of merchant ships equipped with wireless increased enormously, and there was an irresistible demand from the public for wireless to be compulsory for all but the smaller ships. Thanks to Crippen, then, the *Titanic* was fitted with wireless and at least those who took to the boats in 1912 were rescued by the *Carpathia*.

The *Laurentic* ambushed the *Montrose* in the St Lawrence, only 16 hours from Quebec. Dew boarded the *Montrose*, introduced himself to Captain Kendall and then approached Crippen, to whom he said, 'Good morning, Mr Crippen. I am Chief Inspector Dew'. Later, Crippen said, 'I am not sorry. The anxiety has been too much.' He was quick to exonerate Ethel. He insisted that she knew nothing about Cora's death, which seems likely.

On 20 August, after extradition formalities had been completed, Dew set off home for England with his now-infamous prisoners. Once again, no-one on the ship, the SS *Megantic*, knew who they were. Dew, who had been Mr Dewhurst on the *Laurentic*, had now become Mr Doyle − not the brother of Sir Arthur Conan Doyle, surely? − and Crippen alias John Robinson had become Mr Neild. As they travelled from Liverpool to London, they were not only recognized but mobbed by angry crowds. Dew was on the crest of a wave; eventually in 1938 he wrote his memoirs, 'I caught Crippen', though he owed much to the incredible Captain Kendall.

The trial of Dr Crippen, which started on 10 October, 1910, was short and the verdict a foregone conclusion. He was guilty and sentenced to death. It was suggested by the barrister Edward Marshall Hall that Crippen might have given his wife hyoscine to damp down her voracious sexual demands, because he was making love to Ethel and unable to satisfy both women; it was rumoured that this line of defence was put to Crippen and that he rejected it because it would be damaging to Ethel's reputation. It was a strangely gentlemanly thought-world that the mild doctor inhabited, and it is hard to square this fastidiousness with the butchering of Cora's corpse. Cora's arms, legs and head were never found. Crippen in effect succeeded in totally disposing of half of the body, and therefore came close to getting away with murder; without any human remains it is unlikely Dew would have gone any further.

As he waited to be executed, Crippen thought only of Ethel Le Neve, kissing her photograph and writing her poignant letters. In these final days, a new public attitude to Crippen developed, a respect for this quietly dignified and vaguely romantic figure. Many people started to feel sorry for the hen-pecked little man; he had after all been led quite a dance by his awful wife. Crippen was, even so, hanged at Pentonville on 23

November, 1910. Ethel Le Neve, still only 27, was tried a week after Crippen. She was found not guilty of being an accessory after the fact, and slid instantly and deliberately into obscurity. Some said she went to Australia and died there in 1950. Some say she went to Canada or America instead, changing her name to Allen. Some say she ran a tea-room in Bournemouth under another assumed name. I happen to know that she spent her last years in Hove. But it was a half-life, a life in the shadows, a life ruined by the unhappiest of love affairs, and it seems particularly unjust that Ethel must have suffered far, far more than her lover.

Edith Thompson and Frederick Bywaters

'Oh don't!'

EDITH THOMPSON WAS born, as Edith Graydon, on Christmas Day 1893 in a lower middle class family in Manor Park, East London. Her father was a clerk with the Imperial Tobacco Company. Edith was the eldest and liveliest of his five children, and he made a great fuss of her. In fact he spoiled her. She was a talented dancer, and she took part in amateur theatricals until 1920. This interest in drama was her undoing. She was impressionable, tended to over-dramatize things, and read enormous quantities of romantic fiction which fed her rich fantasy life.

Alongside this drama-queen personality there was a harder-headed Edith who knew she needed to make money if she wanted to get on in life. She became a book-keeper at the age of seventeen, at a wholesale milliners in Aldersgate, a firm called Carlton & Prior, and found herself promoted fairly quickly. When she met Percy Thompson, she was earning more than he was.

Percy Thompson was a plodder. He came from a poorer family and started work at the age of thirteen. He was solid, dependable, and usually he took no chances. Even so, on holiday in Ilfracombe in June 1914 Percy had sex with Edith. Edith was far from sure she wanted to spend the rest of her life with dull Percy, but the war nudged her towards marriage. Young men were dying in their thousands, then tens of thousands, and it seemed foolish to wait. They were married in 1916.

Percy Thompson turned out not to be the sort of romantic hero Edith had longed for. He was not even going to be the gallant young soldier Edith saw other young women waving off to the front. He enlisted but was discharged as medically unfit; he boasted to a friend that he had duped the army medical officers into thinking he had a heart condition, so he was either a weakling or a coward and either way he was not what Edith was looking for.

In the summer of 1920, Edith met Frederick Bywaters. He was eighteen, over eight years younger than Edith, with a square jaw, healthy muscular body, light brown wavy hair and a pleasant face. He was in every way the opposite of Percy. Percy had (apparently) tricked his way out of the war; Freddy had played truant from school to fight, signing up for a Merchant Navy convoy when he was only fifteen. Freddy was an old school friend of Edith's brother Billy, which is how he came to be lodging at the Graydons' house while his ship was in the London docks. Mrs Graydon saw Freddy as a possible husband for her second daughter Avis, but before the summer of 1920 came to an end Edith was already showing a serious interest in him.

The following summer Freddy's ship returned from the Far East, and Edith persuaded Percy to invite Freddy – and Avis, for form's sake – to go on holiday with them to the Isle of Wight. Percy liked Freddy, and agreed. The moment they were alone, Edith and Freddy kissed for the first time. Edith recalled in her letters how tightly he had held her. It was a short step to arranging for Freddy to become the Thompsons' lodger in their double-fronted house in Ilford. Two weeks into this new arrangement it was Freddy's birthday, so Edith took the day off work to take Freddy breakfast in bed. She told him she was suicidal. He told her to take her clothes off. They made love then and there, and after that at every possible opportunity. At last it was the passionate relationship that Edith had dreamed of, straight out of her bodice-ripping novellas. Perhaps for Freddy, at just nineteen, it was simple opportunism rather than love.

The Twenties were a time when liberation was in the air among the younger generation, and the liberation of women in particular. They bobbed their hair, wore strapless dresses and daringly short skirts, and won scandalous reputations as reckless flappers. Why shouldn't women be free to do as they like? Unfortunately for Edith, who belonged to this generation, there was another, older generation brought up with late Victorian values and for whom the Great War had meant the loss of their dearly-loved sons. This was the older generation that would shortly pass a terrifyingly harsh judgement on Edith Thompson.

To begin with, Percy knew nothing of the passionate affair going on in his own house, but eventually his suspicions were aroused. Edith unwisely refused to have sex with her husband. This led to a quarrel in which Percy struck Edith and pushed her to the ground. Freddy tried to intervene and Percy threw him out; he had to go back to his parents. After that, Edith arranged to meet Freddy secretly every time his P & O ship docked at Tilbury. Edith became pregnant by Freddy and induced a miscarriage; she was afraid that a baby might scare Freddy off altogether. Meanwhile, Freddy was trying hard to back out of the relationship. He even wrote to her, 'Can we be pals only?' She wrote back in effusive romantic style, saying 'even if you don't still love me, I always shall you.'

Percy, dogged as ever, refused to give Edith the divorce she wanted. 'I have got her and I will keep her', he told Freddy.

In September 1922, Freddy's ship docked again in Tilbury. He travelled into London to meet Edith and they took a train from Fenchurch Street to Ilford, making love in an empty carriage. Now he was with her, Freddy's passion for Edith was as strong as ever. They met again and again, dreading the ending of Freddy's shore leave on 3 October. In her letters Edith called Freddy 'darlint' by which she meant 'darlingest'. She was a great letter-writer. It was to be her downfall. Now she wrote one that would help to send her to the gallows. 'He has the right by law to all that you have the right by nature and love – yes darlint be jealous, so much that you do something desperate.' At her trial, this was interpreted as an incitement to murder. Maybe that is what she meant. Maybe she didn't know what she meant by it. Maybe it was just a string of phrases from a novelette.

Whatever Edith intended to happen, Freddy seems to have taken it as the signal that he was to kill Percy. The Thompsons went out one evening to see a Ben Travers farce at the Criterion. As they walked home afterwards, a man jumped out onto the ill-lit pavement from a front garden, pushed Edith onto the ground, and repeatedly stabbed Percy with a knife. One of the blows severed Percy's carotid artery and blood poured from his mouth. Edith shouted, 'Oh don't, oh don't!' and the man ran off into the night.

The police found Freddy Bywaters still wearing his bloodstained coat and he told them where he had got rid of the knife. There was no doubt about his guilt. Edith's position was precarious, especially in view of the letter she had written, apparently goading Freddy to murder Percy. Stupidly, she made a statement to the police saying that Percy had felt ill and collapsed, that she saw no-one attack him. Presumably she hoped by doing this to avoid giving a description that would lead the police to Freddy, but they had already reached Freddy and knew from him what had happened. Edith made another statement, but by this time she had already done herself irreparable damage.

Edith decided to present herself and Freddy as a romantic hero and heroine, using and defending her letters as witnesses to their great passion. She was not only a great reader of romantic fiction; she was in her way a great writer of romantic fiction too. Her letters are fluent flights of fancy derived mainly from the cheap fiction she read. Freddy's attack on Percy was to be seen as a forgivable crime of passion.

The letters were in fact a godsend to the prosecution. In the letters she came across as a shameless wanton, which did her no good in court. She had written fantasies based on her novelettes about poisoning her husband with quinine or broken light-bulb glass, and these could easily be turned into the raw materials of a conspiracy to murder. Thompson's body was exhumed and tested for poison, but no trace could be found by the two distinguished pathologists who studied it. Freddy Bywaters ceaselessly protested Edith's innocence, but to no avail.

The evidence of poisoning could not be produced, but it was possible to use the letters to suggest that she was guilty of aiding and abetting the murder. The Solicitor General misled the jury when he said that Edith's correspondence contained 'undoubted evidence' of a 'preconcerted meeting between Mrs Thompson and Bywaters at the place', that is, the place where the murder took place. The letters contain no such thing, but the jurors were in no position to check because only half of Edith's correspondence was submitted as evidence. Were the jury to assume or guess that the Solicitor General was lying? That would not have seemed very likely. The judge in effect reinforced this deadly lie in his summing-up, by failing to correct it. He should have explained, then or before, why many of the letters had been withheld; it was simply because they contained material that was deemed too sexually explicit. Her two pregnancies were described. One of the letters described having sex with Freddy in the open air in Wanstead Park.

Even the letters that were deemed fit for the jury to read were fairly raunchy by the standards of the day, though they consisted largely of fantasies. The foreman of the jury said, 'It was my duty to read them to the members of the jury. . . Nauseous is hardly strong enough to describe their contents . . . Mrs Thompson's letters were her own condemnation.'

Both of them were found guilty of murder and sentenced to death. Edith sobbed, 'Take me home, Dad!' as she was taken to the cells.

Edith's appeal was rejected. The Lord Chief Justice declared that this was 'a common and ordinary charge of a wife and another murdering her husband'. There were appeals to the King and Queen and the Prime Minister. A newspaper tried to beg a reprieve from William Bridgeman, the Home Secretary, at his holiday home in Wales. All to no avail.

What counted heavily against Edith Thompson was the fact that she was an older woman, a successful businesswoman, whereas Bywaters was no more than a young merchant seaman.

Obviously the murder was set up by the dominant partner – in this case the woman. Another factor was the explicitness of her letters, which contained references to their sexual activity. She was a brazen adulteress. In the final analysis, Edith Thompson was hanged for sexual wickedness, for adultery. Even the foreman of the jury admitted as much.

In Holloway, as the execution date approached, Edith Thompson disintegrated emotionally and psychologically. The prison doctor was giving her increasingly heavy doses of morphine to deaden her hysteria and terror. She whined constantly, 'Why did he do it? Why did he do it?' Though she was only twenty-nine, by the day of her execution, 9 January, 1923, her hair had turned grey with terror and she was only semi-conscious. To get her through the execution, they had to sedate Edith heavily with strychnine and morphia. They had to carry her to the scaffold and hold her up while the cap and noose were put over her head.

When the body was winched up from the drop, it was seen to be in a terrible state. The dress she was wearing had to be burned. According to reports from the prison, 'her insides fell out'. After the customary post mortem, carried out to make sure that the execution had been done properly, the body was covered in lime and buried in the prison cemetery.

Rumours circulated that Edith Thompson had been pregnant when she was hanged. The odd description of her 'insides falling out' could have been a euphemism for a miscarriage. Edith's weight increased significantly, from 119 pounds on 11 December, the day she was sentenced, to 133 pounds on 9 January, the day she died, though she had eaten very little during that month. Why was she gaining weight? Did they hang not only an innocent woman, but an innocent pregnant woman?

Edith's lover, Frederick Bywaters, was executed, still aged only twenty, on the same day at Pentonville. He had gone to his death fearless and something of a hero in the popular press. Even though he had murdered Percy Thompson, he had remained loyal to Edith throughout the trial and protested her innocence. When he said goodbye to his mother the day before his execution, he said, 'Give my love to Edie'.

Edith Thompson was a silly, spoilt, wayward young woman, but she had not committed murder. She had not committed any capital offence. There was no evidence that she had played any part in Percy's death, other than leading Freddy on. While the attack was taking place she was incapable of doing much because Bywaters had thrown her to the ground, but she did shout, 'Oh don't! Oh don't!' which meant that she had done what she could to stop the killing. It was a self-evident miscarriage of justice, one that would follow the careers of many of those involved in the case and lead eventually to the abolition of the death penalty in Britain.

The British justice system refused to consider Edith's appeal, and has never reversed its wrong verdict. When Holloway Prison was rebuilt in the

1970s, Edith Thompson's body, along with those of three other women hanged at Holloway was transferred to Brookwood Cemetery near Woking. Instead of the customary unmarked grave, Edith now has a granite memorial.

'The Man from the Pru'
and the Anfield murder mystery

WILLIAM AND JULIA Wallace were an ordinary, lower middle class couple living in the Anfield district of Liverpool. They were a quiet, childless and rather sad pair. He was a cold, dull man with a mournful drooping moustache. He made a living as a life insurance agent for the Prudential; she was quite cultured, fastidious and rather more aspiring, hoping for something more from life. They lived in a small Victorian terraced house, No 29 Wolverton Street, which Julia had worked hard to make a genteel, middle-class home.

On the night before Julia Wallace died, her husband received a telephone message at the City Café in North John Street, the café he regularly visited because it was the venue of his Chess Club. The mysterious caller who was to change the lives of both of the Wallaces so melodramatically spoke to the club's captain, Samuel Beattie. He identified himself as Mr R. M. Qualtrough. He left a message asking Wallace to call and see him, apparently about an insurance policy, at 25 Menlove Gardens East at 7.30 p.m. the next day, 20 January, 1931.

The next day, Wallace accordingly set off to

meet the mysterious Mr Qualtrough, who has never to this day been identified, leaving his house in Wolverton Street, as he later told the police, at 6.45 p.m. It is known that William Wallace boarded a tram about three miles away in Lodge Lane at 7.10, so the time that Wallace gave in his police statement is probably correct. Rather oddly, on the tram, Wallace kept reminding the conductor of his destination. After getting off the tram at Menlove Gardens West, he went on a futile search for Qualtrough's house; it turned out in the end that the address Qualtrough had given him was false; it just did not exist. During the search for 25 Menlove Gardens East he called at a newsagent, 25 Menlove Gardens West, and asked a policeman as well, making a point of asking people the time.

Satisfied that 25 Menlove Gardens East did not exist, Wallace gave up the search and made his way home. He arrived back home at 8.45 to find the house in darkness. Feeling his way into the parlour, the front room, Wallace found the battered body of his wife lying face down on the floor on top of his mackintosh. She was lying rather too neatly to have fallen like that; it looked as if someone had straightened the body up and laid it on the raincoat. There was also some money missing.

The photographs of the crime scene have survived. They show the pathetically genteel home that Julia had created, with its traditional set-piece fireplace and a large mirror above. Framed family photographs line the mantelpiece and four large pictures fill the wall on each side. It is a shock to see Julia's body lying too tidily on the carpet, her feet near the fireplace and head towards the door. This position suggested that she was not afraid of whoever killed her; the murderer must have been well into the room, struck her from behind so that she fell towards the door in that way – unless of course the body was moved from a very different position, which is possible.

The police arrived, found no sign of a forced entry, and found Mr Wallace in a remarkably detached and composed state. He said something about a poker being missing from the fireside set. They suspected that he had done it. There was something odd about his account of entering the parlour at 8.45 pm, in near total darkness, apart from the glow from the fire, and going to the gaslights on each side of the fireplace to light them; only then, he claimed, did he see Julia's body. That is peculiar, because Julia's body, as the crime scene photographs show very clearly, filled the space between the doorway and the fireplace. It would scarcely be possible to enter the room and reach the gaslights without tripping over the body. Two weeks later, when Wallace was staying with his sister in Aigburth, the police arrested him and charged him with Julia's murder.

The case for the prosecution hinged on the police view of Wallace as a cold, calculating, scheming man. There was no such person as Qualtrough. The 'Chess Club Murderer' had set up the Qualtrough alibi himself from start to finish. It was Wallace himself, the prosecution alleged, who had phoned the City Café and left the message. The lengthy journey and the non-existence of the address given would explain why he was out of the house for such a long time, round about the time the murder was committed. But the prosecution argued that Wallace could have committed the murder at the beginning of the evening, before setting off to catch the tram. They also alleged that Wallace's persistent reminders about the stop at Menlove Gardens where he wanted to alight were simply a device to make the tram conductor remember him. In a similar way, asking for confirmation of the time in the newsagent's and asking a policeman to direct him to the address he was looking for were ways of ensuring that there were witnesses for his alibi.

The prosecution had more trouble explaining the lack of blood on Wallace's clothing. The scenario the counsel for the prosecution presented in court was as follows. Julia Wallace was in the parlour. Her husband, perhaps upstairs, took all of his clothes off and then came into the parlour wearing only his mackintosh. He then blud-geoned his wife to death, sending spatters of blood in all directions. He spread the mackintosh on the floor, put his wife's body on top to 'explain' the spots and splashes of blood on it, then went upstairs naked to wash the blood off. Then he put his clothes back on and went off for the meeting with Qualtrough.

There were in fact many difficulties with this scenario. One of them was that Wallace was known to have boarded the tram at 7.10, and at a point three miles from the house. It would have taken Wallace a full 25 minutes to cover the three miles, making it likely that he was telling the truth about leaving the house at 6.45. Could he have bludgeoned Julia to death, washed and dressed and been out on the streets by 6.45? The 'forensic' report gave the estimated time of death as earlier than 6 p.m., but it seems likely that the police indicated to the pathologist their preference for a time of death that would fit the scenario they were assembling. A major problem with having Julia dying at 6 o'clock or earlier is that she was seen, alive, by a delivery boy at 6.30. That means that there was only a window of fifteen minutes – at the very most – in which Wallace could have committed the murder and done all the cleaning up. It was not long enough.

There were other problems with the prosecution's hypothesis. The bath was completely dry. There was no sign that anyone had taken a bath in the recent past. If Wallace had indeed committed the murder naked, then climbing into the bath would have been the obvious and only way of making absolutely sure every spot of blood was removed. It is inconceivable that Wallace would have risked missing blood splashes by having a mere wash-down. None of the towels were damp either, so no-one had had a bath or a wash-down in the previous few hours.

The area round the body in the parlour was found to have been sprayed with Julia Wallace's blood. The murderer must have been covered in it. Yet there were no drops of blood outside the parlour. If Wallace had hurried, naked and blood-spattered, out of the parlour to go and wash upstairs, there would be some spots of blood elsewhere. The forensic investigators were delighted when they found one drop of coagulated blood on the rim of the lavatory bowl. This was taken by the prosecution to prove that Wallace had indeed gone to the bathroom to wash. But the single drop of blood could easily have been picked up by one of the police officers on his coat hem, and accidentally transferred from the parlour to the bathroom as he made a tour of the house. The fact that it was a coagulated blob of blood suggests that it was moved a couple of hours after the murder rather than immediately after.

All in all, the prosecution case was unconvincing. Yet, in spite of the evidence, the jury found Wallace guilty, after only one hour's deliberation. He was sentenced to death.

Legal history was made when William Wallace appealed. His case was heard on 18 May by the Lord Justice, who ruled that the verdict must be overturned on the grounds that it had been made against the weight of the evidence. On the evidence as presented at the trial, Wallace should have been acquitted. Wallace came within a hair's breadth of the gallows, and was then freed. He tried to go on living at 29 Wolverton Street, and tried to go on doing his life insurance job too, but the whispering and the gossip just would not stop. People would cruelly call, 'Julia! Julia!' in ghostly voices through his letterbox, just as he had himself that night late in January, and he realised that he could not go on. He had to move away. He went to live in Cheshire, where he died only two years later of renal cancer.

The murderer of Julia Wallace was never caught, and never even identified. The police only considered one suspect, her husband, and there was insufficient evidence against him. But over the years since 1931 a prime suspect has emerged. His name is Gordon Parry. He had worked with Wallace in the insurance business and was a frequent visitor to the Wallace house. At the time of the original murder investigation, Gordon Parry was one of the names given to the police as someone Julia Wallace would have felt safe inviting into her house. She would have opened the door to Parry. The police even got as far as asking Parry where he was on the evening in question, but they were satisfied with his answer.

Gordon Parry was tracked down in the 1960s by two crime writers, Richard Whittington-Egan and Jonathan Goodman, when Parry was living in London. Parry would not let the two writers into his home – but then again why should he have trusted them in his home? The two investigators were surprised how much Parry knew. He seemed to know everything about everyone involved in the murder investigation. That in itself does not strike me as odd. The Wallace murder case was a sensational news story of its time. As a work associate of Wallace and a 'friend' of sorts to both Wallace and his wife, he would naturally have taken a great deal of interest in the case, even if he himself was entirely blameless.

Gordon Parry did however give the investigators one snippet of information that was suggestive. He told them that Wallace was 'sexually odd'. What that meant is very hard to tell, but on the whole people in 1931 did not normally discuss their sex lives; it was not the 1960s. The Wallaces seem very unlikely people to have shared this sort of information about themselves in the course of a social conversation, even with someone they regarded as a friend. So, if it was true that William Wallace had unusual sexual tastes, how did Gordon Parry know about them? One possibility is that Parry's relationship with Julia was more than just a friendship. If they were flirting, possibly even more, maybe Julia revealed one of her reasons for being dissatisfied with her husband. It was found that Julia was not wearing normal ladies' underwear when she was killed, but a nappy, and perhaps that was part of the 'oddity' that Parry was referring to.

In 1980, a radio presenter called Roger Wilkes researched the Wallace case. Startlingly, some new evidence had come to light. A new witness came forward, a car mechanic called John Parkes. He had been given a car to clean by Gordon Parry on the night of the murder. While he was cleaning the interior, he found a bloodstained glove, which Parry snatched away from him, muttering, 'That could hang me'. Parkes did not say anything to the police at the time because he was afraid of Parry, who had a violent streak and a nasty temper. Parry was a dangerous man to cross.

Unfortunately, Wilkes made this breakthrough just too late to confront Gordon Parry with it. Parry had died in North Wales a few weeks earlier.

Parry fits the profile of Julia's killer well. He had worked with Wallace and evidently harboured some sort of resentment against him. He had been in the same insurance business and knew about the pattern of collection. The Prudential worked on a weekly cycle that ran from Wednesday to Wednesday. It was not unusual to be storing a significant sum of money in the cash box on a Tuesday night, representing the week's takings, as Wednesday was account day, when the money was banked. If anyone who understood the insurance system was going to rob someone like Wallace, Tuesday night was the night to do it. Julia was murdered on a Tuesday evening. Parry, as a former work associate of Wallace, would have known all about the pattern of takings. As it happened, Parry or whoever else it was, only got away with £4 from Wallace's cash box, but the attack on a Tuesday does not look random. We also know that Parry was a dangerous thug with a criminal record, easily capable of beating someone to death with a poker.

Although it has been alleged that there is something suspicious about Wallace's account of his discovery of Julia's body, there is not. He did not, as has been said, cross the darkened room, crossing the area where Julia was lying, to turn on the gas lights before he saw the body. According to his own police statement, 'I then came down and looked into the front room and struck a match and saw my wife lying on the floor.' So there was nothing suspicious about his account.

The wild goose chase looking for Qualtrough's non-existent house could as easily have been set up by Gordon Parry, to lure Wallace away from his home for a good hour or two, giving Parry time to go in, kill Julia, take whatever money was there and, in effect, frame Wallace for wife-murder. A marvellous revenge.

Why did Wallace remind the conductor that he wanted to get off at Menlove Gardens? The explanation may be very simple and ordinary. It may be that Wallace had had the bad experience of being whisked past the stop where he wanted to get off, and having to waste time and shoe leather walking back. He was keen not to be late for the appointment. That in turn explains why he kept asking people to verify the time for him: he had an appointment to keep. There is no more to it than that.

The murder of Julia Wallace, with its mysterious, nebulous, unidenitifiable Qualtrough lurking in the background, gripped the newspaper readers of the day and has gone on exercising the imaginations of crime writers ever since. It was even made into a film in the 1990s, *The Man from the Pru*, starring Jonathan Pryce and Anna Massey. Was Gordon Parry the evil genius behind it all, the envious murderer who killed Julia, who widowed and robbed Wallace and then framed him? Or was Wallace, the cold and cunning Chess Club murderer, the real culprit all along, just as the police believed at the time? Raymond

Chandler described the Julia Wallace case as 'unbeatable'. For him it was 'the perfect murder'. No-one was ever convicted for it, and still, even after seventy years, we are no nearer to solving it.

Alma Rattenbury and George Stoner

'the broken heart'

ALMA RATTENBURY, WHO was to become the tabloid press's notorious femme fatale in the 1930s, was born in British Columbia at the close of the nineteenth century. Her German father left her English mother and disappeared without trace when Alma was very young, and after that Alma took the surname of her stepfather, a printer called William Clarke. The young Alma Clarke was a gifted musician. At seventeen she performed with the Toronto Symphony Orchestra, playing the solo parts in concertos for both piano and violin.

When the family moved to Vancouver in 1913, Alma met an Irishman called Caledon Dolling. They fell in love and were married the next year. When the First World War broke out, Dolling joined up and was posted to the town of Prince Rupert. The young couple were well liked there, and Alma pursued her musical interests by joining the Prince Rupert Ladies' Musical Club. The local newspaper praised her performances. 'The most difficult and complex expressions seem to come perfectly naturally to her, and the fact that she plays from memory makes it all the more remarkable.' But the idyll in Prince Rupert was to be short-lived. Almost at once, Dolling was posted to France. Alma wanted to be near enough to her husband to be able to see him when he was on leave, so she went to London and found herself a job in the War Office. Then, in 1916, Dolling was hit by a shell and killed.

Alma joined the Red Cross and spent the next two years working as a nurse in northern France. She was wounded twice and awarded the Croix de Guerre.

When the war was over, Alma found a new man, Captain Compton Pakenham. They were married, far too hastily, in 1921 and moved to America. They had a son, Christopher, who was born in 1921, but the marriage failed almost at once and Alma returned with her young son to Vancouver, where she resumed the piano and gave recitals. Alma had already lived a very full life, and it was as if she had come full circle. But after one of her recitals in the Victoria Empress Hotel, Alma met Francis Rattenbury, a well-known architect, and a new phase of her life began.

Shortly after this meeting, Alma and the much older Francis Rattenbury became lovers, and this in spite of the fact that he was already married. Rattenbury even took the audacious step of moving Alma into his house and forcing his wife Florence to move upstairs. Although we may feel pity for Francis as the undeserving murder victim – and he certainly did not deserve to die – his treatment of his first wife shows a cruel streak in him. He expected Florence to agree to a divorce. She finally agreed, and in 1925 Alma and Francis Rattenbury were married. Three years later, Alma gave birth to their son, John.

There was so much scandal that they decided to move back to England – Rattenbury was himself English, not Canadian – and they took a rented house in Bournemouth, the Villa Madeira. New problems surfaced almost immediately, when the Rattenburys unwisely took on an eighteen year old chauffeur, George Stoner. It was not long before Alma lost sexual interest in her old husband and turned her attentions to the young chauffeur. Alma seduced George Stoner. Francis Rattenbury may have known about Alma's affair with George Stoner, and he must at least have suspected, but he did not intervene in any way.

One spring evening, on 24 March, 1935, while he was sitting in an armchair at his home, Francis Rattenbury was beaten repeatedly over the head with a mallet. Alma and George were the natural suspects.

A few days before he was attacked, Francis Rattenbury was distressed. Alma suggested a trip to a friend's house, with a view to raising money for one of his building projects. The trip away would have entailed Alma sleeping with Rattenbury. George was extremely jealous; he did not like the idea of Alma going back to sleeping with her husband at all. On the day of the attack, Alma and Francis had a quiet evening. At the end of it, Alma went to bed early. At about 10.30 p.m.

she heard a shout and went downstairs to see what had happened. She found Francis unconscious and covered in blood. She sent for Dr O'Donnell and had a couple of whiskies while she waited for him to arrive. When O'Donnell got there, he found Alma hysterical, incoherent and slightly drunk. Francis was unconscious, breathing only with difficulty and his pulse was slow. O'Donnell called the local surgeon, Mr Rooke, and Rooke decided to transfer Francis to a nearby hospital. Rooke went with Francis in an ambulance, while O'Donnell was driven to the hospital by Stoner. Alma waited at home with her maid, Irene Riggs.

Dr O'Donnell had contacted the police, because of the nature of Francis Rattenbury's injuries – it was all too obvious that someone had attacked him – and it was not long before PC Arthur Bagwell arrived at the house. He searched the house, and then Alma, still tipsy, suddenly admitted that she had done it. Then she changed her mind and said that George Stoner had done it. Alma was obviously unhinged by the traumatic events of the evening and their implications, which she must already have appreciated; when the policeman left, she tried to kiss him.

At 3.30 a.m., PC Bagwell returned with Inspector Mills, and Alma again said that George Stoner had done it. Dr O'Donnell came back from the hospital and, seeing Alma's intoxicated and hysterical state, gave her some morphine and sent her to bed. Moments later she was back downstairs again, accusing her husband's eldest son, Frank, of committing the crime; Frank was in Canada and could not possibly have been the attacker. Alma was sent back to bed.

At 6 a.m., Alma was questioned again by the police, and this time she confessed to attacking her husband herself. An hour later she was taken to the police station and formally charged with attempted murder. She said, 'That's right. I did it deliberately and would do it again.'

Three days later, Irene Riggs called the police to tell them about a conversation she had had with George Stoner. He had said, 'I suppose you know who did it,' and the next day he had shown her where he had got the mallet from. Then Francis Rattenbury died. With Irene Riggs' evidence as a lead, the police arrested Stoner and charged him with murder. The charge against Alma was changed from attempted murder to murder.

The trial of Alma Rattenbury and George Stoner began on 27 May, 1935. The case had already attracted a great deal of public interest, and people had queued for up to twelve hours to get a place in court. Alma and George pleaded not guilty. Alma withdrew her confessions, explaining them away as hysterical and irrational ramblings. Stoner stuck by his confession, but claimed he was under the influence of cocaine when he attacked Rattenbury; he had had no intent to kill. Stoner, presumably on instruction from his lawyer, was trying for 'diminished responsibility', presenting himself as guilty but not responsible for his actions at the time in question.

The prosecution's star witness was Irene Riggs.

She testified that Stoner had confessed during a drive to Wimborne. 'I asked Stoner why he had done it. He said because he had seen Mr Rattenbury "living" with Mrs Rattenbury in the afternoon.'

Alma said, 'Stoner had come into the room. He had what looked like a revolver in his hand . . . He said he would kill me if I went to Bridport.' Stoner's lawyer accused Alma of seducing Stoner and manipulating and using him. This image of Alma as an unscrupulous temptress turned the public against Alma.

After five days, the jury retired to consider their verdict. It took them forty-seven minutes to find Alma innocent. They found George guilty, but recommended mercy. The judge ignored what the jury had said and sentenced Stoner to death. The shocked reaction in the courtroom was palpable. Alma almost fainted; women in the gallery sobbed. Almost immediately a petition was started to get a reprieve for George Stoner.

Alma was in such a distressed state after the trial that she had to go into hospital to recover. Released from hospital on 3 June, Alma was like a lost soul. She had lost the husband she still liked, even though she had stopped sleeping with him, and the young lover she had become obsessed with was about to be hanged. She was profoundly depressed. At Christchurch the following day, she walked along the bank of the River Avon near the Three Arches, sat down and smoked a cigarette, and then wrote some notes to loved ones. Then she took off her fur coat, walked forward to the river and plunged a dagger into her chest six times. Incredibly, three of these stab wounds pierced her heart. She fell into the Avon, and was dead before she entered the water. She was watched as she did this by a passer-by, William Mitchell. Horrified by what he saw, he ran to her aid, but there was nothing he could do.

Alma Rattenbury's funeral was another great public occasion, attended by thousands – most of them women. Walking unobtrusively through this crowd was a man collecting signatures for George Stoner's reprieve. By 15 June, there were over 300,000 signatures on the petition

When she died, Alma Rattenbury was still only 38. She was a woman of enormous talent and potential, but somehow incredibly unlucky. The murder trial and the acquittal, followed by her own self-execution, were melodramatic enough. Yet, if she had only waited, there was a happy ending round the corner. Just three weeks after she died, George Stoner was reprieved. In fact he was released from prison in only seven years before being released on parole. Had she waited, Alma might have been reunited with George Stoner. But most of what Alma Rattenbury had done, all her life, had been done on emotional impulse. The case of Alma Rattenbury and George Stoner was remarkable in many ways. The way the two were treated by the justice system was in marked contrast to the way Edith Thompson and Frederick Bywaters had been treated just a decade earlier – yet the crimes and the circumstances were similar. Had something been learnt from the awful mistakes made in the Thompson-Bywaters case?

But there is a more fundamental question still. Was justice really done? George Stoner murdered Francis Rattenbury just as surely as Freddy Bywaters murdered Percy Thompson, out of frustration and jealousy. If it was just for Bywaters to be hanged, it was just for Stoner too. The reprieve for Stoner appears to have been granted as some sort of concession to public opinion, which is no basis whatever for a system of justice.

Ruth Ellis

'dance with a stranger'

RUTH ELLIS DID not kill her husband; she killed her boyfriend instead, but her case has all the characteristics of a wife-husband killing. The Ruth Ellis case has a very special place in British criminal history because Ruth Ellis was the very last woman to be hanged in Britain. As a result, Ruth Ellis has generated far more interest and sympathy than, for example, Louisa Merrifield who was hanged just two years earlier in 1953. The death penalty was suspended in 1965, and abolished altogether in 1970. The Ruth Ellis case has inspired several books and TV programmes and two films, one starring Diana Dors in a remarkable portrayal of Ruth's disintegration in the condemned cell, and another, the more recent *Dance with a Stranger*, starring Miranda Richardson.

There are other aspects of her case that make it particularly poignant. Many have argued that there were extenuating, mitigating circumstances that should have led to a prison sentence, not the death sentence.

Just 5 feet 2 inches tall and born at Rhyl in North Wales, Ruth Ellis was a Fifties good-time girl. She loved the London night-life and was part of the Soho nightclub scene. She met a car racing driver, David Blakeley, at a club and a tempestuous love affair developed. Their troubled relationship disintegrated and both Blakeley and Ellis went on to other partners, but Ellis could not let go.

On Good Friday in 1955, Ruth Ellis created a disturbance outside the hotel where David Blakeley was staying with some friends. She suspected that Blakeley was having an affair with a friend's nanny and she was in a jealous rage. Blakeley, perhaps sensibly, refused to go out and talk to her. It would certainly have done no good. In frustration, Ruth eventually phoned the police from her flat. At 9 p.m. two days later, on Easter Day, Ruth saw David Blakeley go into the Magdala pub, a hostelry on the edge of Hampstead Heath. She waited for him outside. Blakeley came out of the pub with his friends at 9.20, ignoring Ruth who was still waiting to speak to him.

Ruth Ellis took a loaded revolver out of her handbag and fired a shot. It missed Blakeley, but ricocheted off a wall and injured a passer-by. She fired again and this time she hit Blakeley. He fell face down in the gutter. Ruth Ellis walked over to his prone body and cold-bloodedly fired four more bullets into him. She had emptied the revolver. Customers came out of the pub to see what was happening, among them an off-duty policeman. It was all over now, and she gave up the smoking gun without resistance to the off-duty policeman, who arrested her. David Blakeley was found to be dead on arrival at hospital.

There was a good deal of public sympathy for

Ruth Ellis, and the press made much of the case. She had clearly been tormented by her callous lover. It was a crime of passion. Bringing the loaded gun did look like premeditation though. One newspaper paid for two barristers to defend her, but she seemed uninterested in defending herself. The sad truth is that she had loved Blakeley to the point of obsession, could not bear to lose him, and now that he was dead she had nothing to live for. The prosecuting counsel, Christmas Humphries, asked her questions that she answered in the most damaging way.

'Mrs Ellis, when you fired that revolver at close range into the body of David Blakeley, what did you intend to do?'

'It is obvious that when I shot him I intended to kill him.'

She seemed to be defying the jury to find her innocent. She had pleaded not guilty, but everything else she said pointed to her guilt.

Her Old Bailey trial for murder was held in Number One Court two months after the killing. For the trial, Ruth wore a black two-piece suit and white blouse; she had re-dyed her hair to her preferred colour, platinum blonde. The get-up was her defence team's idea, and it was a very bad miscalculation. She looked as brazen as Scarlett O'Hara, and did not win the jury's sympathy. If she had gone into the dock looking dowdy and down-trodden she would have stood a better chance of enlisting support.

The trial opened on 20 June, 1955 and lasted just over a day; the jury took fourteen minutes to reach its verdict. It was a disgracefully hasty business, given that a woman's life was at stake.

There was a considerable and vociferous demand for a reprieve during the next three weeks, but on 11 July the Home Secretary announced there would be no reprieve. The execution would go ahead in two days' time.

Ruth Ellis was hanged in Holloway Prison on 13 July, 1955, and buried in the prison graveyard. She was twenty-eight. A huge crowd had assembled outside the prison waiting for the execution notice to be posted on the gates; few had believed the sentence would really be carried out. As was normal, to ensure that the execution was carried out in the proper way, a post-mortem was carried out an hour later. The distinguished pathologist Keith Simpson carried out Ruth Ellis's post mortem. He found nothing abnormal or unexpected; 'deep impressions around neck of noose . . . fracture-dislocation of the spine at C2 with separation of the spinal cord at the same level . . . fractures of both wings of the hyoid . . . larynx also fractured . . . no pregnancy . . . small food residue in stomach, and odour of brandy . . . deceased was a healthy subject at the time of death'. The clinical detail sounds strikingly ordinary, with no hint at all of the macabre state murder that had been committed on the poor woman one hour earlier. And the final state murder of a woman in the United Kingdom.

During the rebuilding of Holloway Prison, her body along with the bodies of other hanged women was moved. Ruth Ellis was reburied in Buckinghamshire.

Forty-seven years later, in 2003, her sister and other supporters urged the Court of Appeal to review the case and reduce the sentence to manslaughter on grounds of provocation. The case was referred to the Criminal Cases Review Commission, whose job it is to investigate possible miscarriages of justice. Ruth's sister Muriel is now in her eighties, and believes she is pursuing her sister's dying wish by pursuing the appeal. Ruth believed the truth would come out, not thinking who might see that it did; Muriel has made it her mission to save Ruth's reputation. Ruth's son and daughter are no longer alive, but there are surviving grandchildren.

At the original trial the judge ruled out a defence of provocation by David Blakeley. One key piece of information not made known at the original trial is that Blakeley punched Ruth just ten days before the killing, causing her to have a miscarriage; the jury was not told of this or the rest of Blakeley's violent behaviour. Nor was the jury told anything about Ruth Ellis's background. She had been raped by her father as a child and her personality had been affected by her subsequent addiction to anti-depressants; these facts might have been used to argue for mitigation. She was shallow, silly and impulsive, but some at least of this could be explained in terms of damage resulting from a traumatic childhood. A more important fact is that another of Ruth's boyfriends later admitted (more than once) that he gave her the gun, taught her how to use it, and then drove her to the murder scene; he knew that he bore a great responsibility for what happened. Ruth Ellis did herself no favours at her trial. She seemed to be in a state of grief and shock, unable to defend herself.

As her execution approached, she seemed to rally, hysterically recalling the man who put the gun in her hand. She hadn't meant to do it, but she was egged on by this other man. It was true, and the newspapers reported it, but it was unfortunately just too late to help her. And they hanged her.

PART FIVE

POLITICAL
ASSASSINATIONS

Brutus and Cassius

'Caesar's murderers'

BY 45 BC, WHEN he returned to Rome from Spain, Julius Caesar was at the height of his success, the most powerful figure in the Roman world. A problem was that some people, both common people and courtiers, wanted to shower him with ever higher honours, while others were alarmed at the emergence of a personal dictatorship. It is unclear whether Julius Caesar himself really wanted any further aggrandisement. He certainly claimed that he didn't, more than once. On one occasion, while travelling from Alba to Rome, some people saluted him, calling him king. The word had a resonance then that it does not have today; in ancient Rome, 'king' could also mean 'tyrant'.

He could see that the rest of the crowd did not like it and seemed not to like the word himself. He called out that his name was Caesar, not king. Another time when he was in the Senate, he made a point of behaving towards the others present as if they were all equals together, and he said that he should have honours taken away from him rather than added. He had too much already.

But the idea of making Julius Caesar king was put about, perhaps by Caesar's friends, perhaps even by his enemies, who wanted to see him fall. He was in a sense caught in a well-established tradition, the cursus honorum, the honours race, in which men of noble birth competed for honours and gradually climbed up the hierarchy of honours. It was naturally assumed that men who had reached a certain level in the honours race would seek to climb to the next rung. This may be why so many republicans feared Julius Caesar. He could reach up to the next rung, so he certainly would. He in fact accepted some honours and offices without using them. For instance he accepted the power of the magistracies, without actually wielding it; by doing this, he enabled other aristocrats to develop their careers without hindering them.

Julius Caesar spent the last few months of his life planning a huge military campaign against Parthia. The idea was to avenge the defeat of Crassus. It may be that, to him, being away from Rome on campaign was actually preferable to staying there Rome and dealing with the possibly insoluble problem of his precise personal status. It may also be that a war against foreign enemies would unite Rome and make her forget all these petty quarrels.

Although he had said to the Senate that he had too many honours already, he went on accepting them, so as not to appear ungrateful. He was appointed 'perpetual dictator' and he started wearing the knee-high red boots of the kings of

Alba Longa, from whom he was descended. Antony publicly offered him a diadem, a white linen band worn across the forehead; this was the Greek symbol of monarchy. Caesar refused the offered diadem, but it is not clear whether he was feigning modesty; he may have intended to accept it if offered it again.

Then the plotting began. The instigator of the plot to assassinate Caesar seems to have been Gaius Cassius Longinus. Cassius was aggrieved because although Caesar had pardoned him for earlier disloyalty, he felt he had been slighted by not being offered a command in the forthcoming war against Parthia. Cassius persuaded his brother-in-law Marcus Junius Brutus to join the plot.

Brutus was fanatical, merciless, and notorious for being a greedy money-lender. He had fought on Pompey's side at Pharsalus, like Cassius, and also been pardoned by Caesar. Julius Caesar had in effect been more than generous to both of them and they owed him a debt of gratitude. Perhaps that was one of the reasons why they hated him – the sense of obligation. Caesar had genuinely fatherly feelings towards Brutus, partly because he had had an affair with Servilia, Brutus's mother. It was rumoured that Brutus was Caesar's son in fact, but that was not true. Brutus was well-known as a descendant of Lucius Junius Brutus, who lived in about 500 BC and who was thought to have founded Republican government in Rome. It was that earlier Brutus who drove an earlier king, Tarquinius, out of Rome for misrule. The later Brutus came to think of himself as re-enacting that early cleansing of Rome. In killing Julius Caesar, he was destroying the monarchy in Rome for a second time. The idea appealed to his ego.

Neither Brutus nor Cassius had any real reason to assassinate Julius Caesar, but Cassius's minor feeling of slight combined with Brutus's tendency to fanaticism was enough to do it. It became an obsession.

It seems certain that Caesar knew of the plot to assassinate him. The news had leaked out, which is why there was so much talk of omens and portents. Caesar disregarded all of these warnings. As Caesar himself said, 'Cowards die many times before their deaths; the valiant never taste of death but once'.

The Roman Senate traditionally met in a building called the Curia Hostilia, but that had been destroyed by fire. As a result, Caesar summoned the Senate to meet in the Theatrum Pompeium, which had been built by Pompey, on the Ides of March (15 March) 44 BC.

Julius Caesar was attacked in the Senate by a group of conspirators, all senators, calling themselves the Liberators. Ironically, most of them had been pardoned by Caesar and had their careers advanced by him; the attack was a monstrous act of ingratitude. First Casca stabbed him. It was a minor cut in the neck, probably because Casca was disturbed and nervous about being the first. Caesar spun round, seized the dagger and kept hold of it, shouting, 'Vile Casca, what does this mean?' At the same time Casca shouted in Greek to the other conspirators, 'Brother, help!' The conspirators encircled Caesar. Those senators who were not in the conspiracy were rooted to the spot, unable to help Caesar, unable to run, just frozen.

The conspirators had agreed beforehand that each of them should stab Caesar and 'flesh themselves with his blood'. Brutus stabbed him in the groin. Daggers and swords were lifted on all sides and plunged into Caesar. Some who saw it said that he fought and resisted and called for help, until Brutus drew his sword; then he submitted. There was disagreement about what he said, but he apparently said something to Brutus. Perhaps it was 'And you, Brutus?' or 'You too, Brutus, my son!' but those who reported it could not even agree about whether he was speaking in Latin or Greek. After this enigmatic farewell to Brutus, Julius Caesar covered his face with his robes and waited for the death stroke. He fell, perhaps by chance, perhaps because the conspirators threw him there, at the foot of the plinth of Pompey's statue, which was wetted with his blood. He had sustained 23 stab wounds, some of them superficial, some mortal.

There were over sixty conspirators, all with different motives. Some were old enemies with scores to settle, others were men who were disappointed not to have been promoted higher, others were jealous of his power, others were simply jealous of his brilliance, his genius. Some were genuinely fearful that there seemed to be no limit to the pre-eminence that he would achieve.

He was becoming a dictator in the worst sense. Seneca said, 'Glory, ambition and the refusal to set bounds to his own pre-eminence' were the things that drove Caesar to his own doom. The so-called freedom of the Roman republic was a slogan, a pretext rather than a reason for killing him.

One unnerving thing about Caesar was his refusal to accept the Roman class system, and that made him dangerously unpredictable. An interviewer once asked Barbara Cartland whether we live in a classless society, to which she answered, 'It must be, or I wouldn't be talking to you.' If a society is to function well, either everyone has to believe in a class structure, or no-one, and behave accordingly. In Rome, the people at the top, those who wielded power, inevitably believed in the class system. Caesar stood above many of the prejudices of his time; he attempted to stand above class, as well as party and race. He also stood above influence, which must have made him seem almost god-like.

Caesar himself does not seem to have thought of himself as a king, though that is what he was accused of being. If he had thought in monarchical terms he would have appointed an heir, which he did not – at least not in any explicit manner.

The immediate aftermath of Caesar's death was a kind of paralyzed shock, rather like the response of the senators witnessing the assassination itself, but on a city-wide scale. The assassins were all insignificant men, whose lives only had meaning while Caesar used them, really only had the meaning that Caesar gave them. Suddenly, with the power supply cut off, they realised the depth of their own powerlessness, their lack of real ability. Cassius was unpopular. Brutus was a fanatic. Neither of them could organize or bring about reforms or create a new leadership for Rome. They were unable to exploit the hiatus that followed the assassination they had carefully planned. Their action in killing Julius Caesar had been purely and single-mindedly destructive. The sheer pointlessness of the assassination was underlined by the assassins' total failure to create an alternative government in the days and weeks that followed.

Then Marcus Antonius (Mark Antony) took the initiative. He used Caesar's will to inflame the Roman people against the assassins, exactly as portrayed in the famous 'Friends, Romans, countrymen' scene in Shakespeare's play. Roused to a frenzy of revenge, the people of Rome ran off to burn the houses of Cassius and Brutus, and the assassins were forced to flee from Rome. Antony chased them as far as Modena, where he defeated them and looked set to become master of Rome. He had at any rate shown himself capable of purposeful and concerted action when almost everyone else in Rome was in a daze.

But there was a snag. Although Caesar had not nominated a political heir, he had left a huge amount of money to one man. He had left three-quarters of his estate to the eighteen year old Gaius Octavius, known as Octavian, who was the son of his niece Atia. Octavian had been sent to

Greece to serve with the Legions in the preparations for the war with Parthia. Now, of course, he returned at the head of Caesar's legions to claim his inheritance. With that huge fortune, and Julius Caesar's evident blessing behind him, he was bound to wield enormous power.

Antony treated the young Octavian like a child, and relations between them quickly became very tense. There was a gradual slide towards civil war between Octavian and the senate on one side and Antony and Lepidus on the other. Antony and Lepidus were defeated and fled to Gaul and Spain. Brutus and Cassius had entrenched themselves in the east. The Senate controlled Italy. Octavian seemed to be marginalized in the messy struggle for power. But he had a focus, a goal. He was determined to cull Caesar's murderers. To do this, he had to make a reconciliation with Antony and Lepidus. In Rome there was a bloodbath. Where Caesar had been forgiving and issued pardons, Octavian and Antony issued death warrants. 2,500 noble Romans, including Cicero, were murdered.

Then they set off in pursuit of the assassins, meeting and defeating them at the Battle of Phillipi in 42 BC. When the battle was lost, Brutus killed himself by falling on his sword. Cassius too decided to die rather than be captured and compelled his servant to kill him. Within three years of Julius Caesar's pointless assassination, justice of a sort had been done. Every single man who had had anything whatever to do with the conspiracy had died a violent death. The assassination been cruelly violent, and the revenge was the same. This thanks to Caesar's heir, Octavian – the young man who would later change his name, and his image, to Augustus.

Walter Tirel

'a hunting accident in the New Forest'

EVERYONE HAS HEARD of William the Conqueror, the first Norman king of England, but his son, William II, often called William Rufus, is by comparison a shadowy and elusive figure. The main thing we remember him for is his mysterious death while hunting in the New Forest, and this has left us with an iconic rustic image of him on horseback in dappled light under oak trees, felled without warning by an unexpected arrow during the chase. He has become a figure that belongs to a mythic past, a pagan realm where horned gods rule the forests and courtiers conspire against unworthy kings.

In fact, History has a lot to say about William Rufus. He was deeply unpopular as a man, and even more unpopular as a king. He was in many ways like his father, and that may explain why he was the Conqueror's favourite son. It is not known exactly when he was born – that much really is shadowy – but he was certainly born before his father conquered England, and was a boy at the time of the conquest. He was probably born between 1056 and 1060.

He was a short, stocky and rather fat, with wild

red hair and a distinctively ruddy complexion. The red hair and red face gave rise to the nickname 'Rufus'. His personality was distinctively unattractive. He disliked people, he was tyrannical, cruel, greedy, brash and given to fits of violent temper and vindictive paranoia. He offended the Church not only with his blasphemies but by taxing the Church heavily and driving Anselm, the Archbishop of Canterbury, into exile. Largely because of these practices, William Rufus suffered greatly at the hands of chroniclers in the years after his death; most of the chroniclers were monks.

William was also gay and sympathetic towards the Jews. These tendencies were disastrous for any public figure, let alone a king, in an age that was strongly anti-semitic and strongly homophobic. They also made him even less popular with the Church.

Peter of Blois was the most critical of the monastic chroniclers, and he blamed many of the problems on Ranulph, the Bishop of Durham, whose advice William acted upon. It was Ranulph who was the cruel extortionist and the woeful oppressor of the kingdom, rather than William. William was criticized for holding 'in his own hands' the archbishopric of Canterbury, four bishoprics and eleven abbeys; he was 'keeping all these dignities for a long time for no good reason whatever', taking all the income from all of these vast estates.

Peter painted a very dark picture of England under William and Ranulph. 'Holiness and chastity utterly sickened away, sin stalked in the streets with open and undaunted front and, facing the law with haughty eye, daily triumphed.' Godless England was afflicted by alarming portents. 'There were thunders terrifying the earth, lightnings and thunderbolts most frequent, deluging showers without number, winds of the most astonishing violence, whirlwinds that shook the towers of churches. . . fountains flowing with blood, mighty earthquakes, while the sea, overflowing its shores, wrought infinite calamities to the coasts.' These phenomena, which most of us would attribute to natural causes, were implicitly God's warning voice telling England that William was a very bad king.

The general dissatisfaction with the William Rufus régime made it easy for William Rufus's elder brother Robert to gain support. Robert Curthose had inherited the Dukedom of Normandy from their father. Almost inevitably, there was mounting rivalry between them over the throne of England, which must have appeared the greater prize. Many of the barons were ready to support Robert as a replacement for William as king. There was a rising of the barons in 1088, just one year after he came to the throne, organized by his uncle, Bishop Odo of Bayeux, who wanted to replace William with his brother Robert. But William proved to be strong, ruthless and purposeful enough to crush it. There was another rising of the barons only seven years later, in 1095.

William Rufus was a very strong king, in that he was able to fend off major rebellions and maintain control. Under the circumstances, it is a great tribute to his strength of purpose that he remained on the English throne a full ten years. He was able to defeat King Malcolm III of Scotland and replace him with a client-king, the Saxon Edgar Atheling. He in effect gained control of the entirety of his father's legacy when his brother Robert wanted to join the crusade. Robert mortgaged the Duchy of Normandy to him, leaving him in charge during his absence.

When Robert went off to fight in the First Crusade in 1095, William used the respite to secure the borders with Wales and Scotland. He built Carlisle Castle and a chain of forts along the Welsh border to stem the raids on marcher barons by Welsh brigands. His barons continued to complain about the high level of taxation, and in particular they complained to William's younger brother, Henry, who had been waiting ever since their father's death to seize his brother's throne if an opportunity arose.

William never placed any trust in his barons, which is possibly why he never won their loyalty, and he never trusted his brother Henry. Perhaps he had good reason. It was after all Henry who suggested the hunting trip in the New Forest. But why did William agree to ride off into the New Forest with the brother he profoundly distrusted and a band of noblemen whose loyalty he could not depend upon? He must have known that any one of them could have killed him at any time. Or did he trust in the magic aura of kingship? Did he imagine the fact that he was the king was protection enough – that they would stop short of anything as terrible, as taboo, as regicide?

During the night before his final day, William had a disturbing nightmare. He dreamt that the men he was about to ride out with would kill him. At an unconscious level he knew he was taking a terrible risk. Yet still he went. The reasons why he acted as he did that day are still not known.

What is known is that during the hunt, on 2 August, 1100, an arrow was loosed that found its way to the King's chest. It is not known who shot the arrow, but it was said at the time that it was a powerful Norman baron, Sir Walter Tirel, the Lord of Poix. According to Peter of Blois, Walter had recently arrived from Normandy and was welcomed to join the King's table. After the banquet was over, the King invited the new guest to join the hunt. The hunting party spread out through the woods as they chased some running deer. As they did so, the King and Walter Tirel became separated from the others. That was the last time William was seen alive. Walter fired a wild shot at a stag, which missed and hit the King in the chest instead. It was actually not a fatal injury, but William fell from his horse onto the arrow shaft, which then drove deep inside him, piercing his lung. Walter tried to offer aid, but there was no help he could give the dying man. Walter feared he would be charged with murder, panicked, mounted his horse and fled. It was said that it was an accident, but there are several aspects of the story that arouse suspicion.

If the King's death was an accident, why did the rest of the company ride off to leave the King to die alone, quickly drowning in his own blood? Incredibly, the King of England's body was just left unattended in the woods, abandoned at the spot marked today by the Rufus Stone. It is also known that Sir Walter Tirel had a reputation as a master bowman, someone who was unlikely to shoot wild, and someone who was unlikely to make the basic mistake of accidentally shooting his (one) hunting companion. The circumstances make the incident look very much like murder and a conspiracy to murder at that.

The body was picked up by some countrymen in a cart and taken back to the palace. The next day he was buried in a modest grave and with few signs of grief. Contemporary chroniclers say that all his servants were busy attending to their own interests, as would be likely with the change of regime, and that few if any of them cared anything at all about the funeral.

The King died unmarried and therefore with no legal offspring. His younger brother Henry succeeded to the English throne as he had been hoping. The speed with which Henry secured the treasury at Winchester and had himself crowned king – only three short days after his brother's death – suggests a fair amount of pre-planning. That in turn suggests that Henry knew in advance that William was going to die. He stood to gain most by his brother's death, so if there was a conspiracy to kill William it is most likely that Henry engineered it. In the three-cornered struggle for the English throne, this interval when Robert was out of the way was the very best moment Henry could have chosen to have his brother assassinated. With William slain while Robert was in Palestine, Henry was in the strongest possible position to gain the throne, and he made sure of that by having himself crowned immediately, before Robert could return. Everything points to a political coup engineered by Henry.

Henry was not blamed for the assassination by any of the church chroniclers. They were very pleased and relieved to see Henry on the throne, describing him as 'a young man of extreme beauty' and 'much more astute than his two brothers and better fitted for reigning'. He was a safer bet than William, releasing the Church estates, imprisoning Ranulph and recalling Archbishop Anselm from exile. It is possible that Henry did all these things precisely to buy the Church's approval, rather than out of piety. When Robert raced back from the Crusade on hearing of William's death, he mounted an invasion to try to unseat Henry. Peter of Blois was keen to blame this too on Ranulph, who, he said, escaped from prison, 'repaired to Normandy, and in every way encouraged the Duke thereof, Robert, the King's brother, to invade England.'

Walter Tirel was named by chroniclers as the man who shot the fatal arrow, but there is no record of any retribution. There was no trial, no execution, no sanction, no penalty. That too looks as if he was acting as part of a larger conspiracy. Maybe all those who went out with the King that day wanted him dead, and it was simply Tirel who drew the short straw. But it is also possible that Tirel did not kill William Rufus. There is one contemporary document that suggests he was innocent of the killing. The great Norman Abbot Suger was a friend of Walter Tirel's and he gave Walter shelter during his self-imposed exile in France. They evidently liked and trusted one another. Suger had many opportunities to talk to Walter and they evidently had many conversations about the events of that fateful day. What Suger wrote is very revealing:

> It was laid to the charge of a certain noble, Walter Tirel, that he had shot the king with an arrow; but I have often heard him, when he had nothing to fear nor to hope, solemnly swear that on the day in question he was not in the part of the forest where the king was hunting, nor ever saw him in the forest at all.

This means that Walter was afterwards claiming that he was not alone with the king; he was with the main party, elsewhere. If Walter was not alone with the king, who was? The most likely candidate is the king's brother, Henry. Walter Tirel may have accepted the argument that someone had to be blamed for the shooting, but Henry himself could not be tainted with the crime; for the good of the kingdom, and the safety of his tenure of the English throne, Henry must seem to be blameless. Walter Tirel was never given any advancement, but Henry was adamant that he must not be punished in any way for what had happened.

William Rufus was a horrible man, and he had two brothers, one younger, one older, who both wanted his throne. It is not at all surprising that there was a conspiracy to assassinate him and replace him. The thing that is surprising is that after ten years of staving off threats to his safety William went off willingly into the woods with his murderers.

Reginald Fitzurse

'and the martyrdom
of Thomas Becket'

REGINALD FITZURSE WAS a Norman knight of the twelfth century, the eldest son of Richard Fitzurse. He was probably born in about 1130, and inherited the manor of Williton in Somerset when his father died in 1168. He has sometimes been referred to as a baron, because he held his lands from the King. He was certainly a major land-owner. In addition to the land he owned in Somerset, he owned the manor of Barham in Kent and lands in Northamptonshire too.

But Reginald Fitzurse is not remembered for being a country squire, of however many manors in total, and he is not remembered with any favour or kindness by anyone at all. He is remembered for one thing only – a single act of phenomenal brutality and sacrilege, the murder in his own cathedral of Archbishop Thomas Becket, the greatest saint of the middle ages.

Thomas Becket, born the son of a wealthy London merchant in 1118, was educated at Merton Priory, then London, Paris and Italy. Like many ambitious young men, he decided that his best chance of progress lay in the Church. He became secretary to Archbishop Theobald of Canterbury, who thought highly of his administrative abilities and eventually recommended him, in 1154, to Henry II as his Chancellor.

Thomas excelled in this new role, which was the medieval equivalent of Prime Minister. He worked very closely with the King and they became firm friends. Becket appeared to give his absolute support to the King's plan to unify the laws relating to Church and state. In this Henry II misread Thomas's wishes and it led to trouble later. In 1162, Henry decided to select Thomas as the new Archbishop of Canterbury, assuming that Thomas would continue to collaborate from 'the other side'. Thomas warned him not to do this, but Henry insisted. Given the charge of looking after the interests of the Church in England, Thomas did just that, and consequently resisted Henry's attempts to reduce the Church's great power. Within a very short time, the two men were more enemies than friends, and Henry wanted to remove Thomas, who was now an obstacle to his reforms.

Reginald Fitzurse was one of the four knights who were in attendance on Henry II in northern France late in 1170. They heard the King's ill-tempered words regarding the Archbishop of Canterbury; 'Will no-one rid me of this turbulent priest?' Henry II was exasperated with Becket's non-co-operation with the raft of reforms he was trying to introduce, and had already brought him to trial at Northampton Castle in 1164, a confrontation that had led to Becket's flight and self-imposed exile to France. Thomas Becket had fled Northampton Castle in the middle of the night in fear of his life. The King's temper was such that he could have ordered his archbishop's execution or mutilation on the spot. Becket decided then not to risk staying in England any longer.

The exile had lasted six years, while the administration of the see of Canterbury was in effect left in the hands of others. Thomas felt he needed to return to England, even though he knew he risked death from the King or his supporters in doing so. Relations with the King were only a little better than they had been at Northampton in 1164.

Whatever he meant by it, Henry II certainly did utter words such as, 'Will no-one rid me of this turbulent priest?' and 'What a set of idle cowards I keep about me who allow me to be mocked so shamefully by a low-born clerk!' and he uttered them more than once, as he himself admitted afterwards. It sounded to the four knights as if it was an order to get rid of Becket, and they certainly took it as such. Together they plotted how they would murder the Archbishop. The conspirators left Bures, near Bayeux, where the King was staying and travelled secretly, separately and rapidly by different routes to England. When it was noticed that they had gone, an attempt was made to overtake them and bring them back, but it was too late. It is fairly clear that the four barons expected the King to change his mind and countermand the order, and they wanted to act, to solve the problem of Thomas before he could do so.

They arranged to meet at Saltwood Castle, which was held by one of the four, Ranulf de Broc, on 28 December, 1170. Saltwood Castle was close to the English Channel coast of Kent, and not too far from Canterbury.

The following day, they set off with a small entourage of armed men for Canterbury itself. At St Augustine's Abbey, which stood on the eastern edge of the city, they stopped and gathered further reinforcements from the abbot, who seems to have been glad to assist in Becket's downfall. From there they rode into the cathedral precincts through the gate-house in Palace Street and entered the Archbishop's hall to the north-west of the Cathedral, probably at about 3 o'clock in the afternoon, and demanded to see Becket. With them was Robert de Broc, who was the nephew of Ranulf de Broc, one of the four knights; Robert had been in charge of the place during the Archbishop's absence. They left a substantial force of soldiers outside the gate-house, to keep the crowd out and stop the Archbishop escaping.

It is not certain that the four knights intended to kill Thomas. They may have intended to take him prisoner, to coerce him into absolving those he had excommunicated. It may be that they only resorted to murder as a result of Thomas's intransigence, and the presence of an unexpected crowd of people in the cathedral. On the other hand, one of them admitted later that their original plan had been to strike the Archbishop down in his private chamber next to the hall.

When the four knights entered the Archbishop's hall, where the servers were eating, they sat awkwardly and silently, not acknowledging the Archbishop – nor he them. At length, Thomas offered them greetings. None of them replied except Fitzurse, who muttered, 'God help you!' Thomas reddened at this insult.

Reginald Fitzurse told Thomas that he bore a message from the King. All four of the knights were there, but it was Reginald Fitzurse who dominated this exchange, and Reginald Fitzurse who was the most aggressive and offensive of the four. Reginald had been one of Thomas's tenants when Thomas had been Chancellor. Thomas reminded him of this, to make him remember his lower status, but this reminder only made Reginald angrier and he called on everyone present who was on the King's side to prevent the Archbishop from escaping. One senses in Reginald's mounting anger that afternoon a self-conscious effort to make the adrenalin flow and get himself to a pitch where he could assassinate the Archbishop; he needed to be angry to carry it through. Reginald Fitzurse accused Thomas of refusing to absolve the people he had excommunicated.

'The sentence was not mine but the Pope's,' Thomas reminded him.

'You were behind it,' Reginald persisted.

'Granted, but the sentence itself was given by one greater than I. Let those concerned go to the Pope for absolution.'

Reginald Fitzurse went on, 'The King's command is that you and yours shall leave this realm.

There can be no peace with you after your insolence.'

Thomas told Reginald to stop threatening him.

At this the knights went outside to arm themselves and shut the gate-house doors to prevent any help arriving for the Archbishop. They posted guards on the Archbishop's hall. Reginald Fitzurse forced one of the Archbishop's servants to fasten his armour, then snatched an axe from a carpenter who was working on some repairs.

Thomas sat down on the bed in his chamber. There was an animated discussion as to what had been said. Some of Thomas's monks thought the knights were drunk. John of Salisbury criticized Thomas roundly; 'You are doing what you always do. You act and speak just as you think best, without asking anyone's advice'.

Thomas asked him, 'Well, master John, what would you wish done?'

John replied, 'You ought to have called a meeting of your council. Those knights want nothing more than a good reason for killing you'.

'We have all got to die, and we must not swerve from justice for fear of death. I am more ready to meet death than they are to inflict it on me,' Thomas said.

John said, 'We're sinners, the rest of us, and not yet ready to die. I can't think of anyone except you who is asking for death at the moment.'

Out in the Great Court, the knights prepared themselves. The great cloaks they had worn in the Archbishop's Hall to cover their coats of mail were now off and slung over the branches of the mulberry tree. Now ready, they charged at the Hall door, but Osbert and Algar, the Archbishop's servants, had bolted it. Robert de Broc knew the building well, and took the knights round the kitchen, through some bushes and into the orchard on the south side of the Hall. From here there was a staircase up to the Hall. The stairs were being repaired and the workmen had knocked off for the day and thrown down their tools. Ranulf de Broc climbed a ladder to a shuttered window. The others picked up axes and other tools and with these they smashed their way back into the Hall.

Meanwhile, the noise of the splintering wood and shouts of the servants alerted Thomas and his friends to the imminent danger. The monks tried to get Thomas to move, but he was reluctant. 'Not a bit of it. Don't panic. You monks are always afraid of being hurt!' Eventually, when they told him it was time for Vespers, he allowed himself to be swept out of his chamber, behind it, and from there by a private staircase into the south range of the cloisters, which was the normal route into the cathedral via the door into the north transept. The service of Vespers was due to begin. Thomas was reluctant to be hurried, but the monks around him could see that the angry knights were preparing to do murder and thought Thomas would be safe once he was within the sanctuary of the cathedral. How wrong they were! Probably Thomas himself knew there could be no other outcome now but his death, and knew there was no point in hurrying anywhere; these four knights were going to kill him.

Thomas and his small group of monks arrived in the cathedral's dark but crowded north transept just ahead of the knights, who could be heard running heavily along the south range of the cloisters. There were shouts; 'There are armed knights in the cloister!'

'I will go and meet them', Thomas said, but his supporters swept him on towards the choir. Because of the disturbance, the monks who had started to celebrate Vespers abandoned their prayers and moved towards the Archbishop, who they had heard was already dead; for a moment they were delighted to see that he was alive and unharmed, but their pleasure was short-lived. The monks hastened to close and bar the doors in order to keep the knights out, but Thomas stopped them, reminding them that it was not proper to turn the house of God into a fortress, 'and we come to suffer – not to resist'.

It would have been easy, even at this late stage, for Thomas to vanish inside the dark cathedral; had he wished, he could have spirited himself away in the roof or the crypt and the knights would never have found him. But Thomas had no real intention of escaping this time. Thomas was mounting the steps leading up from the north transept towards the choir when Reginald burst in, still taking the lead in every way, shouting, 'King's men!' The four armed knights were there, with their huge swords unsheathed, and a body of men-at-arms, a sight that frightened all of them, though the huge congregation filling the nave saw none of this. With the knights was one of

Thomas's monks, a sub-deacon called Hugh – later called Hugh Evil-Clerk because of his part in this historic murder.

Reginald Fitzurse bellowed, 'Come to me here, King's men! Where is Thomas Becket, traitor to the King and the kingdom?' No-one responded; it must have seemed an unnecessary question, though in the twilight the knights may not have been able to see him. 'Where is the Archbishop?'

Thomas gave an oblique answer, 'The righteous will be like a bold lion and free from fear,' and walked back down the steps to meet the knights. He said in a moderate voice, 'Here I am, no traitor to the King but a priest. Why do you seek me? God forbid that I should flee on account of your swords or that I should depart from righteousness.'

Thomas was now standing in the centre of the transept beside the big drum-shaped Norman pillar. He turned to look straight at the altars dedicated to the Virgin Mary and St Benedict. Perhaps he had an idea that he would die in front of these altars. The knights moved towards him demanding, 'Absolve those you excommunicated and return to office those you suspended'.

'No penance has been made, so I will not absolve them,' Thomas replied.

'Then you will now die and suffer as you deserve.'

'And I am prepared to die for my Lord, so that through my blood the church will attain liberty and peace, but in the name Almighty God I forbid you to hurt my men, either cleric or layman, in any way. If it is me you seek, let them leave.' At this point, most of Thomas's monks sensed what was about to happen and instinctively ran away and hid, John of Salisbury among them.

Then the knights rushed at Thomas. Reginald laid hands on Thomas and tried to drag him roughly back towards the door, so that he could kill him out in the cloisters. Together they tried to hoist Thomas onto William Tracy's back so that they could carry him outside. Thomas grappled with them and rebuked them. 'Don't touch me, Reginald. You owe me faith and obedience, you who foolishly follow your accomplices. Do you bear a sword against me?'

This rebuff made Reginald furious. He did not recognize Thomas as his lord, was not his inferior, and he was not a follower either. He aimed a blow at Thomas's head and said, 'I don't owe faith or obedience to you that is in opposition to the fealty I owe my lord King.'

Thomas bowed his head and raised his hands above his head in prayer, seeing that he was about to die. 'I commend myself and the cause of the Church to God, St Mary and the blessed martyr St Denis.'

All the other monks fled for their lives except Edward Grim, who instinctively tried to defend his master with his arm. The moment Thomas ended his prayer, Reginald Fitzurse at once swiped at Thomas with his sword, knocking his fur cap off, cutting the tonsure off the top of his head and slicing into his left shoulder. The same blow cut Grim's arm to the bone. Grim tried to support Thomas, but fell back. Grim reflected on his master's awful death. What a worthy shepherd to his flock he was to set himself against the wolves so that the sheep would not be torn to pieces! He was abandoning the world, the world that was overwhelming and overpowering him now, yet that same world would one day elevate him beyond any of their dreams. . .

Another sword blow fell on Thomas's head and somehow he remained standing firm. He put his hand to his head, looked at the blood and said, 'Into thy hands, O Lord, I commit my spirit'. A third sword blow, from William Tracy, brought him on to his knees, and he muttered, 'For the name of Jesus and the protection of the Church I am ready to embrace death.' He fell full length, with his arms stretched out in front of him as if in prayer. Now Richard Brito, who had not till now used his sword, aimed a blow at Thomas's head, inflicted a terrible wound, cutting the top of the skull right off and spilling Thomas's brains; the energy of the blow broke the sword's point on the stone pavement. By this stage, Thomas was prone and motionless on the ground – and probably dead.

The fourth knight, Hugh de Morville, had been keeping the huge crowd in the nave back with his sword-point. The evil cleric who had come in with the knights, Hugh, placed his foot on Thomas's neck and dug his sword inside the wound on his head and flicked it, scattering the brains across the floor. He shouted to the others, 'We can leave this place, knights. This traitor will not rise again.' Then the knights, once again shouting, 'King's men, King's men!' made their way out of the place that would from that day forward always be called The Martyrdom, into the cloisters and the great court, ransacking the Archbishop's palace before they left. If they repented their action in killing the Archbishop, that repentance had not yet taken effect.

Thomas was dead. His body lay where it had fallen, face down, with arms outstretched. Edward Grim, who was with him through this nightmare, commented afterwards that Thomas had shown great perseverance. He had not cried out or uttered a word, not so much as sighing when struck. He stood or knelt waiting fearlessly for the blows. A martyr had been born. Thomas's body-servant, Osbert, cut off a piece of his own shirt and covered the mutilated head with it. For a few minutes, the dead Archbishop lay all alone in the darkness. Then, gradually, from the shadows, the monks emerged from their hiding places and were occupied with ushering the huge congregation out of the desecrated cathedral. Then they crept into the north transept to see what they most feared. It was obvious to all who were there that something horrible, but also profoundly momentous and historic, had happened. Pieces of cloth were steeped in his blood and kept as sacred souvenirs.

A thunderstorm broke while the monks washed and dressed the body and laid it to rest overnight in front of the high altar. The prayed in silence as no service could be sung in the desecrated church.

The next morning, astonishingly, Robert de

Broc arrived and called the monks together. He told them that Thomas's body would be thrown to the dogs unless they buried it secretly. He must have known already that Thomas would be seen as a martyr, that there was a danger of a Thomas cult developing – and he vainly tried to stop it. The monks obediently buried Thomas in the crypt, keeping the clothing and bloodstained cloths from the pavement as relics. One of the entrances to the crypt was right next to the spot where Thomas fell. A tomb was built between the two pillars of shining Purbeck marble, a spot which is now an empty space. Later, much later, there would be a great ceremony of translation, in which the remains of St Thomas of Canterbury were carried up and entombed in a spectacular shrine behind the cathedral's high altar. By the early sixteenth century, that shrine would be an Aladdin's cave of gold and precious jewels – too great a prize for Henry II's successor, Henry VIII, to resist. That too is an empty space.

After the murder had been done, the four knights rode to Saltwood. There are two different versions of their mood afterwards. One account says that they gloried in their deed, but William de Tracy, another of the four, said that they were overwhelmed by a sense of guilt. That may of course have been a revisionist view of things, when it became clear that the world as a whole was revolted by what they had done – not just the murder but the sacrilege. The earlier de Tracy's penitence had begun, the more chance he had of being forgiven. On 31 December, the last day of the year, they rode to South Malling near Lewes, one of the Archbishop's manors. There, it is said, they placed their armour on a table, but the table itself rejected it: it was hurled onto the floor.

Reginald Fitzurse and the other knights were excommunicated by the Pope. They were not punished by Henry II, who seems to have genuinely regretted giving them the order to kill Becket, but he advised them that they would be safer if they fled to Scotland. When they got to Scotland they found that this was not so. Both the King of Scotland and the Scots themselves were all for hanging them, so they were forced to return to England. They sheltered at Knaresborough, which belonged to Hugh Morville, one of their number, and stayed there for a year. If they were waiting for the dust to settle, waiting for people to forget about Thomas Becket, they were wasting their time.

No-one wanted to have anything to do with Thomas Becket's murderers, who were regarded by everyone as little better than Judas Iscariot. They were pariahs. They were forced to give themselves up to the King. Henry II did not know what to do with them. Although he himself had quarrelled with Becket over this very issue of benefit of clergy, he had lost, and he now found that he was not in a position to put four laymen on trial for the murder of a priest; they were not bound by lay jurisdiction. So Henry II sent them to the Pope. The Pope's punishment was fasting and banishment to the Holy Land; that was the limit of his power. It was ironic that Thomas, by opposing Henry II's legal reforms, had in effect put his own murderers beyond the reach of natural justice. Just about everyone wanted to see the four knights hanged, but there was neither secular nor ecclesiastical law that allowed it.

Before leaving for the Holy Land, Reginald Fitzurse gave half of his manor of Williton to his brother and the other half to the Knights of St John. Fitzurse and his companions are said to have done their penance at a place called 'the Black Mountain'. It is not known what or where this was, but it may have been some sort of religious retreat near Jerusalem. They died there, all of them within three years of the assassination, and were buried in Jerusalem outside the door of the Templars' Church.

There are alternative versions of the fate of the four knights. One of them has Reginald Fitzurse seeking shelter in Ireland, where he founded the McMahon family. If so, it would be quite appropriate; Thomas McMahon was one of those responsible for the assassination of Lord Mountbatten in 1979.

Miracles were claimed at Thomas Becket's tomb. Pilgrims flocked to Canterbury in ever-increasing numbers as the years passed, and St Thomas of Canterbury became the greatest saint, not only in England but in Europe. His cult was only ended in 1538 when Henry VIII had his huge shrine at the eastern end of Canterbury Cathedral demolished and what were thought to be Becket's bones were (allegedly) scattered or burnt. Recently it has been pointed out that there is no documentation authorizing a burning and that it was quite common in such situations to allow reburial in a more obscure place. A re-buried skeleton found in a unusual grave in the crypt in 1888 may hint at a complex answer. It looks as if the Commissioners reburied Thomas in the 1888 grave, and that someone later, and in great haste, removed Thomas's body in order to bury it in a place of greater safety or greater sanctity. To avert any possible future repercussions, they replaced Thomas's skeleton with one from a common graveyard – any skeleton would do – and in their haste they inadvertently included some earth and a few bones from other burials. It is likely that Thomas's body was taken away in 1546, when this part of the crypt was being walled off to make a wood store for a church official, Richard Thornden. Thornden, a Catholic sympathizer, is likely to have wanted the saint's remains to be properly in the cathedral, not in his wood store. There is reason, though not proof, to believe that Thomas's bones now lie either under the pavement in the Lady Chapel – or even in what is called Coligny's tomb, right next to the site of the shrine.

Charlotte Corday
and 'The Friend of the People'

JEAN PAUL MARAT was born in 1743 and became one of the leading figures of the French Revolution. By then he had already made a significant name for himself as a doctor. But for the Revolution, he would probably have been remembered as a great medic and scholar. It was not until 1774 that he published *The Chains of Slavery*, his first 'revolutionary' piece. The Revolution changed Marat, just as it changed his assassin.

By the 1780s, Marat was deep in politics, heart and soul. He founded a newspaper, *L'Ami du peuple* (The Friend of the People), which became profoundly influential. Above all the frenzy of shouting, it was Marat's voice that everyone heard. He became one of the legendary figures of the French Revolution, standing alone, never joining any political group or faction. His attitude was to suspect those in power, and to speak out against anything he believed wrong. No wrong, no poverty, no misery, no persecution could silence him. He was endlessly shouting, 'We are betrayed!' If anyone suspected anyone else of anything, they had only to denounce them to Marat, and the newspaper did not let up until the accused was found innocent or guilty. He made lots of enemies, and it is astonishing that he lasted so long. To avoid being attacked or arrested, he spent a lot of time hiding in cellars and sewers. It was through living like this that he picked up a horrible skin disease. He was tended by his one trusted friend, Simonne Evrard.

His position in relation to the King was peculiar. He was implacably hostile to the King, and saw him as the one man who must die for the people's good, but he would not hear of the King being tried for anything that pre-dated the acceptance of the new constitution.

After the King's execution, in which Marat played his part, there were five months in which the struggle between Marat and the Girondins went on. Marat despised the Girondins because he thought that they had suffered nothing for the republic, talking too much of their high-flown feelings. They were too self-consciously re-creating the Roman Republic of a bygone age. Marat had no time for that. The Girondins sought to silence Marat by having him tried before the Revolutionary Tribunal, but this backfired badly. Marat was acquitted by the Tribunal on 24 April, 1793 and returned in triumph to the Convention with the people of Paris behind him. The fall of the Girondins on 31 May was now almost inevitable. It was Marat's final triumph.

The skin disease was worsening now and he could only ease the pain by sitting in a bath. He used often to sit in the bath for long periods, writing on a board resting across the sides. On 13

July, 1793, he heard a young woman begging to be let in.

His visitor was Charlotte Corday.

Charlotte Corday or, to give her her full name, Marie-Anne Charlotte de Corday d'Armont, was born in 1768 on a farm in the village of Champeaux in Normandy. She was no farm peasant, though. She was the fourth child of a provincial noble family. They moved to Caen, where Charlotte's mother died in 1782. After that, the teenaged Charlotte and her sister Eleonore went to the Roman Catholic convent as boarders to complete their education, but the Abbaye closed three years later, and Charlotte then went to live with a cousin in Caen (148 Rue St-Jean).

Swept along by the Revolution, Charlotte became more and more committed to the idea of a Republic. She saw herself as devoted to the 'enlightened' ideals of the time, though she had been a monarchist only a couple of years earlier. She was struck by the government's actions against the Girondins, who were taking refuge in Caen. Charlotte Corday favoured the Girondins, who were more moderate than extremists like Robespierre and Marat. With the moderates being persecuted, it began to look to her as if a Girondin Republic would never come about. She saw Marat in particular as the person who was responsible for the misfortunes of the French people, with his daily demands for more heads. She decided that she was the one who had to get rid of him – an unusual sense of mission in an eighteenth century woman.

On 9 July, 1793, Charlotte left her cousin's apartment in Caen and took the mail coach to Paris. There she stayed at the Hotel de Providence, where she wrote a long screed entitled *Speech to the French who are Friends of Law and Peace*. The purpose of this was to explain the action she was about to take.

And so we come to 13 July, 1793, with Charlotte Corday arriving on the doorstep of Jean-Paul Marat's house in the Rue des Cordeliers. She was carrying a table knife with a dark wooden handle and a silver ferrule, which she had bought for a few sous at the Palais-Royal. She knocked at the door and said that she had an appointment. She had information to give Marat – news from Caen, where the escaped Girondins were trying to raise troops in Normandy. Marat was keen to hear news of his enemies and asked for her to be let in.

The interview took place in Marat's bathroom, with Marat still naked in his bathtub. He asked her for the names of the deputies at Caen, and wrote down their names on a piece of paper. Then he said, 'They shall soon be guillotined'. At this, the young woman stabbed him through the heart with her table knife. The painter Louis David painted an unforgettable picture of the scene immediately afterwards, the pale body of Marat slumped in the tin bath, still holding his quill. Only the murderess is missing, dragged off to the Conciergerie prison and shortly to be tried for her life.

The verdict was a foregone conclusion, but she used the trial to assure everyone that she had

Despite the fact that his reign lasted less than two years, Richard III remains one of the most notorious kings in English history. His connection with the disappearance of his two young nephews has caused him to be under suspicion of their murders for centuries. But was he the culprit?

Below is the home of Lizzie Borden (right), where in 1892, Andrew and Abby Borden were axed to death. Lizzie stood trial for the murders of her father and stepmother, but was acquitted of all charges. The scene of the crime was Fall River, Massachusetts, and a play called 'The Legend of Lizzie Borden' was written by Reginald Lawrence.

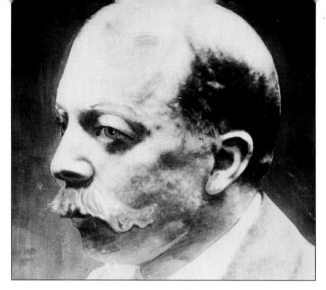

Above: An artist's impression of Dr. Hawley Crippen.
Below: A photograph taken illegally of Dr. Crippen and Miss Ethel Le Neve in the dock of the courtroom where they were on trial for the murder of Mrs. Crippen in 1910.

Twenty-eight year old Ruth Ellis, shown in a photo made prior to her arrest, died on the gallows in London's Holloway prison for the murder of racing car driver David Blakely. The streets outside the prison walls were jammed as the one time model and nightclub hostess went to her death.

Above: Twenty-four-year-old ex-marine Lee Harvey Oswald is shown after his arrest. He received a cut on his forehead and blackened left eye in a scuffle with officers who arrested him. Oswald was charged with the murder of President John F. Kennedy.

Below: The revolver used by Jack Ruby to assassinate Lee Harvey Oswald as he was being taken to the county jail following the assassination of President Kennedy.

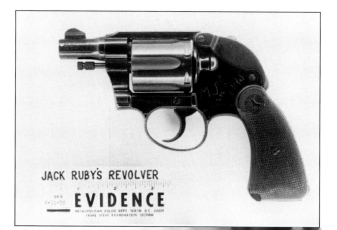

JACK RUBY'S REVOLVER

EVIDENCE

Sixty-two year old Mr. Hanratty stages a lone vigil outside the House of Commons in London to protest against the execution of his son James, who was hanged in 1962 for the A6 murder.

The name of John Wilkes Booth conjures up a picture of one of America's most infamous assassins – the killer of possibly the greatest president of the United States, Abraham Lincoln.

A portrait of Charlotte Corday, a noblewoman who was guillotined for stabbing Jean-Paul Marat, a French revolutionary. She was initially a supporter of the French Revolution, but was so appalled by the actions of the Jacobins that she swore to kill one of the leading revolutionaries.

acted entirely alone. She wanted to avoid another purge. She wanted to assert the contribution that women could make to politics. 'Even the women of the country are capable of firmness.' She also wanted to remind Paris that there was more to France than Paris. 'It is only in Paris that people have eyes for Marat. In the provinces, he is regarded as a monster.' Inevitably, she was condemned to death.

The day before her execution she wrote a letter to her father, asking his forgiveness for 'having disposed of my existence without your permission'. She also wrote a letter in which she complained that 'there are so few patriots who know how to die for their country; everything is egoism; what a sorry people to found a Republic!' She was probably hoping that someone would follow her example and sacrifice themselves by assassinating Robespierre.

Her last request was that a National Guard officer called Hauer should paint her portrait. As a token of gratitude, Charlotte gave Hauer a lock of her hair, 'a souvenir of a poor dying woman'. On 17 July, at 7 o'clock in the evening, she was guillotined. Charlotte Corday refused the ministrations of a priest on the scaffold. A bystander at the execution wrote, 'Her beautiful face was so calm that one would have said she was a statue. Behind her, young girls held each other's hands as they danced. For eight days I was in love with Charlotte Corday'. Charlotte died unrepentant, convinced that she had avenged many innocent victims of the Terror and prevented more unnecessary deaths. By this time, not least because of her performance at her trial and her extraordinary composure on the scaffold, she was becoming a symbolic figure, representing the moderate France that was disgusted by the Terror.

The Convention put Marat's bust in the hall where its sessions were held. Marat had become a hero of the Revolution, and was certainly much safer dead than alive. A year later, his ashes were transferred to the Pantheon with great pomp. But celebrity of the kind Marat achieved is fragile. His is a type of fame that can switch like the batting of an eye to infamy. A decree of February 1795 saw to it that Marat's ashes were removed from the Pantheon. Quite rightly too. Marat proceeded by way of a particularly nasty kind of power play. His was the politics of the tabloid press – the naming and shaming of alleged criminals, regardless of the process of law – his was the ethical standard of the lynch mob. He was ready to send countless numbers of people to prison and death on somebody else's say so.

It was Marat who was the infamous murderer. And Charlotte Corday, the murderer's murderer? Perhaps she was that very unusual creature, the famous murderer!

John Wilkes Booth

'and the death of a tyrant'

FOR A HUNDRED years John Wilkes Booth was America's most notorious assassin, but he led two lives. He was the leading conspirator who succeeded in murdering perhaps the greatest president the United States has ever had, but he was also a much-admired actor; it is often forgotten that, unlike Lee Harvey Oswald, he was a well-known figure, even a minor public figure, before he killed the president.

Like many actors before and since, Booth came from a theatrical family. His father, Junius Brutus Booth, emigrated from England in 1821 and made a big name for himself on the American stage. John was born on 10 May, 1838 on a farm (worked by slaves) in Maryland. He was the ninth of ten children, and his siblings later recalled his waywardness and eccentricity. John went to several private schools including a Quaker school before attending an Episcopalian military academy at Catonsville. During the 1850s, he became a Know-Nothing. This Know-Nothing Party was formed by 'nativists', people who wanted to preserve the country for native-born white citizens. The theme of white supremacy was a crucial element in Booth's psyche, and had a major role in his decision to kill Lincoln – that freer of black slaves.

For a while after his father died in 1852, Booth worked on the farm, but it was just too dull. He day-dreamed about doing something remarkable. According to his sister Asia, he cried 'I must have fame! Fame!' He decided to be a famous actor like his father.

Booth made his stage debut at the age of seventeen in 1855 in Baltimore, as the Earl of Richmond in *Richard III*. He started acting in earnest two years later, but early notices were not favourable and he was inevitably compared unfavourably with his much-admired father. John hated that. Junius Booth was one of the most famous actors of his day, though he had an eccentric personality, problems with alcohol and (significantly) bouts of insanity. In spite of later achieving a great deal as an actor, John may have felt that he could never outshine his dazzling father and this may have driven him to try to make his mark in some other way.

Theatre companies often used big-name touring actors to pull in larger audiences, and Booth eventually succeeded in achieving this 'star' status, though it led him into a punishing lifestyle. Often a different play was performed each night, so after a performance Booth might have to stay up the rest of the night learning a new part, then go to the theatre for a morning rehearsal. This irregular lifestyle involved keeping unusual hours, and may have helped to make him less visible as a conspirator, even though he was recognized wherever he went. Booth began his stock (repertory) theatre appearances in 1857 in Philadelphia, which was then the drama capital of America. His early acting lacked confidence, and he frequently needed prompting; he forgot his lines and missed his cues. The acting and stage manager at the Arch Street Theatre commented that the new actor did not show promise as a great actor. Others in the company were more forthright, saying that he had no future as an actor at all. But he was only nineteen and he was very determined.

In 1858, he moved to Richmond, Virginia for a season of repertory at the Marshall Theatre. Here he became more confident and was liked by audiences. He also became more positively committed to the southern way of life and more entrenched in southern, white-supremacist political views.

In 1859, Booth appeared to make a fresh start altogether, joining the Richmond Grays. But he enlisted, on 20 November, 1959, with the sole purpose of witnessing a political assassination, the hanging of the fiery abolitionist John Brown in Charles Town, Virginia. He was part of the armed guard standing near the scaffold to prevent anyone from rescuing John Brown. Shortly after the historic hanging, Booth was discharged. The episode shows Booth's fanatical support of the southern cause, his desire to be involved in historic events, his morbid interest in political assassination, and his unstable, maverick behaviour.

During the Civil War, Booth promised his mother he would not join the Confederate Army, but he was involved in some covert operations and may have been a southern agent. Possibly he was smuggling medical supplies to Confederate troops.

John Wilkes Booth was a charismatic figure, good-looking, with a slim athletic build and magnetic eyes. Another actor commented that 'when his emotions were aroused, his eyes were like living jewels. Flames shot from them.' He attracted women. Booth was often seen 'lounging' in the arms of Ellen Starr. In 1861, an actress called Henrietta Irving slashed his face with a knife when she realised Booth had no intention of marrying her. After Booth was killed, the photographs of no less than five women were found in his pockets. One of them was a picture of his fiancée, Lucy Hale, the daughter of Senator John P. Hale who, ironically, was a prominent abolitionist. But these are just further signs of Booth's inconsistency and waywardness. He wanted to see Brown hanged, but was also happy to accept Hale as a father-in-law: both were abolitionists.

Booth's acting career took off in 1860, and he played leading roles in many plays. In Shakespeare's *Julius Caesar*, he played Mark Antony with his brothers Edwin and Junius as Brutus and Cassius. In November 1863, Booth acted in front of Abraham Lincoln. The Lincolns saw him in *The Marble Heart* at Ford's Theatre. With them in the box was a guest, Mary Clay. She reminisced that Wilkes Booth twice, when uttering disagreeable threats, came up close to Lincoln and pointed at him. When he came close a third time, Mary Clay said, 'Mr Lincoln, he looks as if he meant that for you.' Lincoln replied, 'Well, he does look pretty sharp at me, doesn't he?'

Now Booth was earning $20,000 a year. He was able to invest in oil. In May 1864, he left the stage and went to Pennsylvania to concentrate on his oil investments. He formed the Dramatic Oil Company with three actor friends. But he was too impatient; when success was not immediate, he dropped out, handing most of his investment over to a friend and his brother Junius.

In October 1864, Booth made a mysterious journey to Montreal, where he held secret meetings with Confederate sympathisers. In November, he returned, carrying a letter of introduction which eventually led him to meet Dr Samuel Mudd. Booth was assembling a conspiracy to capture the President, take him to Richmond as a hostage and use him to compel the Federal government to return the Confederate prisoners of war who were held in Union prisons. The intention was to re-invigorate the Confederate army and enable it to win. It was a plot to kidnap, not to kill.

He must later have wished that he had taken his chance on 4 March, 1865, when he attended Lincoln's second inauguration as the invited guest of his fiancée. Booth must have thought about it when later he said to another actor, 'What an excellent chance I had to kill the President, if I had wished to!'

All through these years, Booth behaved in a secretive, erratic way, but his brothers and sisters seem to have thought little of it. Asia later recalled how when he stayed with her in Philadelphia 'strange men called late at night for whispered consultations'. She knew her brother was a spy, a blockade-runner, a rebel.

The capture of the President was to take to place on 17 March, 1865. But after five months of detailed planning by Booth and the other conspirators, Lincoln changed his plans at the last minute. Instead of visiting the Campbell Hospital outside Washington to see a play, *Still Waters Run Deep*, he decided to attend a luncheon at the National Hotel, where he would speak to officers of the 140th Indiana Regiment and present a captured flag to the Governor of Indiana. Booth was thwarted.

Two weeks later, the Union siege of Richmond ended in Confederate defeat. One week after that, on 9 April, 1865, General Lee was obliged to surrender. Booth was doubly frustrated; his own conspiracy to kidnap Lincoln had failed and the Confederates had lost the war. On 11 April, Lincoln gave his last speech at the White House. Booth and two of his co-conspirators, Powell and Herold, were in the audience. Lincoln proposed conferring rights on certain black people, 'on the very intelligent and on those who serve our cause as soldiers'. Booth was now beside himself with rage. 'That is the last speech he will ever make.' Booth's fury made him think up a wild, last-throw attempt to get the better of Lincoln. Just four days later, he would murder him.

Booth made a big mistake in thinking that the conspirators who had been ready to kidnap were just as ready to kill.

At 9 a.m. on 14 April, 1865, Booth went to a barbershop to have his hair trimmed, then returned to the National Hotel, where many of the guests recognized him. Later in the morning he went to Ford's Theatre to pick up his mail. There he heard from the theatre manager that Lincoln would be attending that evening's performance of *Our American Cousin*. He decided that this was his opportunity to kill Lincoln. He spent some time walking round the theatre. He knew the play well, and knew that the biggest laugh would come at 10.15 p.m.; that would be the moment to shoot. At noon he went to a stable and hired a fast mare before returning to the hotel.

At 2 p.m. Booth visited Lewis Paine and told him he was going to kill Lincoln. He also told Paine that he, Paine, was going to kill Secretary of State William Seward. Booth then went to the boarding house belonging to Mary Surratt and left her a package containing field glasses; she was to take them to her tavern at Surrattsville, where he could collect them that night. At 3 p.m., Booth visited George Atzerodt to tell him to assassinate Vice-President Andrew Johnson, who lived in the same building, but Atzerodt was out. Inexplicably, Booth left a note for Johnson, who was then at the White House. After picking up the mare, Booth went to a tavern for a drink and wrote a letter to the press, which was to be delivered the next day; he signed the letter with his own name and those of three others – Paine, Atzerodt and Herold – in effect condemning them to death. At that stage poor Atzerodt didn't know what was in store for him. It was only by chance that Booth met him in the street at 5 p.m. and told him to kill Johnson at 10.15 p.m. Atzerodt did not want to do it, but he was already fatally implicated.

At 6 p.m. Booth rode to the theatre to rehearse the route he would use in the assassination, everything except the leap onto the stage. Then he returned to the hotel to rest, dine and change. He put on calf-length boots, new spurs and black clothes and picked up a compass, a bowie knife and a derringer, a single-shot pistol. At 8 p.m., Booth held a final meeting with the other conspirators. Paine would assassinate Seward, Atzerodt would assassinate Johnson, Booth would assassinate Lincoln; all the attacks would take place at 10.15 p.m. They would meet at the Navy Yard Bridge and ride to Surrattsville. After that, Booth rode to Ford's Theatre, left his horse round the back and went to a tavern to get a bottle of whiskey. Another customer, assuming he was acting that night, quipped, 'You'll never be the actor your father was.' Booth answered cryptically, 'When I leave the stage, I'll be the most famous man in America.'

At 10 p.m., Booth climbed the stairs to the dress circle, saw the white door of Lincoln's State Box. A footman sat next to it. Booth gave him his card and opened the door into the dark area at the back of the box, wedging it shut with the leg of a music stand he had left there earlier. Then

Booth opened the inner door, approached the President from behind and shot him in the head at close range.

In the confusion that followed, Booth may have shouted 'Sic semper tyrannis!' (Thus always to tyrants), though some in the audience thought he shouted this after he landed on the stage. Major Rathbone, who was sitting in the box, thought he shouted 'Freedom!' immediately after the shot. Rathbone grappled briefly with Booth, but was stabbed in the arm. Booth jumped over the front of the box and onto the stage. One of his spurs caught in one of the decorative flags draped over the balustrade, and he landed awkwardly, breaking his left leg just above the ankle. He managed to run across the stage, out of the theatre to his waiting horse, and he rode away.

At 11 p.m., Herold caught up with Booth and they made for Mary Surratt's tavern. Booth was preoccupied with the pain in his leg and as yet did not know that the rest of the conspiracy had failed. Paine had not killed Seward and Azerodt had not killed Johnson. Booth took some whiskey and got to Dr Mudd's house at 4 a.m. Dr Mudd attended to his broken leg.

It was several days before the army caught up with Booth and Herold. They were rumoured to be in the area between the Potomac and Rappahannock Rivers. Lieutenant Edward Doherty of the Sixteenth New York Cavalry followed their trail, picking up sightings from fishermen and ferrymen on 24 April. It was clear that Booth was assisted along his escape route by a rebel, Captain

Willie Jett. Jett was tracked down to the house of his girlfriend's parents, the Goldmans, where he was found in bed with the Goldmans' son. Jett was compelled to tell the soldiers where Booth was, and he undertook to lead them to the barn where Booth and Herold were hiding. Booth was defiant. He refused to surrender. When Doherty threatened to set fire to the barn, Booth admitted that Herold was keen to surrender, which he was allowed to do. As soon as Herold was out, a fire was started at the back of the barn. Sergeant Boston Corbett shot Booth in the neck for reasons that were left unexplained in Doherty's otherwise very detailed report, and Booth died two hours later. Ironically, Corbett was commended by Doherty for his action in 'bringing the murderers to justice'. Whether Corbett was just over-zealous, or someone had given orders that Booth was not to be taken alive, is a matter for speculation. It may be that there were others involved in the conspiracy who were now to be protected. Similar thoughts revolve round the murder of Lee Harvey Oswald.

Booth had always wanted fame. In the end he achieved infamy. But to an alarming number of people, it seems to make little difference whether they are famous or notorious. Perhaps – even if it is for an evil act – what matters most is to be noticed, to be remembered.

Charles Guiteau

'playing to the gallery'

CHARLES GUITEAU WAS born on 8 September, 1841 in Freeport, Illinois. He was the fourth of six children of Luther Wilson Guiteau and Jane Howe. When Charles's mother died, he was only seven and his father remarried.

As a young man, Charles worked for his father as a clerk, and was then employed as a cashier in a local bank. Luther was against sending his son to college, but in 1859 Charles inherited enough money from a grandfather to enable him to go to the University of Michigan. Charles had been discontented at home. Now he was even more discontented at university. He turned to religion, and in particular to the doctrines of John Humphrey Noyes, who had founded the Oneida Community in New York State; it was a kind of communism based on the Bible. As it happened, his father was already a devotee of Noyes' teaching. In 1860, Charles joined the Oneida Community in New York. But even this did not make him happy, and in 1865 he left the community, convinced that he had been called by God to spread Noyes' millennial communism by founding a newspaper.

Guiteau then settled in Hoboken, New Jersey

and tried to set up his new newspaper, which he called the *Daily Theocrat*. It did not last, and within a few months he was asking to be let back into the community. A year later he left it again.

By August 1867, Charles Guiteau had run himself out of money. His brother-in-law George Scoville generously offered him a job in his law office in Chicago, and a home. Still he could not settle. Within a few months he resigned his post and went back to New York, apparently to work on the *Independent* newspaper, but this work was more menial than he was anticipating; he ended up merely selling advertizing space. By 1868, Guiteau was back in Chicago, where he got a clerical job in another law office.

In 1868, he married Annie Bunn, who was a librarian. It proved to be an unhappy relationship, basically because Guiteau was an unhappy and maladjusted man tottering on the edge of sanity. He maltreated his wife, locking her in a closet for nights at a time. In 1874, she divorced him.

After the failure of his marriage, Guiteau's behaviour became more erratic and peculiar than ever. The inner restlessness was coming more and more to the surface. When he was chopping wood one day, he unaccountably threatened his sister Frances with the axe he was holding; frightened, she ran to tell the doctor, who said she should have him confined in an institution. The Guiteau family as a whole must by this time have realised that Charles was insane.

Guiteau ran off and disappeared. The following year he reappeared as a regular attender of revivalist meetings. He became an itinerant preacher, writing his own sermons.

Guiteau's father died in 1880, and for some reason Charles then turned to politics. He became fired by the Stalwart faction of the Republican movement. The Stalwarts were led by Roscoe Conkling and their enemies were the so-called Half-Breeds led by James Blaine, who supported the president-elect, James Garfield. It was in this way that Charles Guiteau began to see James Garfield as his enemy – a real turning-point in his life. He was at last acquiring a purpose, a mission.

In May 1881 Guiteau conceived the idea of assassinating Garfield, who was now the President of the USA. Remarkably, he publicly explained his action in advance. On 16 June, 1881, he wrote an Address to the American People. He wrote a letter to the White House and another to General Sherman, saying 'I have just shot the President. His death was a political necessity. I am a lawyer, theologian and politician. I am a Stalwart of the Stalwarts . . .' and so on. These were obviously the ravings of a madman, and they were probably consigned to the waste paper basket accordingly, but they were no less dangerous for that. Even madmen can kill.

On the day of his assassination, President Garfield was in high spirits, doing handstands on his son's bed. Luckily we never know what the future holds in store for us.

At 8.30 a.m. on 2 July, 1882, at the Baltimore and Potomac Railroad Station, Charles Guiteau shot President James Garfield, once in the arm and once in the back, as the President was about to set off on holiday. The first shot only grazed his right arm and stuck in a lump of putty in the box of a glass-cutter. The second shot proved to be fatal. The shooting took place in front of a group of the President's staff. Various passers-by reacted in a variety of ways, but doctors were sent for. A well-known Washington physician, Dr Bliss, arrived and, presumably overwhelmed by the gravity of the situation, performed the following actions; he put hot water bottles on Garfield's feet, took them off again, opened a window, closed it again, poked his finger into the wound in the President's back, and then called for a local doctor. One wonders what he charged.

Dr Reyburn thought the call to attend a bullet-ridden President must be a hoax, and took his time travelling to the President's bedside. This unsatisfactory embryonic medical team decided to hoist the President onto a mattress and carry him back to the White House. They gave him a morphine injection. Garfield vomited and this they put down to the injection, whereas it was almost certainly a response to the wound.

It was not until 5.30 p.m., nine hours after the shooting, that the doctors decided to remove the bloodstained suit. They gave him a glass of champagne, which he threw up. He continued vomiting all night. Another doctor appeared, Navy Surgeon General Wales, and he stuck his finger into the President's back wound. He announced that the bullet had hit the liver. Next Dr Frank Hamilton of New York stuck his finger in the wound and encountered a clot, so he promptly pulled it out again. Incredibly, fifteen different doctors in all stuck their fingers into the President's wound. Contemporary commentators said there were just too many doctors involved; but it is their incompetence that is so breathtaking.

All kinds of mad but well-meant suggestions poured into the White House. One telegram proposed hanging the President upside down so that the bullet would fall out.

Joseph Lister had been advocating the use of antiseptic methods in surgery since 1865, but there were still a lot of backwoodsmen in the medical profession. Pus was seen as a good sign in a wound, and some doctors took a pride in the filthy conditions in which they worked. Healing and recovery were expected to be slow. With old-fashioned medics like these around him, Garfield could not expect to survive at all. His death was certain.

Guiteau, meanwhile, was immediately arrested and taken into custody. The train policeman, a man called Patrick Kearney, was so excited to have arrested this important assassin that he completely forgot to take Guiteau's gun from him. It was only when Guiteau reached the police station that he was disarmed. A reporter turned up to draw a sketch of the villain for his newspaper. Guiteau promptly demanded a 25 dollar fee for this. Soldiers were posted outside to stop a lynch mob seizing him. After a time, he was taken to the District of Columbia Jail to await his trial.

The President, who lived on for several weeks,

was given entirely unsuitable food for a wounded man. He was given steak, eggs, brandy. Gradually his body was taken over by blood poisoning. His wound became severely infected. By 19 August, his face had become so swollen that his right eye was completely shut. Several incisions were made in his face to drain the pus. James Garfield eventually died miserably on 19 September. One medical journal commented, 'President Garfield's case has been the most grossly mismanaged in modern history', and accused his doctors of blaming Providence.

Up until the moment of Garfield's death, Guiteau stood a chance of getting off on an insanity plea. But after the death, it looked less certain.

Guiteau's trial opened on 14 November, 1881, and went on until January 1882. A plea of insanity to President Chester A. Arthur was entered by neurologists as well as by the Guiteau family. Guiteau tried to persuade the jury that inspiration for the assassination had come from God himself. Guiteau played the insanity card very clumsily, though. While he was in prison, he had been organizing lucrative lecture tours that he would give on his release and he had also dictated his autobiography to the press. He was clearly expecting to be free in the near future.

He seemed oblivious of many signals that his future was not going to be as straightforward or as pleasant as he liked to imagine. He got a flood of letters while in prison. One of them read, 'You dirty, lousy, lying rebel traitor; hanging is too good for you, you stinking cuss. We will keep you spotted, you stinking pup. You damned old mildewed assassin. You ought to be burned alive and let rot. You savage cannibal dog.'

When Garfield died, Guiteau still misread the situation. He suddenly felt vindicated. God had after all been on his side.

Guiteau's plea began, 'I plead not guilty to the indictment and my defence is threefold: 1. Insanity, in that it was God's act and not mine . . . I am not legally responsible for my act. 2. The president died from malpractice . . . if he had been well treated he would have recovered. 3. The president died in New Jersey and therefore beyond the jurisdiction of this court.'

Guiteau's own brother-in-law, George Scoville, was his defence lawyer. The prosecuting lawyer was George Corkhill. Guiteau's behaviour during the trial was as erratic and bizarre as it had been for several years past. When Guiteau saw the great crowd in the court room, he decided to take advantage of it. He scribbled little notes and passed them back to the crowd. One of the notes read, 'I am charged with maliciously and wickedly murdering one James A. Garfield. Nothing can be more absurd, because General Garfield died from malpractice . . . The issue here is Who fired that shot, the Deity or me?' What he hoped to gain from these performances is hard to tell. They would certainly seem to support the idea that he really was insane.

In his opening statement, Leigh Robinson, who was assisting Scoville, lost his nerve. He asked for a postponement of the trial, mentioning a possible third lawyer who would join their team. This provoked an angry outburst from Guiteau: 'I do not want to hear any more speeches of Mr Robinson's. I want him to get out of the case . . . Mr Robinson came into the case without consulting me. I know nothing about him. I don't like the way he talks. I expect to have some money shortly and I can employ any counsel I please.'

Scoville was evidently also angry with Robinson, saying in front of the whole court room that Robinson ought to say who this mysterious third lawyer was. Robinson had evidently not discussed the postponement proposal or the third lawyer with Scoville beforehand.

And so it went on, with Guiteau interrupting all the time and sabotaging his own lawyers' efforts. At one point he said, to his own lawyer, 'You are about as consummate a jackass, I must say, as I ever saw. I would rather have some ten year old boy try this case than you.' Scoville even resorted to appealing to the court to stop his client from directly addressing the press.

Even Guiteau began to realise that all was not going well when he was in the prison wagon and a bullet whizzed through the grille, piercing his coat though not his body. It was a drunken farmer who had taken a pot-shot at him. The would-be assassin missed, but he was still hailed as a national hero by the press.

Guiteau loved playing to the gallery, though. His trial dragged on into the New Year, and he addressed the crowd in the court room, 'I had a nice Christmas. I hope everyone else did. I had plenty of visitors, high-toned, middle-toned and low-toned people. That takes in the whole crowd. Public opinion don't want me hung.'

On 23 January the jury deliberated for less than an hour before agreeing on a guilty verdict. He was sentenced to death. The insanity plea was rejected, and a writ of execution was issued. Still he did not give up. He tried to sell for a hundred dollars the suit in which he had shot Garfield. He sold his autographs and autographed photographs, which he advertized in local papers. One wonders what he thought he would do with the money.

On 30 June, 1882, Charles Guiteau was led away to be hanged at the District of Columbia Jail. He requested that the flowers he assumed had been sent in by his legions of admirers should be placed in his cell, only to be told that there were no flowers at all. Then, while actually standing in front of the noose, he recited an endless, repetitive, poem that he had written. It went, 'I am going to the Lordy, I am so glad. I am going to the Lordy, I am so glad. I am going to the Lordy, I am so glad' and so on – until he was stopped. In becoming the President's assassin, Guiteau finally found out who and what he was; it was the purpose and the role for which he had been searching all his life until then. And he certainly loved being the centre of attention – that feeling of importance, of being a celebrity, being a part of history. He and the yet-unborn Lee Harvey Oswald had a lot in common.

There is no doubt that Guiteau fired the shots that caused Garfield's death, but with proper medical treatment (even by 1880s standards) even the wound in his back need not have been fatal. Garfield died as much through medical incompetence as through the hands of the mad lone assassin.

Jacques Mornard/Ramon Mercader

'the long arm of Stalin'

THE NAME OF Jacques Mornard is not well known. Nor, though, is the real name of his victim, Lev Davidovich Bronstein. Like Lenin, Bronstein had to adopt a nom de guerre in the run-up to revolution, simply to evade capture and retribution. Bronstein took the name Leon Trotsky when he was on the run after escaping from a prison in Siberia in 1902.

Trotsky was born in 1877 and was a mature forty years old when the Russian Revolution broke out.

Trotsky's role in organizing the 1917 Russian revolution was just as important as Lenin's, even though he did not actually become a Bolshevik until July 1917. He was also the most important figure in the negotiating team for the Brest-Litovsk peace treaty. During the next three years Trotsky and Lenin frequently disagreed, but that was partly because there were massive inconsistencies and shifts in Lenin's strategies and policies.

After Lenin's death, it might have seemed as if the way was clear for Trotsky to lead the political field. But seniority always counted for a great deal in the Communist Party and there were many long-serving members who remembered that Trotsky was a Johnny-come-lately, only joining the party in 1917. But it was also true that there were more ambitious, more determined and more ruthless men around than Trotsky. They mounted a campaign to discredit him, master-minded by Stalin, and he was dismissed as commissar for war. He was given work of little political significance to do, such as heading the electric power development programme. He resigned from this post in 1925. In 1927 he was expelled from the Communist Party for alleged anti-party activities; he had in fact simply become more and more open in his disagreement with Communist Party policy.

In January 1928 he began his life in exile, when he was sent to Turkestan. He was shortly after that banished from the Soviet Union altogether and arrived in Constantinople in 1929. In Turkey, Trotsky tried to establish and co-ordinate a network of followers; he was far from giving up on politics, in spite of the enormous dangers involved in crossing Stalin. But even in Turkey he was being watched by Stalin's agents. KGB (Soviet intelligence agency) agents encircled him. Two of them were brothers, who were later known in America as Jack and Robert Soble. They were Lithuanian and Jewish by birth, but served the Soviet Communist Party throughout their lives. Jack Soble was able to visit Trotsky in various European cities and both he and his brother became well-known among German Trotskyists. Trotsky, with good reason, became suspicious of them and turned them out of his group in 1932. Beria, the head of the KGB, allowed the entire Soble family to leave the Soviet Union in 1940; they were totally trusted by Beria to carry on their espionage work in the United States. This they continued until as late as 1961, when they were both convicted of espionage.

Another important Soviet agent was Mark Zborowski, who was Russian-born and educated at the Sorbonne in Paris. He moved to the USA in 1941, where he resumed his work spying for the KGB. A Soviet spy defecting to the West eventually exposed Zborowski as a fellow agent ten years later, in 1951.

In 1936 Trotsky went to Norway, finally settling in Mexico at the invitation of the artist Diego Rivera in 1937.

Trotsky was accused of joining Zinoviev in a plot to kill Stalin, but he emphatically denied this charge. Stalin was very angry with Trotsky. He saw him as a major political nuisance, and would certainly have had him shot had he still been within his reach in the Soviet Union. He nevertheless decided that he must be eliminated at any cost, wherever he was in the world, and gave orders for Trotsky to be assassinated in Mexico. Trotsky was aware that he was in serious danger. He knew Stalin had agents everywhere and that he had good reason to fear spies and infiltrators. It was one such infiltrator who would shortly murder him.

When Stalin took against people he arranged to have them killed. Stalin was a great lover of movies, and through films knew all the big American movie stars. He liked classic westerns, and seemed to identify with the lone cowboy who rode into town and got his own way by shooting people. Ironically, there was one movie cowboy he particularly hated and that was John Wayne – not for his film acting but for his political activities – and he set in motion the arrangements to have him killed. Khrushchev later boasted that he had intervened, had Stalin's 'fatwah' revoked, and saved John Wayne's life!

One colourful figure Trotsky encountered in Mexico was Frida Kahlo. Frida was born in 1907, though she claimed to be three years younger. She met her future husband, the painter Diego Rivera, when they were both at school. In adulthood, Frida became part of the Mexico City art world; she married Diego Rivera, though both of them had many affairs. Rivera had an affair with Frida's sister – and Kahlo had an affair with Leon Trotsky.

In the summer of 1940, Trotsky's house was attacked by a gang of twenty men. The Mexican painter David Siqueiros organized this band of Spanish and Mexican Communists, who were veterans of the Spanish Civil War. They launched the armed raid on Trotsky's villa in May, riddling the house with hundreds of bullets, none of which hit Trotsky. An American volunteer and a bodyguard were killed in the attack. It was clear to Trotsky that Stalin was determined that he should die and he did what he could to step up the security at his villa. Siqueiros was arrested and freed on bail; he was then spirited out of the country with the help of Pablo Neruda, who was a Communist and also a Chilean diplomat.

Another plan to kill Trotsky was organized and co-ordinated by Pavel Sudoplatov, a mysterious and shadowy figure who functioned as a superspy. Sudoplatov was approached in the post-Stalinist era by a high-ranking Soviet officer who wanted to interview him, General Volkogonov. He was reluctant to be interviewed but, rather surprisingly given that he was a superspy, agreed to the general's suggestion that he should write his autobiography. It eventually surfaced in the west in 1994 as Special Tasks: Memoirs of an Unwanted Witness – a Soviet Spymaster, by Pavel and Anatoli Sudoplatov. Sudoplatov was evidently a thoughtful Stalinist who well understood the political manoeuvrings of the 1940s, and was also ready to do terrible things in Stalin's name.

Sudoplatov's plan involved using Ramon Mercader, who was the son of the wealthy Spanish Communist Caridad Mercader, this time as a lone assassin. Ruby Weil, an American Communist, was very friendly with Sylvia Ageloff, a follower of Trotsky. In 1938, Ruby Weil introduced Sylvia to a man she called 'Jacques Mornard'. Mornard pursued Sylvia until they became lovers. Later, Sylvia travelled to Mexico to do volunteer work for Trotsky. Jacques Mornard was then able to use Sylvia's position as an intimate of Trotsky's household to gain admittance to Trotsky's house and get to know all about Trotsky's security, the location and deployment of guards, and so on.

Jacques Mornard (Ramon Mercader) presented himself as someone who was very interested in Trotsky's ideas, and arranged a meeting with Trotsky to discuss a philosophical treatise he had drafted.

It was on 20 August, 1940 that Trotsky was attacked in his villa in Mexico City by this agent of Stalin's. Trotsky came to trust Jacques Mornard as a friend. He had wormed his way into Trotsky's confidence by associating himself with someone Trotsky legitimately trusted – 'a friend of a friend'. Trotsky invited Jacques Mornard, described as a French Jew, to take tea with him. Because Jacques Mornard was an invited guest, it did not occur to the bodyguards to search him, which turned out to be a fatal mistake. According to the police report, Mornard had a small ice axe hidden inside his trousers.

Jacques Mornard attacked Trotsky suddenly and without warning, battering his skull and injuring his right shoulder and right knee. Trotsky was conscious for a short while before he lapsed into unconsciousness as a result of the brain injury. According to the bodyguards, his last words were, 'I think Stalin has finished the job he has begun'.

Trotsky was taken to hospital, where he did not regain consciousness and died the next day, 21 August, 1940. His death was announced in newspapers all round the world on the day after that, though not in the Soviet Union. All that appeared there was a very indirect report; according to American journalists an attempt had been made to assassinate Trotsky by an intimate friend and follower. Frida Kahlo, who had been Trotsky's mistress, was for some reason accused of committing the murder, but was soon afterwards released.

It became known that Mornard (or Mercader) was a Soviet agent. The Soviets tried various ways of helping him to escape from his Mexican Gaol after his conviction, but it became clear that the American authorities were well informed about these plans, and were able to tip off the Mexican authorities in advance of each break-out attempt. In this way the Americans were able to ensure that Trotsky's assassin was not sprung from prison.

The death of Trotsky became the subject of two films, *The Assassination of Trotsky* (1972) with Richard Burton as Trotsky and *Frida* (2002), this time with Geoffrey Rush playing the exiled and doomed revolutionary. More obliquely, Trotsky became Snowball the pig in George Orwell's *Animal Farm* (1945).

Ramon Mercader was finally released from prison in 1960. After that he retired to the Soviet Union on a KGB pension. Frida Kahlo had to have a leg amputated – it had been damaged long before in a traffic accident – and became depressed. She committed suicide in 1954. Pavel Sudoplatov was awarded orders and medals for organizing and carrying out the vengeful 'special task' of assassinating Trotsky.

Lee Harvey Oswald
'the lone gunman'

LEE OSWALD, the man who killed President John F. Kennedy, was a very different character from John Wilkes Booth, the man who killed President Abraham Lincoln. Until that fateful moment when he killed Kennedy, Oswald had achieved nothing at all. It was as if that was the only thing he could do to make people remember him, that was his only way into history.

Lee Harvey Oswald was born in New Orleans in October 1939. His father died two months before he was born. For a time he was left in an orphanage, and after that he moved from place to place with his mother Marguerite, because she found it difficult to hold down a job. By the age of eighteen, Oswald had lived at an astonishing twenty-two different addresses and he had attended twelve different schools.

As a boy, Lee Oswald became a persistent truant, a street kid, missing 80 per cent of his high school classes. He grew up rootless, insecure, unsocialized, always the odd one out. When he was fourteen all the symptoms of a disturbed personality were apparent when he was remanded in youth custody. He was referred to Dr Renatus

Hartog, a psychologist, for an evaluation; and Dr Hartog found that he had 'personality pattern disturbance with schizoid features and passive-aggressive tendencies'. Dr Hartog believed that Oswald had 'definite traits of dangerousness', and advised that he should be kept on probation and given psychiatric help. Not long after that, Oswald was ordered to be put into a home for disturbed boys and subject to mandatory psychiatric care. All the signs were there. For whatever reason, and presumably an unfortunate collision of nature and nurture, Lee Harvey was developing from being a disturbed youth to being a disturbed and highly dangerous adult.

The mother's response to this analysis of her son was typically unhelpful. She fled from New York, and took him to Texas. It was a flight from treatment and, because of her immature and irresponsible decision, she must bear some of the blame for what followed later. Years later, in the aftermath of the assassination, the New York authorities were asked what action they had taken about Oswald at the time. The Warren Commission was told by the New York Probation Service, 'There is very little one can really do. We don't have the extra-state jurisdiction, and we didn't even know where she [Marguerite Oswald] had gone'.

The young assassin then joined the US Marine Corps, as much as anything to escape from the suffocating clutches of his mother. During his military career he became an expert marksman with a rifle. In 1956 he on two occasions achieved

48 and 49 out of 50 during rapid fire at a target two hundred yards away. These are outstandingly high scores. After the assassination, there were many sceptics who doubted whether Oswald could have fired three shots in rapid succession and score hits with two of them, and this led them on to the idea that there must have been other marksmen in the plaza. But the evidence still exists that Oswald was certainly capable of firing all three shots, in quick succession, and given his record he might even have succeeded in hitting Kennedy with all three shots.

During his military career, Oswald learned Russian, then travelled to Russia in 1959; he seems to have thought of it as defection. The Russians declined Oswald's offer to be a spy, possibly because they sensed that he was a weak and defective personality, possibly because they thought he would play games and attempt to become a double agent. The Soviet authorities wanted to return him to America, but he attempted suicide by cutting one of his wrists and they allowed him to live in Minsk, where he took a factory job. He married a Russian, Marina Prusakova. Oswald maintained that he was a Marxist and tried to renounce his American citizenship. The Soviet authorities recognized his instability after the suicide attempt and handed him over for psychiatric evaluation. Two psychiatrists concluded that he was 'mentally unstable' and warned that he was capable of further irrational acts. How right they were.

Then, in 1962 he changed his mind, as no

doubt the Soviet authorities thought he would, and returned to America. He took his wife and infant daughter with him. He had got tired of Soviet authoritarianism. Oswald hung on to the fantasy that he was a high-powered spy, telling one of his friends that he had been responsible for giving the Soviets the information that enabled them to shoot down the U-2 spy plane. He desperately wanted to be important, to influence historic events.

Oswald took a job in Dallas at a graphic arts firm, producing classified government work that included detailed maps of Cuba. Oswald boasted to friends that not only was he working on the Cuba maps, but the CIA arranged the job for him. Although this may have been true, his CV up to that point does not make it very likely, and his record of indiscretion made him a poor security risk. In the spring of 1963 the Oswald family moved to New Orleans, where he befriended Judyth Vary. According to her, Oswald interviewed female Cuban refugees who came to work at the Reily Coffee Company, where both Oswald and Judyth now had jobs. Oswald was on a mission, finding out the names of safe contacts in Cuba. Oswald's employers seem to have known that he was doing some kind of secret work and nodded at it.

In March 1963, Oswald bought himself a rifle and a handgun. Rather peculiarly, Oswald got Marina to take a photograph of him wearing the handgun at his right hip and holding the rifle and a copy of a Yugoslav newspaper, *Politika*. Why was he creating a trail of evidence against himself in this way? Or was it all juvenile play-acting that eventually got out of hand? And what did Marina think he was doing?

In the summer of 1963, Oswald became secretary of the Fair Play for Cuba Committee (New Orleans chapter). When Oswald gave out 'Hands Off Cuba' leaflets on the streets of New Orleans, he was heckled by anti-Castro Cuban exiles and arrested by the police for disturbing the peace. A local radio show host interviewed Oswald on air. But what Oswald was up to is not at all clear. Although the leaflets supported Castro, the address printed on them, 544 Camp Street, was that of a racist ex-FBI agent called Guy Banister who was running a training camp for anti-Castro exiles preparing to take over Cuba. Oswald spent a lot of time in Banister's office. According to Judyth, Oswald often went through a garage next door to Reily's to reach Banister's office; so as not to arouse suspicion, he befriended the garage owner, Adrian Alba, and took to whiling away time at the garage reading gun magazines. The garage was frequently used by CIA and FBI agents. Alba later testified that he saw the driver of one of these cars pass an envelope to Oswald. It is far from clear, even after all these years, what Oswald was doing or where his loyalties lay.

Before the Kennedy assassination, Oswald had already aimed his rifle at a prominent local politician, trying to shoot him from the street through a window in his home. His target moved, and he missed. At the time the police were unable to identify the would-be assassin but, after the death of the President, when Oswald's life was carefully sifted over, it became obvious that this shooting was his work too. It is a sobering thought that if the earlier assassination had been 'successful', Oswald would probably not have been free to commit the later one, and the course of American history would have been changed.

But he missed, and he was free to kill the President. The chance visit of President Kennedy to Dallas that autumn provided Oswald with a much higher-profile target. By chance he was looking for someone to assassinate. By chance he had a job in a building that overlooked the route of the President's motorcade. The opportunity must have seemed like a gift from destiny.

At 12.30 p.m. on 22 November, 1963, Oswald shot President Kennedy from a window on the sixth floor of the Texas School Book Depository in Elm Street, where he was temporarily employed during the Christmas rush. The window had a view across Dealey Plaza. It is believed that Oswald fired three shots at the President's motorcade as it moved slowly across the plaza away from him, hitting the President twice, fatally, and wounding Governor Connally. Their wives, who were also in the car, were mercifully unhurt.

Whether there were more snipers behind a wooden fence at the top of a grassy bank in front and to the right of the President's car is still not known. Those who favour a conspiracy put one or more snipers in that location, the celebrated 'grassy knoll'. This would account for the grotesque jerking back of Kennedy's head at the impact of the second shot, which implies a shot from in front. The large wound in the back of the head would also be more consistent with an exit than an entry wound. So, there is some circumstantial evidence for a second gunman. One of the bullets appeared to follow a zig-zag path through the bodies of both Kennedy and Connally, and this so-called 'magic bullet' has often been used as evidence that at least one additional shot must have been fired. But recent virtual reality reconstructions have shown that the path followed by the magic bullet was after all a dead straight line. The earlier misinterpretations did not allow for the fact that Connally's seat was positioned significantly lower than the President's, in order to make the President more visible. Nor did they allow for the fact that Governor Connally's body was twisted into an abnormal position because he had turned round to speak to Kennedy.

After the shooting, the dying President was raced to a nearby hospital where the surgeons found that his brain was so badly damaged that they could do nothing for him. Oswald left the Book Depository, took a bus and a taxi back to his room, changed his clothes and (according to the Warren Commission) picked up a pistol. A little later, the official report states that Oswald killed Police Officer Tippit in Tenth Street, though witnesses who saw the shooting describe a different man, someone who did not look like Oswald at all.

Oswald was arrested at the Texas Theatre in the Oak Cliff neighbourhood at 1.50 p.m., initially for the murder of Tippit. He was only later charged with murdering Kennedy. Police Officer McDonald, who arrested Oswald in the theatre auditorium, told him to stand up so that he could handcuff him; Oswald shouted, 'Well, it's all over now', punched McDonald and pulled his revolver from his belt. He was going to kill McDonald as he had earlier killed Tippit. This time, luckily for McDonald, the gun did not respond when he pulled the trigger and Oswald was overpowered.

Oswald's behaviour while in custody was unnaturally calm. When challenged about the two ID cards he was carrying, one in the name of Lee Harvey Oswald and one in the name of Alek Hidell, Oswald smirked at the officer and said, 'You figure it out'. He smiled complacently and appeared to enjoy all the attention; he spoke to the press in a measured, almost pompous way. It was if this was the moment he had been waiting for. This was his inauguration. He still denied shooting anyone, but he was only teasing his audience.

While he was being transferred to the county jail two days after the assassination, a nightclub owner called Jack Ruby shot Oswald in the stomach. Oswald died shortly afterwards. There has been endless speculation about this shooting too. Was it the spontaneous action of a misguided but public-spirited citizen? Or was it part of a conspiracy to ensure that Oswald did not go to trial and reveal in the court room that others had been involved in the Kennedy assassination?

There were many doubts and uncertainties surrounding the assassination, so a week after the assassination the new President, Lyndon B. Johnson, ordered a full investigation by a specially appointed commission. The report the Warren Commission eventually released concluded that Oswald had fired all three shots – the initial shot that missed altogether and the two that hit Kennedy – and that he had acted alone, without accomplices. The conspiracy theories were fuelled by a desire to see this momentous event resulting from a complicated and deep-laid plot involving some powerful underground organization, perhaps the Mafia or the CIA. But the truth seems to be that the catastrophic end to Jack Kennedy's presidency was down to the caprice of one lone, mad gunman desperate for his place in history. And he got it.

Thomas McMahon
'the murder of Lord Mountbatten'

IT WAS HIGH summer in 1979, August Bank Holiday, and the height of the holiday season. In a bay on the west coast of Ireland, a family set off on a boat trip. It was the Mountbatten family.

Lord Louis Mountbatten and his family had been spending a holiday at his Irish castle, a kind of holiday home in County Sligo in the north-west of the Irish Republic. He came out of the castle at 9.15 a.m. and announced that the family would go out for a trip on his boat, *Shadow V.* It was 11.15 a.m. before the family were boarding the boat in the harbour at the fishing village of Mullaghmore. At 11.30, Lord Mountbatten himself steered the boat away from the shore and out across the bay from Mullaghmore. He was watched by the IRA button man. He had been watched for some time, and his movements were very predictable. This had been his routine every August for the past twenty-five years. Mountbatten was also watched from the shore by his bodyguard, one of two Irish policemen who went everywhere with him while he was staying at the castle.

The boat rounded the headland and was just a hundred yards offshore off the next small inlet when suddenly, and with no warning whatever, a bomb hidden on board was detonated. It was 11.30 a.m. The explosion was seen by witnesses. One eye witness said the huge blast blew the boat 'to smithereens'. All seven of the people the boat was carrying were thrown out into the sea.

Nearby fishermen raced to the site of the explosion and found Lord Mountbatten, the cousin of the Queen, the mentor of Prince Charles. They pulled him out of the sea, but he was already dead. He had been blown unconscious by the blast that threw him into the sea. His legs had been terribly damaged – almost severed – by the explosion, and he had drowned. Other survivors were pulled out of the water and rushed to hospital. There were more bodies too. It was not just Lord Mountbatten who was killed in the explosion, but one of his fourteen year old twin grandsons, Nicholas Knatchbull, and a local boat boy, the fifteen year old Paul Maxwell. When Paul's body was brought ashore, his father held him in his arms and found that he was still warm. One of the injured was the Dowager Lady Brabourne, a woman of eighty-two, and she died of her injuries the next day.

The Prince of Wales, who was abroad at the time of the murder, had a special fondness for Lord Mountbatten. He was severely shaken by the news and returned to England at once. Mountbatten's death was a severe shock to Britain as a whole, not least because he did not seem like an appropriate IRA target. He had long retired from any active military or diplomatic service; he was just an old man on a seaside holiday.

Lord Mountbatten was more properly Louis Francis Victor Albert Nicholas, first Earl Mountbatten of Burma, but known to his friends as Dickie. He was born in 1900, and was known until 1917 as Prince Louis Francis of Battenberg. The change of name happened as a response to anti-German feelings in Britain during the First World War, and the Battenbergs changed their family name when the British royal family changed its name from Saxe-Coburg-Gotha to Windsor. As well as being a distinguished and highly supportive member of the royal family, Lord Louis had a distinguished naval career too, especially in the Second World War. He served as Supreme Allied Commander-in-Chief in South-East Asia for the last two years of the war. He then became the last Viceroy of India, presiding over India's violent transition to independence. Towards the end of his life, Lord Mountbatten gave an interview. He said he did not mind the prospect of death but hoped he would have a peaceful one. No-one could have imagined that he was so soon to meet such a gratuitously violent and savage end.

The attack on the Mountbatten family raised many questions. One question related to the level of security surrounding the family holiday. The local police watched Classybawn Castle for the one month of the year that Lord Mountbatten spent there, though by implication not for the rest of the time. There were in any case only two policemen assigned to look after him, and no-one was watching the boat. The village of Mullagh-more is only twelve miles from the Northern Ireland border, in other words in a potentially sensitive area. It was also close to an area that was known to be in use as an IRA refuge.

Mountbatten's boat was left moored, complete-ly unguarded, in the public harbour in Mullaghmore. Lord Mountbatten insisted that the boat should be painted in a distinctive green colour, the colour of an admiral's barge. The colour never changed. Mountbatten liked the limelight and the media, and was happy to have a film made about his life in 1968. This showed him on one of his family holidays at Mullagh-more, including a sequence on the conspicuous green boat. The boat was moored in the harbour, and easily reached by stepping across just one other boat. The cabin was locked, but not the engine compartment. Obviously it was very easy for anyone to tamper with the boat at any time after dark, and install a time bomb or a radio-controlled bomb in the engine compartment – which is exactly what the IRA did.

There was never any doubt in anyone's mind that it was the IRA who were behind this assassination.

On the same day as the Mountbatten assas-sination, 27 August, 1979, there was another incident that was in its way even more horrific. The Mountbatten assassination took place on the west coast; the Warren Point ambush took place on the east coast, on Carlingford Lough, which marks the border between Northern Ireland and the Irish Republic. In the early afternoon, just after the news about Lord Mountbatten's death broke, two IRA men took up their position on a vantage point, overlooking Narrow Point on Carlingford Lough from the Irish Republic side. On the Northern Irish side was a stretch of dual carriageway that made an ideal ambush point.

At 3 p.m. A Troop, 2nd Parachute Battalion, left their base to drive to Newry, ready for a tour of duty patrolling the bandit country of South Armagh. There were thirty paratroopers in the convoy, travelling in several trucks. As the convoy came into view, at 4.40 p.m., it passed a hay-trailer in a lay-by; concealed inside the hay were five hundred pounds of explosives, which the button man detonated. The explosion knocked the rear truck sideways, killing outright seven of the nine soldiers inside.

It was a scene of carnage. A press photographer happened to be passing, stopped and took some photos of the immediate aftermath. A policeman ran past him shouting hysterically, 'Don't go in there. They're all dead! Get away!' There was a lot of smoke and ammunition exploding in the burning vehicles; the surviving soldiers were confused and naturally thought they had come under heavy fire. They saw some people on the opposite bank of the river and started returning the imaginary heavy fire. Luckily there were not many people about, but an English schoolboy who happened to be fishing on the river bank was killed.

A command post was set up by the nearby

castle gate-house, which the IRA had predicted; having studied British army tactics carefully, they knew that this would be their response. The paratroopers gathered at the gate-house, not noticing the milk churns stacked there. They were full of explosives. The paratroopers were running straight into an IRA trap. The IRA men watching the response patiently waited five, ten, fifteen minutes. Once they were all gathered at the gate-house, twenty minutes after the first explosion, with reinforcements already arriving by helicopter and truck, the IRA button man detonated the second bomb. It was even bigger than the first and killed another eleven men. The effect was horrific. The men were not just killed, they were blown to pieces. There were torsos, arms, legs, heads lying in the road, hanging in the trees, floating in the river. The press photographer was traumatized by what he saw; he never took another picture after that.

The IRA had succeeded in killing eighteen British soldiers and inflicting a major propaganda injury on the British government. The deliberate co-ordination of these two separate attacks was designed to make the maximum psychological and political impact. It was revenge for Bloody Sunday, punishment for the war crimes of the paratroopers. The day's events were a major boost to IRA morale. The effect on the Margaret Thatcher government of Britain was to entrench hostility to the IRA and its political objectives. The assassination was controversial, even within the IRA. There were those who saw Mountbatten's involvement in colonialism as Viceroy of India as sufficient justification in making him a target for political assassination. There were others who thought it ill-judged to kill an old man on holiday, and they were aware that killing him and his family in this way would look cowardly and unnecessary. The IRA had considered proposals to kill Mountbatten in previous years, but ruled them out.

Mountbatten and his security advisers should really have seen that the political tensions were increasing, and that by 1979 it was no longer appropriate to continue the Mullaghmore holidays. Mountbatten had indeed wondered about it, but was told by the security service that this was a risk that might reasonably be taken.

Who were the murderers? Clearly the IRA was to blame, but it was very difficult to prove which individuals were involved. Just before the Mullaghmore bomb went off, two IRA men were stopped nearby at a police check-point. The passenger seemed very calm, but the driver was extremely anxious. The policeman was uneasy about them and phoned his police station for support. The driver, who gave the name Pat Regan, was Francis McGurl, a local Republican sympathizer. The passenger was Thomas McMahon, an expert IRA bomber from Armagh.

They were both interviewed at the police station later. McMahon was tough, uncompromising and gave little away; questioning him would lead nowhere. McGurl, who was younger and weaker, broke down under twelve hours of questioning, admitted involvement but denied planting the bomb on Mountbatten's boat. It seemed he had kept watch while McMahon, the bomb expert, had installed the bomb by torchlight. Forensic scientists found specks of the distinctive green paint from Shadow V on McMahon's boots and traces of explosives on his clothing. There was enough forensic evidence to charge – and convict – Thomas McMahon.

The Warren Point ambush was harder to deal with because the incident straddled the border. Tons of dust and rubble were taken away for forensic analysis. The conclusion was that the explosives had come from South Armagh and were of the same type as used in earlier IRA bombs. Two men were stopped on the Irish Republic side of the Lough leaving the scene just after the ambush. They were Joe Brennan and Brendan Burns, both known to be members of the Provisional IRA. Burns was a particular friend of Thomas McMahon's, so it looked increasingly as if the two attacks were linked. Forensic evidence showed that Brennan and Burns had been lying down at the vantage point overlooking the scene of the ambush at Narrow Point.

There was no doubt in the authorities' minds that these were the two men responsible for detonating the Warren Point bombs, but the case against them stalled because of a lack of co-operation from Dublin. In Dublin, the matter was seen as politically explosive and likely to lead to big trouble in the Republic. In the end, the two men could only be charged with traffic offences.

There was a plot to capture the two men on a seven hundred yard stretch of road where it passed into Northern Ireland out again. This half-baked plan came to nothing when the look-out soldier at the beginning of this short stretch of road fell asleep and therefore failed to give warning that the car with Brennan and Burns inside was on its way. They got away.

Joe Brennan was convicted for another attack in 1994, but released early under the Good Friday Agreement. Brendan Burns blew himself up with his own bomb in 1988. McGurl was acquitted in 1980, and crushed to death by a tractor in 1995. Thomas McMahon was sentenced to life for the murder of Lord Mountbatten. In August 1998, as part of the Good Friday Agreement, which included an amnesty for political prisoners, the decision was made to release Thomas McMahon. It caused a great deal of political controversy in Britain. Conservative and Unionist politicians condemned the decision to release McMahon, believing it would be seen as an inappropriate concession. McMahon was a notorious killer, who had according to Democratic Unionist Peter Robinson 'carried out the foulest of deeds . . .' It was also seen as inappropriate to release potentially dangerous prisoners when the fighting had not entirely ceased.

But the father of the Irish boat boy killed in the explosion off Mullaghmore unexpectedly sup-ported the release of Thomas McMahon. In a statement showing remarkable generosity of spirit, John Maxwell said, 'Thomas McMahon has served his time and, if he is no longer a danger to society, then he should be released. Keeping him in prison will unfortunately not bring my son back. Peace is the imperative now, and we must look forward so that perhaps Paul's death and those of thousands of others from both sides of the political divide here will not have been entirely in vain'.

Peace is the imperative now.

PART SIX
CHILD VICTIMS

St William of Norwich

'and the blood lie'

ST WILLIAM OF Norwich was born in 1132. He is thought to have died on 22 March, 1144, though his body was not found until three days later, on Holy Saturday, the day between Good Friday and Easter Day. The timing of the boy's death in relation to the Church calendar held strong symbolic significance to the Norwich clerics, which helps to explain how both the boy and his death acquired mythic status in the Middle Ages.

The starting-point of the story is simple enough. A boy's body was found in Thorpe Wood near Norwich; it bore signs of a violent death. No-one touched it until the feast of Easter was over. On Easter Monday the corpse was buried where it was found. In the meantime a number of boys and young men had visited the spot, which means that the body could easily have been mischievously tampered with, and significant wounds added in imitation of the wounds of Christ. Jews were suspected of murdering the boy on account of the nature of the wounds.

The body was identified as that of a boy called William, a tanner's apprentice. It was later said that he had frequently visited the houses of certain Jews with his master, a fact which seemed to implicate the Jews.

William's uncle, who was the priest Godwin Stuart, opened the grave to be sure of the identification. The burial service was read and the corpse re-buried. A few days later the diocesan synod met under Bishop Eborard and Godwin Stuart took the opportunity to accuse the Jews of committing the murder of his nephew. He offered to prove his accusation by ordeal. The Jews of Norwich were the king's men and directly under the sheriff's protection; the sheriff had to point out that the Bishop had no jurisdiction over the Jews. No formal condemnation of the Jews was possible because of the strength of character and purpose of the Sheriff of Norwich, who conscientiously and strong-mindedly protected the Jewish community from Church interference.

The only thing Godwin Stuart was able to achieve was the 'translation' of his nephew's body from Thorpe Wood to the monk's cemetery. This was done on 24 April.

An attempt was made to develop a cult of St William, but it never really caught on. A couple of miracles were reported in the five years following his death. Probably the story of poor St William's (alleged) murder by the Jews would have faded and been forgotten, but for another murder in 1149.

The Jew Eleazar was murdered by the retainers of Sir Simon de Novers. The Jewish community demanded that the murderer should be punished. Bishop Turbe, who had succeeded to the see of Norwich in 1146, acted for the accused, who was his own tenant, and took the opportunity to bring up the murder of William five years before as a counter-charge. The case was tried before the King at Norwich, but had to be put off, according to the chronicler, because the Norwich Jews paid a large sum of money to the King and his councillors.

Bishop Turbe was keen to revive the blood lie, the dangerous myth that Jews performed human sacrifices, and this was his reason for bringing up the case of William. He was partly responsible for perpetuating the cult, as was Richard de Ferraiis, who became Prior in 1150, after the bones of St William were translated to the chapter-house. Thomas of Monmouth, the chronicler, became the saint's personal sacrist. Thomas had three visions in which he saw Herbert of Losinga, the cathedral's founder, ordering the boy's body to be exhumed and reburied in the chapter-house. This was done in 1151. The body was moved again, in 1154, to the apsidal chapel of the Holy Martyrs, now known as the Jesus Chapel.

Once the body was inside the cathedral, the miracles started to multiply, and St William's cult really took off. Thomas of Monmouth wrote down the story of what had happened to St William. This was now some long time after the boy's death, and Thomas seems to have believed whatever anybody told him. The result is a highly coloured and prejudiced version of events, and probably does not represent what really happened at all. But this, in summary, is what he said.

William had been in the habit of visiting the houses of Jews and was forbidden by his friends to have anything to do with them. On the Monday of Holy Week in 1144, he was lured away from his mother by a messenger who offered him a job in the archdeacon's kitchen. The next day William was seen with the messenger going into a Jew's house. William was never again seen alive.

On the Wednesday of that week, following a service in the synagogue, the Jews lacerated his forehead with thorns, and then crucified him. A Christian servant carrying some hot water ordered by her master saw, through a crack in the door, a boy tied to a post; she assumed the water was to cleanse the boy's body. Later she found a boy's belt in the room. Many years later she pointed out to Thomas the evidence of the martyrdom in the same room. A month after the boy's martyrdom, thorn-points were found on William's head and the wounds of the martyrdom in his hands, feet and side.

(Significantly, this servant's testimony was not produced until Thomas was preparing his book.)

On the Thursday, the Jews discussed how to dispose of the boy's body.

(If the Jews really had premeditated the killing as a human sacrifice, they would have planned this beforehand. If there is any truth at all in Thomas's story, the boy's death must have been an accident, possibly some rough horseplay as at

Inmestar. In AD 415 at Inmestar in Syria, some Jews in a drunken frolic accidentally killed a Christian child in a mock Crucifixion.)

On the Friday, Good Friday, Eleazar and another Jew carried the boy's body in a sack to Thorpe Wood.

(Eleazar was a cunning choice; he had just been murdered himself, and therefore in no position to defend himself. The charge also somehow vindicated his killing by a Christian.)

On the way to dispose of the body, they were met by a man called Aelward Ded, who saw what was inside the sack. The Jews bribed the sheriff (always Thomas's enemy, because he was the Jews' protector) *to extort an oath of silence from Aelward. It was only five years later, after the sheriff's death and when on his own death-bed, that Aelward told his story. (Here Thomas was explaining away the late emergence of corroboration for his story. The Jews may well have stumped up large amounts of money. They were besieged, frightened people, and would naturally have resorted to paying protection money if it meant they would be left alone for a while; even if these payments were made, they do not in any way prove their guilt.)*

The most destructive piece of 'evidence' that Thomas produced was the testimony of Theobald, who was a converted Jew and a monk at Norwich

Priory. Theobald told Thomas that in the ancient writings of the Jews it was said that they could only obtain their freedom and return to their fatherland if a certain ceremony was performed. This was the annual sacrifice, somewhere in the world, of a Christian; in the year 1144 it had been the turn of the Norwich Jews to perform this human sacrifice.

This was the infamous 'blood lie', which has been described as 'one of the most notable and disastrous lies of history'. It has been widely used, right through the last thousand years, as the justification for persecuting Jews everywhere and provides the backdrop to horrors such as the Holocaust. The idea of the blood lie may seem preposterous, but there were scholars in the late nineteenth century who were ready to support it by writing learned dissertations proving that throughout history the Jews have indulged in the sacrifice of children.

The cruelly prejudiced accusation that the Jews killed St William was, thanks to Thomas of Monmouth's lie, inevitably going to be repeated again and again in subsequent decades. There were five more such accusations in the twelfth century, fifteen in the thirteenth century, ten in the fourteenth, sixteen in the fifteenth, thirteen in the sixteenth, eight in the seventeenth, fifteen in the eighteenth and thirty-nine in the nineteenth century. The most remarkable aspect of the St William story is not that a case was fabricated against the Jews way back in the middle ages, but that the situation was far worse in the nineteenth and twentieth century. Instead of leaving medieval prejudices behind, we have exaggerated them.

What did happen to William? Unfortunately, the surviving evidence is so tainted by the prejudices and personal and professional agendas of medieval churchmen that it is impossible to tell. William was a boy apprentice, and as such he would have been exposed to both physical and sexual abuse from his master and by other, older workers; that was the common lot of apprentices. He may have died as a result of excessive punishment for inadequate work, or as a result of a campaign of bullying. The fact that the boy's trousers were missing would in any modern murder case be interpreted as a sure sign that he had been sexually molested, though this was evidently not inferred at the time. There is, sad to say, nothing exceptional about William's untimely death. Once the master, the bully or the sexual predator found that William was dead, removing the body to some deserted place well outside Norwich and dumping it there was an understandable act. It made it harder to connect the death and the killer – and it succeeded. One thing I am certain of, and that is that the death of St William of Norwich was nothing whatever to do with the Jews.

Little St Hugh of Lincoln

LITTLE ST HUGH of Lincoln was the son of a poor woman named Beatrice, who lived in Lincoln. Hugh was born in about 1246 and died at the age of nine or ten in 1255. His story has many parallels with that of William of Norwich, except that his body was found in the town rather than the countryside. He disappeared on 31 July, 1255, and his body was discovered a month later in a well on 29 August. He was said to have been crucified by the Jews of Lincoln. His body was found at the bottom of a well belonging to a Jew named Copin.

Copin was accused of enticing Hugh into his house. Then a large number of Jews gathered there to torture, scourge, crown with thorns and crucify the boy in imitation and mockery of the death of Christ. The story, as reported by the medieval chronicler, goes on to say that the earth refused to accept Hugh's body, and that was why it was thrown down a well. Some time after Hugh had gone missing, his friends told his mother they had seen him following the Jew. It was on going to Copin's house that she discovered her son's body.

Copin (or Jopin) confessed the crime when

under threat of torture, and stated that it was a Jewish custom to crucify a boy once a year. Both the confession and the annual child sacrifice will have been put into Copin's mouth by his torturers.

A tomb was built for the boy who died the death of Christ, and miracles were claimed by those who prayed there. The canons of Lincoln translated the body from the parish church where he was first buried, burying it with great pomp in Lincoln Cathedral. A feast of Little St Hugh was instigated on 27 July. Copin himself was made to suffer a cruel death; the confession under threat of torture had done the poor man no good at all. But that might have been the end of the story, but for a series of external events.

About six months before the death of St Hugh, Henry III had sold his right to tax the Jews to his brother, Richard of Cornwall. Having lost this source of revenue, Henry III decided that he would be eligible for the Jews' money if they were convicted of crimes. As a result, the authorities were encouraged to convict Jews. The number of charges brought against Jews was therefore not just a result of a surge of anti-Jewish feeling following the death of Little St Hugh of Lincoln; it was a result of a shift in fiscal policy. In the wake of all this, ninety Jews were thrown into prison in London, presumably on trumped-up charges. The London Jews were found guilty and condemned to death, but they were both released and pardoned when they agreed to pay large fines. Eighteen more Jews were hanged in Lincoln as well. This was the first time the death sentence was given for ritual murder by a civil government. The King was able to confiscate their property too. In this way Henry III kept his coffers filled – it was nothing to do with justice or the prevention of crime.

The 'martyrdom' of St Hugh became a popular theme for ballads – both poems and folk songs – in the middle ages. Little St Hugh entered the realm of popular culture. As the story spread, so the shrine of Little St Hugh became a focus for pilgrimage. Chaucer refers to Hugh of Lincoln in his *Canterbury Tales*. One of the popular ballads was recorded in the eighteenth century:

> She's led him in through ae dark door,
> And sae has she thro' nine;
> She's laid him on a dressing-table,
> And stickit him like a swine;
> And first came out the thick, thick blood,
> And syne came out the thin;
> And syne came out the bonny heart's blood,
> Then was nae mair within;
> She's row'd him in a cake o' lead,
> Bade him lie still and sleep;
> She's thrown him in Our Lady's draw-well,
> Was fifty fathom deep.

The untruths and internal inconsistencies here are all too obvious, but the ballad does show how a murder story has its own engine, driving it further and further from the circumstances of the actual crime. Cecil Sharp, who collected some versions of the ballad, commented that the charge against the Jews was 'groundless and malicious'.

The cult of St Hugh continued even into the early twentieth century, when a new well was constructed in the former Jewish quarter of the city and unscrupulously advertized as the well in which St Hugh's body was found.

As with the death of St William, it is very difficult to know whether there was any truth in the medieval account of events. We can be sure that Hugh went missing and was eventually found dead. It is quite possible that he was found dead in the bottom of a well. But that is quite a common accidental death among children. Children are often fascinated by wells, liking to peer down them and drop stones down into the water. They have often died as a result of leaning too far and falling in. If they survive the fall, there is usually no way of climbing out. The well may even have been in the garden of a Jew, but that does not incriminate the Jew Copin.

The problem is doubled by the clear evidence in the chronicler's account that accusations were brought against Jews for the sake of extorting money from them.

The story of Little St Hugh is another example of the blood lie levelled at the Jews repeatedly during the middle ages – and later. Beside the site of the gothic shrine of Little St Hugh in Lincoln Cathedral is a plaque that tells the important part of the story:

Trumped-up stories of ritual murders of Christian boys by Jewish communities were common throughout Europe during the Middle Ages and even much later. These fictions cost many innocent Jews their lives. Lincoln had its own legend, and the alleged victim was buried in the Cathedral in the year 1255. Such stories do not redound to the credit of Christendom, and so we pray;

Lord, forgive what we have been,
Amend what we are,
And direct what we shall be.'

Sarah and Sally Metyard

SARAH METYARD WAS a milliner in Bruton Street, Hanover Square in London. Sally Metyard was her daughter and assistant. In 1758, Sarah Metyard had five apprentice girls. They had come to her from different workhouses. Among the unfortunate five apprentices were Anne Naylor and her sister.

Anne Naylor was a weak girl, physically unable to do much work, and this made her a target for some ferocious bullying by Sarah Metyard and her daughter. Their cruelty to her caused her to run away, but she was brought back and shut in an upper room, kept alive on only bread and water. She saw an opportunity to escape, and managed to get out into the street. She ran to a milk-carrier and begged for help. She feared the women would kill her. Sarah Metyard's daughter Sally came out and dragged her back into the house. She was seized by the older woman, who held her down while the younger woman beat her with a broom handle.

Then they imprisoned Anne in a back room, tying her to the door in such a way that she could not sit or lie down. They left her like this for three days, though they did allow her to go to bed in the normal way at night – an odd concession, given the level of cruelty to which they were subjecting her. They gave her no food at all for three days. While Anne Naylor was imprisoned and tortured in this way, the other apprentices were made to work in an adjoining room, so that they could see what would happen to them if they were disobedient. They were forbidden to offer her any kind of help.

On the fourth day, ill, exhausted and starving, poor Anne Naylor's speech faltered and she died, still strung up on the door. The whole weight of her body was held up by the ropes that tied her to the door. She could not fall, even when dead. She just hung there, as if crucified. The apprentices called out to the younger woman, 'Miss Sally, Miss Sally! Nanny does not move!'

Sally Morgan came up to see. 'If she does not move, I will make her!' Then she took off one of her shoes and hit the dead girl over the head with the heel. Sally Morgan could see no sign of life, called her mother and had the girl cut down. Sarah Metyard and her daughter then ordered the apprentices to go downstairs while they moved the girl's body into the garret.

They told the girls that Nanny had had a fit but had now recovered; they had locked her in the garret in case she should run away again. To make it seem as if all was relatively well, the younger woman took a plate of meat up at midday, saying it was for Nanny's dinner.

On the fourth day after the murder, the two

women locked the body in a box, left the garret door open and the street door ajar. Then they set up a little charade, sending one of the apprentices up to call Nanny down to dinner, and to tell her that if she promised to behave well in future she would not be locked up any more. The girl came back downstairs with the news that Nanny was not there. After a show of searching the house, the two women came to the conclusion that Anne Naylor had run away once more.

The two women had not reckoned on Anne Naylor's sister, though. The little girl mentioned to a lodger in the Metyard household that was sure her sister was dead. Some of her clothes were still in the garret and she would not have run away without them. The little girl's confidence was not respected, and the two women were furious that they might be given away. They murdered her and hid her body, like her sister's.

Anne Naylor's body was kept in the box for two months. For all of that time the garret was kept locked, because the smell of the decaying body would give them away. In fact the smell became so penetrating and over-powering that the women decided to get rid of the body altogether. On Christmas Eve, they cut Anne Naylor's body up. The head and trunk were tied up in one piece of cloth, and the arms and legs in another. One hand was kept to one side. It had one finger missing, which might make it recognizable as the hand of Anne Naylor; the two women burnt it straight away.

The plan was to burn the entire body, bit by

bit, but Sarah Metyard and her daughter were afraid the smell would arouse suspicion. Instead, they did something far riskier, which was to take the body parts to Chick Lane and tried to throw them over the wall into the public sewer, an open drain. They found that too difficult, and so just left them in the mud by the drain.

It was only a matter of hours before the watchman found the parts of Anne Naylor's body and reported his discovery to the constable. They were examined by the coroner, Mr Umfreville, but he assumed they were parts of a corpse illegally exhumed from a churchyard by resurrection men and took no further action. He did not suspect a murder.

Four years passed, and Sarah Metyard and her daughter must have begun to believe that they had got away with the two murders. There was a new difficulty now. There were now continual quarrels and fights between the mother and the daughter. The mother thought she could remain in control by continuing to beat her daughter, but the daughter, now older and more assertive, naturally had other ideas. She tried threatening suicide to stop her mother's ill-treatment; she then threatened to inform on her mother as a murderer, which is what she did. She must later have regretted it.

At last it came out, and both the mother and the daughter were imprisoned. At their trial, both were sentenced to be executed the following Monday and their bodies dissected.

Mrs Metyard was in a fit when she was put in

the cart to take her to her execution, and just lay on the floor of the cart. When the cart reached the scaffold, she was still unconscious, and was – very unusually – hanged in that state. The daughter, meanwhile, wept incessantly until she was dead. After being left to hang for an hour, the bodies were taken to Surgeons' Hall, where they were put on view to a curious public before being dissected.

William Andrew Horne

'justice delayed'

WILLIAM ANDREW HORNE'S father was a scholar, an educated man who tried in vain to educate his son. William was interested only in pleasure and his indulgent father decided to allow the youth his head. William acquired horse and hounds and ended up becoming a classic dissolute country squire.

He seduced several girls, two of whom were his mother's servants. Another was the daughter of a local farmer; she died, it was said, as a result of this unhappy liaison. William Horne had two illegitimate daughters, one of whom lived to the age of fifteen; the other was still living in 1759 and might have been respectably married if only Horne had given her financial support, but he refused to give her anything. He was miserly.

But these were not the only vices. William Horne also had sex with his own sister, who gave birth to his son in February 1724. Horne told his brother Charles three days later, at ten o'clock at night, that they must take a ride. He then put the new-born baby in a bag and mounted his horse. William and Charles Horne rode together to Annesley in Nottinghamshire, taking it in turns to carry the bag. When they got near Annesley,

William dismounted and asked Charles if the baby was still alive. Charles said it was. William took it and told his brother to wait until he came back. When he returned, Charles asked him what he had done with the baby. William said he had put it behind a haystack and covered it with hay.

The following morning, after a very cold night, the child was found dead.

Not long after this incident the two brothers quarrelled, and Charles told their father what had happened. The father probably understood all too well that both brothers would hang for what William had done, and swore Charles to secrecy. Charles kept his word until the old man's death; he lived to the age of one hundred and two, dying in 1747.

William Horne had not treated his brother Charles well. Now his severity would be rewarded. After their father's death, Charles had some business to attend to with Mr Cooke, a solicitor in Derby, and decided to tell him of the infanticide many years before, asking his advice. The lawyer told him to go to a Justice of the Peace and make a full statement about the whole affair. Charles Horne then went as advised to a magistrate and told him about it, but the magistrate hesitated to take action on the matter, saying there was a danger that half the family might be hanged for it; since it had happened so long ago, surely it would be better to let it rest.

So, in spite of Charles Horne having told three other people, his father, a lawyer and a magistrate, about the infanticide it remained a close secret.

In 1754 Charles Horne became seriously ill and called in a Mr White of Ripley. Charles assumed he was about to die and so he unburdened himself to Mr White and asked his advice. Mr White did not want to give Charles Horne advice on the matter; he did not want to know about it; he did not want to get involved at all. Charles recovered within a few days. Mr White was surprised to see him looking so well and Charles said he had begun to recover as soon as he had told him about the death of the baby.

Some time after this, William Horne, the bumpkin squire, quarrelled with a man named Roe at an inn regarding the killing of game. In the heat of the argument, Roe called Horne an 'incestuous old dog'. Horne unwisely prosecuted Roe for libel in the Ecclesiastical Court at Lichfield and made a dangerous enemy. Roe lost his case and was forced to pay all the legal costs. Roe swore revenge and heard a second-hand version of the not-so-close secret about the dead child which he thought he could use against William Horne. He heard that Charles Horne had mentioned something along the lines of his brother having starved an illegitimate child to death.

Roe went off to a magistrate in Derbyshire and obtained a warrant. Charles was due to appear before the magistrate the following day. William heard about this and was worried that Charles was going to do him damage. William sent for Charles and told him he would (now) be his friend if he would deny the story about the child. Charles refused to do this unless William gave him five pounds, a startlingly small sum in the circumstances, in which case he would go straight to Liverpool and leave the country. It was, in fact, a very generous offer on Charles's part, but William was too miserly to agree to part with five pounds to save his own life.

Charles was examined by magistrates in Derbyshire, but they did not want to pursue the case. Then Roe applied to a Justice of the Peace in Nottinghamshire; this man issued a warrant for William Horne to be taken into custody. A constable went from Annesley with Mr Roe to William Horne's house. They found that Horne was not there. They searched the house, but there was no sign of him. They made a second search. This time they noticed something they had not noticed before – a large linen chest. They asked Mrs Horne what was in it. She said it was full of table and bed linen. Roe wanted to see inside and was all for breaking it open, but Mrs Horne unlocked it for him, presumably not wanting to see her furniture damaged. As soon as it was opened, William Horne popped up out of it like a Jack-in-the-Box.

He said, 'It is a sad thing to hang me, for my brother Charles is as bad as myself, and he cannot hang me without hanging himself.'

William Horne was taken into custody. Two Justices of the Peace committed him for trial at the next assizes. He had not been in prison very long when he applied for a writ of Habeas Corpus. On the strength of this application he was taken to London, where his counsel argued that he should be allowed bail, but the judges disagreed and he was sent to Nottingham Gaol.

On 10 August 1759 he was tried before Lord Chief Baron Parker. His trial lasted nine hours, at the end of which he was found guilty and sentenced to death. He was hanged just after his 75th birthday, for a murder he had committed twenty-five years before.

Captain John Sutherland

'and the murder of a cabin boy'

DURING THE NAPOLEONIC Wars, a British transport ship, *The Friends*, was anchored in the Tagus estuary about a mile downstream from Lisbon, within sight of the beautiful white Belem Tower. It was 5 November, 1808. During the day both the captain and the mate were ashore along with the other two crew members. The only people left on board were the captain's servants, a 13-year-old cabin boy called William Richardson, and a negro called Jack Thompson. It was Jack Thompson who was to be the principal witness at the trial, though even he was unable to explain what happened.

At about eight o'clock in the evening, the captain came back on board, went to his cabin and called the cabin boy down. A few minutes later, the cabin boy went back up on deck and told Jack Thompson the captain wanted to speak to him. The captain wanted to know from Jack how they were to manage the watch that night, given that the mate and the other two seamen were staying ashore. Jack Thompson volunteered to keep watch until twelve o'clock. The captain agreed to this and asked Jack to be sure to call him at twelve, implying that he would take over the next watch himself. Meanwhile, Jack was to let him know if any ship came alongside.

The captain then asked Jack Thompson to send William Richardson down to him, which he did. It is not known what went wrong in the next few minutes. There seems to have been no build up to the violence that erupted at all, but only about five minutes after the cabin boy entered the captain's cabin, Jack Thompson heard the boy shouting his name, as if calling for help. Unfortunately, Jack did not go down straight away, as he assumed the captain was 'only beating the boy', which was not unusual. If he had gone down immediately, he might have saved the boy's life. But the boy went on calling out, so Jack at last went down to see what was happening.

Jack Thompson saw William Richardson lying wounded on the floor and Captain Sutherland standing over him waving a dagger. The cabin boy was obviously relieved that Jack Thompson had come in, and said straight away, 'Jack Thompson, look here. Captain Sutherland has stabbed me.' The boy lifted his shirt and showed him a terrible wound in his abdomen, near the groin, and his intestines were falling out. Jack Thompson turned to leave the cabin with the idea of fetching medical help for the boy, and Captain Sutherland said, 'Jack, I know I have done wrong.' Rushing out, Jack called back, 'I know very well you have.'

Up on deck, Jack called out to the next ship, another transport called the Elizabeth, to try to get assistance. There was apparently no surgeon on the Elizabeth. Jack then went ashore with Captain Sutherland to find a surgeon. They met a couple of soldiers and told them what had happened, and then returned to the ship. When they got there they found that two surgeons had already tended the cabin boy, dressed his wound and put him to bed.

The next morning, William Richardson, Captain Sutherland and Jack Thompson were all transferred to another ship, the *Audacious*. *The Friends'* mate had meanwhile gone back on board and heard the story about the attack on the cabin boy. He had asked Captain Sutherland what he had been doing with the dagger. Sutherland said that he would never hurt anyone else with it, and threw the weapon into the sea.

When all three were on the *Audacious*, the murderer, his witness and his still-living victim, Jack Thompson heard Captain Sutherland apologizing to the boy. He was very sorry for what he had done, and said so more than once.

William Richardson died of his wound nine days later.

It was not until 22 June, 1809, seven months later, that Captain Sutherland was brought to trial. Sutherland was tried at the Admiralty Sessions before Sir William Scott and Sir Nash Grose, indicted for the wilful murder of William Richardson. Although the incident had taken place in Portuguese waters, it had taken place on a British ship and was therefore still under the jurisdiction of the Admiralty. Several witnesses were called, but the main one was Jack Thompson.

It took the jury very little time to agree a guilty verdict, and Sir William Scott passed sentence of death. Sutherland was to be hanged at Execution Dock in London and his body afterwards handed over to the surgeons for dissection. Sutherland was overcome after the sentence was passed. He had a wife and five children to consider, as well as his own awful fate. He was close to fainting and had to be helped away by attendants.

It is still not clear what happened in the captain's cabin that could have led to an armed attack on a defenceless boy. It appears to have been an act of sadistic and unprovoked violence without any justification at all.

Esther Hibner
(mother & daughter) and Ann Robinson

THE VICTIM IN this case was Frances Colpitt, a ten-year-old pauper. This poor little girl was apprenticed to Esther Hibner, who lived at Platt Terrace, Pancras Road in London. The apprenticeship, which started in April 1828, was to learn the making of tambour-work (embroidery).

It was in the October of 1828, after Frances had been working for the Hibners for six months, that the ill-treatment started. It was not just Frances who suffered, but the other children in the Hibners' care as well.

They were kept short of food, compelled to get up and start working at three in the morning, kept working until eleven at night, and sometimes later. They were given no beds, but made to sleep on the floor with only an old rug to cover them at night. They were allowed no exercise. The breakfast they were given consisted of a slice of bread and a cup of milk; after that they were given no more food all day. Sometimes Esther Hibner declared that Frances and the other children had not earned their breakfast. Then they were given a few potatoes at midday, and afterwards nothing more until the next day. They were given meat to eat only once a fortnight. On Sundays they were locked in the kitchen all day.

This cruel regime took a terrible toll of the children, and three of them died as a result of it.

Frances Colpitt was reduced to a very low state. She had sores on her feet and abscesses on her lungs, and it was the bursting of an abscess on the lung that led to her death. Esther Hibner's daughter, also called Esther, had taken Frances from her work, knocked her to the ground, picked her up and knocked her down again. When Esther Hibner senior was told that Frances was lying 'ill' in the work room, instead of showing any concern for her welfare and making sure she was allowed to recover, she said, 'Let her lie there'.

After that, Frances could scarcely crawl about the house. Esther junior told her to clean the stairs. Frances tried to do this, but collapsed in a state of exhaustion. For disobeying her order, Esther beat her with a cane and then made her carry on cleaning the stairs. It emerged at the trial that both Esther Hibner junior and Esther Hibner senior had caned Frances, and that Ann Robinson had caned her too.

A doctor attended Frances Colpitt both before and after she died. He found large sores on Frances' feet. Her toes were 'mortifying' and falling off. After her death, Frances Colpitt's body was examined closely and found to be in a dreadful state as a result of sustained maltreatment by the Hibners and Ann Robinson.

At the trial of the three people who had abused Frances Colpitt, the apprentices themselves gave evidence of the cruel regime they had been subjected to. Mrs Hibner said she would leave her defence in the hands of her daughter. The daughter said the apprentices had lied about the way they were treated. Ann Robinson took the same line of defence – that the apprentices were lying. She also claimed she had less responsibility for what happened to the apprentices, as she was employed by the Hibners and went home every night at eight.

The jury acquitted Ann Robinson and Esther Hibner junior, but found Esther Hibner senior guilty. She was sentenced to death and ordered to be executed the following Monday. Meanwhile the other two prisoners were to be tried for assault on Frances Colpitt.

Throughout the trial, Esther Hibner senior showed no remorse for what she had done and no fear of what might happen as a result. When she was accused of murdering another apprentice, she pleaded not guilty with all the firmness of a clear conscience. She had evidently persuaded herself that she was not responsible for the children's deaths. Once a verdict of guilty had been reached on Frances Colpitt's murder, it was decided not to proceed on the charge relating to the other murder; Esther Hibner could after all only be hanged once.

Esther Hibner was taken to the condemned cell, where she became aggressive and violent. She told the prison governor, Mr Wontner, that she would not be hanged; he had other ideas. She met her daughter for the last time the day before her execution. Afterwards she went out into the yard. The warder thought there was something suspicious about her behaviour, and sent someone after her to watch what she was doing. In the meantime, Esther Hibner had made an attempt to cut her own throat, though she was not fatally wounded. She was bandaged up, but then needed to be confined in a strait-jacket to stop her from ripping the bandage off. She told Mr Wontner that she had not attempted suicide; she was only hoping to gain a few extra days of life. But it made no difference. The execution date remained fixed for the next day.

The prison chaplain, Mr Cotton, spent a lot of time with Esther Hibner, but to no avail. She said she knew enough of the Bible already. At eight o'clock on the Monday morning, regardless of the cut throat, Esther Hibner was taken out to be hanged. She looked terrible. She wore a white cap, and a white bed gown over a black gown; together with her sallow complexion the outfit made her look very unearthly. She refused to walk to her death, so two men had to carry her. When she arrived at the scaffold, she was greeted by a crowd of yelling women. After her death, which seemed to be instant, her body was handed to the surgeons for dissection.

On the same day, the younger Esther Hibner and Ann Robinson were tried for their many death-dealing assaults on Frances Colpitt and the other apprentices. Their sentences – twelve and four months in prison – seem startlingly and disproportionately lenient by comparison with the punishment visited on the elder Esther Hibner.

John Bell

'the boy who killed for nine shillings'

JOHN BELL WAS an unusual murderer in two ways. He was only fourteen years old (his victim was only thirteen), and he does not seem to have minded about being hanged. The unfortunate victim was Richard Taylor, the son of a poor tallow-chandler who lived at Stroud in Kent. Richard was described as a having a peculiar intelligence and an amiable disposition.

On 4 March, 1831, Richard Taylor was sent on an errand. He was to go to Aylesford to collect an amount of money for his father; it was his weekly parish allowance of nine shillings – a kind of social security. The errand was a regular one and on that account more dangerous; people could observe a pattern in the journey and plan an ambush accordingly. The boy set off in a sou'wester with a kerchief tied round his neck, a shirt, a blue jacket and waistcoat, brown trousers, shoes and stockings. He also asked his father to lend him a knife so that he could cut a bow and arrow on his way home.

Richard arrived safely at Aylesford, where he met Mr Cutbath. Cutbath was the relieving officer of the parish, and he gave Richard the usual nine shillings. The boy concealed the money in the way he had been shown by his father. He put it into a little bag and held it in the palm of his hand and covered it by pulling a mitten over it. Mr Cutbath watched him hide the money in this way before he set off on the return journey.

Usually Richard arrived back home at about three o'clock in the afternoon, but on 4 March, 1831 he did not return. When night fell, Mr and Mrs Taylor became alarmed. When the boy had still not come back in the morning, Mr Taylor decided to set off for Aylesford to find out what had happened. He discovered when he got there that Richard had indeed been there and collected the money but he was unable to find out what had happened to him after that. There was just no sign of the boy.

Days passed.

On 11 May, Richard was found. A man by the name of Izzard was following a path through a wood about two miles from Rochester, some distance from the public highway, when he found the boy lying dead in a ditch. Murdered for nine shillings. The mitten had been cut from his left hand and his clothes were all pulled about as if he had fought for his life. The body was badly decomposed, but it was still obvious from the bloodstains on the shirt, coat and neckerchief that he had had his throat cut. The wound made in his throat by a sharp-pointed weapon could still be seen. The woodland area was searched and an ordinary white horn-handled knife was found nearby; it looked as if that had been used for the murder.

The knife gave some clues as to the identity of the murderer, and the Bell family was suspected. The authorities took the father and his two sons, John aged fourteen and James aged eleven, into custody. These three lived in the poorhouse right next to the place where the murder was carried out. The constable discovered that the knife found in the wood belonged to the boy, John Bell. This pointed to him at least being involved in the murder.

The murder was investigated in front of magistrates in Rochester. The result was that the two boys were both implicated. After that it was seen to be necessary to exhume the body of Richard Taylor. For some reason the boy had been buried without his body having been searched; this was a mistake and it was clear that a search was essential. The authorities decided to take the two Bell boys to the graveyard to witness the exhumation, in order to see what effect this would have on them. The older boy maintained a sullen silence. When the younger boy was told to get down into the grave and search the dead boy's pockets, he did so cheerfully, rooting about until he produced the knife Mr Taylor had lent Richard when setting off for Aylesford. This was the only item found on Richard's body, so robbery must have been the motive for the murder.

The two boys were then questioned again in front of the magistrates. This time the younger boy admitted that he and his brother had together conspired to kill Richard Taylor. John had waylaid Richard in the wood, while he, James, had kept watch at the edge of the wood. The younger boy's version of events was accepted. The father was released, although there was a strong suspicion that he was an accessory after the fact. It was just the older boy who was committed for trial for murder, though then younger boy was clearly just as depraved. James Bell's statement revealed that they had been planning to kill Richard Taylor for a long time, ever since he had freely told them why he so frequently made this journey from Stroud to Aylesford and back. They would have killed him sooner or later. John had given him one shilling and sixpence as his share of the proceeds.

As he was being taken to Maidstone for his trial, John Bell pointed out a pond where he had washed Richard Taylor's blood off his hands on his way home after the murder. He also pointed out to the constable, from the road, the opening in the wood that led to the place where the murder was known to have been committed, and where Richard's body was found. 'That's where I killed the poor boy.' Then he said, 'He is better off than I am now, don't you think he is, sir?' The constable readily agreed with him. He probably guessed the boy would hang.

The trial of the fourteen year old John Bell on 29 July, 1831 was a strange affair. John Bell himself seemed completely detached and indifferent. He seemed to have no apprehension of the terrible consequences of the proceedings. He remained firm throughout. Whether this was due to bravery – the British stiff upper lip – or lack of imagination or sheer stupidity is impossible to tell. The judge gave an emotional address leading up to the sentence of death, yet the boy showed no emotion. The only point in the proceedings where he showed any emotion at all was when it was revealed that his body would be handed over to the surgeons in Rochester for dissection.

There was no reprieve for John Bell on account of his age, no mercy shown. But then, he had shown none to Richard Taylor, whom he had knowingly killed for just nine shillings. He was hanged at Maidstone at 11.30 a.m. on 1 August, 1831.

Revd Thomas Hunter

'revenge on the tell-tales'

THOMAS HUNTER WAS born in Fifeshire, Scotland, the son of a wealthy farmer. Thomas Hunter was educated at the University of St Andrews, where he took his Master of Arts degree. It was customary in the 17th century for young graduates intending to take holy orders to spend a year or two acting as tutors to the children of rich families. This was partly due to the need to wait for an appropriate benefice. While the young graduates performed this role as tutors they were often called chaplains.

It was in this state, or station, that Thomas Hunter lived as chaplain in the household of a rich merchant called Mr Gordon. Mr Gordon was a bailey (or alderman) of Edinburgh. Mr Gordon had a wife, two sons and a daughter. Also in his household were a maid who attended Mrs Gordon and her daughter, some clerks and household servants. Hunter was to be responsible for educating Mr Gordon's sons. The Gordons were to begin with well pleased with Thomas Hunter, seeing him as a highly intelligent and well-meaning young man, a young man with a good heart.

Hunter then became emotionally and sexually

involved with the governess. Their liaison continued for some time without the family being aware of it. Generally Hunter and the girl made love when Mr and Mrs Gordon were out. On one occasion they were together in Hunter's room and they forgot to lock the door. The children by chance came into the room and found them locked in an embrace. The children were young, the oldest was only ten, and probably did not understand what they had seen. Hunter assumed that they would say nothing, simply because they would not know what to say.

Unfortunately, when the parents returned and the family were at supper together, the children said just enough about what they had seen in Hunter's room to leave no doubt in Mr and Mrs Gordon's minds as to what Hunter and the governess had been doing. The governess was dismissed the following day. Hunter, rather surprisingly, was forgiven, after he made a full apology for his misbehaviour and undertook never to do anything like it again. The incident was written off by Mr Gordon as *folie de jeunesse*, and Hunter was kept on.

Instead of being grateful to Mr Gordon for giving him a second chance, Thomas Hunter wanted revenge on him. He wanted to hurt Gordon. He also wanted to punish the children who had betrayed him. He decided to murder them, but he would have to wait for a suitable opportunity. When the weather was fine, he used to walk across the fields with the two boys for an hour before lunch, and the boys' sister usually went too. That would be the time when he would kill them – all three of them.

Just before the murder, in mid-August, 1700, the Gordons were staying at their country house just outside Edinburgh. Mr and Mrs Gordon were invited to lunch in Edinburgh, and they were due to set off at just about the time when Hunter usually set off on his midday walk with the children. Mrs Gordon was keen that all the children should go with them into the city, but Mr Gordon was adamant that they should not, and he would only agree to take the daughter. The boys must stay with Hunter. In this way, Hunter's original plan to kill all three children was frustrated, but he was still going to kill two of them.

After Mr and Mrs Gordon had set off, Hunter took the boys into the fields and sat down as if he was preparing to relax on the grass. He sharpened his knife as if passing the time while the two boys ran about catching butterflies and picking wild flowers. Then he called the boys to him to explain to them why he was going to kill them. He rebuked them for telling their parents what they had seen in his room and told them they must die for it. The boys were terrified and tried to run away from him, but they were small and he was able to catch them quite easily. He held one down with his knee while he cut the other's throat. Then he cut the second boy's throat.

Thomas Hunter had not even taken the precaution of committing the murders in a private, secluded place. The field he had chosen was within half a mile of Edinburgh's Castle Rock, a spot where he might easily be seen. As it happened, a man was walking on the Castle Rock, and he witnessed the terrible double murder from that vantage point. In a state of shock, he called out to some other people in the area and they ran with him to the place where the two boys lay dead.

Hunter had run to the bank of a nearby river, intending to leap in and drown himself. The group of people who had run down from the Castle caught up with him there and recognized him as the Gordons' chaplain. They decided that one of them should contact Mr and Mrs Gordon to tell them the awful news about what had happened. The Gordons were distraught.

Old Scottish law has it that 'if a murderer should be taken with the blood of the murdered person upon his clothes, he should be prosecuted in the Sheriff's Court and executed within three days after the commission of the fact'. Hunter was accordingly dealt with in unusual haste. He was committed to prison immediately and chained down to the floor all night. The following day the sheriff ordered a jury to assemble; they ordered that Hunter should stand trial. Hunter pleaded guilty, and worsened his already hopeless case, if that were possible, by expressing regret that he had not killed Mr Gordon's daughter as well as his sons. The sheriff then passed sentence that Hunter should be executed the very next day on the spot where he had committed the murders. He was also sentenced to have his right hand cut off at the wrist with a hatchet. He was to be hanged by being drawn up to the gibbet by a rope. After his death, he was to be hung in chains on the road between Edinburgh and Leith, with the murder weapon stuck through his severed hand and mounted over his head.

Thomas Hunter was executed in this barbaric way, a revenge execution in every way appropriate to Hunter's barbaric revenge double-murder, on 22 August, 1700.

Constance Kent

'the dead baby in the privy'

IN JUNE 1860, Constance Kent, who was then
sixteen, and her younger brother William Kent
were back from school for their summer holiday.
Their home was Road Hill House in the village of
Road (now spelt Rode) on the border of Wiltshire
and Somerset, not far from Frome. Constance's
father, Samuel Kent, had several daughters and a
new wife and since he was socially ambitious he
decided it would be a good idea to move close to
Bath, which was still a fashionable place where
his daughters might be seen and pick up good
husbands. Road Hill House seemed ideal. It was
eight miles from Bath. It was big, with stables, a
fine garden and a shrubbery and pleasant views
across fields and lanes.

The Kent household was affluent, respectable,
but rigidly so, and not everyone in it was happy.
Constance was profoundly unhappy. The Kents
had a new baby, Francis Saville Kent, and their
affection for him completely displaced any feeling
they might have had for Constance, who became
acutely jealous of Saville.

On 29 June, 1860, Saville had been put to bed
early. He slept soundly because he been unable

to sleep during the day; the chimneys had been swept that day. The Kents kept two dogs. One was allowed to roam about inside the house. The other was kept chained in the yard. As was his usual custom, Mr Kent went out into the yard at 10 p.m. to feed the outside dog. Constance and William went to bed at the same time, as did Mary Anne and Elizabeth their older sisters. Mr and Mrs Kent stayed up for about another hour talking before they too went to bed.

Mr and Mrs Kent slept right through that night without being disturbed at all. Mrs Kent woke at dawn when she thought she heard a sound like a drawing room window being opened. During the night, a man fishing in the River Frome heard a dog barking. The village constable heard the dog bark too, and saw a light in a downstairs window and in the nursery window. Elizabeth Gough, the children's nurse, woke up at 5 o'clock, to see that the baby Saville was not in his cot. She noticed that the sheets had been put back neatly, so she assumed Saville had been taken by his mother and that he was safely in his mother's room. She fell asleep, not thinking anything was wrong.

Mrs Kent was pregnant, so when Elizabeth Gough got up at 7 o'clock and went to Mrs Kent's room and got no answer to her gentle knock she returned unconcerned to her own room and read her Bible. An hour later the assistant nurse arrived, and Elizabeth Gough went back to Mrs Kent's room. Saville was not there, and Mrs Kent was angry with her for thinking that she was well enough to go wandering round the house at night looking for children. Miss Gough was now worried. She had no idea where the baby was. She went to the children and asked them if they knew what had happened to Saville. None of them knew anything. Miss Gough was getting frightened. She asked Sarah Cox, the parlour maid, if she had seen Saville. She had not seen Saville, but she had found the drawing room window open.

At this point Elizabeth Gough raised the alarm. The boot boy was sent to the parish constable, then to the village constable, who always insisted that the parish constable should attend because the parish was in Wiltshire and the village in Somerset. The two policemen arrived and came to the conclusion that baby Saville Kent had been kidnapped. The policemen advised Mr Kent that the matter should be reported to the Wiltshire police; Mr Kent rode off at once to Southwick, a short distance along the Trowbridge road, to report the crime.

Meanwhile, the villagers organized a search. They disliked the Kents, and freely admitted it. Samuel Kent was brusque and high-handed. He did not like the idea of being overlooked by the row of cottages near his house, and had had a high fence erected to block their view. He had also insisted on having sole fishing rights to a particularly rich stretch of the river. The Kents' unpopularity was underlined by the behaviour of the village children, who jeered at the Kent children and openly taunted them. Even so, the plight of a lost baby touched the villagers and they set about trying to find it. Two of them, William Nutt and Thomas Benger, began searching the grounds of the Kents' house. Constance had once run away dressed as a boy, first cutting her hair and leaving her locks in an old privy in the shrubbery. Nutt and Benger went there and found an ominous pool of blood on the floor, but no splashes on the seat. They could not see down into the cess-pit, so Nutt went off to get a lamp. Benger's eyes gradually became accustomed to the dark and he saw something pale. He picked it up and found it was a blanket, heavily bloodstained. Nutt came back with a candle. By its light they saw the baby, resting on a splashboard under the seat; the blanket had been resting on the baby. The water was later drained from the cess-pit, revealing a bloodstained piece of flannel, a fragment of women's clothing and a newspaper that had been used to wipe a knife.

Messengers were sent off to fetch Mr Kent from Southwick and the doctor, Mr Parson, from Beckington. By this time, Kent had reached Southwick toll gate, and was reporting that his child had been stolen in a blanket and that anyone with a child in a blanket was to be stopped. This was an odd thing for him to report; no-one knew that a blanket was missing, and the baby had not been found together with the blanket until well after Kent had left for Southwick. How did Mr Kent know that his son had been carried to the privy in a blanket? There was something else very peculiar about Mr Kent's ride to Southwick. The messenger who went after him to tell him the baby had been found dead, discovered that Mr Kent had only reached the tollgate. He had not reached Southwick itself, which was only a mile away, yet he had been gone an hour and a half. The lost hour was never explained. What was Mr Kent doing during this crucial time, when he should have been riding as fast as possible to get help?

Back at the house, the case had been taken over by Inspector Foley. Foley's policeman found a bloodstained shift, belonging to a woman above the boiler in the kitchen, though this was only mentioned three months later. All the night dresses in the house were inspected. Only one of them had blood on it, and that, the doctor confirmed, was menstrual blood - nothing to do with the murder. The investigators rapidly came to the conclusion that no outsider was involved. The murderer knew the layout of the inside of the house perfectly, knew that the window could only be opened a certain way without creaking, knew about the privy in the shrubbery, and so on.

The nightdresses were inspected for blood because of the way the baby had been killed. The poor little boy had had his throat cut with a razor and died instantly. There was another injury too, one that was harder to explain. A weapon of some sort had penetrated the child's night gown and made a smaller wound in the chest. This had not bled. There were also two more tiny wounds in the left hand; they too had not bled. When the parlour maid collected the laundry, she took Constance's nightdress along with the others. The girl followed her and asked her if she would get her a glass of water; the maid later thought this odd, as the girl had a jug of water in her room. When she returned she went on with her tasks, but next day discovered that Constance's nightdress was missing. It was never found. The boodstained shift in the kitchen was a different garment, and no-one knows who that belonged to.

The inquest was opened in the Red Lion Inn. There was evidence that the amount of blood spilt in the privy was about a pint and a half, not enough given the nature of the wound. The jury wanted to question the children, who were clearly emerging as suspects, especially William and Constance, but among the crowd there was such a strong feeling against the children that the inquest had to be adjourned to the Kents' house. Constance said she knew nothing, had gone to bed at half past ten, had heard nothing unusual, knew of no resentment against the boy, and found the nurse always kind and attentive. William said much the same. The verdict was wilful murder by person or persons unknown.

There was great local outrage about the crime, and Scotland Yard became involved in the case. Inspector Whicher quickly concluded that Constance had murdered her half-brother and charged her accordingly. She broke down in tears and pleaded her innocence. The nurse suported Constance; she had never known Constance behave other than well towards the child. She also made the point that the walls of Constance's room were so thin that she could not have gone out in the night without others hearing what she was doing. Constance mentioned giving the child a present and that they had played together.

But two school friends of Constance's gave a different story entirely at the committal hearing at Devizes in July 1860. They said Constance had told them how much she resented her stepmother's attitude, that her parents favoured the two youngest children and treated the children of the first Mrs Kent as servants. William, she had said, was made to use the back stairs, like a servant, and was always compared unfavourably with the baby. Constance and William had always stuck together.

Overall there was insufficient evidence, but Whicher was sure she was guilty and she was not acquitted. Instead she was discharged into her father's care.

Samuel Saville Kent had married Mary Anne Windus in 1830, when he was 28 and she 21. They were both from middle class commercial families and to begin with they lived in London. Samuel Kent became ill and the doctor's advice was to move to the coast for better air, so they moved to Sidmouth, where Kent took a job as a factory inspector at £800 a year. A son, Edward, was born in 1835, but the four children born between 1837 and 1841 all died in infancy. Mrs Kent was herself not constitutionally strong, and she had already shown symptoms of consumption when she was pregnant with Edward. She then started to show signs of mental instability. She took the children out and got lost. She also had a knife hidden under her bed.

The doctor advised Samuel Kent to hire a housekeeper, to keep a close eye on his wife. In 1844, Mrs Kent gave birth for the ninth time in fourteen years - this time to Constance. Under the care of the new housekeeper, Miss Pratt, Mrs Kent gained strength and then gave birth to William. By this time Mary Kent was completely insane and, in typical Victorian style, Samuel Kent shut his wife away without any treatment and pretended everything was normal. Then, in 1853, while Miss Pratt was away visiting relatives, Mary Kent developed a bowel problem and quickly died.

The children were used to Miss Pratt, who had been with the family for a decade, but they were nevertheless shocked when their father announced that he and Miss Pratt were to be married. Edward was so disgusted that when he returned home from school he had a blazing row with his father about the marriage, left the house and went to sea.

Then Samuel Kent and his new wife moved to Somerset, but the problems simmered away. Constance was as angry and resentful as Edward. She became hyper-sensitive to what were probably never intended to be slights. She became sullen, sulky, often rude. The jeering of the Road village children probably made matters worse, and she became paranoid. The second Mrs Kent seems to have been a very patient woman, but she must have found Constance very hard to deal with. In the end Constance just became a nuisance and Mr and Mrs Kent decided she should go away to school in London, which she also resented deeply. When she returned from school on holiday, it was to find that Mrs Kent had had another baby. This was the unfortunate Saville, and the Kents doted on him.

In 1854, the news came that Edward had been lost at sea. Mr Kent was distraught. Then, eventually, a letter came from Edward to say that other officers had died, but that he had survived. In 1858 he died of yellow fever. Only William was left, and he too was sent away to school. They were reunited in the holidays, and at the end of one of them, rather than be separated again they decided to run away. Constance disguised herself as a boy and they walked to Bristol. They tried to get a room in a hotel, but they were turned over to the police. Forced to explain herself to her father, Constance said that she wanted to leave England and was not sorry.

Mr Kent decided to try a new school nearer to home, and her behaviour there was better, though she was still just as churlish at home. After the murder of Saville, Samuel Kent sent her to a French convent, probably to get her away from the village children and the English press. Constance stayed there for two years - and it was her kindness to children that was remarked on. It seems that she became deeply religious. In around 1864, Constance confessed to the murder of Saville and asked for her confession to be made public, probably encouraged by the priests she came in contact with.

On Lady Day 1865, Constance appeared at Bow Street Magistrates Court dressed in black and confessed publicly to the murder. Then she collapsed in tears. Her father read about the extraordinary confession and visited her. She was then sent to Salisbury to stand trial in July 1865. Again she appeared in black, looking tall, grave and noble. She added a few details to the earlier confession.

She claimed she had taken a razor from her father's wardrobe a few days before the murder, though he did not notice. She had placed candles in the privy, then went to bed, waited for everyone in the house to go to sleep. She went downstairs and opened the window shutters. Then she went to the nursery, picked Saville up from his cot, took out one of the blankets, replaced the other covers, then wrapped the boy in the blanket. She took the baby downstairs, put on galoshes, climbed out of the window, walked to the shrubbery and cut Saville's throat with the razor. She thought blood would gush out but it did not come. She thought this meant Saville was not dead, so she tried to stab him in the chest with the razor. This was a peculiar claim, because the post mortem showed that this wound could not have been caused by a razor. She put the body still wrapped in the blanket into the privy. This too was inconsistent with what the men found; the blanket was definitely on, not round the body.

Constance went on to explain in detail how she had found only two spots of blood on her nightdress. This is almost incredible, given the act she had just committed. She washed the blood out herself and the next day her nightdress was dry, which also seems unlikely.

The bloodstained shift in the kitchen was never explained, by Constance or anyone else. There are several disconcerting and unsettling things about Constance's confession, apart from the details already mentioned. One is the fact that her description of the murder – her murder – was lifted almost word for word from an account published in a book written by someone else in 1861. The details she added were unconvincing attempts to explain things that no-one else understood either. How could she possibly have put on her galoshes and climbed out of a half-open window while carrying a sleeping baby wrapped in a blanket?

Constance spent 20 years in prison at Portland and Millbank. She was released in 1885 at the age of 41, and after that moment she disappeared completely. No-one knows what happened to her after that. One sensational theory is that she washed up in the East End of London three years later and, using perhaps not Papa's razor but someone else's, carried out the Whitechapel murders – not Jack the Ripper but Jill.

It is rather more likely that she emigrated, possibly to America or Australia.

Constance may have murdered her half-brother, Francis Saville Kent, out of hatred for her stepmother. Certainly she could have done the awful deed if she inherited her own mother's insanity and latent violence. But I am left with a peculiar sensation that in spite of Constance's confession she was not telling the truth. Was she telling this version of events in order to cover up for someone else? For her brother William, perhaps, or her father? It is certainly not beyond the bounds of probability that she and William carried out the murder together. But what was behind Mr Kent's one hour delay in riding to the next village? What was he doing during that time? And how did he know the baby would be found wrapped in a blanket? If Mr Kent was the murderer, what possible motive could he have had? If he committed himself the murder, it is hard see why the churlish and discontented Constance would have confessed on his behalf - unless of course her inherited mental instability and her time at the convent conspired to convince her that she had done something she hadn't. Perhaps she brainwashed herself into taking on the burden of the sins of the world, in imitation of Christ. It is after all not all that uncommon for innocent suspects to sign confessions after they have been interrogated for a while by experienced police officers; priests and policemen are quite capable of persuading people they are guilty when they are not.

Carl Bridgewater
'the death of a newspaper boy'

THE JAMES HANRATTY case was a classic example of a police investigation that was engineered to produce a conviction. Hanratty was hanged, yet it is still uncertain whether he was really was the A6 murderer, or simply targetted by the police as someone round whom a prosecution case could be built. The Carl Bridgewater case, coming a little later, at least did not result in a hanging, so the possibility remained of putting a wrong judgement right.

Carl Bridgewater, the unfortunate victim in this murder case, of course remains dead. No amount of legal back-tracking can change that. Carl was a thirteen year old schoolboy, taking on a newspaper round to earn a little pocket money. It seems that during the course of delivering the newspapers one day he accidentally stumbled on a burglary. The case against the burglar-murderers was that they must have killed the boy in order to prevent him from reporting the crime and make sure that he would not be able to identify any of them later.

Carl died on 19 September, 1978. He had not been doing the paper round for very long, just two months, and the last call he made was one of the last in the round. He was delivering a newspaper to Yew Tree Farm near Stourbridge in Staffordshire. This isolated farmhouse was the home of an elderly couple with mobility problems, and the arrangement they made was for the newspaper to be left on a particular chair inside the house. The owners, Mary Poole and Fred Jones, were both disabled. As it happened, they were out for the day. The boy let himself into the house by the back door, as was expected by the couple, and evidently walked right into the middle of a robbery. The boy was taken through into the sitting room and shot in the head at close range immediately, in cold blood. Carl's body was discovered by a friend of the family at 5.30 p.m., less than an hour after he had been killed. A blue estate car was seen near the farmhouse at around the time of the robbery.

The innocent boy's callous murder shocked the whole country and there was enormous pressure on the police service to find the people who killed him and bring them to justice. The inquiry was led by Detective Chief Superintendent Robert Stewart, who commented that the killing of a young boy seemed completely unnecessary. 'Every police officer on this inquiry is appalled by the viciousness of this unmerciful killing. It's possible, however, that Carl had to be silenced because he recognised someone.' That final point later proved very telling. The high profile of the case meant that the police were less likely to produce a fair and just result; they were being pressed for a quick result. A large number of extra police was drafted into the investigation from the West Midlands Regional Crime Squad.

Not long after the murder at Yew Tree Farm, on 30 September, 1978, a similar robbery to the Yew Tree Farm robbery took place not far away at Chapel Farm, Romsley. At least it was similar except that no murder took place. The police quickly connected this crime to a small-time criminal called Patrick Molloy and his associates. It turned out, from the way the police constructed the evidence, that Molloy and the other three, James Robinson and cousins Michael and Vincent Hickey, had all taken part in the Yew Tree Farm robbery. Under aggressive and highly pressured police questioning, Molloy made a statement that he had been at Yew Tree Farm on the afternoon when Carl Bridgewater was shot. According to the statement he was upstairs looking for things to steal when the boy was shot. Arrests quickly followed.

On 9 November, 1979, at Stafford Crown Court, Robinson and the Hickeys were found guilty of murder, sentenced to life: a recommended twenty-five years in prison. Molloy was found guilty of manslaughter and aggravated assault, and sentenced to twelve years in prison. Patrick Molloy died in prison in 1981, less than two years after his ordeal.

In November 1981, five months after Molloy's death, a new name was introduced into the Yew Tree Farm case. This was an ambulance driver. There had until now been no eye-witness identification of the four men who committed the Yew Tree Farm robbery and murder, but an eye-witness did report seeing a man in a blue uniform leaving the farm house round about the time of the murder. The uniformed ambulance driver had in fact got a serious criminal record; he had been found guilty of murder and robbery at another location and had dealt with his victims in an equally brutal way. It also turned out that he knew Carl Bridgewater; that fact alone meant that it would have been essential – in his mind – to dispose of the boy, who would certainly have been able to make a positive identification.

The defence of the so-called 'Bridgewater Four' now argued that there was reasonable doubt as to their guilt. The appeal judge, Lord Lane, wrote off the argument based on the new evidence as a red herring.

In February 1983, the Hickeys attempted to draw public attention to their beached case for a re-trial by staging a rooftop prison protest. It was done in very cold weather, yet they managed to stay out on the roof for several days. The protest had the desired effect, and the following month the Home Secretary ordered a new enquiry into the case, in view of complaints about the conduct of the police in the case. The police insisted there was no case to answer and the enquiry petered out.

In October 1987, when Douglas Hurd was Home Secretary, the case was referred back to the Court of Appeal, where it was investigated for over a year. In March 1989 the court threw out the appeal, saying that the original verdicts had been correct. A few months later, the defendants were denied the right to make further appeals, in spite of the fact that the situation was changing significantly. Members of the West Midlands Regional Crime Squad, who had been directly involved in the Yew Tree Farm investigation, were under investigation themselves now, on 97 charges of malpractice. The malpractices were so widespread that the squad was disbanded. The policeman who conducted the key Yew Tree Farm interview, the interview with Molloy which induced the 'confession', was indicted and cautioned for 'violence towards suspects and helping to fabricate evidence'. Seventeen other charges were brought against this same officer. Yet the appeal court ruled that this newly emerging information was irrelevant to the convictions for the murder of Carl Bridgewater.

In 1993 another Home Secretary, Kenneth Clarke, refused to refer the Bridgewater case back to the Court of Appeal. In 1994, the High Court ordered Michael Howard to release the documents considered by his predecessor in order to see the evidence on which an appeal had been turned down. The High Court took the view that vital evidence had been ignored, evidence that could lead to the convictions being overturned. Gradually public concern over the unsafe – and probably unjust – convictions grew.

The police had clearly ignored key forensic evidence found at the crime scene: an un-accounted-for set of fingerprints found on Carl Bridgewater's bicycle. The murderer had picked the bicycle up and thrown it into a nearby waste silo. This crucial new evidence should have led to a new trial, but the Home Secretary decided not to send the case back. Eventually in 1996 he gave way and the case was referred back.

Further new evidence emerged that the discredited police officer who had taken Molloy's statement, together with another officer, had fabricated and forged a confession from Vincent Hickey, which they had then used to force the confession from Molloy. No fingerprints were found, other than the fingerprints on the bicycle, and not even those were produced. No murder weapon was ever found. The only evidence to support the convictions were the statements that were produced by forgery, deception, bullying and – there is no other word for it – torture. Molloy was subjected to days of violent inter-rogation during which his teeth were broken and was repeatedly hit in the face and round the head. He was given food that had been heavily salted and denied liquids; in desperation, he had had to drink from a toilet. He was kept away from a lawyer for ten days; once he had access to a lawyer, he retracted the 'confession' extorted under duress. Molloy said that he had not made the confession at all. The discredited police officer had dictated the confession while the other officer wrote it down; Molloy had been in a state of physical and psychological trauma after days of maltreatment when he signed. On this evidence, the Court of Appeal immediately overturned the verdict; the forensic evidence, statements and admissions on which the first trial had been based were seriously contaminated.

Michael Hickey, Vincent Hickey and James Robinson had been in prison for eighteen years before their convictions were overturned. Patrick Molloy died in prison. The real house-breaker at Yew Tree Farm – the real murderer of Carl Bridgewater – has never been brought to justice.

Michael Helgos
and JonBenet

'the Boulder City Pageant Queen'

IT WAS ON Christmas night in 1996 that a couple in Boulder City found that their daughter was missing from her bedroom. John and Patsy Ramsey were frantic when they found a hand-written ransom note left for them on the stairs. It began, 'Mr Ramsey, Listen carefully! We are a group of individuals that represent a small foreign faction. We do respect your business but not the country that it serves. At this time we have your daughter in our possession . . . You will draw $118,000 from your account . . .'

Minutes later Patsy Ramsey called the police, who arrived within a few minutes. From the beginning the police suspected that the Ramseys themselves were responsible for the disappear-ance of JonBenet Ramesy. Their suspicions were confirmed when they asked John Ramsey to search the house and he found his daughter's body in a small cellar. By the time the little girl's body was removed from the house a few hours later, the Boulder Police had made up their minds about the Ramseys' guilt. Almost immediately there was a leak from the police to the local media of a few 'facts' about the case, including the 'fact' that there was no evidence of a break-in and no possibility that anyone outside the house could have got in. This disinformation was clearly aimed against the Ramseys and intended to signal to the people of Boulder that the Ramseys must be guilty. Another leak to the press involved the discovery of child pornography and evidence of child sex abuse at the Ramsey house. Another leak included the idea that Patsy had killed her daughter in a fit of temper over JonBenet's bed-wetting and concocted the kidnap story to avoid detection.

A police interrogation tape shows a policeman outlining the police hypothesis. Patsy listens, shaking her head in anger and disbelief and saying very emphatically, 'You're on the wrong path, buddy'. The police officer tells her there is 'trace evidence, scientific evidence' connecting Patsy to the murder. This infuriates Patsy, who knows perfectly well that this cannot possibly be true, because she knows she didn't commit the murder. She tells the officer that her daughter was the most precious thing she had and that her life has been hell ever since she died. She erupts: 'Quit screwing around asking me questions and find the person who did this!'

The police were implacable. A move was made to indict the Ramseys, but the indictment was dropped because it was found that the case did not hold up. Much of the alleged evidence was spurious and untrue. There was, for instance, no evidence whatever of child pornography or child abuse at the Ramsey house. Police photos taken on the day of the crime showed clear evidence of a break-in at the cellar window. The post mortem evidence showed that JonBenet was not killed by a single blow to the head, which was necessary to fit the police hypothesis, but had a died a more complicated and tortured death. She had been immobilized with a stun gun, sexually assaulted, strangled, and finally hit over the head. That did not fit the case the police had been trying to build against Mrs Ramsey. So the indictment had to be dropped 'for lack of evidence'.

In fact, as far as the Ramseys were concerned, they had been found guilty and condemned by the leaks and the consequent media frenzy. As far as the people of Boulder were concerned, the Ramseys were guilty. The unfortunate couple and their eleven year old son had their lives totally wrecked. Not only had they lost JonBenet, a pretty little girl who had won beauty contests, they now stood to lose everything else too.

But a few people continued to have faith in the Ramseys. A television documentary drew attention to the evidence from the crime scene pointing clearly to a break-in, and suggested that the abductors may indeed have intended to take the child outside through the window where they broke in, but for some reason decided not to abduct her but to kill her there. The ransom note certainly implies a change of mind - or perhaps that more than one person was involved in the attack and the two (or more) men had different motives. The documentary led to a new investigation co-ordinated through the District Attorney's office, though on limited funds.

The new investigators were concerned that there were several other suspects who had not been pursued by the police in 1996, simply because they had decided the Ramseys were guilty. There had been no routine house-to-house search of the neighbourhood, for the same reason. There had been two men living close by, both with criminal records, who moved away straight after the murder; there were also two paedophiles in the area who were not checked out. The police had decided on John and Patsy Ramsey, but there was plenty of evidence pointing elsewhere.

There were two small spots of blood on JonBenet's clothing. One of the bloodspots contained her DNA, but also traces of some DNA belonging to someone else. There was similar 'alien' DNA under one of her fingernails. The 'alien' DNA was not Patsy Ramsey's or John Ramsey's, but someone else's. The DNA from the second blood spot was from the same stranger, a white male. These blood samples were available in 1996 but the implications were not followed through. The investigators tried to match the stranger's DNA through the US national DNA database, but there was a strong possibility that the killer was a first offender, or at any rate had never been caught.

The investigators found a dozen new suspects, and one of those became the prime suspect. The investigators gave a press conference in which they gave the impression that they now knew who they were looking for and that the net was closing in on him. They hoped that this pressure might push the suspect into coming out into the open. It had an immediate and melodramatic effect that they could not have foreseen.

John Kennedy, a mechanic living in Boulder, went to the police to tell them that he thought he knew the killer. It was a man called Michael Helgos, who had committed suicide the day after the press conference. Kennedy thought the timing of Helgos's suicide was significant. He also knew that Helgos was a bizarre, deranged, violent man who took pleasure from shooting cats and speculated what it would be like to crack a human skull. Michael Helgos had also said in the period just before the murder that he was going to make a lot of money, which could have been a reference to the ransom he was hoping to get from the Ramseys.

In fact, shortly after the murder, the police had been informed about Helgos. Home videos were found showing him playing with a very young girl. A neighbour had returned home to find him naked with her daughter. He had a video collection containing some very violent scenes, but it also included a Disney film in which a very young girl is shown being woken up by Santa Claus; was this a scenario Helgos wanted to re-enact, and the mainspring of the decision to wake little JonBenet up on Christmas night?

Helgos had several stun guns, one of which

was of the type used on JonBenet. Two footprints were found in the Ramsey house. One was a HITEC trainer. Helgos owned a matching pair.

But there were peculiar circumstances surrounding the death of Michael Helgos too. The fatal shot was fired through a pillow. Why would Helgos have wanted to muffle the shot? It would not have mattered to him, when dead, whether anyone heard the shot. But perhaps it was not suicide at all; perhaps someone else shot Helgos. The bullet passed through his chest from left to right, which is a very odd wound for a right-handed man to inflict on himself, especially given that most people committing suicide with a gun shoot themselves in the head. Given that the ransom note mentions 'we' and there were two different footprints in the Ramsey house, it begins to look as if two people were involved in the killing. Michael Helgos was one. Who was the other? Was Helgos sufficiently unnerved after the press conference for his associate to fear that he would give them both away and could not afford to let him live? It begins to look that way.

The associate's name is known to the investigators (though not to me!) and they even know where he lives.

As Patsy Ramsey feared, the man or men who attacked her daughter went on to attack again. In an affluent part of Boulder, nine months after the Ramsey murder, a girl of about the same age as JonBenet and who even went to the same dance studio as JonBenet was attacked in her own home. Her parents found an intruder in the house who presumably got in while they were out. The parents went to bed, and then some time later the intruder went into the little girl's room, put his hand over her mouth, called her by her name and sexually assaulted her. Luckily the mother was a light sleeper and woke up, sensing something was wrong. She went into her daughter's room and saw the intruder, who ran past her and jumped out of the window and off the roof to get away. He was dressed completely in black. Michael Helgos is known to have liked dressing completely in black and stalking people at night. This attack is very likely indeed to be linked to the Ramsey case, though the Boulder police denied any connection. The later investigators discovered that although the second attack was known, in full detail, to the police, they had taken no action on it.

The case seems to be tantalizingly close to a conclusion. One of the major suspects, Michael Helgos, is dead, probably killed by his even more dangerous associate. David Williams, one of the detectives involved, says the killer could be taken into custody. They have his DNA. 'It's a travesty that it isn't happening.' It would take perhaps six detectives six months to solve the crime. But the District Attorney's office does not have unlimited funds and the case may have to be closed before the final solution is reached.

Meanwhile, the Ramsey family have had to endure the horrible bereavement inflicted on them by total strangers, the loss of JonBenet; they have also had to endure a painful hostile interrogation by the authorities; they have been vilified in the press; they have been assumed to be guilty by their neighbours. They have been forced to move away and make a new home for themselves - in Charlevoix in Michigan – where they live in poverty. Their lives have been destroyed.

Francisco Arce Montes

and the French youth hostel murder

IN THE SUMMER of 1996, a party of forty students and five teachers from Launceston College in Cornwall stayed at a youth hostel in the village of Pleine-Fougères in Brittany. One night, 17 August, the teachers ordered lights out towards midnight and, some time in the small hours of the following morning, an intruder entered the building, probably through a door that had been left unlocked.

He crept upstairs to the girls' dormitory and picked Caroline Dickinson, apparently at random. He put his hand over her mouth, raped her and suffocated her with a pad of cotton wool to stop her from making any noise. None of her friends woke up fully to witness what happened, though some remembered half-waking to hear groaning, which they took little notice of assuming it was one of the girls having a dream.

Caroline's death was only discovered at 8 o'clock, when one of her friends tried to wake her and found she was cold. Teachers were called, and they frantically tried to revive her. Ambulance workers were called, but she was already dead, and had been dead for hours.

By the time the death was discovered, the

murderer had escaped. He may by that time have been many miles away. The French put fifty police on the case, and showed a real determination to solve the case quickly. It seemed to pay off because within days they had a result. A convicted rapist called Patrice Pade confessed to killing Caroline and the hunt was over. The examining magistrate, Gerard Zaug, was convinced that Patrice Pade, a vagrant in his forties with a long history of rape and violence towards women, was the killer. Zaug held a new conference in which he identified the killer.

A week later, the results of the DNA tests on traces of semen found on Caroline's body emerged, and they decisively proved that Pade was not the killer. The examining magistrate had got it wrong, but he did back down immediately. For one thing, Pade's description of the interior of the youth hostel was so accurate that Zaug was convinced he must have been there. He demanded more tests and argued that Pade could have been an accomplice to the killer, whose identity for the time being remained unknown. But it was clear to others that Patrice Pade had confessed to a crime he had not committed. People do sometimes confess because they want attention, but it may be that because he had an appropriate criminal record he was put under pressure to confess.

On 7 August, 1996, Patrice Pade was released and the inquiry had to begin all over again. All the teachers, hostel staff and the boys on the trip were DNA tested, but none provided a match, so all of them were cleared of suspicion. As the months and years passed various leads emerged, but none leading to an arrest and conviction.

The strongest lead was a very similar attack 25 miles away from Pleine-Fougères. This attack, another nocturnal attack on an English girl, happened only hours before the attack on Caroline. It seemed very likely that this earlier attack and the attack on Caroline were committed by the same man. Unfortunately there were no leads on the man involved in the earlier attack either and a definite link could not be made. There was speculation that Caroline might have been the victim of a serial killer, which made it all the more urgent that he should be found and arrested.

The net was widened. DNA tests were carried out on four hundred men aged between fifteen and sixty in the Pleine-Fougères area. There were still no matches. The examining magistrate's conduct of the affair was strongly criticized by Caroline's parents, John and Sue Dickinson, among others, and before the end of 1996 he had been taken off the case. The Dickinsons welcomed his replacement, Judge Reynaud Van Ruymbeke, and approved of his early efforts to move the case forwards.

In February 1998 Van Ruymbeke issued a photofit picture of his prime suspect, a man who had been seen in the village just before the murder. The photofit showed an alarming-looking individual with long dishevelled hair, sunken eyes and a cruel mouth; it was like a sketch of an ape-man. The picture was circulated widely in France and the UK. In December 1999, police had an anonymous tip-off from a man who worked on a building site near Pleine-Fougères. He said one of his work-mates looked rather like the photofit picture and had been acting suspiciously during the days before the murder.

But by this stage Reynaud Van Ruymbeke had decided to leave the case to take up another job.

The years passed and the trail, such as it was, had gone cold. It began to look as if Caroline Dickinson's killer would never be caught. The breakthrough that led to a conviction happened as a result of a hunch by a US Immigration Officer called Tommy Ontko. He worked for the Immigration Department at Detroit airport. In one afternoon he did what the French police, Interpol and Special Branch had failed to do in five years. Tommy Ontko stopped work halfway through a busy day at work, and called at the British Airways desk to get a copy of the *Sunday Times*. He usually did not eat lunch, but liked instead to read a British paper with a doughnut and some coffee. He read the story about the hunt for Caroline's killer. For the first time Francisco Montes was being named as a suspect and the news story gave his approximate age.

Tommy Ontko speculated that after the time that had gone by Montes could easily have gone to America to 'disappear'. So, Tommy tapped the name Montes into the immigration service database, and found five possible matches. He needed an accurate date of birth to get an exact match, so he phoned the police in Rennes in Brittany. The French police assumed he was

English and brushed him off with a number for the British Consul, Ronald Frankel. It was just a mistake, but for Ontko it was a lucky break. Frankel was excited by the possibility of a breakthrough as he had been closely associated with the case from the time of the murder, having visited the murder scene and tried to comfort the Dickinson family. It was Frankel's keenness to get the case solved that took the investigation the next significant step forward. Tommy Ontko asked Frankel if he could get the date of birth he needed. Frankel said he could. A relative of Frankel's was a translator for the French judiciary and, as it happened, was in a car travelling with the detective and investigating magistrate who leading the Dickinson investigation. Mrs Frankel found the translator's mobile phone number and Ontko rang it. They pulled the car over to the roadside and read him Montes's date of birth along with lots of other information from the file.

Tommy Ontko ran the new details through the criminal records database and found he had been arrested twice, once just three weeks before in Miami. Ontko then phoned an old police friend in Florida, who sent him Montes's photos and fingerprints, which Ontko forwarded to France and Portsmouth. At 7 that evening, Ontko went home to eat alone. As he did so, he started wondering if this Montes really was the same Montes and, if so, whether he was still in prison. When he went in to work the next morning he discovered that Montes was still in prison and for a very significant offence. He had broken into a youth hostel, where he was caught masturbating while standing over a sleeping teenage girl. The previous October Montes had been arrested near another Miami youth hostel carrying a torch and a small pair of scissors, but on that occasion had not been jailed. The scissors were a regular feature of Montes's attacks; he used them to cut his way through the clothes of his victims.

More checks on Montes were made in the USA, and Ontko found that Montes was wanted in Germany, Switzerland, Spain and Venezuela for questioning in relation to similar crimes. Tommy Ontko knew then that Montes was the man who had killed Caroline Dickinson.

Two years before he attacked Caroline Dickinson, Francisco Montes was caught in the act of trying to abduct an Irish teenager from a French youth hostel. The French police released him without charge. He had stalked Valerie Jacques, who was then aged fourteen, for days, following her and her school party from Paris to the Loire valley in 1994. She noticed him following her and staring at her. He broke into the room Valerie was sharing in a hostel at Bléré and tried to attack her. He asked her to go outside and help him fix his car. She looked round the room and saw that everyone else was asleep. She screamed and he ran away. The incident was reported to the hostel proprietor, but the following night Montes got into the hostel again. Valerie was now very frightened. She and the other four girls in her room were the only girls to have no proper security. There was no lock on their door, so they slid a chest of drawers against it. Once again she was woken up by the sound of Montes calling her name and trying to push his way in. She was terrified, jumped out of bed and ran to the far corner of the room. Then she heard the police arriving. The police asked her to identify Montes, but in spite of her identification, he was released with a caution.

Valerie Jacques only told the rest of her family about the incident when she saw his photograph on television after he was arrested in 2001 for Caroline Dickinson's murder.

Montes admitted the sexual assault on Caroline, but denied intending to kill her. In June 2004, at the age of fifty-four, he was sentenced to thirty years in prison.

Francesco Javier Arce Montes was born on 14 March, 1950 in Gijon in northern Spain. His father, Geraldo Montes, ran a grocery store; he died in 1997. Since the arrest of 'Javi' in 2001, the Montes family have moved away, and don't want to talk about him; 'you do not choose your relatives'. In a statement to the court in Rennes, Montes's mother elderly mother disowned him. She moved out of her house when he returned there in 1996 after murdering Caroline. She said, 'I could not stand living with him any more', and admitted to being frightened of him. The family pleaded with a Spanish judge to keep him in prison when he was arrested near Gijon for the attempted rape of a teenage girl in 1997, but after only three months in prison he was released. The mother had made three complaints to the police that he had threatened her with violence.

Montes complained that his upbringing had been difficult, but knew that he had been a difficult person. He admitted to having a poor relationship with his mother and his sister, and blamed them for everything that had gone wrong. He even accused his mother of poisoning his food.

Montes spent some time living in Britain during the 1990s. Given that he was a serial offender, the British police are now wondering whether he was responsible for sex attacks while living in the Earls Court area of London. Detectives from Swansea will seek permission to interview Montes in relation to a series of unsolved sex attacks in Wales that coincided with a four-year period when he was in Britain. The South Wales Police inquiry has a particular case as its focus; a man attempted to rape a thirteen year old Girl Guide on the Gower Peninsula in 1993, a girl who only escaped when holiday-makers heard her screams and went to her aid. At that time, Montes was working in a restaurant in Swansea. There was also an attack on a fifteen-year-old French girl at Oxwich Bay about seven miles from Swansea. Devon and Cornwall Police are asking all British police forces to re-examine unsolved sexual assaults from 1993 to 1996, though so far there has been little active research, and Scotland Yard said it had already ruled Montes out of any serious sexual assaults in London.

The one positive result from this sad story is that John Dickinson's campaign to press the French police into higher levels of activity has led to the routine use of DNA testing in France. John Dickinson is using the successful conviction of his daughter's killer as the basis for a new campaign for the creation of a global database of DNA to prevent other families suffering the same fate. Interpol is aiming to simplify the process of DNA identification by using a numerical process that will enable rapid preliminary matching; this is then followed up with further laboratory testing to make sure the match is exact. But, as in all such collaborative ventures, 'We are reliant on the contributions of each member state. While some, such as Britain, are advanced, others are slowing down.'

PART SEVEN

THE
LADY-KILLERS

William Corder
'and the Murder at the Red Barn'

THE INFAMOUS MURDER at the Red Barn was probably the murder that most caught the public imagination in the nineteenth century. It was a dramatic news story, a story of love turned sour, and it soon became one of the stock Victorian melodramas.

The victim of the crime was Maria Marten. She was born in 1801, the daughter of a humble mole-catcher at Polstead in Suffolk. She was given a good education, rather better than was normal for a girl of her station. She was also a very good-looking young woman with a fine figure and a pretty face. Not surprisingly she was surrounded by admirers, and not very surprisingly she gave way to temptation, not once or twice but several times. She became pregnant by 'a gentleman of fortune' who lived in a house nearby, and at the time of her death the child was three years old. She formed a new liaison in 1826, this time with William Corder.

Corder was the son of a rich farmer at Polstead. He was a smartly and fashionably dressed young man of twenty-four, with a florid complexion. He was naturally attracted to the good-looking Maria, a relationship developed and she had another child - Corder's child. The infant died shortly after it was born and Corder took the body away at night and disposed of it in haste, by means that he would never discuss. Naturally people wondered whether the child had been deliberately murdered by Corder and disposed of to destroy the evidence. Maria used the scandal that was circulating as a lever on her father to make him agree to a marriage.

On 18 May, 1827 William Corder called at old Mr Marten's house to tell Marten that he was willing to marry Maria. He added that no time should be lost, and in order to get the marriage through as quickly as possible it should be as private as possible and by licence rather than by banns. He and Marten agreed on the following day as the day of the wedding. Corder persuaded Maria, who was very unhappy at this way of doing things, to dress in a suit of his own clothes and go with him in disguise to a barn on his farm. It was called the Red Barn.

At the Red Barn, she could change into her own clothes and from there he would take her in a gig to a church in Ipswich – where they would be married. Maria reluctantly agreed to this strange set of arrangements and Corder went home. Maria followed soon after, carrying an outfit that she could wear for the wedding. Corder had meanwhile managed to persuade Mrs Marten, Maria's stepmother, that he was determined to make Maria his lawful wife, and that they had to rush the marriage through immediately as he knew there was a warrant out against Maria for her bastard children.

A few minutes after Corder had left Maria, he was seen by Maria's brother walking towards the Red Barn with a pickaxe over his shoulder. From that moment on, nothing more was heard of Maria, except Corder's lies. It was expected that Maria would return from Ipswich within a day or two, but her earlier visits to Corder had been of varying lengths and Corder had undertaken to find her lodgings in Ipswich. Her delayed return was not regarded as ominous or alarming.

After a fortnight, the Martens began to wonder where Maria had got to. Mrs Marten pressed Corder for an explanation. He said she was safe and well and that he had lodged her some distance away, so that his friends would not discover the fact of his marriage and be annoyed with him. Corder used this style of answer repeatedly when the Martens wanted more news of their daughter.

In September Corder said he was unwell and visiting the Continent for the sake of his health. Before he went, he expressed concern that the Red Barn should be well filled with stock, and he saw to it himself; it is not clear why he did that. Presumably if the barn was full of cattle it would be rather difficult for anyone to take a spade to the earth floor; in fact in a barn full of cattle no-one would even think of doing that. He took £400 with him before setting off.

Several letters arrived subsequently, addressed to his mother and Maria's parents, to say that he and Maria were at Newport on the Isle of Wight, living together as man and wife, yet all the letters carried a London postmark. He also expressed surprise that they had had no answer to Maria's letter to them describing the marriage ceremony. In a letter to someone else, Corder explained that Maria was unable to write herself because she had hurt her hand. William Corder was now very obviously lying. People started to speculate about what was going on. Mr and Mrs Marten became more and more dissatisfied and alarmed.

In March 1828, Mrs Marten (Maria's stepmother) had the same dream on three successive nights. She dreamt that her daughter had been murdered and buried in the Red Barn. Mrs Marten was terrified. These dreams seemed to make sense of her daughter's disappearance and William Corder's endless lies and evasions. She was initially reluctant to say anything to her husband because it would sound silly and superstitious, but she became convinced that the dreams contained the truth of what had happened. Eventually she told him and his reaction was as she had anticipated. He would do nothing. She nagged. On 19 April she persuaded her husband to apply for permission to examine the Red Barn, specifically to look for Maria's clothes. The grain that had been stored in the Red Barn had been removed and at the moment it stood empty. Mrs Marten's repeating dream had been so vivid that she even knew the exact spot where her husband ought to dig.

Poor Thomas Marten went into the empty barn, its timber-frame interior latticed with vertical, horizontal and diagonal struts. Marten dug where his wife said he should, in the middle towards one end. The soil was softer there. Before long he turned up the green silk handkerchief (belonging to Corder) which he knew his daughter had been wearing on the day she left their home. Filled with fear and apprehension about what he would find next, he went on digging. Eighteen inches down he found part of a human body. Overwhelmed with horror, Mr Marten dropped his tools and staggered outside to raise the alarm. He knew what he had found and when help arrived and more digging was done his worst fears were realised. He had indeed found the grave of his murdered daughter.

Maria's body was badly decomposed, but the dress, which was still in perfect condition, allowed no doubt to remain about whose body it was. The corpse's teeth were still intact and there were sufficiently distinctive features of the teeth to make it absolutely certain that this was Maria. Maria's sister Ann recognized the set of teeth from the position of a missing tooth.

The whole village was in uproar at the discovery. John Wayman, the Bury St Edmunds coroner was notified and a surgeon, John Lawden, examined the body. The coroner opened an inquest at the Cock Inn at Polstead. Lawden said the victim had died violently; there was blood on her face and clothes and on a handkerchief tied round her neck. There was also a visible wound in the throat, which had been inflicted by a sharp instrument. There was another wound in the orbit of the right eye; something had been thrust in which had broken the bones and penetrated the brain. When the body was found, it was partly inside a sack and dressed only in a shift, petticoat, stays, stockings and shoes.

Everyone's thoughts turned to William Corder as the murderer. The local constable, Ayres, went off to brief a London policeman, Constable James Lea, in an attempt to find Corder. Lea was given little to go on except a single London address where Corder had been, in the Gray's Inn Road area, but traced Corder's movements from address to address, eventually finding him towards the end of April at Grove House in Ealing Lane near Brentford. He was there with his wife of three weeks, and he was - almost incredibly - running a boarding-house for young ladies. Lea had some difficulty in gaining access to Grove House, but Lea pretended to have a daughter he might wish to place at the boarding house, and was shown into a parlour. There he found William Corder sitting at breakfast in his dressing-gown with four ladies. He was holding his watch, timing the boiling of some eggs.

Constable Lea called Corder to one side to tell him discreetly that he had a serious charge against him. Corder was alarmed and asked if they could discuss it in the drawing room. Did he know a person named Maria Marten at Polstead? No, he knew no-one of that name. Lea handcuffed him and set about searching the house. Amongst other things he found a passport to France dated December 1827 and some threatening letters from a man called Gardener, suggesting that some other offence had been committed that Corder needed to cover up. In the course of the search he found a pair of pistols, a powder-flask and some balls in a velvet bag. The pistols had been bought immediately before the murder from Harcourts in Ipswich. Later, when Mrs Marten saw the velvet bag she recognized it as the bag Maria was carrying when she left their house for the last time. Lea also found a sharp-pointed dagger. This was later identified by a cutler named Offord as being the one he had sharpened for Corder a few days before the murder.

Corder was taken before magistrate Matthew Wyatt at the Lambeth Street police station and charged with the murder. After that, he was taken straight to Polstead to be questioned by the coroner. Corder's behaviour seems to have varied between extremes, rather like his complexion, which was seen to change colour from minute to minute during the trial. In London he had been frightened. On the roof of the coach from London to Colchester he was in high spirits, cracking distasteful jokes. At the trial he was overwhelmed by the gravity of what he had done and seemed unconscious of what was going on.

On arrival at Colchester, Corder and the policemen stayed at the George Inn for the night; Corder was secured by one hand to the bed-post all night.

Crowds gathered to get a look at Corder when he arrived. He was already an infamous celebrity. Confronted by the coroner, he seems to have realised that it was all lost; he became very agitated. The coroner concluded that Maria Marten, aged 26, had been wilfully murdered by William Corder. Meanwhile, Corder's unfortunate wife, who knew nothing at all about Maria Marten or the murder in the Red Barn, was still under the impression that Corder was arrested on a charge of bigamy; no-one had the heart to tell her the truth.

His trial opened on 7 August, 1828 in the shire hall at Bury St Edmunds. Everyone in the neighbourhood wanted to be there. Hundreds of people gathered round both entrances to the shire hall, some arriving as early as five in the morning. The rain fell in torrents, but many stood in the rain for four hours waiting for the doors to open. At 9 o'clock so many people poured into the shire hall that the barristers had to struggle against the press of the crowd, and were repeatedly driven back. When the judge had taken his seat, the names of the jurors were read out, summoning them to take their places, but there were so many people in the building that it was almost impossible for them to get into the courtroom. Nearly an hour later, the jury was still incomplete and they had to be passed over the heads the crowd, some arriving with their coats torn, their shoes pulled off and fainting from shock.

There were crowds elsewhere too, at the gaol and along the road from the gaol to the shire hall. Everyone wanted to catch a glimpse of the infamous murderer, William Corder. Corder dressed carefully for the occasion in a new black suit. He brushed his hair down over his forehead, instead of his usual style which was brushed up in front.

Perhaps he thought it made him look less raffish. Corder challenged several of the jurors, so it was some time before a full jury was empanelled. Corder pleaded not guilty. Then the evidence of the identity of the body in the Red Barn – his barn – was described, and the surgeon's evidence of her violent death. Maria Marten's brother was also able to give evidence that when Corder left the house of Mr Marten he was carrying a loaded gun.

Corder was asked to defend himself. He read, quietly and tremulously, from a piece of paper an account of what had happened. When they had reached the barn, he said, Maria had flown into a temper, which had made him angry with her. He had told her he would not marry her after all and made to leave the barn. Then he heard the sound of the gun going off. Maria had shot herself. He had tried to revive her and failed. He had panicked.

'The sudden alarm which seized me suspended my faculties, and it was some time before I could perceive the awful situation in which I was placed and the suspicions which must naturally arise from my having delayed to make the circumstance instantly known. I at length found that conceal- ment was the only means by which I could rescue myself from the horrid imputation, and I resolved to bury the body as well as I was able.'

It was no good. The forensic evidence of stab wounds in the throat and eye socket told a differ- ent story. Maria could not have shot and stabbed herself to death. A verdict of guilty was passed. Corder wiped his eyes with a handkerchief. He knew he was guilty. Then he was sentenced to death, which had a huge effect on him. When he got back to the gaol, the governor, Mr Orridge, pressed him as hard as he could to confess. Corder shouted, 'I am a guilty man', and then produced a written confession. After that, he quietened down. He attended a service in the prison chapel before being taken off for execution. Just before the hanging he said feebly, 'I am justly sentenced and may God forgive me'.

After the execution, there was spirited bidding for the rope. People were prepared to pay as much as a guinea an inch for it. Huge sums were offered for the pistols and dagger used in the Murder at the Red Barn, but they became the property of the Sheriff of the county.

James Greenacre

IT WAS 1836 and there was building work going on in the Edgware Road in London, about a quarter of a mile from the place where the Regents Canal emerges from under the pathway.

The buildings under construction were dwellings, to be called Canterbury Villas, and they were very nearly finished. On 28 December, 1836, a bricklayer on the site by the appropriate name of Bond noticed a package wrapped in sacking, carefully and very deliberately hidden behind a paving-stone. He moved the stone to get a better look and was horrified to see a pool of frozen blood. He called the clerk of works and another of the building workers over and together they opened the package. Inside they were horrified to find the trunk of a human body; the head and legs had been removed. It turned out to be the body of a woman aged about fifty. The head had been removed in a clumsy and amateurish way, the neck part sawn through, part broken off. The legs had been taken off in the same clumsy way.

In truth, the busy building site was a very foolish place to try to hide a body. It was bound to be discovered very quickly. The murderer must have been either stupid or insane. In the event, in the very swiftest of murder trials, it was never really established which.

An inquest held on the body on 31 December, 1836 at the White Lion in Edgware Road returned a verdict of 'wilful murder'. The victim remained unidentified.

Shortly afterwards, there was great excitement in the locality when it was reported that a human head had been discovered. It was found in the Ben Jonson Lock on the Regents Canal, in the reach running through Stepney Fields. The trunk, which by then had been buried, was exhumed to see if it matched the head. A surgeon named Girdwood declared that the head and trunk did indeed belong to one and the same body. This was a step forward, but there was still no clue as to the identity of the murderer or the identity of the victim. The head was preserved in spirits and kept at Mr Girdwood's house, where people could go and inspect it if it was thought that they could contribute to an identification.

No further progress was made on this unusual and macabre case until 2 February. Then a labourer named James Page was cutting osiers in a bed near Cold Harbour Lane in Camberwell, when he saw a large bundle covered with sacking lying in a ditch, partly under the water. He just happened to see it as he stepped over the ditch while he was working. Page was curious and lifted the bundle out of the water. He saw what looked like human toes sticking out of it and became alarmed. He called to a fellow worker who was close by, and together they opened the package.

It contained a pair of human legs. They were taken off to Mr Girdwood, who confirmed that the legs too belonged to the body found in the Edgware Road.

On 20 March, a major breakthrough came. A broker from Goodge Street in the Tottenham Court Road applied to the Paddington church-warden for permission to inspect the remains of the dead woman. This was Mr Gay, and he was concerned about the sudden and inexplicable disappearance of his sister, Hannah Brown, who had left her lodgings on Christmas Eve and had not been seen or heard of since. He was now very worried about what might have happened to her. Obviously he feared that she might have been murdered. When Mr Gay saw the head floating in the bottle of spirits, he identified it as that of his sister; his horror at this recognition can only be imagined.

The police made enquiries about Hannah Brown, and discovered that she had recently been courted by a man called James Greenacre. She had been about to marry Greenacre. She left her lodgings in Union Street Middlesex Hospital, to accompany her husband-to-be to his house in Carpenter's Buildings, Camberwell, to prepare for their wedding the following Monday. She had last been seen in the company of James Greenacre. James Greenacre was naturally the man the authorities most wanted to speak to next.

The magistrates at Marylebone police office issued a warrant for Greenacre's arrest. After great difficulty, Greenacre was taken into custody on 24

March at his lodgings at No 1 St Alban's Place in Kennington Road. It was discovered that he was living there with a woman called Sarah Gale and her child; he was not just living with Sarah Gale, he was cohabiting with her. The arrest of Greenacre and Gale took place under circumstances that confirmed the mounting suspicion of guilt. Inspector Feltham and a police constable went to Greenacre's lodgings and found him in bed with Sarah Gale. Inspector Feltham told Greenacre the reason for his visit and at first Greenacre said he did not know anyone called Hannah Brown. Later he admitted that he had known her and had been on the point of marrying her but that she had disappeared. He did not know where she was.

Greenacre and Gale got dressed. Greenacre then told Feltham it was lucky he had come to see him that night as the next day they were sailing to America. It was an odd way of expressing the situation. Lucky for Inspector Feltham, certainly, and lucky for justice too; but certainly very unlucky for James Greenacre and Sarah Gale. The story about the imminent voyage to America certainly had every appearance of being true, because there were boxes all round the flat that were packed, closed and tied up with rope ready for travel. The boxes were opened by the police, and they were found to contain many items that had belonged to Hannah Brown. There were even more incriminating items still, including pieces of an old cotton dress that corresponded exactly with the cloth that the body had been wrapped in when first discovered in the Edgware Road.

The trial of Greenacre and Gale opened at the Old Bailey on 10 April, 1837. Greenacre was charged with the wilful murder of Hannah Brown. Sarah Gale was charged with being an accessory after the fact, in other words with helping Greenacre in the full knowledge of what he had done. The judges were Lord Chief Justice Tindal, Mr Justice Coleridge and Mr Justice Coltman. Public interest in the case was very great, because of the macabre dismemberment of the victim and her dispersal round London: the court was packed. The trial was very short, reaching its conclusion on the second day. The judge began his summing up at 6.15 pm. The jury returned a guilty verdict after only fifteen minutes. Greenacre was sentenced to death and hanged on 2 May, 1837; Gale was sentenced to transportation – she would have to spend the rest of her life in Australia, which some would say was a fate worse than Greenacre's.

Oscar Slater

'the murder of Marion Gilchrist'

IT WAS ON 21 December, 1908 that Marion Gilchrist
was battered to death in her apartment in Glasgow.
Miss Gilchrist was what used to be called 'a maiden
lady' of 82. She was looked after by a servant,
Helen Lambie, and the violent murder happened
during the very short time when Helen was out
buying a newspaper. She was out for as little as ten
minutes, yet in that time an assailant managed to
get into Miss Gilchrist's apartment, beat her to
death and make off with a small diamond brooch.
One peculiarity of this case is that the police
discovered that only the one small diamond
brooch was stolen, when Marion Gilchrist had a
large collection of jewellery.

The family in the apartment underneath Miss
Gilchrist's, the Adams family, heard noises, unusual noises, and Arthur Adams went upstairs to
investigate. It had sounded like three knocks on
the ceiling. Miss Gilchrist was an old lady and was
perhaps in difficulties of some kind, possibly
having a stroke or a heart attack or possibly she
had fallen over and broken her leg; maybe she
was signalling for help. When Mr Adams reached
Miss Gilchrist's door he rang the bell. There was

no answer, though he could hear noises inside the apartment. He went downstairs again, but was urged by his sisters to check that Miss Gilchrist really was all right. He went back upstairs and was standing in front of the door when Miss Lambie arrived back from her errand. It was at this moment that they both saw a man down in the hallway of the building. This was a semi-public area, so it did not strike either of them as unusual – perhaps another tenant or a visitor. There was no reason to connect this person with Miss Gilchrist.

Mr Adams told Miss Lambie what he had heard and the two of them went into the apartment. Together they found Miss Gilchrist; she was lying near the fireplace with her head brutally smashed in.

Oscar Slater, the man who emerged as the chief police suspect, had been living in Glasgow for about six weeks, with his French girlfriend. He claimed to be a diamond-cutter. Whether he was or not, the police – and others – thought he was a 'bad lot'. This assessment of Slater was based mainly on the lowest of prejudices; Oscar Slater was German, he was Jewish and he had a French mistress. But it must be admitted that he was also running an illegal gambling operation.

The day after the murder, Mary Barrowman, a girl of fourteen, told the police that at about the time when the murder had been committed she had bumped into a man hurrying out of the Gilchrist address. Mary described this man as tall, young, and wearing a fawn cloak and a round hat. This description was evidently of a different man from the one Mr Adams and Miss Lambie saw. They described their man as 'about five feet six inches, wearing a light grey overcoat and a black cap'.

The police found out that Oscar Slater tried to sell a pawn-ticket for a diamond brooch just four days after the murder, and assumed that this brooch must be Miss Gilchrist's brooch. Even more suspicious was the fact that Slater and his girlfriend had then sailed for America on board the *Lusitania*, and Slater had used an assumed name for the passenger list. The police had been under a great deal of public pressure to find the villain who had committed this murder. Within five days they had their man – or, at least, a man. They cabled the police in America to take Slater into custody and then showed a picture of Slater to the three witnesses. The two girls, Helen Lambie and Mary Barrowman, obligingly identified Slater as the man they saw immediately after the murder; Mr Adams did not. It was the two girls who were sent off to America, on a free return trip, for the extradition proceedings. The trip to America looks suspiciously like a bribe.

Slater turned out to be very accommodating. He was very willing to return to Scotland to answer the accusation. He knew he was innocent, could prove it, and was positive that this 'misunderstanding' could be cleared up relatively easily. He could not know that the authorities were already determined to pin the murder on him and would stoop to any depth to secure a conviction. He could not know how close he would come to being hanged.

The initial British court hearing was in the Edinburgh High Court on 3 May, 1909, over four months after the murder. The police had by this time decided not only that Slater had committed the murder, but that he had committed it with a small hammer that he owned. They had also mustered a dozen witnesses who claimed to have seen Slater near Miss Gilchrist's apartment on the day of the murder. This was hardly significant as Oscar Slater and Marion Gilchrist lived only four blocks apart.

This 'evaporation' of the evidence against Oscar Slater is another of the hallmarks of his case, especially in view of the apparent determination of the authorities to get a conviction. That Slater should have been seen a number of times on the streets of Glasgow two hundred yards from his own home could hardly be presented as significant evidence tying him to the murder, at least not in any trial that was fair. The pawn-ticket turned out to be even weaker evidence against him. The defence lawyer was able to show that the pawn-ticket belonged to a brooch pawned several weeks before the murder, so it could not possibly have been the one stolen from Marion Gilchrist. Similarly, the voyage to America had been booked six weeks before the murder; it was very far from being a 'moonlight flit'.

Slater said in court that he had been at home with his girlfriend and her servant at the time when the murder was committed. This alibi was simply swept aside. The Lord Advocate, Alexander Ure, decided that Slater must be hanged. The jury was not so sure. It was not a unanimous verdict, but a majority found him guilty. Oscar Slater was sentenced to be hanged on 27 May, 1909.

A petition for clemency was launched immediately, raising 20,000 signatures. Two days before the execution was due to take place, the sentence was commuted to life imprisonment, with hard labour. Slater had his life, but it was still a cruel and unjust sentence. Naturally he wanted to prove his innocence and get out of prison. Doyle had read about the case some years earlier in the book Notable Scottish Trials and had been struck then by the fact that Slater had been convicted on suspicion based on prejudice, and on no solid evidence whatever. Doyle did not approve of Slater as a person. He thought him a reprobate, but he was sure he had not committed the murder for which he was convicted.

It proved a long, slow process interesting people in Slater's case. Many people felt that even if he had not committed the murder he probably had something to do with it. He was an unpleasant person and generally regarded as immoral. Doyle took his time. He spent three years thoroughly researching the case and in 1912 produced a book called *The Case of Oscar Slater*. It went through all the evidence raised against Slater at his trial and showed, detail by detail, how it could not be made to prove Oscar Slater's guilt.

The matter of the assumed name, for instance, was less suspicious than it was made to appear in court for the simple reason that Slater was travelling with his mistress; he was trying to avoid being detected by his wife, not the police. Slater had indeed possessed a small hammer as mentioned in the trial, but it was far too small to have inflicted the wounds on Miss Gilchrist's head. Doyle said that a forensic investigator at the crime scene had declared that a large chair, dripping with blood, seemed the likeliest murder weapon. The matter of Miss Gilchrist opening the door and letting someone she knew into her apartment strongly suggested that the murderer was well-known to her in some capacity or other. Oscar Slater and Marion Gilchrist did not know each another at all.

Sir Arthur Conan Doyle's book raised a storm of indignation against the injustice that had been done against Slater. Now many people were ready to demand either a pardon or a re-trial. But the authorities were adamant, and nothing changed. Even Doyle's book made no difference. Then, much later, in 1925, William Gordon was released from Peterhead Prison; unknown to the authorities, Gordon was carrying a desperate message written on greaseproof paper and hidden under Gordon's tongue. It was Oscar Slater's cry for help to Sir Arthur Conan Doyle. Slater hoped to re-activate his old ally and enlist his help in getting justice for him.

Doyle was moved by this desperate plea and tried once again to help. He fired off a fusillade of letters. But there was no new evidence that Doyle or Slater knew of. They were no further forward.

But even after this long period, it was possible for new information to emerge.

In 1927 a new book about the case came out, *The Truth About Oscar Slater*, written by William Park, a Glasgow journalist. Park decided, just as Doyle had done, that Miss Gilchrist had known her murderer and went on to speculate that Miss Gilchrist had had a disagreement with the man about a document that she possessed. Park inferred this from the fact that Miss Gilchrist's documents had been disturbed and rummaged through, presumably by the murderer. During the argument she was pushed and hit her head. Her attacker then had to decide. He could leave Marion Gilchrist to recover and then probably have him charged with assault – or he could make sure she did not recover, in other words kill her. He decided to kill. The laws of libel made William Park hesitate and stop short of naming the killer, but he believed that Miss Gilchrist's nephew murdered her.

The book was a sensation. The newspapers were full of the story and it was then that significant new information – or information long withheld – started to come out. A grocer called MacBrayne confirmed Slater's alibi; he had actually seen Slater on his own doorstep at the time of the murder, when he had said he was at home. Mary Barrowman and Helen Lambie were traced. Now they were ready to admit that they had been bribed and coached by the police to make a false identification. One wonders how many innocent people have been sent to their deaths or to long prison sentences, over the centuries, by bribed perjurers like these two women. A detective called Trench said he had never believed Helen Lambie's identification. For breaking ranks in this way, Trench was persecuted by his fellow officers, charged with concealing evidence, and he had to leave the police force. As this new information was published in the newspapers it became impossible for the authorities to keep Slater in prison any longer. On 8 November, 1927, the Secretary of State for Scotland issued a statement: 'Oscar Slater has now completed more than eighteen and a half years of his life sentence, and I have felt justified in deciding to authorize his release on licence as soon as suitable arrangements can be made.'

A few days later, Oscar Slater was released, though not pardoned.

Arthur Conan Doyle despaired at the sheer wickedness of the Scottish authorities who refused to admit that they were wrong. But he also despaired of Slater. It says much about Conan Doyle's probity that he was prepared to put himself to considerable trouble and expense to help a man he really disliked intensely. Because Slater was released but not pardoned, his case had to be re-opened and re-tried if he was to be exonerated. It would be only then that Slater could apply for compensation for the eighteen years of wrongful imprisonment.

Conan Doyle and others gave money so that Slater could pay the legal fees. In the end Slater was cleared of all the charges brought against him and awarded £6000 in compensation. Conan Doyle naturally assumed Slater would pay back his supporters for the legal fees they had given him, which is what the honourable Sir Arthur would have done in the same circumstances. But Slater was embittered by his time in prison, and resented the fact that he had been put in a position where he had been forced to buy a re-trial; he should not have been asked to pay anything. He regarded the £6000 as his. Conan Doyle was a wealthy man and did not really need to have back the £1000 he had put into Slater's fund, but he was shocked that Slater was not prepared to pay him back. Slater was not an honourable man. Conan Doyle wrote to Slater, 'You seem to have taken leave of your senses. If you are indeed responsible for your actions, then you are the most ungrateful as well as the most foolish person whom I have ever known.'

When Oscar Slater died in 1949, the newspaper notice read, 'Oscar Slater Dead at 78, Reprieved Murderer, Friend of A. Conan Doyle'. Slater, Conan Doyle and many other people had gone to a lot of trouble to prove that Slater was not a reprieved murderer. It is doubtful whether Conan Doyle ever thought of Slater as a friend, either. But then, not everything we read in the newspapers is true.

Oscar Slater certainly did not kill Marion Gilchrist, but somebody did. Who was the real murderer? Nobody knows who killed Miss Gilchrist, though several theories have been floated. There are some significant pieces of evidence that point to the possible motive and the curious 'coincidence' of Helen Lambie's popping out to buy a newspaper.

Marion Gilchrist was well-off. She had collected jewellery for years. By the time she was murdered she had a collection worth £3,000 then, and probably worth £60,000 in today's money. To build this collection, she often bought from shady back-street dealers. It may possibly have been one of these who attacked her. Helen Lambie also revealed that she was expected to make herself scarce whenever one of these less than legitimate dealers was due to call. Was there rather more than coincidence to Helen Lambie's absence from the building at the time of the murder? Had she been asked to make herself scarce by Miss Gilchrist so that she could have a confidential conversation with a caller she was expecting? Or was she asked to make herself scarce by the murderer himself? Either way, it seems likely that Helen Lambie may have known more about the situation than she ever revealed.

The murderer was also able to let himself in with his own doorkey, or was let in by Miss Gilchrist; either way, he must have been well known to the old lady, probably a regular dealer, a friend, or a relative who hoped to inherit. Maybe the theft of the brooch was meant to put the police off the scent and make them think the motive was robbery, when the real motive was something else, such as inheritance. And that brings us back to William Park's intriguing theory about the unnamed nephew.

PART EIGHT

BODIES IN
BOXES

Kate Webster

'and the Barnes Mystery'

KATE WEBSTER WAS born in 1849 in County Wexford in Ireland. She was born as Catherine Lawler and started her life of crime very early on. Most of her crimes were small-scale: theft, deception and dishonesty. She claimed that she married a sea captain called Webster, by whom she had four children, but it is not certain that any of that is true. She stole the money for the ferry across the Irish Sea and sailed to Liverpool, where she went on stealing. At the age of eighteen she was sentenced to four years in prison for theft.

Released from prison she moved to London to make a sort of fresh start. She became a domestic servant, a cleaner. She would clean conventionally, though fairly incompetently, for a while, before cleaning out her employer's valuables and then moving on to a new job.

In 1873 she was living in Rose Gardens, Hammersmith. She got on well with her neighbours, Henry and Ann Porter, who were to reappear later in her story and become implicated in the most bizarre way imaginable. Then she moved to Notting Hill, where she became cook and housekeeper to Captain Woolbest. While she was there she met a man called Strong, by whom she became pregnant. After the baby boy was born in April 1874, Strong disappeared. Kate Webster fell back on stealing and this in turn led to her being sent to prison again.

Coming out of Wandsworth Prison in 1877, Kate looked once again for domestic work. She worked for a while for the Mitchell family in Teddington, but complained that the Mitchells did not have anything worth stealing. She shifted from job to job, sometimes using the name Webster, sometimes Lawler. She became friendly with another domestic called Sarah Crease, and it was Sarah who looked after Kate's son while Kate was in prison.

A photograph of Kate Webster exists. She stares blankly into the camera. The face is plain, severe, determined, with a cruel and aggressive mouth and deep-set staring eyes. Looking like that, every inch a murderess, it is surprising that anyone employed her at all.

In January 1879 Kate Webster took a job as a domestic servant with Mrs Julia Thomas at No 2 Vine Cottages, Park Road, Richmond. It went well at first. Kate was happy working for Mrs Thomas who was a rather eccentric woman in her fifties, and fairly well off. Problems began to develop when it became apparent to Mrs Thomas that Kate's work was poor. Mrs Thomas was also irritated by Kate's frequent visits to local pubs. A series of reprimands followed, and then Mrs Thomas gave Kate Webster notice. This period of notice was fatal. Mrs Thomas seems to have realised it, too, as she started asking friends and relatives to come and stay with her. She did not like being alone in the house with Kate Webster.

The day of Kate's dismissal arrived, 28 February, and she still had no new job to go to, so she pleaded with Mrs Thomas to let her stay over the weekend. Mrs Thomas reluctantly agreed.

On the Sunday, 2 March, 1879, Mrs Thomas went to church in the morning as usual. This Sunday afternoon, Kate was to visit her son, who was being looked after by Sarah Crease. She called in at a pub on her way back to Vine Cottages. She arrived back late, which annoyed Mrs Thomas, who expected Kate to be back before she went to the evening service. Mrs Thomas rashly took this opportunity to deliver one last reprimand, which with hindsight seems foolish, in that Kate Webster was supposed to be leaving for good the next day.

At church, Mrs Thomas appeared agitated. It is possible that Kate's behaviour had been threatening. It is possible that Mrs Thomas suspected Kate might be stealing her possessions. Yet, when the evening service was over, Mrs Thomas unwisely did not persuade any her friends to escort her home. She went home alone – and to her death.

What happened when Julia Thomas got home is unclear. Kate Webster's later version of events was straightforward enough. 'We had an argument which ripened into a quarrel, and in the height of my anger and rage I threw her from the top of the stairs to the ground floor. She had a heavy fall. She was seriously injured and I became agitated at what had happened, lost all control of myself and to prevent her screaming or getting me into trouble, I caught her by the throat and in the struggle I choked her.'

Mrs Thomas's next-door neighbour, Mrs Ives, heard the fall, but that was followed by silence. Probably there was no struggle. Probably Kate Webster's confession was full of lies.

Kate Webster then decided to try to cover up what had happened by disposing of the body. She began to dismember it, with the idea of dropping it in bits into the river. She cut off Mrs Thomas's head with a razor and meat saw. Then she cut off the arms and legs. She boiled the torso and limbs in a copper on the stove and burnt the internal organs. Even Kate Webster found all of this revolting, but she kept at it until she had burnt or boiled all the body parts. She packed them all into a wooden box, all except the head and one foot, which she could not fit in. It was said later that she even tried to sell the boiled-off fat as dripping, but this seems unlikely.

Mrs Thomas's next-door neighbour, Mrs Ives, noticed a strange smell, which was probably the burning.

Kate threw the spare foot onto a manure heap, but was unsure what to do with the head. She put it into a black bag for the moment and set about cleaning up the cottage. She borrowed one of Mrs Thomas's silk dresses to visit the Porters on the Tuesday afternoon, taking Mrs Thomas's head with her, in the black bag. She told the Porters she had inherited a house in Richmond from an aunt; she was going to sell it and return to Ireland. She asked Henry Porter if he knew of an estate agent who would help her. Kate had given Henry Porter and his son Robert the black bag to carry from the station, via two pubs, and the Porters both noticed how heavy the bag was. It is not at all clear why she took Julia Thomas's head on this macabre outing, or how she disposed of it. As far as I know it was never found.

Kate enlisted the help of young Robert Porter to help her move the wooden box. She and Robert together carried the box to Richmond Bridge, where she said someone was meeting her to collect it. The young man was told to walk on; she would catch him up. Robert did as he was told, but he had not walked on very far when he heard a splash, as of something heavy hitting the water. A few moments later Kate caught up with him again.

The box was picked out of the water by a coal-man, who must have had a very nasty surprise when he opened it. He reported it to Barnes police station. The police got a doctor to look at the remains, and he confirmed that they were parts of a female and that they had been boiled. Without the head, identification was impossible.

Meanwhile Kate Webster took to calling herself Mrs Thomas and wearing all of the dead woman's finery. She sold the contents of the cottage to a Mr John Church, who was a general dealer. The two of them seem to get on well, and were later seen drinking together. The real Mrs Thomas had not been reported missing yet, so the newspapers called the case 'the Barnes Mystery'. The Porters read about the case in their newspaper. Young Robert noticed that the box described in the press was much like the one Kate Webster had made him carry to Richmond Bridge for her. He had good reason to remember it, and the very peculiar way in which it had ended up in the Thames.

Kate agreed a price for the furniture and some of the clothes with Mr Church and he arranged to have them moved. This aroused the curiosity of Mrs Ives, who asked Kate what was going on. In amongst the dresses, Mrs Church later found a purse and a diary belonging to Mrs Thomas as well as a letter to a Mr Menhennick. Mr Church and Mr Porter decided to go and visit this Mr Menhennick, who evidently knew the real Mrs Thomas. The three men realised from what they now knew that the body in the box was probably that of Mrs Thomas. Together with Mr Menhennick's solicitor, they went to Richmond police station.

The next day, the police searched No 2 Vine Cottages. They found an axe, a razor, some charred bones and one of the handles belonging to the box found floating in the river. It was obvious now that not only was the body in the box that of Mrs Thomas but that Kate Webster was the murderer. On 23 March a detailed description of Kate Webster was circulated by the police.

Kate Webster had meanwhile fled to Ireland with her son. This was not a very intelligent move, partly because it was predictable – it was where she had originally come from – partly because she had told the Porters that that was where she was going. The Irish police found her fairly easily and arrested her on 28 March. She was escorted back to England. At Richmond police station she made a statement and was formally charged with murder. Typically, Kate Webster included some lies in her statement. She tried to incriminate John Church. He, she said, had been responsible for the murder. Poor Church was arrested and charged with murder. Luckily he had a good alibi and had conspicuously helped the police in uncovering the crimes. The charges against him were eventually dropped at the committal hearing, but only after an unnerving interval.

Kate Webster's trial opened at the Central Criminal Court, the Old Bailey, on 2 July, 1879. It was presided over by Mr Justice Denman. The prosecution was led by the Solicitor General, Sir Hardinge Gifford. Kate Webster was defended by Mr Warner Sleigh.

The prosecution called Mary Durden as a witness. She was a hat maker, and she said that on 25 February, several days before the murder, Kate Webster had told her she was going to Birmingham to take possession of the property left to her by a deceased aunt. This was clear evidence of premeditation. The prosecution encountered difficulties with the matter of identification. There was no direct evidence that the remains found in the box were actually those of Mrs Thomas. The head had still not been found, and without that there was, at that time, no way of being certain whose body it was. Medical evidence was produced to show that all the body parts belonged to one body, and that the body had belonged to a woman aged between fifty and sixty. But that still did not mean that it had to be Mrs Thomas.

The defence weakly argued that even if it was Mrs Thomas, she could have died of natural causes, which seemed rather unlikely. Whoever chopped her up, boiled and burnt her, could not have meant her well or cherished her memory. Henry Porter and John Church gave evidence against Kate, and once again the defence tried to cast suspicion on them and implicate them in the murder. In his summing up, the judge went out of his way to vindicate both Church and Porter, pointing out that they were both men of previous good character.

On 8 July, the jury retired to consider a verdict. It took just over an hour to reach a guilty verdict. Kate once again denied committing the murder. Just before sentence was passed she claimed to be pregnant. She was examined by some of the women present in court and this claim was written off as just another lie. She was taken to Wandsworth Prison to await execution. While she was there, Kate Webster told yet more lies. She made two more confessions. One of them implicated Strong, the father of her son. Her solicitor told her that there would be no reprieve even though there was (surprisingly) a small public lobby to have her death sentence commuted. The day before her execution, Kate made a second confession to her solicitor, one that seemed to be rather nearer the truth. She said she was resigned to her fate and that she would almost rather be executed than go back to a life of misery and deception. The 'heat of the moment' excuse that she used was almost certainly a lie. The murder of Mrs Thomas was a brutal, cold-blooded killing that Webster had been planning for several days beforehand. Whether the motive was simple revenge for dismissal, or another of Kate Webster's 'cleaning-up' jobs, is hard to tell – probably both.

There were still questions unanswered. Why did Kate Webster turn to murder? She had a very long history of lying and petty theft, but no history at all of violence. Why did she suddenly commit a violent murder at this stage in her life? Also, if Kate pushed Mrs Thomas down the stairs as she claimed, why were there bloodstains at the top of the stairs? Kate must have attacked Mrs Thomas with the axe before she fell down the stairs. Probably already fatally injured, Julia Thomas was finally silenced by strangulation. Kate Webster could not own up to the exact details of the murder, because they showed her as a cold-blooded killer.

Kate Webster was hanged at Wandsworth Prison on Tuesday 29 July. Wandsworth had taken over the responsibility for housing Surrey's condemned prisoners when Horsemonger Lane Gaol had closed in 1878, and Kate Webster was only the second person to be hanged there. In fact she had the distinction of being the only woman ever to be hanged at Wandsworth.

She was taken to the execution shed, which housed the large white-painted gallows. The noose lay on the trap door. The hangman, Marwood, stopped her on the chalk mark on the double trap door, fitted the leather body belt round her waist and secured her wrists to it while his assistant strapped her ankles with a leather strap. She was supported on the trap by two warders standing on planks, just in case the prisoner fainted and fell prematurely. Marwood, fitted the white hood and the noose, leaving the free rope hanging down her back. He stepped quickly aside and pulled the lever. Marwood's newly perfected 'long drop' meant that Kate Webster fell about eight feet out of sight into the pit, dying instantly of a broken neck.

The new execution method ensured that the whole business was over within two minutes, and was thus much more humane than Calcraft's 'short drop' executions, in which prisoners took as much as fifteen minutes to die. There were usually two newspaper reporters present, who were there to reassure the public that executions had been carried out 'expeditiously'.

Kate Webster was buried in an unmarked grave, Grave No 3, in one of the exercise yards. In all, 134 men and one woman were to be executed at Wandsworth. The last prisoner to suffer hanging at Wandsworth was Henryk Niemasz, who was executed for murder in 1961.

Arthur Devereux

'out of sight, out of mind'

ARTHUR DEVEREUX'S WAS one of the earliest trunk murders in England. It is a peculiar and eccentric notion – to think that locking a corpse in a trunk is a good way of evading detection. It may be that murderers who seek to hide their crime in this particular way have a special additional delusion, that hiding the body away out of sight is a way of 'vanishing' not only the body but the crime itself. Out of sight, out of mind.

One summer's day in 1898, Miss Beatrice Gregory was walking in Alexandra Park in Hastings. She was a pretty young woman and it was natural that a polite and neatly dressed young man should try to engage her in conversation. He was a chemist's assistant called Arthur Devereux. Beatrice was on holiday with her mother. She saw no reason why she should not see Arthur again; in fact she saw him every evening for the rest of her holiday. Beatrice's mother met him and she too liked him. He seemed different from many other young men: a cut above. He was ambitious and he had some imagination. He talked about the future in a way that was exciting, and Beatrice longed to be part of Arthur's future. When he proposed, she accepted.

Mrs Gregory was not so happy about the engagement, and could not believe that Arthur could deliver all the promises he was making. The marriage went ahead regardless, but within a few months Beatrice too was beginning to wonder whether Arthur's vision of the future was just fantasy. He was child-like, impractical, and increasingly he found married life on his low pay much less exciting and romantic than he had pictured. He became pensive, preoccupied.

Beatrice gave birth to a son, Stanley, and Arthur loved him dearly. It began to look as if the child might save the marriage – but, as usual, that was a forlorn hope. Then Beatrice became pregnant again. That really worried Arthur; he knew they could not afford to have two children and his affections were already completely engaged with Stanley. Then Beatrice gave birth to twin boys, Evelyn and Lawrence. Arthur had no love left for them.

Over the following two years, the Devereuxs moved to Kilburn in north-west London. They were living in a flat, Arthur was still working as a chemist's assistant, and Beatrice was under-nourished. Arthur increasingly felt trapped by circumstances, by marriage, by the two sons he had no interest in, by Beatrice. In his child-like way, he saw the removal of Beatrice, Evelyn and Lawrence as the solution to his problem; life would then be better.

It was probably late in 1904 that Arthur Devereux decided to kill them. First he asked the landlord if, when the tenants in the flat below theirs moved out, he could rent the extra flat. Then he brought home a big tin trunk and put it in the empty flat. Then, on 29 January, 1905, he brought home a bottle of morphine. He managed to get Beatrice to swallow nearly the whole bottle, perhaps by telling her it was a cough medicine. By the next morning, both she and the twins were dead.

Devereux put the three bodies in the tin trunk, arranged for it to be collected and taken into storage in Harrow, and then moved with little Stanley to another part of London. He was hoping to disappear, but he had reckoned without Mrs Gregory, the concerned and caring mother of Beatrice. Mrs Gregory called at the Kilburn flat and was surprised and concerned to find that it was empty. She wrote to Arthur and the letter was forwarded, but his answer was very unsatisfactory and suspicious. He said Beatrice had gone on holiday and he would prefer it if Mrs Gregory did not try to contact her. That was very strange. Mrs Gregory instinctively feared the worst. She heard about the furniture van that had called to collect a trunk, successfully traced it to a warehouse in Harrow, and eventually succeeded in getting an order giving her the authority to open the trunk.

The next day, the story of the discovery of the three bodies in the tin trunk was in all the newspapers. Arthur Devereux decided to change address again. This time he went to Coventry, where he found a job as a chemist's assistant again. The police inspector in charge of the investigation, Pollard, had little difficulty in finding Devereux. It was simply a question of under-taking a nation-wide trawl of chemists who had recently taken on new male assistants with six-year-old sons.

Arthur Devereux made Inspector Pollard's task even easier. When Pollard went to arrest him, Devereux gabbled, 'You're making a mistake. I don't know anything about a tin trunk.' Pollard had not mentioned a tin trunk. Devereux had just proved his own guilt.

At Devereux's Old Bailey trial, Devereux tried to make out that his wife had killed herself and the twins, and that he had lost his nerve and hidden the body. But he was given away by a telegram he had sent to a chemist in Hull on 22 January. It was in reply to a job advertisement, and he had written, 'Will a widower with one child aged six suit?' And this was sent when Beatrice and the twins were still alive. There was only one way he could have known that his next job was going to be as a widower with one child - and that was by deciding that he was going to kill Beatrice and the other two children. He could not have known in advance that Beatrice was going to commit suicide after killing the twins.

A psychologist decided that Devereux was sane, but to make the sort of decisions that Devereux made surely took him to the very outermost edge of sanity. He must have known that killing his wife would lead to his own execution and therefore leave Stanley as an orphan. He must have known that his mother-in-law would come looking for Beatrice. He must have known that the three bodies would be discovered sooner or later, identified and traced back to him. But with the trunk, it was a case of 'out of sight, out of mind' – and Arthur Devereux was certainly out of his mind.

Arthur Devereux was found guilty and hanged at Pentonville Prison on 15 August, 1905.

Maria Goold
'the Monte Carlo trunk murder'

THE MONTE CARLO trunk murder took place only two years after the Devereux case. The psychology of the second case has similarities with the first, though this time the killer was a woman, an adventuress called Maria Vere Goold. For business purposes she liked to call herself Lady Vere Goold: it gave her better credit. It was true that her feeble-minded and alcoholic husband was in line to inherit an Irish baronetcy, but she was certainly not a lady yet, and she never would be.

Maria Goold was born Maria Girodin, and she had already lost two husbands in suspicious circumstances before she met the third, the dim-witted Vere Goold. He had little money, but that did not deter Maria, as she was used to living on credit and loans. One year into their marriage, in early 1907, the Vere Goolds tried what gambling could do for them. They lost money, and had little choice but to try to get it dishonestly.

Maria scraped acquaintance with a rich old Swedish lady, Madame Levin, and succeeded in borrowing forty pounds from her. But Madame Levin would not part with any more, and nagged ceaselessly for the return of the £40. This was frustrating for Maria.

On 4 August, 1907, 'Lady Vere Goold' invited Madame Levin to her home, the Villa Menesimy, where she and her husband were living in considerable poverty. The old lady was sitting chatting with 'Sir Vere Goold', who was mumbling drunkenly, when Maria stole up behind Madame Levin and struck her very hard over the head with a poker. The old lady collapsed. Maria took a knife and cut her throat with it. Then Maria began cutting the body to pieces and pack them into a large trunk.

A niece who was staying with the Goolds – it is tempting to call them the Ghouls – returned that evening and was alarmed to see the place spattered with blood. Maria passed this off with the facile explanation that her husband had had a fit and vomited blood.

As with the Devereux case, it is hard to see what Maria Goold had in mind, long-term, but she and her husband left Monte Carlo that evening, taking the trunk with them, and went to Marseilles. The trunk was labelled 'Charing Cross, London'. It was handed over to the baggage clerk to send on while the Goolds went to a nearby hotel to breakfast and sleep. But the baggage clerk, an observant and conscientious man named Pons, noticed blood seeping from the Goolds' trunk. It was also August, and a hot August in the south of France at that; the trunk was beginning to smell unpleasantly. Pons went off to find the Goolds at their hotel to ask them what was in the trunk. Maria said dismissively that it was poultry and ordered the clerk to send it off at once. Pons did not send it off at once. He was suspicious and went to the police instead, where a police inspector told him that the Vere Goolds must not be allowed to leave Marseilles until the contents of the trunk were examined by the police.

It is odd that the police left it to the baggage clerk to detain the Vere Goolds, rather than doing that job themselves, but Pons obediently went back to the hotel, where he found the Vere Goolds on the point of leaving. Pons asked them to go with him to the police station. Maria coldly agreed and took with her the big carpet bag she had brought with her from Monte Carlo. She tried to maintain the façade of aristocratic contempt for this little man who was her nemesis, but in the cab she broke down and offered Pons ten thousand francs to let her go. Pons would not hear of it. On they went to the police station.

An hour later, the police had the trunk opened. Inside were the torso and arms of Mrs Levin. The police found her head and legs in the carpet bag. It was very obvious to everyone that Vere Goold was a drunken dimwit and incapable of organizing or doing anything, so he was sentenced to life imprisonment. Maria was sentenced to death. The death sentence was not carried out, though. While Maria was in prison in Cayenne, she died of typhoid. Goold himself went to pieces without the support of drink and drugs, and killed himself.

Maria's motive for killing Mrs Levin is obscure. It would seem that she may have had some twisted idea that she would somehow be able to get her hands on the old woman's money, but if she had thought hard about it she would have realised that that was not so, unless she was a legatee. It is more likely that she killed her in anger and frustration. She knew the old woman had lots of money, but would not hand it over. Resorting to the trunk suggests a deep level of psychological inadequacy. Hidden in the trunk, the crime was out of sight and Maria was safe. But at some level of her mind, Maria must have known that the body would begin to decompose and the smell would give it away, and that in Marseilles or London or some point in between, a railway official would be bound to report it to the police.

Perhaps it was a simple, unconscious, need to be caught.

The Brighton Trunk Murder

'the perfect murder?'

THE IDEA OF hiding a body in a trunk is an extra-ordinary one, because detection is certain. Sometimes the identity of the victim is obvious, and sometimes it has to be deduced as a result of forensic investigation. Usually there are enough clues on or in the body to point to a killer, too. The trunk itself may furnish clues.

The Chief Constable in Brighton was optimistic of success when on 17 June, 1934 he went to the left-luggage office at Brighton station to look at the naked torso of a woman. The remains had just been discovered in a plywood trunk. The clerks could remember nothing about the man who had left the trunk there on Derby Day, which was ten days earlier, on 6 June. It had been the busiest day of the year.

Even so there seemed to be lots of clues. The renowned pathologist and forensic expert Sir Bernard Spilsbury looked at the human remains, which were incomplete. She had been a young woman, probably in her early twenties. Her general physical condition suggested that she belonged

460

to the middle or upper classes; she was well nourished, with a good figure, no slack flesh, and well-toned muscles that implied plenty of exercise. The golden brown of the skin also suggested that she could afford to spend a good deal of time in lower latitudes; that suggested wealth. At the time of her death she had been pregnant.

The Brighton police sent out an alert to all other left-luggage offices in England to search for mysterious abandoned packages. At King's Cross station in London, the young woman's legs were found in a suitcase. Each leg had been severed at the thigh and the knee, and they were the legs of a well-proportioned and athletic young woman. Some clues were emerging as significant. The body had been wrapped in brown paper and on one sheet was the suffix '-ford'. It looked as if it was the second half of a place-name, perhaps Guildford. In the trunk there were two newspapers, copies of the *Daily Mail* for 31 May and 2 June. They were of an edition only circulated within fifty miles of London.

Then a porter remembered helping a man to carry the trunk on Derby Day. The man had travelled from Dartford to Brighton. Dartford was a place-name ending in 'ford' and it was a place where the London edition of the *Daily Mail* might be bought. It began to look as though the murderer was a Dartford man. It also began to look as though the case was about to be solved. A girl who had sat in the same train compartment as the man from Dartford was able to give a general description of him. Five cheap day returns had been bought that day, and the ones that could be traced were eliminated by the police. The makers of the trunk and the suitcase were traced, but they were unable to connect the items with particular purchasers. Suddenly the trail had gone stone cold. There were no more leads.

The pathologist said the young woman had died on about 30 May, a week before the trunk was left at Brighton station. The man who killed her must have had plenty of spare time, and presumably a home where he could safely conceal a body for a whole week without detection; this would have to be a man with a large property or a single man who had (and expected) no visitors. The fact that a whole week went by before the body was dumped suggested that the murder was not premeditated; the disposal of the body had not been planned, and it had taken several days for the murderer to work out how to do it. A certain amount of reconstruction was possible.

A fairly well-off, strong and athletic man had a secret love affair with a rather similar girl - also well-off, strong and athletic. He lived in Dartford, in the stockbroker belt. The girl became pregnant. On 30 May she called on him to ask him what to do about it. His reactions perhaps revealed that he had no serious intention of marrying her. There was a quarrel, perhaps developing into a fight, and he hit her over the head with something heavy that happened to be to hand. The young woman's head was never found, but there were no injuries to the rest of the body, so it can be assumed that she died of some head injury.

The man was severely shaken by the girl's death, which he never intended or wished - he probably loved her and was very distressed at what had happened, but could not face the exposure of the affair or the accusation that he had murdered the girl. He needed time to decide how to dispose of the body. He decided to dismember it. He deposited the trunk in Brighton, travelling on a third class ticket so as to lose himself in the crowd and not be remembered by witnesses. He deposited the suitcase containing the girls' legs at King's Cross. Probably after that, he left the country, knowing that it was only a matter of days before the body parts would be discovered.

In theory, the crime should have been solved by finding out which Dartford resident emigrated immediately after Derby Day. The sports clubs and riding stables of the Dartford area would almost certainly reveal both the missing man and the missing woman. In reality, the police investigation revealed nothing whatever that led to the Brighton trunk murderer. None of the obvious leads led anywhere at all. Careful searching of left-luggage offices did not reveal the whereabouts of the young woman's head, which was never found - though they did uncover the bodies of three children, opening up other murder enquiries. From that day to this, the Brighton trunk murder has never been solved. There is not even so much as the name of a suspect.

PART NINE

MURDER FOR PROFIT

Thomas Wynne

THE STRANGE CASE of Thomas Wynne, who lived in England in the reign of Elizabeth I, reads like a piece of fiction, but it is a true story. Thomas Wynne was born in the port of Ipswich and at the age of fifteen he went to sea. When he was about twenty-four, his ship docked in London, where he was unable to resist the lure of the whore-houses. He liked London low life and quickly sank into every kind of crime, and became the greatest expert known in the art of house-breaking.

He even had the impudence to burgle the royal lodgings at Whitehall Palace, almost making off with more than £400 worth of plate. Stealing from Elizabeth I was a rash move. He was caught and sent to Newgate Prison. He was very lucky, as it happened, because Elizabeth I's Act of Grace was passed just at that time, granting free pardons to all prisoners for all offences except treason and murder, and so it was that he was released.

Wynne made poor use of Her Majesty's clemency, and he went straight back to the criminal career that had landed him in Newgate. He was close to being caught again, when he had the good luck to be taken into the service of the Earl of Salisbury as a scullion. While in this very lowly position as a mere kitchen boy, he had the audacity to pay court to the Countess's maid, who was much higher up the social scale, and was as scornful and contemptuous as might be expected. Wynne's love for the maid instantly turned to hatred. One night, as she was coming downstairs after helping her ladyship undress, he gave her a beating. The young woman was in such a bad way afterwards that she had to be carried to her bed to recover and inevitably the Earl was told of the incident.

The Earl of Salisbury took it on himself to punish the young man. He ordered him to be stripped and severely whipped by his coachman. The Earl threatened to repeat this punishment every week for the next month. Thomas Wynne had other ideas about this. He decided to pack his few possessions and prepared to take his leave of the Earl's household, though not before helping himself to a few valuables. He broke open the trunk belonging to the coachman who had whipped him and took £9 – just for revenge. He took £15 from the cook, a silver dish belonging to the Earl and the best clothes of the maid he had just given a beating. Then he made his departure.

Wynne dressed himself in a porter's uniform and went to one of the best inns in town. He set his sights on a bundle or parcel that looked promising and, once the coast was clear, picked it up and walked off with it. The servants at the inn thought he was just another servant, and no-one thought anything of a porter carrying a bundle. He carried on doing this for two years, making over £200, which was a great deal of money in Elizabethan England.

These and many other tricks kept Wynne occupied for around eight years. Then he set his sights on an old retired linen-draper. The draper had made a lot of money from his trade and was living on his capital with his wife in Honey Lane off Cheapside. He developed a plan to rob the old couple. He broke into their house at night, and made the huge mistake of murdering them. He cut the poor old couple's throats as they slept together in their bed, fearing that they would wake up while he was rummaging round their house, and then, even he could make his escape, see him and later identify him. After these cold-blooded murders, he went round the house collecting the draper's treasure. Altogether he made off with £2,500, a huge sum in those days. He realised that he had to leave London and wisely decided to emigrate. He made arrangements to take his wife and four children to Virginia.

The day after the murder, the neighbours were concerned to see that the shutters remained shut. Day followed day, and there was still no sign of the old couple and the house remained shuttered. The constable was called and the door broken open. All were horrified to see the old couple in their bed, their throats cut from ear to ear. The murderer was not hard to find. It had to be the poor beggar who was often seen walking to and fro in front of the house, and often sat on a bench belonging to the house. The beggar was arrested, tried and even though there was no evidence against him whatever he was sentenced to be hanged in front of the murdered couple's house.

He protested his innocence to the bitter end, but it made no difference. They went ahead and hanged him; someone had to be to blame.

Meanwhile, Wynne's arrangements were completed and he and his family sailed safely to Virginia, where he prospered with his ill-gotten gains. He became rich.

Twenty years passed, and he often hankered for the old country. He decided that he wanted to see England once more before he died, so he travelled back to England on a sentimental journey, with the idea of taking a last look before returning to Virginia to die. He left his wife, children and grandchildren and sailed back to England.

Wynne went into a goldsmith's shop in Cheapside one day, with the idea of choosing some plate to take home with him to Virginia. He was haggling with the goldsmith, who was weighing the plate for him, when there was a disturbance outside in the street. Some constables had arrested a man, but the man had broken away from them and was making his escape. Wynne instinctively went out into the street, just like everyone else in the neighbourhood, to see what was happening. The crowd in the street was surging along in one direction, and out of curiosity Wynne went with the crowd. Some people behind started yelling, 'Stop him! Stop him!'

Wynne was suddenly transported back in time to his earlier life as a criminal in these very streets and it seemed that the mob behind him were shouting at him. He, Thomas Wynne, was the thief that had to be stopped. His conscience had caught up with him. He suddenly stopped in his tracks and shouted, 'I am the man!' The mob shouted, 'You the man? What man?' Wynne found himself saying, 'The man that committed a murder in Honey Lane twenty years ago for which a poor man was wrongfully hanged.'

Wynne was taken into custody and led before a magistrate, where he repeated his confession. After spending some time in Newgate Prison, he was tried, condemned to death and executed. He too was hanged in front of the house where the murder was committed, like the poor beggar twenty years earlier. After the hanging, Wynne's body was taken to Holloway, where it was hung in chains. When word got back to Virginia, his wife had a mental breakdown and died insane. Two of Wynne's sons turned to crime like their father and they were hanged in Virginia, for robbery and murder. The plantations Wynne had invested in were confiscated by the Crown, as forfeited by his conviction. The surviving members of his family were reduced to poverty. Thomas Wynne not only lost his own life, but wrecked the lives of his entire family.

Stephen Eaton,
George Roades and
Sarah Swift

'killing the curate'

THE REVD JOHN Talbot served as a chaplain to a regiment in Portugal during the reign of Charles II. When the time came for his regiment to be recalled to England, Talbot came back too, serving for a few months in the parish of St Alphege in the Wall in London. Then he went as curate to Laindon in Essex. A dispute of some kind developed between Talbot and some of his new parishioners, and it escalated into a lawsuit. To try to resolve this, he went to London.

What happened to him there on 2 July, 1669 was remarkable. He was in effect hunted down by a gang of seven strangers, who doggedly followed him round London for several hours before finally attacking him. It is still not known what the gang's motive might have been. Was it robbery pure and simple, or had they been hired by Talbot's enemies in Laindon to kill him? Either way, they followed him from four o'clock one afternoon, on 2 July, 1669. Talbot had been warned that his enemies intended to arrest him, or clap a writ on him, so he did his best to lose them. Even so, wherever he went he seemed to bump into them.

Talbot went to Gray's Inn, where he took shelter for a while and wrote letters to several acquaintances and friends, asking them to come to his aid. None of them answered, and none of them came. He was nervous about going out and being accosted by the gang, who he knew had followed him there. In desperation, he spoke to one of the gentlemen at Gray's Inn and was offered shelter in his chambers until he thought it safe to go out again. He took some refreshment, then thought it was safe to risk going out into the streets. He slipped out the back, through Old Street and across the fields towards Shoreditch.

Not long after he entered the fields at Anniseed Clear he saw the same gang as before coming after him. He was now frightened, as it was eleven o'clock at night and he was far from any kind of help. They were evidently determined to get to him. The only way he could see of getting away from them was by breaking through a hedge to reach a house, but the gang caught up with him before he could manage that.

The ruffians grabbed him and went through his pockets, taking twenty shillings from him and a knife. Then they tried to cut his throat with the knife. They inflicted a most peculiar wound on the Revd Talbot. They cut out a piece of his throat about two inches in diameter, then stabbed him deeply in the centre of this hole. Surprisingly, and presumably not intentionally, neither of these wounds was immediately fatal. The windpipe and main arteries and veins in the neck were not touched, though the second wound seems to have reached Talbot's lung.

The dogs in the area were apparently aware that something unusual was happening, as they started barking. This made several gardeners get up, thinking it was time to get ready for market. Shortly after this there was thunder and torrential rain. This drew the local brick makers out to secure their bricks against the weather. So, although the Revd Talbot lay in the field in his shirt and drawers, soaked and badly wounded, and his attackers had done the deed unwitnessed, they were soon apprehended.

The brick makers found Mr Talbot lying covered in blood, and gave him a drop of brandy. Talbot was fully conscious in spite of his terrible ordeal and able to point which way the murderers had gone. Nightwatchmen from Shoreditch were raised and one of them found a man lying among nettles with a bloody knife on one side of him and the curate's doublet on the other. The watchman arrested him on the circumstantial evidence. The man at first pretended to be asleep, then jumped up and tried to run away. A pewter pot was lying near him and one of the watchmen resourcefully picked it up and hit him smartly over the head with it, which made him a good deal more tractable.

Mr Talbot, meanwhile, was carried to the Star Inn by Shoreditch church, where he was put to bed and a surgeon was sent for to dress the wound. The man from the nettle bed was brought into Talbot's presence. Talbot confirmed in writing that he was the man who had cut his throat. It must be the only occasion in criminal history where such an accusation has been made. The man's name was Eaton, and he was a confectioner. He was taken off to Justice Pitfield, who committed him to Newgate Prison. Then another of Mr Talbot's assailants was found, a woman, who also pretended to be asleep. She too was shown to Talbot, who was certain that she was the woman in the gang that attacked him. He asked the constable whether her name was Sarah, as he had heard one of her associates say to her, earlier in the day, 'Shall we have a coach, Sarah?' The constable asked the woman her name and without suspecting the significance of her answer she told him it was Sarah.

Two more of the attackers were caught, one of whom Talbot recognized. They too were sent to Newgate.

Meanwhile, the Revd Talbot was attended by doctors, and his condition improved steadily during the following week. By the eighth day the wound was looking fairly well healed and Talbot was in good spirits. But then he had a coughing fit. This broke the jugular vein and caused a haemorrhage. He fainted from loss of blood before the flow was staunched. Then he coughed again and the bleeding began again. In spite of the fact that he had survived a week, his condition improving all the time, he was now obviously dying. The Vicar of Shoreditch, Dr Atfield, went to see him. Talbot spoke in an easy and familiar way with Dr Atfield, who asked him if he was absolutely sure he had identified the right people. Atfield was evidently thinking that Talbot was about to die and that the people he was identifying as attackers would have to hang for it; he wanted to be sure. He also asked if he would forgive them. Talbot said he prayed for the welfare of their souls, but wanted the law to be executed on their bodies. Two hours later, John Talbot died.

At the trial of the four prisoners, there were several witnesses who attested to the fact that the prisoners had dogged Talbot before murdering him. All the circumstances of the strange events of the day were told. The various letters and statements John Talbot himself wrote during his last week were offered in evidence. He wrote several letters to friends giving an exact and detailed account of his seven-hour manhunt and the barbarous throat-cutting incident. It is quite exceptional in a murder case for the victim to be able to give a detailed eye-witness account of his own murder.

In his writings about the incident, Talbot in particular denounced Sarah Swift, using the word 'bloody' every time he mentioned her. He evidently saw her as the prime mover in the attack. He heard her say to her associates several times, 'Kill the dog, kill him!'

Talbot had been keen, after the attack, to know whether the gang had been hired by his enemies at Laindon to attack him. This point came out in the trial, but Stephen Eaton denied it vehemently, swearing that he never in his life had seen Mr Talbot until he had been taken before him after the attack. Sarah Swift similarly denied being hired to murder Talbot. She said she would burn in Hell before she would admit anything of the kind.

The verdict was a foregone conclusion. On Wednesday 14 July, 1669, Sarah Swift, George Roades, a broker, and Stephen Eaton were taken in a cart from Newgate to Tyburn. There the men confessed the murder, but Sarah Swift obstinately refused to admit anything at all. The fourth assailant they apprehended that night, Henry Pritchard, a tailor, was reprieved when some favourable circumstances relating to his part in the attack were brought forward. The two others in the gang were never caught. It is by no means clear why this motley crew, a confectioner, a broker, a tailor and a bloodthirsty harridan, should follow a curate round London for seven or eight hours. Were they after his money? How much money would they have expected a curate to be carrying? The Revd John Talbot seems scarcely worthwhile as a target for a mugging, and not worth investing so much time in following him. There must have been far more lucrative subjects for them to target. But no connection back to Laindon was ever established either. The whole business remains a rather peculiar and spine-chilling mystery.

Tom Kelsey

'a wrong-headed reprieve'

TOM KELSEY WAS born in Leather Lane, Holborn, in London. His mother was Welsh, and she had an income of forty pounds a year left her by an uncle who lived at Wrexham, so the Kelsey family – mother, father and their only son Tom – went to Wrexham in Denbighshire to live on the estate.

Tom was from the beginning a very difficult child, contrary and stubborn. As he grew older, his personality deteriorated and he developed a dangerous temper. At fourteen he left his parents and returned to London to seek his fortune. He was encouraged in this by a friend called Jones. They had no money and were obliged to beg. They called at a gentleman's house. The gentleman took a liking to them and gave them jobs, Jones as a falconer, Kelsey as a stable boy. It seems that Jones was even more awkward than Kelsey, as it was Jones who was dismissed first. But it was not long before Kelsey was caught pilfering, and then he too was turned out.

It was not long after this that Tom Kelsey fell among thieves. He already had a leaning towards dishonesty, and this seemed like the only way he could make a living now.

One day he was walking past the house of a silversmith, called Mr Norton, when some of his companions snatched Tom's hat and threw it into the silversmith's window, which happened to be open. Tom could put on an innocent expression that would fool anyone, and he adopted this when he went up to Mr Norton and told him what had happened. Mr Norton had seen for himself what happened and said, 'Poor lad! You shall not lose your hat. Go upstairs and fetch it, for I cannot leave the shop.' Tom went upstairs, collected his hat and a dozen silver spoons that happened to be lying around. He came straight down, thanked Mr Norton and ran off, dividing the spoils with his companions.

But not all of Tom Kelsey's exploits went as well as this one, and he was to find himself condemned to hang when he was only fifteen.

He broke into the house of a grocer in the Strand and stole a huge amount of silver as well as forty pounds in cash. He was caught, arrested, tried and condemned to death. His father heard of the trial verdict and travelled up to London at once to see what could be done. He arrived in London the day before the execution, yet succeeded in getting his son not only reprieved but granted a full pardon, on the grounds of his extreme youth.

Mr Kelsey did what he could to keep his son out of further trouble, but he must have known, deep down, that it was a lost cause. The misbehaviour was not a sudden aberration; it was a part of the boy's dysfunctional personality. He was bound to come to a bad end. Mr Kelsey managed to get Tom apprenticed to a weaver, but it did not last. The boy ran away after only a few months with his master.

Tom Kelsey took pride in making everyone he came in contact with as wicked as himself. He decided to corrupt another boy, David Hughes, who was a cousin of his. The two boys attended Kingston Assizes only a few days after David arrived in London from Wales. Tom persuaded David to pick a pocket in the courtroom. The boy was inexpert and was caught immediately and condemned the next day to be hanged within sight of the Bench, 'as a terror to others'. It was a bad week for David Hughes. He arrived in London on the Monday, spent the ten pounds he had brought with him on the Tuesday and Wednesday, picked a pocket on the Thursday, was condemned to death on the Friday and hanged on the Saturday. David Hughes died at Tom Kelsey's hands just as surely as if he had been murdered by him; Kelsey even boasted of his 'success' with David Hughes.

Another of Tom Kelsey's exploits was the robbing of Lord Faversham's lodgings. Lord Faversham was General of the Forces in the time of James II, and always had a guard at his door. Tom Kelsey dressed in foot-soldier's uniform and approached the guard, chatting affably with him for a time before offering to stand him a drink at a nearby inn. The guard said he could not leave his post. Tom good-naturedly offered to stand in his place while he went for the drink and gave him sixpence. The guard went off and Tom and his companions went into the house, rifling it as fast as they could. The soldier came back before they had finished, so Tom gave him twopence to go and get some tobacco. When the poor sentry came back, Tom had gone, with more than two hundred pounds' worth of plate, and his musket. The sentry was ordered to run the gauntlet for losing his musket and imprisoned in Newgate, where he died nine months later.

After another daring robbery, this time at Thistleworth, he was betrayed by one of his companions and had to leave the country. He fled to the camp of King William in Flanders. There he had the audacity to steal a considerable amount of loot from the king's tent. He succeeded in getting this to Amsterdam, where he sold it and then sailed again from Rotterdam for England.

He had not been in England long before he was caught breaking into a house in Cheapside. This led to imprisonment in Newgate. He despaired of ever getting out of prison and decided to do as much mischief as he could while he was there. He may even have committed the murder in order to bring the prison sentence to an end. Mr Goodman, who was one of the turnkeys or warders at Newgate, was sitting drinking when Kelsey without warning and without cause or provocation stabbed him in the stomach. Goodman died immediately.

For murdering Mr Goodman, Tom Kelsey was sentenced to death. He was executed on a gallows erected in Newgate Street, near the prison, on 13

June, 1690. He was only twenty. With hindsight, it would have been better if his father had not procured the pardon for him when he was fifteen. David Hughes' life would have been saved. The gullible sentry's life would have been saved. The turnkey's life would have been saved. But it was a father's natural instinct to try to save his son.

Jack Blewit

JACK BLEWIT WAS born near Bull Inn Court in the Strand. His father was a cobbler and Jack was brought up to follow the same trade. He had been apprenticed only a short time when his father died, and without his father to control him he became unmanageable.

Jack Blewit was unscrupulous as well as headstrong, switching from Protestantism to Roman Catholicism in the reign of James II in the hope of gaining some advantage. He entered the service of the Earl of Salisbury, and in this way got himself a horse, but he did not stay long in military service; once William III acceded to the English throne the new Catholic regiment he had joined was disbanded.

Blewit then decided to try his luck at sea. He boarded a ship sailing for West Africa to collect black slaves. After the cargo of slaves had been got on board, the captain ordered the boatswain and three other hands, one of whom was Jack Blewit, to unload the copper bars they had on board and take them ashore to sell. The boatswain asked for weapons, not entirely trusting the peaceable reputation of the native population, and with some justification. He was given a pistol and three muskets. Unfortunately as their boat

481

was being lowered, they dropped their match into the sea, but were too ashamed of their ineptitude to go back and get another.

Once ashore, Jack Blewit was seized by ten 'Moors' and taken half a mile inland. There he was thrown down and stripped. His captors were so keen to get their hands on his canvas clothes that they cut them off him, along with bits of his flesh. The canvas was cut up to make aprons or loin-cloths. The other three sailors made their way back to the ship without him, while Blewit was sold to a master. He learned the local Tata language and after four months his master presented him to the 'King of the Buccaneers', Esme, who gave him to his daughter Onijah. When the King travelled round his country, which had a circumference of only twelve miles, Blewit attended him as a page. Even though the country was very small, the chief gave himself high status and thought himself very grand to have a white slave to carry his bows and arrows.

A neighbouring chief called Mancha heard about Blewit and bought him for a cow and a goat. Mancha was sober and more moderate in his behaviour than Esme – a better master. Mancha was interested to know what sort of country Jack Blewit came from, whether it was bigger than his own. Blewit tried to convey the dignity of the state of England and its division into shires and counties, its cities and castles. Mancha was profoundly impressed by the huge size of this foreign country and the grandeur of its monarch and wanted to inform Queen Anne of his great respect for her. He planned to send her two goats, which was a very great gift, since he had only eighteen altogether.

Jack Blewit was happy enough living with Mancha, but wanted to return to England. Mancha promised him that he could go back when an English ship next arrived. An English ship did eventually anchor, under the command of Captain Royden. He had come with the intention of collecting more negro slaves. Mancha sent Blewit out in a canoe to tell the English crew who he was. He startled the crew when he stood up, stark naked, in the canoe and addressed them in perfect English. Royden paid a ransom of five iron bars for Blewit and hauled him on board. Royden's crew kindly gave him items of clothing, as he had nothing whatever to wear.

Back in England, Jack Blewit decided to make his way as a highwayman. He stole a horse from a field at Marylebone, then sold it to buy the saddle, pistols and other gear he needed for the job, before attempting to steal another horse, this time to ride. Unfortunately, this time the owner caught up with him before he had ridden any distance. He was taken before a magistrate, then tried and condemned. He begged for any punishment but death. As it was his first offence and the owner had his horse back, he was reprieved. After only four months in prison he was pardoned and set free.

The brush with the law over the horse-stealing did not deter Jack Blewit from pursuing a life of crime and he tried his luck again as a highwayman. One evening on Clapham Common he stealthily overtook a man as he rode along and knocked him off his horse by hitting him under the ear. The blow killed the man outright. Blewit took forty guineas in cash from his victim's pockets and a gold watch worth another twenty guineas. Afterwards, Blewit put the dead man's foot into one of the stirrups. The horse wandered up and down the Common for a couple of hours before someone saw what had happened. The coroner called an inquest, and it was concluded that the man had died accidentally by falling from his horse; his empty pockets were explained by his being dragged along while upside down. The money had simply fallen out somewhere.

Jack Blewit next went to Yorkshire, where he bought new clothes, a horse, sword and pistols. Then, returning to Hertfordshire, he attacked a farmer's daughter, shooting her through the head and taking fourteen pounds. He stayed at an inn at Ware, but he was pursued there and arrested on suspicion. It was seen that he had spots of blood on his lapel. He was overwhelmed by remorse and confessed to the murder. He was taken before a magistrate, who questioned him closely before committing him to Hertford Prison.

Blewit was deeply depressed by his crime, and tried to lose himself in drunkenness every night before his trial, in the spring of 1713. He was found guilty and condemned to death. Jack Blewit was hanged at the age of forty-five, having lived the remarkable life of a cobbler, a soldier, a sailor, a white slave, a horse thief, a highwayman and a murderer.

Dick Turpin

'smuggler, house-breaker and highwayman'

THE INFAMOUS HIGHWAYMAN, Richard Turpin, was born in Hempstead, near Saffron Walden in Essex. His father, John Turpin, apprenticed him to a Whitechapel butcher, who must have regretted taking him on. From the beginning, Dick Turpin was a disorderly, naughty boy. When he completed his apprenticeship he got married and moved back to Essex, but he was not by any means 'settling down'. He now had a wife to support and he did this by stealing cows, sheep and lambs.

Turpin's criminal career nearly ended early, after he stole a couple of oxen from Mr Giles at Plaistow. He cut them up back at his own house, but was suspected by Mr Giles's servants, who made enquiries as to where Turpin sold the hides of his animals. They were told he generally sold them at Waltham Abbey, so they rode there, found the hides of the two lost oxen, recognized them and went back to Turpin's house to take him into custody. He saw them coming, jumped out of the window and escaped. His wife later disposed of the incriminating ox carcasses.

After this close call, Dick Turpin decided to

become a smuggler, and so went off to look for a gang to join. He encountered a band of deer-thieves, who saw that he was game for any mischief and welcomed him into their gang. In this way, he met and got to know Gregory, Rose, Fielder and Wheeler, later to become notorious as the Essex Gang. It was Turpin's idea to diversify into nocturnal house-breaking. The method was bold and crude. They identified houses with items of value inside, knocked on the door at night, and when the door was opened simply rushed in, tied up the occupants and looted the place.

The first victim of these house-breaking raids, which started in 1734, was Mr Strype, who ran a chandler's shop in Watford. The gang took the little money he had, but did not injure Mr Strype in any way. The next raid was on the house of old woman at Loughton. Turpin was sure she had seven or eight hundred pounds in the house. He and the others rushed in and tied up the old woman, her son and their two servants. Turpin then tried to make the old woman tell him where the money was. She insisted that there was no money. Turpin told her that if she didn't tell him where the money was he would put her on the grate. The old woman thought he was bluffing and stayed silent, but Turpin meant what he said, and sat her on the grate. She suffered for a time, but could not stand the pain, so she gave in and told Turpin where the money was. It was only half of what Turpin had been hoping for, but still a good sum.

In January 1735, the gang visited the house of

Mr Sheldon in Croydon. They saw a light in the stable and went to it. They found the coachman there, tending his horses, and tied him up. Coming out of the stables, they met Mr Sheldon in the yard, seizing him and making him show them the way into the house. They took eleven guineas and several pieces of jewellery and plate. Rather oddly, they gave Mr Sheldon back two guineas of his money, apologized to him for what they had done and said goodnight.

At about 7.30 p.m. on 4 February, they visited the house of Mr Lawrence at Edgewarebury near Stanmore and took £26 in money as well as plate and possessions. After this raid, they did not distribute the proceeds fairly. Wheeler, who was keeping watch, was told they had only taken three guineas altogether and was therefore given a small share of the actual total. Something similar happened in another robbery three days later. Turpin, Fielder, Rose Walker, Bush, Wheeler and Gregory met at the White Bear in Drury Lane, ready to attack the house of Mr Francis, a Marylebone farmer. In a similar way, they arrived there at about seven in the evening, capturing and tying up the menservants they found in the outbuildings. And they also cheated each other as before. Those that did the looting lied about how much they were pocketing, while those keeping watch had no means of knowing by how much they were being cheated. Gregory stood guard over Mrs Francis and her maid and daughter; Turpin and Bush guarded Mr Francis and the two menservants.

There was general alarm in the home counties. No-one felt safe from the Essex Gang. One of the King's keepers got a promise from the King that a one hundred pound reward would be paid for anyone apprehending any member of the gang. When the gang heard about this, they became a little more wary. Even so, they were very nearly caught when drinking in an ale-house in Westminster. Officers of the law heard where they were and burst in on them. There was a fierce struggle and Wheeler, Rose and Fielder were captured. Dick Turpin made his escape out of a window, jumped on his horse and galloped away.

After these unsatisfactory developments, Turpin decided he would not get mixed up with another gang, but in future work alone. He rode off towards Cambridge, where he was not known, and make a fresh start. On this journey he had a strange encounter. A highwayman called King had been working the countryside near Cambridge for exactly the same reason as Turpin, but was now travelling back to London. Turpin saw that he was well-dressed and well-mounted, and decided he must also have money in his pockets. Turpin told him to stand and deliver. If he would not he would be shot through the head. King laughed and said, 'What? Dog eat dog? Come, come, brother Turpin, if you don't know me, I know you and should be glad of your company.' The two men swore loyalty to one another and agreed to pull off some robberies together.

Turpin and King committed their first joint robbery that same day, and continued working together for almost three years. Both King and Turpin became very well known figures, so much so that they could not stay in anyone's house - and no-one would have wanted them. They decided that they should make a cave. They chose a place within a dense thicket between Loughton Road and King's Oak Road in Epping Forest, and made a cave big enough to hold themselves and their horses. While they lay completely hidden from view, they were able nevertheless to watch people passing along either of the two roads. If they saw someone likely coming along one of the roads, they could dash out and rob them. They took to living, eating, drinking and sleeping in the cave. Mrs Turpin used to supply them with food and drink and they often stayed in the cave all night.

On one occasion, King and Turpin rode to Bungay in Suffolk. There Turpin saw two young women in the market taking thirteen pounds for corn and decided to rob them. King was against this, but Turpin impetuously went ahead and robbed the women. The two men quarrelled over this. On their way back to the cave in Epping Forest, they robbed Mr Bradele, who was taking a ride in his carriage with his two children.

Shortly after this, an escapade went wrong and got Turpin even deeper into crime than he was already. Turpin and King took on another associate, Potter, and the three of them were riding through Epping Forest towards London when Turpin's horse began to tire. They overtook a man called Mr Major and robbed him, even though they were very near the Green Man inn. Turpin saw that Mr Major had a better horse than his own, and made him dismount and change horses, though not before changing saddles. Turpin and the others rode on to London, while Major went to the Green Man with his second-hand highwayman's horse, and there told Mr Bayes his story. Bayes said he had almost certainly encountered Dick Turpin.

Two days later, Bayes heard that a horse just like the one Mr Major had had stolen from him had been left outside the Red Lion inn in Whitechapel. Bayes went to the Red Lion, checked that it was the same animal and patiently waited to see who would come to collect it. It was at about eleven o'clock at night that King's brother arrived to take it away. He was seized by Bayes and his friends and taken into the house. The man said he could prove it was his own horse, but Bayes threatened to have him arrested and this seemed to frighten him. Bayes said he didn't believe he was a rogue, but that he had been sent by rogues. If he would just tell Bayes where the rogues were waiting, he would be released. The man told him there was a 'lusty' man in a white duffel coat waiting for the horse in Red Lion Street.

Mr Bayes went outside into the street and identified the man described almost straight away. He circled round and attacked him from behind. Turpin was near at hand and came out to see what the scuffle was about. King shouted out, 'Dick, shoot him or we are taken, by God!' Turpin did as King asked, and fired his pistols. Bayes must have thought his time was up, but instead of hitting Bayes, Turpin's bullets hit King and killed him. Once Turpin saw this he rode away. It is not clear whether Turpin intended to kill Bayes or King. He may have decided on the spur of the moment that he, Turpin, was probably safer with King dead than taken alive. He was certainly ruthless enough to have sacrificed King in this way.

After this killing, Dick Turpin remained in Epping Forest for a time, but he was now a hunted man. His situation was made even worse when his cave was discovered. He decided to leave the area. He adopted the name John Palmer and went to Lincolnshire, staying for a time at Long Sutton. Then he went to Yorkshire, again living in caves for some months. While he lived in Yorkshire, he often went hunting and shooting with the gentlemen of the area, but he was still too disorderly and impetuous for his own good.

In October 1738, he was returning from one of these shooting parties. He saw his landlord's cock in the street and shot and killed it. His neighbour, Hall, saw him do it and told him it was a bad thing to do. Palmer replied, 'If you'll stay while I charge my piece, I'll shoot you too.' Hall was concerned enough to go and tell the landlord what had happened – not just the shooting of the cock, but what Palmer had said afterwards - and the landlord went straight off to Justice Crowley to get a warrant for Palmer's arrest.

The following day Dick Turpin was arrested and taken in front of a bench of justices, who happened then to be sitting in Quarter Sessions at

491

Beverley. The justices demanded sureties for his good behaviour, and because he refused to offer any he was imprisoned in the house of correction. Some of the residents of Brough and Welton, where Turpin had been living recently, gave information to the justices that Palmer frequently went off to Lincolnshire and usually came back with plenty of money and several horses. They thought he must be either a highwayman or a horse-thief. The justices then went to 'Palmer' and questioned him closely. Who was he? Where had he lived? What was his occupation?

Turpin told them that two years before he had lived at Long Sutton and was a butcher by trade, that his father had lived at Long Sutton too and his sister kept his father's house there. He said he had got into debt over some sheep that had proved rotten, and he had been forced to leave Long Sutton for Yorkshire. This ambitious and risky lie was put to the test at once. The justices sent a special messenger to Lincolnshire bearing a letter to Mr Delamere, who was a Justice of the Peace at Long Sutton. They would soon know how much, if any, of what John Palmer had told them was true.

Mr Delamere's reply confirmed the Beverley justices' suspicions. 'John Palmer' had lived at Long Sutton for nine months and was accused of sheep-stealing. He had been arrested but escaped from the constable. Soon after Palmer's escape, Delamere had received additional complaints about Palmer's horse-stealing activities. Palmer's father did not live at Long Sutton. Mr Delamere wanted Palmer kept in custody to answer the charge of stealing livestock.

Mr Justice Crowley read the letter and decided John Palmer was too dangerous a man to keep in the house of correction and arranged for him to be committed to York Castle on 16 October 1738. He had been in York Prison for about four months when his real identity was discovered. He was not John Palmer the small-time sheep-stealer and horse-thief of Long Sutton after all - he was Dick Turpin the infamous Essex highwayman.

On 22 March, 1739, Turpin was tried at York Assizes before Sir William Chapple, on two charges of horse-stealing at Long Sutton. He was convicted and condemned. After this, to prove that he was Richard Turpin, the noted highwayman, two witnesses were called to identify him. One of them was James Smith, who said he had known the prisoner since childhood, that his name was Richard Turpin and that he had been born in Hempstead in Essex. The other witness was Edward Seward, who swore that the prisoner was Dick Turpin, the son of John Turpin, landlord of The Bell at Hempstead; 'When I spoke to him at the castle I knew him again, and he confessed he knew me.'

After Dick Turpin was convicted of murdering his own associate, King, he was as jovial and light-hearted as if he was a completely free man.

As word got out that the notorious highwayman who had terrorized southern England was in York, people poured into the city to see him. The morning before his execution he gave three pounds ten shillings for five men to follow the cart as mourners. He also left a gold ring and two pairs of shoes and clogs to a married woman that he knew in Brough, though he acknowledged that he had a wife and child of his own.

He was conveyed by cart to the place of execution in York, on 7 April, 1739. Turpin carried his own execution off with amazing assurance, as if it was his last feat of reckless daring. It was a bravura theatrical performance from one of the most charismatic criminals of all time. He even bowed to his admirers from the cart as he passed them in the street. He finally mounted the ladder to the gallows, looked about him with great self-assurance, chatting to the hangman for about half an hour before throwing himself off the ladder. He died in about five minutes.

The Benjamin Tapner Gang

'the smugglers' revenge'

IN 1748, AN unusually daring large-scale robbery was carried out at the custom house at Poole. A shoemaker called Daniel Chater and a custom-house officer named William Galley were sent from Fordingbridge in Hampshire to Stansted in Sussex to give evidence in connection with this robbery to a magistrate by the name of Major Battine.

These two men, who were no more than unfortunate witnesses to a crime, never reached Stansted and were never to return home. They were brutally murdered as they approached Stansted. The body of William Galley was buried, and only found by the use of blood-hounds. The body of Daniel Chater was found six miles away in a well in Harris's Wood near Leigh, in Lady Holt's Park, and covered up with stones, wooden railings and earth.

The smugglers who were responsible for these two appalling murders were tried at a special hearing in Chichester, the county town of West Sussex, on 16 January, 1749. The three principals in the case were Benjamin Tapner, John Cobby and John Hammond, and they were accused of the murder of Daniel Chater. Richard Mills, father and son, were accused of being accessories before the fact, in other words they assisted the other three knowing that murder was planned. William Jackson and William Carter were accused of murdering William Galley.

The evidence produced at the Chichester hearing revealed what had happened to the two witnesses. On their journey, they passed Havant on their way to Stansted and stopped at the New Inn at Leigh. There they met a man called Austin and his brother-in-law. They asked these two men the way and were guided to Rowland's Castle, where they were told they would get better help. At Rowland's Castle they went into the White Hart and the landlady there, Mrs Payne, suspected what their business was and sent for Jackson and Carter. They were soon afterwards joined by other members of the gang.

They all sat together. Carter asked Chater to speak to him outside. There he asked him where Diamond was; Diamond was one of the suspects in the Poole robbery. Chater said he was in custody and that he himself was going against his will to give evidence against him. William Galley followed them out into the yard to find out what was going on and was knocked down by Carter; then they all went back into the pub. The smugglers pretended to be sorry for what had happened, plied Galley and Chater with rum until they were both helplessly drunk. When they fell asleep, they were searched. A letter which they were evidently going to deliver to Major Battine was found. The smugglers read it – and destroyed it.

Another smuggler, John Royce, came in and Jackson and Carter told him about the letter. They also said they had got the shoemaker of Fordingbridge, the old rogue who was going to inform on John Diamond the shepherd. At this point another of the smugglers, John Steele said they should take the pair of them to a nearby well, murder them and throw them down. This idea was rejected, and other ideas for disposing of the two men were discussed.

Then a saga of needless cruelty began. Jackson put on his spurs and jumped on them as they lay on the bed sleeping off the rum. He spurred their foreheads and then gave them a whipping. The smugglers then took Galley and Chater out of the house, bloodied, and tied them both onto the same horse, with their feet tied together under the horse's belly. They set off, but had not gone more than two hundred yards before Jackson shouted, 'Whip 'em, cut 'em, slash 'em, damn 'em!' At this all the smugglers started whipping the two unfortunate victims – all except Steele, who was leading the horse they were tied to. The whipping continued for half a mile, until they reached Woodash, where the two victims slipped round so that they were hanging with their heads under the horse and their legs in the air.

The smugglers pulled them upright again and carried on whipping them round the head and shoulders until they reached Dean, where they fell upside down as before; with every step the horse took their heads were struck by its hoofs. William Galley was shortly after this found to be dead and they threw his body across the horse and took it to the house of a man called Scardefield who had the Red Lion at Rake. Meanwhile Jackson and Carter took Chater to another house where he was chained up.

The smugglers went and drank gin and brandy at the Red Lion. When it was dark, they borrowed spades, a candle and a lantern. They dug a pit in which to bury the customs officer, making Chater help them. After that they separated, but met again the next day with some more associates, in order to decide what to do with the unfortunate Daniel Chater. They decided that he must be killed, and they decided also that they would throw him down Harris's Well as this would be the most painful death.

The whole of this time poor Daniel Chater was in a terrible state of unimaginable misery and suffering, knowing that he would be killed, and being visited again and again by one or other of the smugglers as they came to abuse and beat him. One of them, Benjamin Tapner, decided he would be the one to kill Chater and took out his knife to do it there and then. The others persuaded him not to as they wanted Chater to suffer longer, so Tapner had to content himself with slashing his knife deeply across both Chater's eyes. Then they put their blinded victim on a horse and set off for Harris's Well. It was night. The well was thirty feet deep, dry and fenced in.

Tapner fastened a noose round Chater's neck and forced him to step over the fence. They tied one end of the rope to the fence and pushed him in. The rope was too short, though, so he was only half in the well, leaning on the edge of it with his thighs. They let him hang there for a quarter of an hour, but he still lived. Then they untied him and pitched him head first down the well. They waited and heard Chater groaning at the bottom of the well. He was still alive. Then they threw down some of the fencing round the well on top of him along with some large stones, and the groaning stopped.

The killings were unbelievably heartless and cruel, and it took the jury at Chichester only a quarter of an hour to decide that all the prisoners were guilty of all the charges. The crimes were so serious that the judge ordered that the executions should take place the very next day. Somehow, Jackson managed to escape execution by dying that evening. All the others were hanged as sentenced, the next day, on 18 January, 1749.

John Holloway and Owen Haggerty

'the Hounslow Heath murder'

ON THE NIGHT of Saturday 6 November, 1802, John Cole Steele, the owner of the Lavender Warehouse in Catherine Street in London's Strand, was murdered on Hounslow Heath. His pockets were rifled and the murderers escaped from the scene, even though a carriage passed the spot only a few moments later. Rewards were offered for the arrest of the assailants, but there was no result. Several men were arrested on suspicion, but all were discharged after questioning. It seemed, as the months passed, that it would remain an unsolved case.

Then, four years later, there was an unexpected breakthrough. A man called Benjamin Hanfield was convicted at the Old Bailey of grand larceny and sentenced to seven years' transportation. He was taken onto a prison hulk at Portsmouth to await his departure for Australia, and on board he fell ill. In the fever of his illness he was apparently revisited by guilt for the murder. He started raving and eventually said he wanted to make a confession before he died. A message was sent to

Bow Street magistrates and an officer was sent to Portsmouth to escort him back to London.

When Hanfield arrived in London, he was taken, still in police custody, to Hounslow Heath, where he pointed out the very spot where the murder of John Cole Steele was committed. He told the story of what had happened at the time of the murder. His story implicated two other men, John Holloway and Owen Haggerty, and the police set about finding and arresting them. Hanfield was admitted to King's evidence, in other words promised immunity for providing information that would convict others, and it began to look as if the murderers, or at least two out of three of the murderers, would be brought to justice at last. On 9 February, 1807, Holloway and Haggerty were brought before the magistrate at Worship Street police office.

There was a lot of evidence against the prisoners, but unfortunately all of it came from Hanfield, their accomplice. The prisoners denied all knowledge of the crime they were charged with. In spite of these problems, the magistrates decided to commit Holloway and Haggerty to trial at the next Quarter Sessions at the Old Bailey. No fewer than twenty-four people were bound over to appear to give evidence in their trial, though their evidence was scarcely strong enough to produce a safe conviction.

The long delay in apprehending the prisoners was one of the peculiar features of the case that excited public interest. So too was the fact that one of the murderers had turned King's evidence.

There was huge public interest in the trial, which opened on 20 February, 1807. Holloway was a man of about forty, tall, obviously immensely strong and muscular, with a brutal and ferocious face, with large thick lips, a shallow nose and high cheek bones. Haggerty was very different: a small, slight figure and aged twenty-four.

The trial opened with a dramatic reading of the King's pardon for Hanfield. He was now not only exonerated from the current charge but had his seven-year transportation sentence revoked by the Crown. Hanfield was already doing very well out of the trial that would end in death sentences for his two associates.

What really happened that night in November 1802 on Hounslow Heath will probably never be known. The only coherent version we have to go on is Hanfield's, so here it is:

'I have known Haggerty eight or nine years and Holloway six or seven. We were accustomed to meet at the Black Horse and Turk's Head public houses in Dyot Street. I was in their company in the month of November, 1802. Holloway, just before the murder, called me out of the Turk's Head and asked me if I had any objection to be in a good thing. I replied I had not. He said it was a 'Low Toby', meaning it was to be a footpad robbery. I asked when and where. He said he would let me know. We parted and two days after we met again and Saturday the 6th of November was appointed. I asked who was to go with us. He replied that Haggerty had agreed to make one. We

all three met on the Saturday at the Black Horse, when Holloway said, 'Our business is to 'sarve' a gentleman on Hounslow Heath who, I understand, travels the road with property.' We then drank for about three or four hours and about the middle of the day we set off for Hounslow. We stopped at the Bell public house and took some porter. We proceeded from thence upon the road towards Belfont, and expressed our hope that we should get ourselves a good booty. We stopped near the eleventh milestone and secreted ourselves in a clump of trees. While there the moon got up and Holloway said he heard a footstep and we proceeded towards Belfont.

We presently saw a man coming towards us and, on approaching him, we ordered him to stop, which he immediately did. Holloway went round him and told him to deliver. He said we should have his money and hoped we would not ill use him. The deceased put his hand in his pocket and gave Haggerty his money, I demanded his pocket-book. He replied that he had none. Holloway insisted that he had a book, and if he did not deliver it he would knock him down. I then laid hold of his legs. Holloway stood at his head and said if he cried out he would knock out his brains. The deceased again said he hoped we would not ill use him.

Haggerty proceeded to search him, when the deceased made some resistance and struggled so much that we got across the road. He cried out severely; and, as a carriage was coming up Holloway said: 'Take care, I will silence the bugger,' and immediately struck him several violent blows on the head and body. The deceased heaved a heavy groan and stretched himself out lifeless.

I felt alarmed and said, 'John, you have killed the man.' Holloway said that it was a lie, for he was only stunned. I said I would stay no longer and immediately set off towards London, leaving Holloway and Haggerty with the body. I came to Hounslow and stopped at the end of the town for nearly an hour. Holloway and Haggerty then came up, and said they had done the trick, and as a token put the deceased's hat into my hand. The hat Holloway went down in was like a soldier's hat. I told Holloway it was a cruel piece of business and that I was sorry I had had any hand in it. We all turned down a lane and returned to London. As we went along I asked Holloway if he had got the pocket-book. He replied that it was no matter, for as I had refused the danger I should not share the booty. We came to the Black Home, in Dyot Street, had half-a-pint of gin and parted.

Haggerty went down in shoes, but I don't know if he came back in them. The next day I observed Holloway had a hat upon his head which was too small for him. I asked him if it was the same he had got the preceding night. He said it was. We met again on the Monday, when I told Holloway that he acted imprudently in wearing the hat as it might lead to a discovery. He put the hat in my hand, and I observed the name of Steele in it. I repeated my fears. At night Holloway brought the hat in a handkerchief and we went to Westminster Bridge, filled the hat with stones and, having tied the lining over it, threw it into the Thames.'

Under cross-examination, Hanfield revealed that he had been with other prisoners in Newgate and the subject of various robberies came up. The Hounslow murder and robbery came up in the discussion and Hanfield had inadvertently said that there were only three people who knew the truth of the Hounslow Heath murder. This very significant remark was passed round Newgate and a rumour spread that he was about to turn informer. He was forced to keep silent after that to avoid being beaten up.

So far, there was only Hanfield's evidence to incriminate Holloway and Haggerty. His version of events might conceivably have been completely false; he might even have committed the murder, solo, and be shifting the blame in order to get out of two major convictions. There was little in the way of corroboration from other witnesses.

A police constable named James Bishop described the layout of the Worship Street police office. There were some cells for the prisoners, places where they could be kept in between successive interrogations. Holloway and Haggerty were confined in two adjacent cells. Immediately behind the two cells was a privy. Bishop stationed himself in this privy regularly after each day's session of questioning. Because the privy ran along behind both cells, he was able to hear the conversation of the prisoners fairly clearly as they spoke to each other through the party wall. Bishop took notes of these conversations, which he later turned into fair copies; he read them out in court.

The defence counsel, Mr Andrews, objected to this evidence on the grounds that Bishop could not have heard all that was said. Recording only parts of a conversation would inevitably lead to misunderstandings. The officer might have motivated by the prospect of a reward and the report was bound to be prejudicial to the prisoners.

The judge overruled Andrews and Bishop's lengthy notes were read out. They were not very revealing, as it happened, except that they had told one very large and significant lie. They had claimed that they had not known each other or Hanfield at all before this case; it was evident from what they were saying through the wall that they had all known one another. It was a significant lie, but proving that people are liars is a long way from proving that they are murderers.

Haggerty protested his innocence and tried to point out some inconsistencies in Hanfield's evidence. One curious feature in Hanfield's account is the one hour delay between Hanfield leaving the scene of the murder and the departure of the other two. What on earth were Holloway and Haggerty doing on the heath for a whole hour. Hanfield had fled when he thought Steele was dead. All that remained was for the other two to check all the dead man's pockets for the pocket book. Then, surely, they would have left the scene with all speed. They should have caught up with Hanfield within ten minutes. The longer the two murderers lingered by the body the greater was the chance that they would be caught. This suggests that Hanfield was not telling the truth.

Holloway also claimed he was innocent. He admitted he had been to Hounslow more than once, might have been in the company of Haggerty and Hanfield but did not know either of them.

The judge summed up, pointing out that the jury needed to be very cautious about the sort of testimony given by Hanfield. The jury discussed the case for a paltry fifteen minutes before returning a verdict of guilty. The judge passed sentence; Holloway and Haggerty were to be hanged the following Monday. They left the dock still protesting their innocence.

Haggerty and Holloway were then confined in the same cell – it is not clear why they were subjected to this unusual treatment – and they spent their last few days in calm, almost indifferent, preparation for death. On the Saturday when their cell door was opened it was found that they were each reading a prayer-book by candle-light as the cell was very dark. On the Sunday night, they prayed through the night and did not attempt to sleep. They intermittently protested their innocence.

At five o'clock on Monday 22 February, 1807 they were called, shaved and dressed. At about seven o'clock they were taken out into the yard. The warders had some difficulty in striking the irons off Haggerty. Holloway sent a message to the sheriffs saying that he wanted to speak to them in private. There was a frisson of expectation. Was this going to be the last-moment confession? It turned out that Holloway wanted to speak to them more publicly and asked them to make a circle round him. Holloway, standing solemnly in the centre of this circle, energetically and earnestly spoke to them: 'Gentlemen, I am quite innocent of this affair. I never was with Hanfield, nor do I know the spot. I will kneel and swear it.' Then he knelt and shouted, 'By God I am innocent!'

It did no good. Owen Haggerty ascended the scaffold wearing a light olive greatcoat and a white cap. He looked down and was silent. The noose was fixed round his neck. Then the hangman brought up John Holloway, who wore a smock-frock and jacket, which was what he was said by Hanfield to have worn at the time of the murder. He carried his hat in his hand. On mounting the scaffold, he jumped and made an awkward bow. Then he said again, 'I am innocent, innocent, by God!' he turned round and bowed again. 'Innocent! Innocent, gentlemen! No verdict! No verdict!' He kept this up for some time, until the hangman tired of waiting for him to stop. He was still shouting when the hangman pulled the cap down over his face. Once the noose was round his neck he stopped talking.

Another prisoner was hanged that day. She was Elizabeth Godfrey. She was nothing to do with the Hounslow Heath murder, but had murdered Richard Prince by stabbing him in the eye with a knife.

One remarkable feature of this case was the colossal crowd the public hanging attracted –

forty thousand people were there. There was not an inch of space to be seen anywhere. The press of the crowd was so great that, even before the prisoners were brought out, some people were already in difficulties and crying out. Short women and boys were in particular danger of being suffocated. Some who fainted and fell to the ground were trampled on and died. There were shouts from various parts of the crowd of 'Murder! Murder!', the standard shout of alarm for people in fear of their lives. It is not known for certain how many people died in front of the gallows that day: perhaps as many as forty. A mother was later seen carrying away her dead son. A sailor-boy carrying a small bag with bread and cheese in it was killed by suffocation. After the dead and dying were carried away, there followed a cart-load of shoes, hats, petticoats and other items of clothing picked up from the streets.

It was a gruesome end to a gruesome murder case. John Holloway and Owen Haggerty were vilified, and maybe rightly so. Maybe they did kill John Steele on Hounslow Heath. But in the end we have only Hanfield's word for it, and what was his word worth? Hanfield was a known criminal, who must have been desperate to avoid the seven years' sentence to transportation to New South Wales, and who may have seen informing on two old enemies, or even friends, as the only way of doing it. One thing is certain - that many innocent people died that day.

John Williams
'and the Ratcliffe Highway Murders'

TOWARDS THE END of 1811, the City of London was shaken by the violent and inexplicable murder of an entire family. It happened on Saturday, 7 December, at midnight. The traders were only then shutting up shop for the night. Timothy Marr, who ran a draper's shop, was one of them. On the night in question, he was still behind the counter after a busy day, gathering up the lengths of cloth out on display in the shop and putting them away on the shelves, helped by his shopboy, James Gowen. There were various types of cloth, rough worsted, dyed linen, canvas for seamen's trousers, serge for their jackets, and cheap printed cotton. Marr also had silk and muslin for his better-off customers.

Marr sent his maidservant, Margaret Jewell, out to buy oysters for a late family supper, and she had left the shop door ajar, expecting to be back in a few minutes. It was midnight, but there were still shops open and it seemed safe to be walking the streets at that hour. Unfortunately, the shop where she was expecting to buy the oysters, Taylor's oyster shop, had shut for the night and she had to try elsewhere. This brought her back past Marr's shop, and as she walked past she looked in through the window and saw Mr Marr and the boy still at work. In the event she found no oyster shop open, though she was able to pay the baker's bill, which was another of Marr's errands.

A gang of criminals meanwhile walked into Timothy Marr's shop, pushed him to the floor and cut his throat. Then they grabbed hold of his shop-boy and murdered him too. Mrs Marr was in the kitchen, feeding her baby. She heard an extraordinary noise and scuffling upstairs, as she thought, so she laid the baby in its cradle and ran up to see what was happening. Then she was met by the men who had murdered her husband. She too was murdered – in the same way. The baby started crying in its cradle, and the intruders went in to silence it, fearing that the noise might attract the curiosity and concern of the neighbours; they cut the baby's throat as well.

Then the maidservant came back without the oysters. She found the shop door shut and locked, so she rang the bell. No-one answered. But she did hear the soft tread of footsteps on the stairs, which she thought was her master coming down-stairs to open the door for her. Then she heard the baby give a single low cry. Then nothing. No footsteps. Nothing. The watchman George Olney passed down the other side of the street, taking someone to the lock-up; he noticed Margaret standing at the door. She became angry and frightened. She could not understand why no-one was answering the door. She started banging on the door and kicking it. Not knowing what to do, she just waited on the doorstep for half an hour, banging on the door from time to time.

In due course, George Olney the watchman came round again, calling the hour at one o'clock, and asked her what she was doing. She explained that she had been locked out and thought it very strange, and he agreed that the family must be in. He had seen Mr Marr putting the shutters up, but later had noticed that they were not fastened. Olney remembered calling out to Marr at the time and hearing an unfamiliar voice answering, 'We know of it'. Now he could see that the shutters were still unfastened. Olney knew there was something seriously wrong. He tugged vigorously on the bell and shouted through the keyhole, 'Mr Marr! Mr Marr!'. The intruders, who were still in the house at this time, realised that they needed to get away. They scrambled out of a window at the back of the house, across some mud and followed a route that showed an intimate knowledge of the area. It included passing through an empty house in Pennington Street. The man living in the house next to it heard a rumbling noise as 'about ten or twelve men' rushed through it from the back and out into Pennington Street.

The watchman wondered what to do. Mr Murray, a pawnbroker, lived next door. He was not a man to interfere in his neighbours' lives, but he and his wife were being kept awake by Margaret's banging on the door and wondered what was wrong, especially since there had been mysterious noises earlier on, including the cry of a boy or woman. Murray assumed that Marr was tired and irritated at the end of an exhausting day and was chastising the maid or the shop-boy. Murray went out to see what was going on and discussed the situation with Margaret and the watchman. Murray decided to climb over the fence separating Mr Marr's back yard from his own. This was quickly done and he got into the Marrs' house from the back. Inside it seemed very quiet and still. He saw a light from a candle burning on the first floor and went up. The door into the Marrs' bedroom was shut and he did not like to go in. He came back downstairs and found the first of the bodies. The fourteen year old James Gowen was lying near the door into the shop. The bones of his face had been shattered by blow after blow with a heavy object; his head had been beaten to a pulp. Blood and brains hung from the ceiling. This was the first of a series of the most appalling tableaux. He saw the body of Marr on the floor in the shop, and the body of his wife in the passage. The bodies were all still warm, still bleeding.

Sickened, Murray stumbled to the front door and got it open. 'Murder! Murder! Come and see what murder is here!' Someone asked about the baby, which Murray had not seen. The people in the street crowded in and saw the baby with its head almost completely severed. The whole neighbourhood was soon in a state of alarm. The night watch mustered and a drum sounded the call to arms. By midnight a huge crowd had gathered in the street outside Marr's shop to hear what had happened.

One of the murder weapons was found in the

Marrs' bedroom. The bed was undisturbed. Beside it stood a chair, and resting against it was a heavy iron mallet or maul, completely covered in blood and human tissue.

The bodies were laid out in the bedrooms and sightseers from all over the neighbourhood came to have a look. Scores of people of every class tramped up and down the narrow staircase to see the murder victims.

An inquest was opened on 10 December and a verdict of 'wilful murder by person or persons unknown' was brought in. The burial of the Marr family took place on 15 December, 1811 at the church of St George's in the East, attended by an enormous crowd, silent apart from groans of pity.

No-one knew who had done the murders - or why. Was it simple robbery? If so, why choose such a humble shop? Was it something to do with Timothy Marr's past, perhaps the settling of an old score? Marr was only twenty-four, but that was old enough for him to have had a past. He had been to sea with the East India Company, sailing his last voyage in the *Dover Castle* in 1808. He had not sailed before the mast but as the captain's personal servant. He was an agreeable young man, keen to please, but also ambitious. The captain, a man called Richardson, had promised to help him if he continued to serve him well. Timothy Marr wanted to leave the sea, marry the girl he was in love with, Celia, and set up a small shop. Ironically, he thought it would be a safer life than his life at sea. When the *Dover Castle* docked at Wapping, Marr was signed off with a significant sum of money - enough to set him up in business. In the April of 1811, Marr and his new wife found what they were looking for, cheap premises not far from the docks. Marr knew about the clothing needs of sailors, and there were huge numbers of sailors passing through the London Docks. Every year 13,000 ships passed through.

But there were dangers in living so close to the docks, which were a focus for crime. In 1800 it was estimated that around 10,000 thieves preyed on the ships that were docked on the open river. Things improved when the London Dock opened in 1805, but only a little. There were still huge numbers of criminals in the area. Within a stone's throw of Marr's shop was the twenty-foot high security wall of the London Dock.

The Marr murders were horrible enough, but they were soon to be followed by more. Everyone in the vicinity of the Marrs' shop felt vulnerable to attack by the merciless gang of murdering burglars, who were still at large, still unidentified; everyone was waiting for the same thing to happen again.

On 19 December, it did. At around 11 o'clock at night, Mr Williamson, the licensee of the King's Arms, No 81 New Gravel Lane, put up the shutters. He was fifty-six, a big, strong, burly man well able to deal with late drinkers or most kinds of trouble-makers. It was a noisy, squalid area full of ship's chandlers, lodging houses, pawnbrokers and pubs packed out with sailors. Every ninth building was a pub. New Gravel Lane was no stranger to disorder. The King's Arms had a tap-room and a private kitchen behind it on the ground floor, and a cellar with a flap-door opening onto the pavement for delivering barrels of beer. The Williamsons' bedroom and that of Kitty Stillwell, their fourteen year old grand-daughter, were on the first floor. Above those bedrooms were a couple of attic bedrooms, one occupied by Bridget Harrington who worked behind the bar, and the other by a young lodger, John Taylor.

Williamson relaxed with a beer drawn by his wife and chatted with his neighbour, Anderson, who was a constable. Williamson suddenly sat up. 'You're an officer,' he said. 'There's been a fellow listening at my door, with a brown jacket on. If you see him, you should take him imme-diately into custody. Or tell me.'

Anderson said he certainly would, and for his own safety as well as Williamson's. He said good-night to the Williamsons, then returned to his own house. The man Williamson described as listening at his door was at the inquest described by John Turner, who remembered Samuel Phillips calling in for a drink with Williamson at 10.40. It was Phillips who told Williamson that 'there was a stout man with a very large coat on, peeping in at the glass door in the passage'. Williamson went off to challenge him, brandishing a candlestick, but came back having seen no-one.

Twenty minutes after returning to his own house, Anderson was aware of a disturbance in the street. There were cries of 'Murder!' People started to gather in the street in front of the King's Arms pub. The shouts of 'Murder!' were coming from a near-naked man climbing down the outside of the house from an attic window on a rope of sheets, shouting and crying incoherently. The watchman stood below, holding his lantern and rattle. The half-naked man was John Turner. Anderson rushed back indoors to get his constable's sword and staff, and came out just in time to see John Turner come to the end of his rope. The last sheet ended eight feet short of the ground, and he fell this distance to be caught by the watchman, Shadrick Newhall. Then John Turner shouted, 'They are murdering the people in the house!'

Anderson quickly decided to force his way into the house through the cellar flap. This was done with the help of Mr Hawse, an axe-wielding butcher. Another man, Mr Fox, managed to get in through some wooden bars at the side of the house; for some reason he was carrying a cutlass. On looking round, the first thing they saw was the body of Mr Williamson, lying head downwards at the foot of the cellar steps, a terrible wound on his head, his right leg broken, his throat cut and a crowbar covered with blood by his side. They then went upstairs to the kitchen and found the body of Mrs Williamson, also with a head wound and a cut throat. Near her was the body of Bridget Harrington, her feet under the grate, with exactly the same injuries. Her throat had been cut right back to the neckbone. By some miracle, the granddaughter was still in her bed, unharmed, fast asleep. Someone carried her out into the street; she could not be left there.

Many enquiries, discussions and investigations followed, in the attempt to identify the criminals who carried out the two violent attacks. The Shadwell Police Office was very active in the investigation, as was Mr Graham of the Bow Street office.

The second set of murders seemed like a replay of the first set, but with one important difference. There was a witness – John Turner. Anderson reported that a tall man in a long Flushing coat had been seen loitering outside the King's Arms that evening. Turner saw a tall man dressed in just this way bending over Mrs Williamson's body. He had stayed in the doorway just long enough to take in what was happening, before tiptoeing back upstairs to make his rope of sheets. Initially, Turner had been taken into custody as a suspect, but it became clear that the murderer or murderers had got out of a window at the back of the house; there were bloodstains on the sill. Outside was a high clay bank with a footprint on it. The murderers, who would have clay on their clothes, must have got away over the waste land of the London Dock. Someone recalled that there were several points in common here with the Marr murders. The savage wounds inflicted, the timing, the escape route, the lack of theft. Once again, money that could have been taken was left in the house.

Attempts were made to find links between the Williamsons and the Marrs, but there seemed to be none. Two men were spotted running away from the scene of the murder at the right time. One was tall. The other seemed slightly lame or exhausted by some exertion. The tall man had said something like, 'Come along Mahoney (or Hughie), come along'.

Of the many suspects interviewed, the one the authorities eventually settled on was a man called John Williams. He was twenty-seven, 5 foot 9 inches tall, slim, 'of an insinuating manner and pleasing countenance'. He had connections with both Marr and Williamson, which the authorities seized upon; he had sailed with Marr on the *Dover Castle*, and he had been seen drinking in Williamson's pub many times, including the fatal evening. They were slight enough connections, but they seemed like a breakthrough. It was also to emerge later that Williams knew Jeremiah Fitzpatrick and Cornelius Hart, the carpenters at the Marrs' house. John Williams had returned from the sea in October 1811 and resumed his old lodgings at the Pear Tree pub, where he returned after all of his voyages. He treated Mr and Mrs Vermilloe as if they were his parents, with trust and respect. He handed over his earnings to Mr Vermilloe as his banker and was a tidy, clean and courteous lodger. He was a cut above normal seamen in his fastidious dress and education. He was occasionally mistaken for a gentleman.

But alongside these undoubted qualities, and in spite of his slightly weak and foppish appearance, Williams was extremely hot-tempered and easily got entangled in brawls. He was easily provoked and men found it entertaining to goad him. He not surprisingly had many female admirers, few male friends.

He was arrested as one of the gang of murderers, though it is very clear from the published evidence that there was no more evidence against him than there was against a hundred other men. Certainly there was not enough to justify a guilty verdict or a sentence of death which is what, in effect, he got. There was a piece about him in *The Times* of 24 December, 1811 that suggested there was no case against him at all. The piece sarcastically listed points against him including that he was short with a lame leg, that he asked a foreign sailor to put out his candle for him, that previous to the murders he had been short of money, that he was Irish. Unfortunately, the tone of the newspaper piece was a little too witty and sly to be effective, given the terrifying national demand for a scapegoat. The juggernaut of Justice was rolling towards Williams and nobody was trying to rescue him. The evidence was being allowed to pile up against him but without proper analysis. If, for example, John Williams was the shorter of the two men seen running away from the Williamsons' house, the lame man who had to be hurried up – why did the taller man call him Mahoney or Hughie? Neither of these names is anything like John or Williams.

Aaron Graham was meanwhile more interested in an Irishman called Maloney – much closer to the reported 'Mahoney' – after he had a letter from Captain Taylor of the frigate *Sparrow* at

Deptford. Taylor reported that Maloney answered the description of one of the murderers. Graham sent for Maloney and was not satisfied with Maloney's account of himself. At Marlborough in Wiltshire the tall man was identified: he was a remarkably tall man with badly bloodstained clothing and it was alleged that there were letters connecting him with Maloney. He was named by the Home Secretary and the Prime Minister in Parliament as William Ablass, commonly known as Long Billy. He was a close friend of John Williams and had been to sea with him. The Times commented that Ablass looked remarkably like Williams, as if that were in itself a condemnation of the man. The torn and bloody shirt that had been noticed in Marlborough was explained by a pub brawl in Reading. Ablass in any case, for reasons not disclosed, had to be released.

The missing piece in the jigsaw as far as the authorities were concerned was a connection between the suspect, John Williams, and the murder weapon, the maul. Mr Vermilloe, the landlord of the Pear Tree, provided the connection. He had himself been in Newgate Prison for a debt of £20 for seven weeks at the time, so the lure of a reward that would pay off the debt was probably a major factor in his evidence. What he said was that he could identify the maul, which was shown to him in Newgate, as having belonged to a German sailor who had lodged at the Pear Tree inn. The sailor's name was John Peterson. Peterson had left his chest of tools with Vermilloe when he went to sea. Most of the tools were marked with Peterson's initials. Vermilloe would not perjure himself totally by saying that this maul was definitely one of Peterson's tools, but he had used one of the mauls for chopping wood and had himself broken the tip. The murder weapon had a broken tip. At a hearing in which the new 'evidence' about the maul was heard, John Williams tried to speak, but he was told by the magistrate to be silent. It is impossible to guess what he might have said; soon he would be silenced altogether.

The authorities hoped that by holding Williams long enough they could get him to tell them the names of his accomplices, so that they could round up the whole dangerous gang. Cornelius Hart was getting himself implicated. He looked like the gang member responsible for stealing the ripping chisel that was left in Marr's house, and he had secretly sent his wife to the Pear Tree to find out if Williams had been arrested, while denying that he was a friend of Williams.

But the holding plan went wrong. When the gaoler at Coldbath Fields Prison went to collect him to answer questions before the Shadwell police magistrates, he found him dead in his cell, hanging from a beam The investigation proceeded as if Williams had admitted his own guilt, though of course he may have committed suicide for some other reason, such as despair at being wrongly charged, or he may have been murdered. The Coroner, Mr Unwin, addressed the jury in terms that were strongly biased, referring to John Williams as a 'miserable wretch' and accusing him of seeking to escape justice by recourse to self-destruction; by killing himself, Williams had proved himself a murderer, and so on. On the last day of the year 1811, Williams' body was moved, late at night, from the cell where he died to a watch-house near the London Docks, ready for burial.

The magistrate, Mr Capper, met the Home Secretary to discuss the possibility of departing from the usual custom of burying suicides at the nearest cross-roads. They decided that something nastier was appropriate - a public exhibition of the body through the neighbourhood where the crimes had been committed.

In line with this extraordinary decision, a procession led from the watch-house at 10.30 in the morning, It consisted of several hundred constables carrying staves to clear the way, the newly formed patrol carrying drawn cutlasses, more constables, the parish officers of the three parishes concerned (St George's, St Paul's and Shadwell), peace officers on horseback, yet more constables, the High Constable of Middlesex on horseback.

Then came the body of John Williams, stretched full length on a sloping board on the back of a cart, to give the best possible view of the murderer's body. Williams was dressed in blue trousers and a blue-and-white striped waistcoat, but no coat, just as he was found in his cell. On the left side of the murderer's head was displayed the maul, and on the right side the ripping chisel or crow bar; these were believed to be the murder weapons. The face of John Williams was awful to look at, and the corpse as a whole was too horrible for observers to describe in any further detail. Yet more constables brought up the rear.

This almost-medieval procession made its way slowly up Ratcliffe Highway, accompanied and followed by a huge crowd of people, all eager to get a good look at John Williams' body. When the cart reached Mr Marr's house, it was halted there for a quarter of an hour. Then the procession moved off towards Old Gravel Lane, Wapping, New Crane Lane and into New Gravel Lane. At Mr Williamson's house the procession again came to a halt for a while. Then it moved off into Ratcliff Highway again, Cannon Street and St George's Turnpike, to the point where the road was intersected by Cannon Street. There, at the cross-roads, a six-foot deep grave had been prepared. At about midday John Williams' body was untied from its platform and stuffed into the grave. A stake was driven through Williams' heart with the blood-stained maul, and then the grave was filled and the paving stones replaced.

The authorities managed for a short time to sell the public the idea that John Williams was a lone killer, but it was obvious from many witness statements that at least two and maybe as many as twelve men were involved. Whether John Williams really was one of the murderers remains uncertain. And who were the others who were with him? There was a mystery surrounding the crowbar used as the second murder weapon. Mr Pugh was the clerk of works who had overseen the modernization of the shop for Marr. His carpenter had asked for a crowbar (or ripping chisel) which Mr Pugh did not have, but borrowed one from a neighbour. When the carpentry job had been done the carpenter had been laid off, but he went without returning the chisel. Pugh asked the carpenter about it and the carpenter replied that he had left it in the shop, though he could not find it. Some days later, Marr told Pugh that he had searched his house thoroughly and was sure the chisel wasn't there. On the day of Marr's murder the chisel was still missing from Marr's shop, only reappearing on the discovery of the bodies of Marr and Gowen, when it was seen lying on the counter. It is reasonable to suspect the carpenter of being one of the murderers. It was not immediately seen as a significant object because it was not covered in blood, but its return during the raid on the Marrs' house was a significant clue.

One peculiar aspect of the evidence is that The Times studiously avoided naming the carpenter. It would later emerge that there were three carpenters, Cornelius Hart and two joiners called Towler (or Trotter) and Jeremiah Fitzpatrick. Of the three, Cornelius Hart is the likeliest. Was he one of the murderers?

The motive seems not to have been simple robbery. There was cash to the value of £150 in the house, yet it was not taken. A score from Timothy Marr's seafaring days seems possible. It is also possible that there was some family rivalry. A man called Thomas Taylor said that he knew Marr's brother had employed six or seven men to commit the murders. He also said he knew one of the men involved, who had been unable to cut the child's throat. Unfortunately, Taylor later said he had no memory of saying any of this and that he had been wounded in the head while serving in the forces; he admitted that he was sometimes so deranged, especially when drunk, that he did not know what he was saying. The magistrates agreed with him that he was insane and let him go. There were, even so, other sources that said Marr's brother hated him. There had been a lawsuit which Timothy Marr had won; the two had not spoken for years.

There were other leads too. A week or two after the murders, when the bloodstained maul had been in the possession of John Harriott at the River Thames Police Office for some time, someone took a look at it with a magnifying glass. A detail had been overlooked. The caked blood and hair was carefully scraped back to reveal the initials I.P. punched in dots. Presumably these were the initials of the maul's owner. The description published at the time wrongly gave the initials as 'J.P.' and, thanks to that useful misprint, Mr Vermilloe's identification of the maul as belonging to John Peterson is seen to be a piece of pure perjury. (The Vermilloes got their £60 reward in due course.)

The other murder weapon, the knife or razor, was invisible through most of the enquiries. So also was the supposition that John Williams was the sort of man who cut people's throats. After his death, discreet investigations into his past revealed no violence with knives whatever.

The strange errand of Margaret Jewell may hold one of the keys to the mystery. She would certainly have been murdered if she had been in the house when the gang arrived; her life was saved by her fruitless search for oysters. Was she in fact sent out by Marr as she said? In one statement she said it was Mrs Marr who had sent her out. The inconsistency suggests that perhaps neither of them sent her out, that it was her own idea to go out on a fruitless midnight shopping expedition. This may mean that she set it up, or had been bribed to go out, leaving the front door open. Her spectacular swoon at the inquest was seen at the time as quite consistent with guilt. She may have colluded with Marr's brother, assuming that some lesser crime was to be committed, maybe theft or some minor assault; finding out later that she had connived at the murder of the whole household might well have made her feel faint.

This was the line of thought followed by one of the investigators, Aaron Graham. Working on this hypothesis, Graham interrogated Marr's brother for two days. Marr had no interest in Margaret Jewell, had never even known her. Nor had there been a murderous family feud. Marr's brother also had an alibi.

Indeed this whole line of enquiry began to disintegrate when the Williamson household was murdered. After Williams' suicide, the investigators lost their way, having decided too soon that he was one of the murderers. What, in the end, did the most serious contemporary investigator make of it? In February 1812, Aaron Graham wrote his report. He concluded that two people had committed the Williamson murders, that Ablass was not one of them. He was sure that Hart was involved in the Marr murders, but doubted if the case could ever be made to hold up in court; he had proved that Hart's statements contained lies. But it is a profoundly unsatisfactory report. He had to release his prime suspect, Ablass, yet he did not say why. He also missed the obvious point that John Turner, who saw the tall man, did not recognize him as Williams, whom he knew well and had seen earlier that evening. If the (relatively) tall man was not Ablass and, as Graham says, Williams' accomplice was shorter than Williams, then Williams must have been the 'tall' man seen at the King's Arms. The only conclusion can be that Williams was not there at all - indeed not involved in either of these horrible cases.

It is also possible that Williams himself was murdered. It would be obvious to the real murderers that if Williams came to trial and was acquitted, the man hunt would resume and they would still be in danger. If he appeared to commit suicide, his guilt would be taken for granted - as indeed it was. So it was simply a matter of bribing a turnkey in a prison with virtually no supervision to hang an already fettered prisoner. The state of Williams' body showed that he had 'struggled very hard' for life, yet when he was found his hands were free, his bed was close by and the iron beam was only five inches higher from the ground than he was; he could have reached up and held onto the beam while he found the bed with his feet. It is very unlikely that he died voluntarily.

The two murders gripped the attention of the whole of England. The poet Southey, avidly reading about them in the Lake District, declared that it was a rare case of 'a private event which rose to the dignity of a national event'. The Marrs were given a tall tombstone bearing a long inscription, relating how they were 'most inhumanely murdered in their dwelling house, No 28 Ratcliffe Highway, Dec 8, 1811.

> *Stop, mortal, as you pass by,*
> *And view the grave wherein doth lie*
> *A Father, Mother and a Son,*
> *Whose earthly course was shortly run.*
> *For lo, all in one fatal hour,*
> *O'er came were they with ruthless power;*
> *And murdered in a cruel state -*
> *Yea, far too horrid to relate!*

John Thurtell

'an unfair trial'

JOHN THURTELL, WHO was at the centre of one of the most sensational murder trials of the nineteenth century, was born on 21 December, 1794. He was the son of the Mayor of Norwich. He was comfortably off as a young man, with enough money to spare to indulge in gambling.

Then he got into debt. He accused one of his fellow gamblers, William Weare, a solicitor, of cheating in a game of cards: and not only that but of cheating him of three hundred pounds, which was a huge sum of money in those days.

John Thurtell invited William Weare to spend a weekend gambling with him and some friends at a cottage at Radlett in Hertfordhsire. The cottage was owned by another of their gambling circle, William Probert. Thurtell and Weare travelled down to Hertfordhire from London together in Thurtell's gig on 24 October, 1823. As they got near to their destination, Thurtell confronted Weare with his behaviour. The confrontation happened outside an inn called the Wagon and Horses in Radlett. Thurtell drew a pistol and fired it at Weare's face. The gun misfired and the under-powered shot glanced off Weare's cheekbone, causing no serious damage.

Thurtell then set upon Weare, who was still dazed and confused by the gunshot, and cut his throat with a penknife. He also beat Weare about the head with the muzzle of his pistol. William Probert and another of Thurtell's friends, and actor named Joseph Hunt, helped Thurtell dispose of the body. To begin with, they put it into a pond in the garden at Probert's cottage. Later, when it was dark, they fished it out and took it to another pond in Elstree. The murder was taken up by the newspapers as 'the Elstree murder'.

The murder was as badly planned as it was executed, and suspicion quickly descended on the circle of gamblers. A labourer found the bloody penknife and the pistol, which was also coated with blood, hair and tissue, beside the cottage and took them to the authorities. William Probert immediately fell under suspicion as the owner of the cottage. Probert was unnerved to find himself being questioned first and realised the danger of his predicament. Suddenly he was the prime suspect. He decided to turn King's Evidence - to buy immunity from prosecution by providing evidence against John Thurtell. He immediately implicated both Thurtell and Hunt. It was Hunt, when questioned, who led the officers to the body in the pond at Elstree.

Thurtell and Hunt were arrested and came up for trial before Mr Justice Park in January 1824 at the Hertford Assizes. Thurtell was on trial for murder, Hunt for being an accessory. The trial was unfair, to the extent that everyone assumed they were guilty before it even began. The press had decided against them. Even the judge was moved to comment, 'if these statements of evidence before trial which corrupt the purity of the administration of justice in its source are not checked, I tremble for the fate of our country.' It was a plea for the sort of restrictions on prejudicial press reporting that are normal in Britain today. The newspapers of the time had shown avid interest in every detail. Nevertheless the trial went ahead regardless.

The John Thurtell case is interesting for another reason as well. His trial was the very last trial in England to be conducted on the old sixteenth century principle that the accused had to fend off a prosecution case by making only a speech after the evidence against him had been delivered - and without the right to cross-examine any prosecution witness. It was clearly unfair, and heavily weighted in favour of a guilty verdict. It was in a sense the last formally unfair trial in England. Neither John Thurtell nor Joseph Hunt had a lawyer to represent or defend them. Thurtell made a long and rather rambling speech to the court in which he attempted vainly to shift the blame onto William Probert, presumably in retaliation for Probert's turning King's Evidence. He made references to his Christian upbringing, to St Paul and to Voltaire. None of this cut any ice as far as the jury or the judge were concerned.

Some of the witnesses called were fools. One who was supposed to be there to support Thurtell made the comment, 'I always thought him a respectable man'. The judge understandably asked him what he meant by that, possibly expecting that some biographical detail showing a solid and worthy side would emerge, such as regular church-going or giving sovereigns to paupers every Christmas, but what he got for a reply was, 'He kept a gig'.

It took the jury only twenty minutes to find Thurtell and Hunt guilty. The judge sentenced Thurtell to death and ordered his body to be dissected after death. Hunt was also sentenced to death, but his sentence was commuted to transportation for life; he lived on at Botany Bay for many years to come.

Thurtell was taken back to Hertford Prison to await execution. There were not many hangings at Hertford. The previous one had been a year earlier. The authorities decided that a new gallows should be built to hang John Thurtell. The new design, copied from others in use round England, incorporated a single trapdoor (a 'falling leaf') that could be made to drop instantly by pulling back bolts and so did away with the need for ladders and carts. There was a stout cross beam about twelve feet long held up on equally substantial uprights eight feet high. The area under the drop was completely enclosed by boards seven feet high and tongued-and-grooved so that there was no possibility of seeing into it from outside. The walls of the platform rose about two feet above the floor, so that most of the prisoner's body was hidden from view after the drop. The enclosure was about thirty feet long and fifteen feet deep with a short steep flight of steps leading directly up from the prison door. The whole structure was painted black and looked very menacing. Round the platform was an outer enclosure where militiamen were stationed with spears; they stood guard to prevent any attempts at escape or rescue.

James Foxen, the hangman, came down from London on the Thursday before the execution. John Thurtell dressed up for the occasion, in a brown greatcoat with a black velvet collar, light breeches and gaiters and a smart waistcoat with gilt buttons. At noon on 9 January, 1824, the hangman pinioned John Thurtell's hands in front of him (unusually) with handcuffs before leading him from his cell to the accompaniment of the tolling prison bell. He mounted the five steps onto the scaffold and positioned himself on the trap. Foxen removed Thurtell's cravat and loosened his collar, before pulling the white hood and the noose over his head. Thurtell shook hands with the Governor and Chief Warder of the Gaol and said goodbye to each of them, before Foxen adjusted the noose.

At two minutes past twelve, Foxen drew the bolts and Thurtell dropped into the box with a crash. It was said that Thurtell's neck could be heard breaking, but the short drop makes this unlikely. In any event, Thurtell died easily and quickly. After leaving his body hanging for the customary hour, it was taken down and sent to the Surgeon's Hall in London for dissection.

A waxwork model was made of John Thurtell for Madame Tussaud's wax museum in London.

His presence in the Chamber of Horrors was the hallmark of Thurtell's infamy.

William Probert had, it seemed, got away unpunished for his role in the murder of William Weare, but only a year before he was in trouble again. He was convicted of horse-stealing and hanged by Foxen at Newgate.

François Courvoisier

'the murder of Lord William Russell'

ON 6 MAY, 1840, Lord William Russell was found dead in his bed. He was elderly, the posthumous son of Francis, Earl of Tavistock, who in his turn was the eldest son of the fourth Duke of Bedford; he was the youngest brother of the two last Dukes of Bedford and uncle to the present Duke, an illustrious member of an aristocratic family who might have been expected to die peacefully in his bed, full of years. He was a good age – seventy-two – but actually he had had his throat cut and his death scandalized London.

Lord William Russell lived at 14 Norfolk Street, Park Lane, where he kept a very modest house-hold. He was attended only by his five servants. He kept a housemaid, Sarah Mancer, and a cook, Mary Hannell, as well as a coachman, a groom and a valet. The coachman and groom lived out, but Sarah and Mary lived in the house with Lord William - and his valet, François Courvoisier.

In the basement were kitchens and stores and a room used by Courvoisier as a pantry. On the ground floor were two parlours used as dining rooms. On the first floor were the drawing room and library. On the second floor were the bedroom and dressing room of his lordship. Above that were the servants' bedrooms.

Lord William was a member of Brooks's Club in St James's and he usually spent much of the day there, but generally dined at home before spending the evenings reading. He went to bed at around midnight.

The valet had been with Lord William only five weeks and they had been an unhappy five weeks. Courvoisier had been heard to say that he disliked his lordship, whom he described as bad-tempered and dissatisfied; if he had been able to afford to do so he would return at once to Switzerland. It would have been better if he had returned anyway.

On 5 May, Lord William had got up at 9am and breakfasted. At noon he had gone to lunch at Brooks's, after summoning the valet to give him several messages to deliver, including one to the coachman to collect him at five. When the valet went into the kitchen after this, he said he feared he might forget some of the errands. He went over them, missing out the message to the coachman to prepare the carriage to fetch him from his club at five o'clock. It is not clear whether this was a genuine or a deliberate mistake on Courvoisier's part. At half past five, his lordship arrived home for dinner in a cab, mildly irritated at his valet's neglect to sent the carriage, though not showing a level of anger that could reasonably inspire hatred.

Lord William took dinner at seven, then coffee, and at about nine he retired to his library. By now, only the three house servants were at home, the housemaid, the cook and the valet. Hannell had been out, but the valet had let her in and she noticed that he locked and chained the street door after she came in. Supper was prepared at ten and Courvoisier fetched his lordship some beer. At 10.30 p.m. the cook and the house-maid went to bed. The valet alone was left to attend Lord William. At half-past midnight, Lord William rang for his valet to help him to bed.

The next morning at 6.30, Sarah the house-maid rose, dressed and went downstairs, knocking on the valet's door to wake him. When she reached the lower floors she found confusion, with furniture strewn about, drawers pulled open, and the street door unchained and on the latch. She was alarmed, and ran upstairs to tell cook, who told her to go and tell Courvoisier. She was very surprised to find Courvoisier already dressed; it usually took him half an hour to dress, and it was only ten minutes since she had knocked on his door. Together they went downstairs. Courvoisier shouted, 'Oh God, someone has robbed us!'

Then Sarah Mancer said they should check that his lordship was all right. She and Courvoisier went to his room. Courvoisier went to open the shutters, and Sarah Mancer went straight to his lordship's side. She saw at once what had happened. The pillow was saturated with blood and his lordship lay there with his throat cut. Sarah screamed, ran from the room and out into the street to raise the alarm. She enlisted the help of their neighbours, who called the law officers and a surgeon. Throughout, Courvoisier's behaviour had been odd. He was agitated, leaning on the bed where Lord William lay dead, saying nothing and taking no part at all in the general activity. Then he seemed to recover and suggested they should tell Lord William's son in Belgrave Square what had happened.

The valet seemed keen to persuade Sarah Mancer that the intruders, whoever they were, had gained entry through his pantry. He showed some damage to the door as evidence. 'It was here that they entered,' he said

Then the police took over the house and examined it carefully. They quickly deduced that the murder had been committed by someone living in the house and the disorder was to make it look as if there had been a robbery. A parcel was found, containing many items belonging to Lord William: his gold opera glasses and so on, but also a gold toothpick, a caddy spoon and a thimble, and it was obvious that it would have been much easier for a real thief to have slipped these into his pocket than to go to the trouble of tying them up in a big parcel. So the idea of thieves breaking in from outside and looting the lower floors was evaporating. Conversely, various significant items had gone missing from his lordship's bedroom, including a ten pound note that was known to have been in his note-case.

The fact that items so close to Lord William had been taken suggested strongly that Courvoisier was behind this. But there was still nothing that specifically incriminated him, so he could not as yet be arrested. The police decided to keep him under surveillance.

A couple of days later, a police officer found five gold rings belonging to Lord William behind the skirting board. He also found five gold coins, a piece of wax, a Waterloo medal and the missing ten pound note. The bank note was a very important piece of evidence. If it had been stolen by any ordinary thief breaking into the house, he would have made off with it, not hidden it behind a skirting board. Really, there was no other explanation but an 'inside job'. It must have been the valet.

Then the police found about Courvoisier's person a locket containing a lock of Lord William's wife's hair. Lord William had mislaid the locket and been upset by its loss; his wife was dead and he treasured the locket. Obviously Courvoisier had taken it to spite Lord William some time before he murdered him. On 13 May, a police officer examined the sink in the valet's pantry. He noticed something odd about the appearance of the lead that sheathed part of the sink. He prised it up and underneath found the gold watch that had been placed by Lord William's bed on the night of the murder, but which had been removed by the time the murder had been discovered. This too implicated Courvoisier.

These were the pieces of evidence against Courvoisier, and many suspected him of being the murderer, but there was also a sense that he would escape conviction on such indirect evidence.

Courvoisier was defended by an experienced lawyer called Flower. His services were paid for by a subscription raised by the foreign servants in

London. There was a feeling among them that it was assumed they would be dishonest because they were foreign. They were right; xenophobia was widespread. Mr Hobler was engaged for the prosecution. The trial of François Courvoisier for the murder of Lord William Russell opened on 18 June at the Central Criminal Court before Lord Chief Justice Tindal and Mr Baron Parke. The trial excited enormous public interest, and there were many titled people among those present. The Duke of Sussex was there, together with Lords Sheffield, Mansfield, Cavan, Clarendon, Lucan and Louth and many others besides.

Courvoisier pleaded not guilty.

The court then heard evidence concerning the fake burglary. The police had come to the conclusion, now presented to the court, that many of the items secreted behind skirting boards and elsewhere had been spirited away during the days and weeks before the murder, and not on the night of the murder itself. There were some items of plate that had gone missing some while before and the police had been unable to find it. But Mr Hobler, the counsel for the prosecution, had discovered it in the possession of the owner of a French hotel in Leicester Square. Those familiar with the stolen plate had positively identified it as having belonged to Lord William.

This led to an extraordinary turn of events. Courvoisier caved in completely and admitted that he had taken the plate. This created a serious problem for his lawyers, who saw that they had no case to defend any more. They decided to continue their defence of the prisoner, though along different lines. Their original line of defence had been preposterous in the extreme. They had been urged, presumably by Courvoisier, to blame the murder on the cook and the house-maid, who had done the deed in conspiracy with the police, who were to be charged as their associates in crime. It was all a conspiracy to secure the conviction of the valet. The lawyers were doubtless relieved that they now had to give that up, though they still accused the police of fabricating some of the evidence in order to excite the jury's hostility towards the prisoner. They also managed to argue with great skill that the only real evidence against Courvoisier was that of suspicion, which was not adequate as evidence.

But it was all in vain. Courvoisier was found guilty and the judge passed a sentence of death. The next day Courvoisier made a confession;

'His lordship was very cross with me and told me I must quit his service. As I was coming up stairs from the kitchen I thought it was all up with me; my character was gone, and I thought the only way I could cover my faults was by murdering him. This was the first moment of any idea of the sort entering my head: I went into the dining room and took a knife from the sideboard. I do not remember whether it was a carving knife or not. I then went upstairs, I opened his bed-room door and heard him snoring in his sleep; there was a rushlight in his room burning at this time. I went near the bed by the side of the window, and then I murdered him. He just moved his arm a little; he never spoke a word.'

One very odd aspect of the crime is that Courvoisier seems not to have realised that murdering Lord William took his petty criminal campaign against him onto a different plane. Obviously the house would be carefully examined by the police and the various items pilfered over the previous five weeks would come to light - and equally obviously their displacement would be attributable to his dishonesty rather than a burglar's. It is just possible that at the moment when he decided to kill Lord William, Courvoisier had forgotten about the stolen goods he had secreted round the house. And if he remembered them during the following few days, he may not have realised their significance.

François Courvoisier, the Swiss valet who killed an English lord to cover his faults, was hanged at Newgate on 6 July, 1840.

Maria and Frederick Manning

MARIA MANNING WAS born in Switzerland as Maria de Roux, in 1821. One of the few things about her that the English came to like about her at the peak of her notoriety was this simple fact - that she was foreign. In the end, she did not reflect badly on England, because she just wasn't an Englishwoman. Maria de Roux moved to London to work as a lady's maid in the household of Lady Blantyre, the wealthy daughter of the Duchess of Sutherland.

It was while she was in service that Maria de Roux developed a taste for high life and finery; she loved the clothes that her mistress wore and the elegant style of her employer's homes. At the same time that she was developing ideas above her station, she came to fear poverty acutely. Above all she wanted to set herself up in a comfortable, genteel household of her own – and for many a young woman in the nineteenth century that meant marrying very astutely indeed.

In 1846, Maria crossed the English Channel on the ferryboat to Boulogne, accompanying Lady Blantyre. It was there that she met Patrick O'Connor. He was a man of fifty, Irish, and he worked as a customs officer in the London dock-lands. Patrick O'Connor was a man of independent means, a man with capital invested, he unwisely told her in an unguarded moment, in foreign railway stocks, and this immediately attracted Maria. She was very taken with him and his railway stocks.

Unfortunately, Maria was at this time entangled with another man. Frederick George Manning was a humble guard on the Great Western Railway. Manning was a weak character and did not have much money. Maria obviously harped on about money a good deal, and he had rather pathetically promised her that he would shortly inherit money, presumably so that she would not give him up. But in Maria's eyes, the new catch was much better: George O'Connor had his money already. Maria had to choose.

Rather surprisingly, Frederick won and the couple were married in St James's Church, Piccadilly in 1847. They were not well off, but they were able to afford a fairly stylish house in Miniver Place, Bermondsey. By this stage, Maria had realised that Frederick Manning was not going to inherit anything at all. She may in fact have used this to humiliate and disadvantage Manning and buy his acquiescence in her infidelity. Maria was still in touch with O'Connor and probably having an affair with him. The three of them even dined together at Miniver Place from time to time.

After a while, Maria decided she had married the wrong man. She should have married

O'Connor. She decided that she might not be able to have the man, because she was already married, but at least she would have his money. She would kill him. It was an odd decision, and she might equally have decided to kill the useless Manning and go off with O'Connor. But it was O'Connor she decided must die.

Maria Manning bought some quicklime and a shovel. On 8 August 1849 she asked Mr O'Connor to dinner. He came but unexpectedly brought a friend with him, so Maria had to shelve her plan. Undaunted, she invited him again the following evening, but asked him to come on his own this time - so that they could be more intimate. When O'Connor arrived the next evening, Maria suggested he might like to wash his hands before dinner. As he stood at the sink to wash his hands, Maria raised a pistol to his head and fired.

The bullet wound did not kill O'Connor though, and Frederick attacked him at once, beating his head with a crowbar. The two of them, Maria and Frederick, husband and wife, buried the battered and bloodied body in a grave they had dug earlier under the flagstones on the kitchen floor, and covered it with quicklime.

The next day, Maria went to O'Connor's lodgings and successfully talked her way into his rooms. She systematically went through his belongings, taking everything of value, including the share certificates. She went back again the next day, just in case she had missed anything.

Two days later, Maria naturally became very frightened when two colleagues of O'Connor's called to see if they knew anything about O'Connor's whereabouts; he had told them he would be eating there on 9 August. Maria said O'Connor had dined with them on 8 August, but they had not seen him since. The two acquaintances went away, but left Maria and George feeling very nervous. They wondered if the couple were actually detectives, so they decided to leave London.

Maria sent Frederick off to sell the furniture. Once he had gone, Maria packed all the valuables she could carry, ordered a cab for King's Cross, where she caught a train to Edinburgh. Frederick decided that he too would leave the country, and took a train and a ship to reach Jersey. Meanwhile, O'Connor's colleagues had become worried by his disappearance, and they told the police of their suspicions about the Mannings. The police decided on a thorough search of Miniver Place. They found that the mortar round two of the flagstones was still moist.

The police lifted the two flagstones and under them they found Mr O'Connor's battered body. Then a massive manhunt was mounted. The cabbie who had taken Maria to the station came forward. He told how he had taken her to one station where she deposited two trunks, and then taken her on to King's Cross. Superintendent Haynes who was in charge of the investigation discovered that Maria had bought a ticket for Edinburgh. Haynes telegraphed the Edinburgh police, to alert them to the fact that Maria Manning was in their city. Remarkably, the Edinburgh police had already arrested her. She had tried to sell some of O'Connor's railway stock, which had been bought in London, and they were uneasy about her French accent; it had looked to them as if a fraud of some kind was being attempted. She was in custody, so it was relatively easy to have her sent back to London and charged with O'Connor's murder. She was held on remand in Horsemonger Lane Gaol in Southwark.

Frederick Manning was arrested a week later in Jersey. He was unlucky enough to be sighted there by a man who had known him in London, and who had read about the murder in the newspapers. The man who saw Manning in Jersey returned to London and reported his sighting there to the police. After that a Scotland Yard detective called Sergeant Langley, who happened to know Manning, was sent out to Jersey to arrest him. Sergeant Langley traced Manning to a rented room in St Laurence and caught up with him, asleep in his rented bed, on 21 August.

Once in the hands of the police, Frederick Manning told the police it was Maria who had killed O'Connor, but he also admitted, rather foolishly, 'I never liked him, so I battered his head with a ripping chisel'. He too was taken to London, charged with O'Connor's murder and, like his wife, remanded in Horsemonger Lane Gaol.

Maria was motivated purely by greed. She granted O'Connor sexual favours, but it seems likely that this was simple 'stringing along'. She was most concerned with getting her hands on his money. It is less clear what Frederick's motive may have been. He may have wanted to get his hands on O'Connor's money to put his own financial plight to rights. He may have killed O'Connor because of sexual jealousy. He may have killed him, as he said, because he disliked him. He may have killed him because his wife told him to; he was a very weak man and dominated by his wife's ego. Or he may have killed him because once Maria had shot him, he could not be allowed to survive to testify against her. At this time, even attempted murder was a capital offence, so if O'Connor had survived Maria's cold-blooded shooting, he could have seen her, and possibly both of them, sent to the gallows. Given that that was the situation, it was safer to go on and finish the job – kill O'Connor – and hope that the body would never be found.

The Mannings were moved to Newgate Prison, next door to the Old Bailey, in readiness for their trial, which opened on 25 October. Justice Cresswell presided and the trial lasted only two days. The Mannings' lawyers each tried futilely to shift the blame to the other partner. Evidently both Frederick and Maria expected the other to take all the blame for the murder. Neither would. In the end, it took the jury only forty-five minutes to conclude that both were guilty.

The Mannings' case attracted a huge amount of public interest. There was a scandalous sexual intrigue, a naughty French-Swiss woman, a connection with the aristocracy, a grisly burial, and the unusual elements of the woman as the dominant partner in the marriage, making all the decisions, and the woman as the prime mover in the murder itself. The spectacular attempts at escape added further excitement. It turned into one of the 'Great Murders' of the nineteenth century.

At the end of the trial, Maria Manning lost her self-control, screaming at the jury, 'You have treated me like a wild beast of the forest'. She went on shouting at the judge as he passed the death sentence on her. The husband and wife were taken to Newgate, then across London to Horsemonger Lane Gaol to await execution. Maria Manning asked the warders accompanying her how they liked her performance in court.

Horsemonger Lane Gaol was built in the 1790s and if the name is unfamiliar it may be because it was renamed Surrey County Gaol in 1859 or because it was demolished in 1880 and no longer exists. Its role was taken over by Wandsworth Prison.

The normal custom was for executions to take place three clear Sundays after sentence was passed. According to this custom, the Mannings were to spend a little over two weeks in the condemned cells. Maria was watched round the clock; this had become the custom after Mary Milner had hanged herself at Lincoln Castle two years before. Maria Manning too attempted suicide, in spite of being closely watched by three wardresses who even slept in her cell with her; she hated it. Maria let her fingernails grow long. While the wardresses slept, she tried to strangle herself and pierce her windpipe with her fingernails. It took all three wardresses to stop her, but it seems unlikely that she could have killed herself in that way.

Maria wrote a letter from her cell to Queen Victoria to ask for a reprieve. She had met the Queen when she was Lady Blantyre's maid, but that made no difference now. Queen Victoria did not believe in overturning death sentences, and this case was no exception: there was no reprieve. In fact the Queen did study Maria's letter carefully, and took an interest in the case, but it was all too clear that Maria was guilty. Maria apparently also wrote to her husband, telling him to accept all the blame for the murder, but he refused. Instead he wrote a confession in which he said that Maria had shot O'Connor and he had finished him with a ripping chisel, and it seems likely that this is what happened.

The executions took place on Tuesday 13 November 1849 at Horsemonger Lane Gaol. They attracted the biggest crowd that ever attended a public hanging. It is estimated that up to 50,000 people went to see the Mannings die. Every possible space was filled with spectators and hundreds of policemen were needed to control the huge crowd.

The gallows, described at the time as 'a huge, gaunt and ominous looking structure', was erected as was usual on the flat roof over the main gate. The hangman was William Calcraft, and Maria Manning was his twentieth woman victim. At 8.15 am, the Mannings went into the prison chapel to take communion, then the prison governor arrived to hurry them along, no doubt alarmed at what the crowd might do if kept waiting. Calcraft came forward and Maria and Frederick Manning were taken to different parts of the chapel to be pinioned. Maria almost fainted while this was happening, so she was revived with brandy. She then produced a black silk handkerchief and asked to be blindfolded with it. This was allowed. She also had a black lace veil over her head, so that the public could not see her face at all.

A procession formed up at the back of the chapel. From there, with the prison bell ominously tolling, the Mannings were made to process to the gallows along a maze of narrow passages, incidentally walking over their own graves along the way, just as they had made their victim walk over his. Maria Manning managed to walk without faltering, led in her black silk blindfold by the prison doctor, Mr Harris. She was wearing a fine black satin gown, which deeply shocked the ladies of quality who watched the hanging. This lady's maid had certainly stepped well above her station.

Frederick Manning faltered and tottered on the long steep flight of stairs up to the roof where the gallows stood. Manning turned to look, awestruck, at the colossal crowd gathered to watch him die and Calcraft drew a white hood over his head and fixed the noose round his neck. Then Calcraft moved to Maria Manning and pulled a similar white hood over her head and fitted her noose. He also tied a rope round her legs, to stop her dress billowing up when she dropped. After that, everybody left the roof except the husband

and wife condemned to die side by side. Immediately, Calcraft pulled the bolt and the drop fell. Frederick hung almost motionless. Maria writhed for some seconds. Probably it took them five or as much as fifteen minutes to die; this was a short-drop hanging. Their bodies were left hanging for the customary hour before being taken down.

The huge crowd began to disperse at or even before the moment of death. This often happened, and some have suggested that it was perhaps a feeling of shame at being present at a public hanging that made people hurry away afterwards.

Charles Dickens was one of the many spectators at the Mannings' hanging and wrote to *The Times* about it. 'I believe that the author has not seen a sight so inconceivably awful as the wickedness and levity of the crowd collected at that execution this morning . . . When the two miserable creatures who attracted all this ghastly sight about them were turned quivering into the air there was no more emotion, no more pity, no more thought that two immortal souls had gone to judgement, than if the name of Christ had never been heard in this world.' Dickens was among those campaigning to have public hangings stopped, and they were finally abolished in Britain in 1868.

Dickens' concern was evidently for the effect the hangings were having on the spectators. They were a sadistic and voyeuristic form of entertainment, a kind of pornography of violence, and can only have fed feelings of morbidity or sadism.

The victims often entered into their parts as entertainers. The Mannings appear to have dressed up for their execution, as many others had done before them. Maria's role as an entertainer continued well after her death. An artist from Madame Tussaud's was probably sent to the Old Bailey in anticipation, to draw her face to ensure a good likeness; Calcraft seems to have sold the wax museum the dress she was wearing for her hanging. Shortly after the execution, the waxwork image of Maria Manning took its place in the Chamber of Horrors.

One spectator at the execution commented in a letter to *The Times*, with an almost audible sigh of relief, 'Thank God she wasn't an Englishwoman'.

Alfred Arthur Rouse

'and the Blazing Car Murder'

IT WAS BONFIRE Night, the Fifth of November, 1930. People were lighting bonfires and letting off fireworks in the usual way. One fire more or less, one explosion more or less would not have been noticed.

Just to the south of Northampton is the small village of Hardingstone, and connecting the two was a short stretch of lane threading through open country. It was on verge of this quiet country lane that, in the small hours of 6 November, Arthur Alfred Rouse's car was seen blazing furiously, with a charred corpse sitting at the wheel.

At first sight it looked like a road accident. Mr Rouse had perhaps driven into the verge and the car exploded into flames, burning him alive before he could escape. It appeared to be just a tragic accident involving the car and its owner. But Rouse was still alive and shortly afterwards he was arrested and charged with the wilful murder of a stranger.

Why had Rouse picked up a stranger and murdered him?

On 23 November, *The News of the World* revealed that the police had taken a statement from a 'mystery woman' who had given them important information. But there were several mystery women in Rouse's life – and that was the root of the problem. As the weeks passed, more and more mistresses and flocks of illegitimate children came to light. At his trial, evidence was given by three of his mistresses. The prosecuting counsel explained that he had called the women to give evidence 'to show that Rouse's domestic life was not what it should have been.' It was a major understatement. Rouse had hoped that the body in the car would be identified as his, so that he could walk away from all of these problems and start afresh.

Alfred Arthur Rouse was a commercial traveller working for a firm selling braces and garters. He had been brought up by an aunt and behaved well in childhood, and he was happily married just before the outbreak of the First World War. He served with distinction in the Territorial Army in the war, and had been wounded in the head in 1915. This injury, perhaps combined with the traumatizing experience of war, changed his personality completely. His life became disorderly and he became sexually promiscuous on a grand scale. His occupation as a sales representative took him all over England and it was an ideal job for someone with his appetites. Eventually over eighty of his mistresses were traced, along with a string of illegitimate children. He even married some of the women, becoming that rare criminal type, a polygamist.

He was in deep trouble. As his various women became pregnant, they wanted financial support.

He could not afford to give it. He was only earning £8 a week, and out of that he had to pay the mortgage and running expenses of his (proper) marital home in Finchley, as well as the hire purchase payments on the car and foster parents' wages for his illegitimate children. By the summer of 1930, Rouse was in deep financial trouble. To crown it all, he heard from one of his London girlfriends that she was pregnant by him for a second time. He could not go on like this.

In June 1930, a girl named Agnes Keeson was murdered in a car near Epsom. The Keeson case baffled the police. Reading about this in the newspaper gave Rouse the idea that, if he planned his hoax carefully enough, the police could be outwitted. The plan was to fake his own death in a road accident, leaving him completely free to start a new life with no financial obligations. He had to choose a man who would take his place, someone who was so marginal to society that no-one would miss him. This part of Rouse's plan worked brilliantly, because no-one knows, even today, who Rouse's victim was – the charred corpse sitting in the driver's seat of his burnt-out car.

Rouse picked a man up in a London pub at the beginning of November. Rouse could probably tell from the man's clothing and demeanour that he was a homeless vagrant and fell into conversation with him. It no doubt emerged that the man's problems were rooted in his inability to get work. Rouse was in business, he said, and could fix him up with a job in the Midlands. The bait worked exactly as Rouse had hoped. The man went with him that night and they set off for the Midlands.

The second part of the plan was to set the car on fire, with the unknown man inside and Rouse outside. The general build of the man was similar to Rouse's, and when badly burnt it would be impossible to guess that the charred corpse, which Rouse intended to turn him into, was actually someone else's. Whether Rouse had Hardingstone Lane specifically in mind as part of his plan is not known, but the quiet stretch of country road just on the southern edge of Northampton suited his purpose well enough. As it turned out it was not quiet enough. He drew the car off the road onto the verge and made an excuse to get out. Perhaps he pretended he felt a wobble in the steering and wanted to have a look at the rear wheels. Perhaps he pretended he was going to relieve himself in the hedgerow. He found some pretext to get out of the car and – exactly what happened next is uncertain. Rouse said that he overpowered the stranger, rendered him unconscious and got him into the driver's seat. It seems Rouse had a mallet with him for the purpose. Alternatively, it is possible that Rouse got the man to sit in the driving seat, perhaps by promising him a turn at the driving, locked the door and set the car on fire with the stranger still inside and still conscious, no doubt frantically struggling to get out as the car filled with flames.

This part of the plan failed. Quiet though Hardingstone Lane was, there was intermittent traffic on it. Someone happened to drive along the road just at the wrong moment, and saw not only the blazing car but Rouse leaving the scene of the crime. Rouse was probably unnerved by the enormity of what he had done and made several mistakes, including saying things that were incriminating. He was arrested.

The circumstantial evidence against Rouse was not really enough to hang Rouse. There was no evidence against him as far as the death of the stranger was concerned, and at this stage Rouse was still denying everything. The local police mishandled the case. They failed to take scene of crime photographs and they allowed the body to be removed from the car before it was inspected by a pathologist. The validity of the 'forensic' evidence was therefore suspect. The police officers involved gave evidence from recollection, not from notes taken at the time. There was also an incredible leakage of information by the police. By 7 November, the day after the murder, and well before the start of the trial, all the information about the case, including witnesses' statements, were in the newspapers, and this inappropriately high level of publicity continued through the trial.

The trial of Alfred Arthur Rouse took place in Northampton on 26–31 January, 1931, under Mr Justice Talbot.

Obviously, the jurors' view of the case and of Rouse in particular must have been tainted by what they read in the press, where the case was handled in sensational style. Rouse's wives and mistresses were being described as his 'harem'.

The judge was aware that undue influence might occur, and warned the jury to take no notice of what the papers said, but by then of course the damage was already done. The jury had made up their mind. The guilty verdict was almost inevitable.

Rouse did himself no favours. He seemed unable to give the same date twice. His testimony sounded unreliable, and he was obviously a liar. Even so, he was treated unfairly. His morals were available for comment and discussion by the lawyers, yet the likely effect of his 1915 war injuries (to head, thigh and leg) was never discussed. The personality change resulting from the injuries and the shell-shock might have been used as a mitigating circumstance. The head injury, which almost certainly damaged his brain, might explain his inconsistency about dates; in other words, the lying might have been inadvertent. A modern lawyer would be able to make a reasoned case for diminished responsibility, and get the murder charge reduced to manslaughter. A shell-shocked serial philanderer, Rouse had behaved so oddly and irrationally that his actions could fairly easily have been presented in way that supported a plea of insanity. In 1930, the same might have been done for Rouse, but for some reason nobody bothered.

The jury brought in its inevitable verdict of guilty. Judge Talbot declared Rouse guilty of murder of an unknown man and sentenced him to death. Alfred Arthur Rouse was accordingly hanged at Bedford Prison by Thomas Pierrepoint on 10 March, 1931.

The identity of Rouse's victim is still not known. Rouse's gaoler claimed that Rouse did reveal his victim's name, but if he did it has not been recorded. The unknown man was buried in the local churchyard at 6 in the morning on 21 March, 1931, in a private service attended by the police officers involved in the case. His gravestone reads, 'In memory of an unknown man. Died Nov 6th 1930'.

Even though Rouse confessed the crime, there is much he did not reveal. He would never say who the man was, and never gave a satisfactory account of the murder itself. Did Rouse hit the man over the head with the mallet to render him unconscious, then move him into the driving seat, or did he somehow persuade the man to sit there, and then lock him in and leave him to burn alive?

Rouse's crime was horrible, but when his case is seen objectively there are mitigating circumstances. He was brain damaged and not fully responsible for his actions, cunning and devious though they were. Rouse is long forgotten. His victim was in effect removed from the map even while he was still alive – the murdered man nobody missed. Even the place where the murder took place has gone. The stretch of lane connecting Hardingstone to Northampton has been quarried away and re-landscaped to make a large and complicated multiple road junction.

James Hanratty
'the A6 murder'

One August evening in 1961, Michael Gregsten, a married man, drove his girlfriend Valerie Storie out into the country for sex. They worked together at the Road Research Laboratory near Slough. Gregsten's wife knew about the affair. Gregsten drove his Morris Minor, as he had done many times before, to the chosen spot and parked on the roadside next to Taplow Meadow, just outside Maidenhead. As they embraced each other and kissed in the front of the car, there was a sharp tap at the window behind Valerie. Michael could see the man, but Valerie couldn't. The man threatened Michael with a gun, said, 'I am a desperate man', and climbed into the back seat of the car. Then he ordered Gregsten to drive off, insisting that they keep looking ahead; they were not to turn round and look at him. They set off through the outskirts of Slough, then onto the open road. After a tense two-hour drive, the stranger ordered Michael to stop in a lay-by on the A6. It was fairly sheltered, surrounded by bushes and known as Deadman's Hill. It was a favourite spot for courting couples.

The menacing stranger asked Michael Gregsten

to hand him a duffel bag, and either Gregsten saw this as an opportunity to take a look at him or tackle him and disarm him, or the stranger interpreted his movement as a threat. Maybe the gunman had realised that Gregsten had already taken a good look at his face through the passenger window and would be able to identify him; he had had time during the drive to decide that Gregsten could not be trusted to leave the scene alive. Whatever the reason, as Michael Gregsten passed the bag, the stranger fired twice and Gregsten was killed outright instantly.

By now it was dark, and the terrified Valerie found herself alone with a homicidal maniac. The stranger savagely raped her, shot her in the back several times at close range and left her for dead in the lay-by. She in fact survived, but remained disabled for the rest of her life. In spite of spending as much as six hours at close quarters with the gunman, Valerie only really saw his face clearly once, for a few seconds, as it was lit up by the headlights of a passing car. She was able to supply police with a description, but it remains uncertain whether that description is at all reliable. By the time she caught the single glimpse of the gunman's face, she had already been traumatized by the shooting of her lover. The police circulated a picture of the wanted man.

Recognition by voice played a key part in the prosecution case at the trial. Just before the man raped her, he said, 'Shut up, will you? I'm thinking'. He spoke with an accent that was very distinct but Valerie could not identify it geographically. It wasn't London. It wasn't Glasgow. But a distinct way of speaking just the same. He pronounced the word 'thinking' as 'finking'.

As soon as Michael's body and the scarcely-living Valerie were found in the A6 lay-by, a massive murder hunt was launched. It was a very peculiar case. The man had appeared from nowhere, disappeared into nowhere, seemed to have no connection with Michael or Valerie, and seemed to have no motive whatever. There was really nothing at all to go on, except the knowledge that there was a violent madman on the loose, a man who said 'finking'.

The police had a suspect, a man called Peter Louis Alphon. His face fitted the identikit picture, and he could not give any account of his movements on the night of the murder. The police even got as far as arresting him, and they were probably right.

At this point, bizarre things began to happen in the development of the case. Michael Gregsten's widow happened to be in Blackpool on holiday, after the murder of her husband, when she spotted a man, a total stranger, about whom she had an intuition. She got in touch with the police. The man was James Hanratty. It says something about the strange and desperate mindset of the police involved in this case that they acted on this absurd contact. Mrs Gregsten had not been at the scene of the murder, had no reason to think she had ever seen the murderer, and so could not have expected to recognize him. She only had the identikit picture. The police picked Hanratty up and questioned him. Initially he could not account for his whereabouts on that fateful evening – but how many of us could do that? – and they started investigating his recent movements.

The police discovered two .38 cartridge cases from bullets fired from the murder weapon in the Vienna Hotel; one of the rooms had been occupied by a Mr James Ryan, which was an alias used by James Hanrattty. The police decided they need look no further. There was nevertheless no forensic evidence from the car to connect Hanratty to the murder.

Hanratty was lined up in an identification parade. Valerie was unable to pick anyone out that she recognized. 'I'm sorry. I only saw him for a few seconds. It's very difficult.' She knew and freely admitted that she had been badly traumatized during and after her ordeal and that this had blocked and distorted her memory. The police ran a second identification parade. This time the police asked the men to repeat the line, 'Be quiet will you? I'm thinking'. Valerie felt sure Hanratty was saying 'finking'. The police thought they had got their man.

Hanratty made himself doubly vulnerable at this point by producing an alibi. He had not mentioned Rhyl before, but now he claimed he had been in Rhyl, 250 miles from the murder scene, on the night in question. It looked like an improvised smoke screen, and the police saw no reason to make no more than a cursory check on his alibi.

James Hanratty was arrested in Blackpool on 9

October in 1961, identified by Valerie at an identity parade, and sent for trial at Bedford Assizes. Much of the trial proceedings turned on Hanratty's alibi, that he had been at Rhyl in north Wales on the day in question.

The jury took a long time – nearly ten hours – to come to the decision that Hanratty was guilty. The use of a gun in the murder was crucial. As the law stood at that time, if Hanratty had strangled or poisoned Michael Gregsten he would have been sentenced to life imprisonment; using a gun meant death. He was sentenced to death and hanged on 4 April 1962.

Hanratty's conviction was controversial. Britain was phasing out capital punishment at the time, and Hanratty's was one of only three executions that took place between 1961 and 1965, when hanging ceased altogether. Had the suspect been correctly identified? Had enough enquiries been made into the validity of Hanratty's alibi? Had any motive been established for the murder? Had sufficient evidence altogether be gathered to justify a conviction, let alone an execution? Had alternative suspects like Alphon really been investigated properly? Hanratty himself stoutly denied that he was involved in any way with the murder, and went to the gallows protesting his innocence. Many people have campaigned to have the case reopened and get some of these questions answered.

The police check on Hanratty's alibi was no more than token. They had already decided that he was the killer, so he could not have been in

Rhyl. Shortly after the hanging, no fewer than fourteen people came forward to say that they had seen or spoken to Hanratty in Rhyl, and that the police had interviewed none of them. The police enquiries had led them to the Vienna Hotel, where Hanratty had certainly stayed. In the Vienna Hotel, the police found cartridge cases that connected the place to the murder scene. But Hanratty was not the only person who had stayed at the Vienna Hotel. As it turned out, it was for him an unlucky choice. Also staying at the Vienna Hotel was Peter Louis Alphon, who up to that moment had been the police's main suspect. Alphon was not identified by Valerie at an identification parade, but then neither really was Hanratty. But once the police had decided that Hanratty was the killer, further enquiries into Alphon were dropped.

Alphon, it must be remembered, had no alibi at all for the night of the murder. He was a friend of Michael Gregsten's wife and therefore had a connection with Michael and Valerie that Hanratty did not. Alphon later claimed that Mrs Gregsten had paid him £5000 to frighten the lovers into separating so that she could get her husband back. Here – at last – was a possible motive. Alphon pronounced the word 'thinking' as 'finking'. He looked remarkably like the identikit picture.

There was also the manner in which the Morris Minor was being driven as the murderer left the murder scene. Many witnesses saw the car as it drove away from the scene; they noticed it because it drew their attention. It was being driven very erratically. This is very peculiar if the murderer was Hanratty, because Hanratty was a very experienced driver. Alphon, on the other hand, had not even passed his driving test, and is therefore far more likely to have been the driver that night.

In a similar way, the personality of Alphon fits the events of the night better. Hanratty was a city character, sociable and well liked by the people he worked with; he had never shown any sign of psychological hang-ups. He does not seem very likely to have behaved in the neurotic and irrational way that the A6 killer behaved that night. Alphon on the other hand was neurotic, psychologically fragile, a petty criminal, a loner, roaming about with no proper job, Any psychological profiling would have identified Alphon as far more likely to have committed the A6 murder than Hanratty. He also had an odd, very distinctive way of speaking. His voice was recorded by investigators years later as he spoke about the A6 shootings – I have heard the tape – and the neurotic peculiarity of his speech fits Valerie's observations.

All this could have been established by the police in 1961. All this could have been presented in court to ensure that the right man went to the gallows. What was not available at the time was Alphon's confession. It was not until many years later, when the events of that summer had preyed on his mind to such an extent that he wanted other people to know what had happened. He claimed in his confession that he was paid a large sum to 'damage' Valerie and Michael. What appears to have happened is that family friends seeking to help Mrs Gregsten by ending the Michael-Valerie affair hired Alphon to surprise and frighten the lovers at Taplow Meadow, where there were known to meet. Maybe Alphon took the gun as a prop, to wave at Gregsten, knowing that it would thoroughly frighten him. Alphon's fundamental instability as a person meant that he got carried away with his gangster role and the situation ran away with him. Maybe he didn't know how to bring the frightening episode to a satisfactory close and panicked. The apparent lack of purpose to the attack is certainly consistent with this scenario. The story is unfortunately muddied by Alphon's retraction later on. By the time Paul Foot interviewed him for his book *Who killed Hanratty?* He had thought better of his confession, perhaps fearing he would be put on trial.

Whether there would have been a watertight case against Alphon is impossible to tell now, since the forensic trail has gone cold, but if all these facts had been made known to the jury at Hanratty's trial it would have been clear that there was 'reasonable doubt' about Hanratty's guilt. It was not a safe conviction.

Immediately after the execution, many began to wonder whether justice really had been done. Even Mrs Gregsten, who had pointed the finger at Hanratty in the first place, began to have doubts. The gathering uncertainty led the British government further towards the abolition of hanging. At least if a man is given a life sentence for murder there remains the possibility of release and restitution; the mistake can be put right. There is no possibility of putting right a hanging.

Over the years since the murder, Hanratty has increasingly looked like the wrong suspect, Alphon the right suspect. But very recently the situation has become startlingly more complicated with the emergence of some DNA evidence. In 1999, the Hanratty family, which has remained firmly convinced of Hanratty's innocence throughout, won their fight to have his case reviewed.

Since 1962, forensic tests have advanced significantly, so in March 2001 James Hanratty's body was exhumed from Carpenter's Park Cemetery near Bushey in Hertfordshire. DNA from his teeth was found to match two samples found at the scene of the crime (trial exhibits 26 and 35); one was on Valerie Storie's underwear and the other was the handkerchief wrapped round the murder weapon, a .38 revolver. As a result of the DNA matching, the Court of Criminal Appeal ruled that Hanratty's conviction was safe and that there were no grounds for a posthumous pardon. In other words, even though serious errors may have been made in the process of bringing Hanratty to justice, he was nevertheless the man who committed the crime, so justice was done.

The Hanratty family remain unconvinced, though. The exhibits were from the beginning never handled in a forensically sterile environment, and could easily have become cross-contaminated. During the trial at Bedford Assizes, the exhibits were regularly taken to and from court in the same boxes; the samples repeatedly came in contact with one another, including the samples of Valerie Storie's and James Hanratty's clothing. In that context it would not be at all surprising if some of Hanratty's DNA found its way onto the other trial exhibits, especially in the minute quantities that were actually present. Officers and witnesses took the exhibits and handled them freely; people were not to know at that time about the possibility of damaging the evidence, simply because no-one knew about DNA.

The forensic scientists who carried out the tests counter-argue that if Hanratty was not the killer, the killer's DNA is unaccountably missing from the exhibits; no other man's DNA was found. The Appeal judge, Lord Woolf, took the view of the forensic scientists: 'In our judgement . . . the DNA evidence establishes beyond doubt that James Hanratty was the murderer.' But if Hanratty did it, why on earth did he do it? And how did Mrs Gregsten identify him in a crowd at Blackpool? The A6 murder remains one of the greatest murder mysteries of modern times. The DNA breakthrough has opened a new phase in the controversy. Maybe further new techniques, not yet invented, will solve the mystery in the future. Let us hope so, for the sake of justice.

Jeremy Bamber

'evil beyond belief'

EARLY IN THE morning of 7 August, 1985, Jeremy Bamber picked up the phone to hear his father shouting, 'Sheila's got the gun. She's gone crazy. Come over quickly.' Ralph rang off and though Jeremy tried phoning back he was unable to get through.

Ralph and June Bamber had adopted Jeremy and Sheila. Sheila had been married, becoming Sheila Caffell. Now Sheila and her six-year-old twin sons lived with Ralph and June at White House Farm in the village of Tolleshunt D'Arcy, not far from Jeremy's cottage. Sheila had gone crazy before, but never with a gun. Jeremy rang the police, then phoned his girlfriend, Julie Mugford, unsure whether he had done the right thing. Then he drove the short distance to White House Farm, to find the police already there. Armed police arrived at 5.30.

At 7.30, after a discussion about Sheila's state of mind, the police broke the door down. They found Ralph Bamber's body first. He was in the kitchen, where the phone was off the hook; Ralph had been calling for help when attacked. His wife June, upstairs in the main bedroom, had been shot once while in bed, then several more times as she tried to get out of the room. The twins had been shot several times in the head as they lay in bed. Sheila was lying beside her parents' bed in the main bedroom. She had died of a gunshot wound to the throat. She was holding a .22 rifle.

Sheila's marriage had broken down. She became depressed and slid into paranoid schizophrenia. She had only been discharged from a mental hospital days before the shootings. Psychiatric reports recorded that her illness was centred on the twins, whom she referred to as 'the Devil's children'. The psychiatrist noted that she had suicidal tendencies. Before the shootings she had stopped taking the medication prescribed to control her dangerous state of mind.

Jeremy Bamber said that there had been a discussion the day before the shootings, when it had been proposed that the twins should be fostered, or that they needed some other care arrangements. Possibly this triggered a schizophrenic episode; Sheila could have decided that killing the whole family would solve the problem. The police concluded that Sheila had murdered her sons and her parents, then committed suicide.

Then something extraordinary happened, which took the murder case into a new dimension altogether and ensured its place in criminal history. The police changed their minds. Sheila had not committed suicide. Jeremy had killed her and the other members of the household. On 29 September Bamber was arrested and charged with the murders.

The police decided that Bamber had a good motive. He stood to inherit over £400,000 as well as the Bamber estate, consisting of five farms, a farming co-operative and packaging factory in which Ralph had a 20% share, and a caravan park with an annual turnover of a million pounds. Why did the police change their minds? They interviewed a number of friends, relations, business contacts, some of whom had a vested interest in seeing Jeremy Bamber convicted of the murders so that he could not inherit. The police seem not to have considered that possibility that the statements might contain bias. Jeremy Bamber's girlfriend gave an account of his actions, but he had broken their relationship off after the murders and it is hard to know how much credence can be put in her version of events. Had he really phoned her saying, 'Tonight's the night'? Evidence motivated by cash or revenge should have been discounted.

The main evidence brought forward by the prosecution was the blood in the silencer. The victims were shot at close range, so their blood splashed back into the silencer. Blood in the silencer was of the same group as Sheila's. If that was the case, Sheila could not have committed suicide. With the silencer attached to the rifle, it was too long for anyone to shoot themselves. Obviously Sheila did not shoot herself using the silencer, then detach the silencer and put it in the cupboard downstairs before returning to the bedroom to die. The presence of Sheila's blood in the silencer seemed certain proof that someone else had shot her.

But there was another possibility, that the blood was a mixture of Ralph's blood and June's blood. The forensic evidence did not conclusively prove that Sheila had not killed herself. More recent tests using DNA profiling have produced an interesting result. There is no sign of Sheila's DNA in the blood in the silencer, but there is a trace of June's DNA and that of an unidentified male. This more advanced test proves that Sheila could have carried out the shootings with the silencer, then removed the silencer, knowing that she needed to shorten the rifle in order to kill herself with it.

Both Jeremy and the police saw a figure in the main bedroom when they first arrived at the house. If the figure had been either June or Ralph, he or she would have opened the window to make contact with the police. The figure was too tall to have been either of the twins. It could only have been Sheila, preparing to kill herself. If it was indeed Sheila, and it is difficult to see who else it could have been, the police who saw her knew perfectly well that Jeremy was outside the house. Given that he was there, with them, he could not possibly have been responsible for Sheila's death, and therefore not for the deaths of the others either. When the police and Jeremy saw the figure in the bedroom, they retreated along the lane. The .22 rifle does not make a loud noise, so Sheila may very well have shot herself at that moment without the police hearing anything at all.

It was said by some witnesses that Sheila knew nothing about guns, but that was untrue. She had been on a shooting holiday in Scotland and taught how to shoot.

Two witnesses claimed that the bathroom window was open, implying that an intruder, Bamber, had broken in, but the police investigators found all the doors and windows secure. DS Ainley wrote in his report, 'DCI Jones did in fact examine the inside of all the ground floor windows and noted that they were all shut and secure on their latches. . . After the inspection by DCI Jones some person partially opened the transom window in the kitchen and also opened the catch on the ground floor bathroom window. I have been unable to discover the person responsible.' Someone - after the murders - opened windows to make it look as if there had been an intruder.

At Jeremy Bamber's trial, the prosecution alleged that he planned to buy a Porsche. This, they alleged, showed that Bamber knew he was coming into a lot of money. But what Bamber planned to buy was not a Porsche but a replica Porsche kit car; this would have cost him about £2500, which he could have afforded without murdering his parents.

It has become clear over the last 20 years that the jury did not hear all the evidence. What they heard was carefully adapted to produce a conviction. It was not only a miscarriage of justice; attempts were made, for more than one reason, to frame Bamber.

In October 1986, Jeremy Bamber was convicted at Chelmsford Crown Court for the multiple murder. The judge described him as 'evil almost beyond belief', recommending that he serve no less than 25 years. He has become one of a small, elite group of convicted murderers whose crimes are so appalling that they can never be released. Bamber has consistently protested his innocence and has tried to have his case reviewed. Two appeals have been rejected.

Was it Jeremy or Sheila who carried out the killings at White House Farm? The open, bloodstained bible beside Sheila's body suggests to me a deranged state of mind. If he is telling the truth, Jeremy Bamber has been the victim of a serious miscarriage of justice. If he is not telling the truth, then he is indeed an infamous murderer.